Practical Guide to
Business Forecasting

AF149346

Edited by
Chaman L. Jain
St. John's University

GɔC **GRACEWAY PUBLISHING COMPANY, INC.**

ii

Copyright © 2001 By Graceway Publishing Company, Inc.

All rights reserved. No part of this book may be used or reproduced in any manner without written permission except in case of brief quotations embodied in critical articles and reviews.

Manufactured in the United States of America
Library of Congress Card No. 00-092568
ISBN 0-932126-41-3 (Softcover)

Published by:

Graceway Publishing Company, Inc.
P.O. Box 670159
Flushing, New York 11367-0159
(516) 504-7576

PREFACE

This book is written with practicing forecasters in mind. As such, the objective of this book is five fold: One, it should be easy to understand so that a person with little or no background in statistics can follow. Two, it should be geared towards practitioners, that is, it should emphasize more on the practical aspects and less on the theoretical aspects of forecasting. Three, it should deal with business forecasting rather than economic forecasting. However, some of the models and issues discussed here are equally applicable to economic forecasting. Four, it should cover not only various models of forecasting but also other issues which are equally important in business. These issues are how to set up a forecasting process/system, which forecasting approach to use, how to select a forecasting software, how to present/sell forecasts to the end-users, how to set up a forecast training program, etc. Five, it should bring in the experience of practicing forecasters so that one can get a clear understanding of the problems encountered in the real world and how they are handled.

The book is divided into twelve parts. Part I deals with the 'Basics' of business forecasting. It covers issues such as who are our customers (end-users), what their expectations are, which forecasts are easier to prepare, who should participate in the forecasting process, what role judgment plays in forecasting, what is the cost of being wrong, how much error we can tolerate, and so on.

To succeed in the forecasting function, both the forecasters and end-users have to work as a team. Part II describes why it is important to work as a team, and what they have to do to achieve it. Forecasters have to learn, among other things, the culture and language of the organization they work for. The end-users have to learn the basics of forecasting — not the nitty gritty of preparing forecasts but the general idea of how forecasts are generated. It is very difficult to evaluate forecasts without having any idea how they are created.

Part III deals with the role of marketing research in forecasting. The marketing research plays an important part in forecasting the demand for brand new products, detecting competitive activities, determining promotional lift and sensitivity of sales to price, and so on.

Before preparing forecasts, one has to decide about the approach, that is, whether forecasts should be initiated from the top, bottom or somewhere in the middle. Part IV deals with such issues.

For a forecasting function to work efficiently and effectively, one has to have a good and efficient forecasting process/system in place. The process deals with the issues such as what kind of data/information should be used to prepare forecasts, from where it will come, where the forecasting function should reside, who should participate in the process, who should have the authority to override over forecasts, how and who should monitor them, and so on. The forecasting system, on the other hand, is nothing more than mechanization of the process so that each step is followed efficiently, as well as in an orderly fashion. Part V deals with the issues of the forecasting process, and Part VI, of the forecasting system.

Data plays an important role in forecasting. To make any sense out of it, one has to clean and message the data. Part VII describes what types of data is available internally and externally, and what to do with it before using a forecasting model.

The forecasting models are the tools of forecasts. Parts VIII and IX describe the forecasting models. Part VIII describes the time series models, whereas, Part IX, regression models. One needs to measure forecast accuracy to determine the quality of forecasts. Furthermore, understanding the forecast error is the basis for improving it. Once one knows where a forecast went wrong, one may figure out what to do to correct it. There are many ways of measuring a forecast error, but which one to use depends on the objective of a forecaster. The Part X describes different measures of forecast accuracy, and when and where each one should be used.

No matter how accurate the forecasts are, they are useless unless they are used. This brings out the question of presenting and selling forecasts to end-users. The Director of Forecast of one company once remarked, " I would rather spend my time in preparing and improving forecasts than selling them, but selling is an equally important part of the forecasting function." Part XI deals with the issues of presenting and selling forecasts to forecast customers.

To have an efficient, on-going forecasting function, one needs to have a forecast training program in place. Part XII describes how to go about to set up such a program, and how to monitor and update it so that it runs efficiently and effectively.

There are some special terms used in every discipline. Forecasting is not an exception. In the last section, we have given a glossary of forecasting related terms, which will help not only in understanding the forecasting discipline as such but also the people you deal with as a forecaster. The forecaster has to work with various functions including production, logistic, finance and marketing. For that reason, we have included some of the terms used particularly in production in the context of forecasting.

There are a number of people who have played an important part in completing this book. To begin with, I wish to express my gratitude to those whose articles have appeared in this book. I am also grateful to Steve Preziosi and Murad Kuliyev, graduate assistants, for their computer help as well as their comments on certain chapters. Special thanks to Jack Malehorn who meticulously edited this book from the beginning to the end. Also, I would like to express my gratitude to Dr. Thomas Chen for reviewing the chapters on regression.

Chaman L. Jain
St. John's University

TABLE OF CONTENTS

TABLE OF CONTENTS

TABLE OF CONTENTS

viii

PART I

BASICS

INTRODUCTION

Forecasting is much more than generating numbers. To get a handle on forecasting, one needs to know why we need forecasts?; who are the users of forecasts?; where and how they are used?; why some people view forecasts as a "voodoo magic" and others are disillusioned by their high expectations?; which forecasts can be prepared more accurately than others and why?; when forecasts should be revised?, who should participate in the forecasting process?, how to win the confidence of upper management?; why it is necessary to integrate the strategic forecasts with tactic forecasts, and consumer demand forecasts with customer demand forecasts?; what role the judgment plays?; what are the consequences of being wrong?; why the accuracy of forecasts is not always as important as we normally think?; what role politics plays in forecasting?; and so on. This part attempts to answer all these questions.

CHAPTER 1

EXPLOSION IN THE FORECASTING FUNCTION IN CORPORATE AMERICA

Chaman L. Jain
St. John's University

In recent years probably no business function grew as rapidly as the forecasting function. In fact, it has just exploded. About ten years ago, only utility companies including telecom, gas and electric had a forecasting department, staffed by full time forecasting people. Now most of the large corporations including Coca-Cola, Eastman Kodak, Hewlett Packard, Johnson and Johnson and Pfizer have a full time forecasting staff – something unheard of ten years ago.

Most of the companies not only now have dedicated forecasters on their staff but also their number is growing. According to the IBF (Institute of Business Forecasting) survey conducted in 1998, 77% of the companies hired one or more full time forecasting persons during the last ten years. The growth has been even stronger in recent years. More than half of the respondents (62%) indicated that they hired full time forecasting persons during the last five years.

Levi Strauss started a separate forecasting department in November 1995. It has now a full time forecasting staff of 30 people. It has even the Vice President of Forecasting. Duracell recognized the need of a forecasting function in mid 1970's. At present, it has a staff of 8 full time forecasters – 5 in operational forecasting and 3 in strategic forecasting. Reckitt & Colman has a forecasting department headed by the Director of Forecasting, with a full time staff of nine people. Mary Kay Cosmetic has a full time staff of 8 persons. According to the IBF survey, 32% of the companies that responded have 5 or more and 15% of them have 12 or more full time forecasters on their staff.

JOB MARKET

Another way of observing the growth in the forecasting function is to look at its job market. There has been a significant growth in listings in the newsletter, "Job Opportunities in Forecasting and Planning," which is geared toward this function. The Spring 1998 issue listed 29 jobs in the area, and the Summer 1999, 51 jobs — 76% increase. A good number of jobs remain unfilled over a long period. In this newsletter, about 13% of the jobs are repeated from one issue to the next because companies fail to find the right person. A few years ago, a Connecticut based company, advertised the forecasting job in New York Times. The company received 55 responses, but none of them had any background in forecasting, according to its forecasting manager.

The survey of US Labor Department also shows growth in jobs in this area. The 1998-99 Occupational Outlook Handbook, published by Bureau of Labor Statistics, states, "Those skilled in quantitative techniques and their application to economic modeling and forecasting, using computers, coupled with good communications skills, should have the best opportunities." The 1996 Spring issue of Occupational Outlook Quarterly states," for economists and marketing research analysts, faster than average growth is expected ... due to increased reliance on quantitative methods of analyzing business trends, forecasting sales, and planning."

SALARY

Salaries offered for positions in the area of forecasting are quite competitive. The median salary of Forecast Analyst, Sr. Forecast Analyst, Manager of Forecasting, Director of Forecasting, and Vice President of Forecasting are $45,000, $56,000, $71,000, $100,000 and $153,000 respectively. These numbers are also based on the IBF survey conducted in 1998. The position of a Forecast Analyst is merely an entry-level position. The median salary for this position in forecasting is much higher than of a marketing major, $45,000 vs. $29,000. The median salary of Vice President of Forecasting is also much higher than its counterpart in marketing, $153,000 vs. $133,000. (Keep in mind that the salaries of forecasting positions are of 1998 because the survey was conducted in 1998, but of marketing are of 1997, the latest figures available.)

CONFERENCE AND SEMINAR ATTANDANCE

The large attendance in the forecasting conferences/seminars also reflects the growth in the forecasting function. The IBF holds conferences in the area of forecasting and planning. In 1998, it held five conferences, two on Best Practices in Forecasting, one on Tutorial in Forecasting, one on Strategic Forecasting, Budgeting and Planning, and one on Forecasting and Planning in Telecom, Electric and Gas. All these conferences were well attended. It should be borne in mind that these conferences are attended primarily by practicing forecasters and not academicians.

VENDORS OF FORECASTNG SOFTWARE AND SYSTEMS

The emergence of new multi-million dollar industry (vendors of forecasting software and systems) that provides support to the forecasting function is also an evidence of growth in the forecasting function. The forecasting software is a stand-alone package. It generates forecasts either by the model selected by the forecaster or by the model chosen by the software package. There are many software packages, which have a built-in automatic feature, that is, they select the best model based on the predefined criterion.

The forecasting system, on the other hand, does much more than preparing forecasts. Depending on the system, it can, in addition to preparing forecasts, help in devising plans for distribution, manufacturing, transportation, sales and marketing. Most of the vendors in the area started their business in last 15 years or so.

Among the vendors of forecasting packages, Business Forecasting System is the leader with a market share of 32%. It started its business in 1986. Among the vendors of forecasting systems, Manugistics is the leader with a market share of 24%. This multi-million dollar company was started only in 1986. Although SAP is in business since 1972, it introduced its forecasting system only in 1998.

The emergence of journals directed toward forecasting, and upsurge in the number of books and articles published in the area also point toward the growth in the forecasting function. At present, we have three journals in the area – Journal of Business Forecasting (started in 1981), Journal of Forecasting (started in 1982) and International Journal of Forecasting (started in 1985). However, the Journal of Business Forecasting is geared toward practitioners, while the other two, toward academicians. In recent years, there has been a tremendous growth in articles on forecasting. At present, practically every business related journal publishes articles on forecasting. The book, Bibliography on Forecasting and Planning, lists 4200 articles on forecasting and planning published during 1979 and 1993.

DRIVERS OF FORECASTING FUNCTION

The forces that have brought the forecasting function to the forefront are: (1) recognition by business that they need forecasts for better decisions, (2) development in technology for processing, storing and accessing data, and (3) willingness among business partners to share information.

More and more businesses now recognize that forecasts are the key to good decision-making. To improve forecasts, they have to allocate more resources to this function. They have to have dedicated forecasters who can spend all, not a fraction, of their time on the forecasting function. They have to make forecasting more objective and less intuitive.

Businesses have been using forecasts all along, even though they did not call them as such. They prepare budget, which is based on some estimates about the future. They prepare a production plan (how much to produce, and when and where), which is also based on some estimates about the future. In fact, every business decision is based on some expectations about the future. Forecasts can be prepared intuitively (based on gut feeling) or systematically using a well-defined procedure. In the past, forecasts were mostly prepared intuitively. It is very difficult to improve forecasts if they are prepared intuitively. With intuitively generated forecasts, forecasters are less likely to know where they went wrong, making them difficult to improve. If forecasts are prepared systematically, forecasters have better chances of recognizing the problems and then fixing them. It is true that forecasting is not rocket science. A lot of judgment goes into it. But the forecasters are trying their best to move away from judgment as much as they can.

The innovation in technology has also played an important role in bringing the forecasting function to the forefront. It has done it in two ways: (1) By improving the data processing capability, which is very vital to forecasting. Data processing capability includes accuracy and speed by which data can be entered, stored, exchanged, manipulated and analyzed. The advancement in computer technology has made possible to solve even the most complex mathematical problems in matter of seconds, something we could not even dream of before. The availability of all kinds of software has made possible for the forecasters to concentrate more on how to improve forecasts than on how to compute them. (2) By improving data accessibility, which is equally important in forecasting. Data accessibility includes accuracy and speed at which data can be accessed. The innovation of EDI (electronic data interchange), where one computer talks to another, has made possible for the forecaster to obtain data from any corner of the world at no time. As such, it gives more data to forecasters to work with. Scanning data technology has provided an access to consumption data to vendors, which tell them rather quickly how consumers are responding to their products in different markets, and also how their products are doing in relation to those of competitors. The EDI technology also allows partners to communicate interactively about forecasts.

Above all, willingness to share information across a supply chain has also provided impetus to the forecasting function. For example, under VMI (Vendor Management Inventory Program), retailers provide access not only to the point of sale data but also share information about changes in their store layout, opening and closing of stores, promotional plans, and their forecasts. At present, Retail Link, Wal-Mart's electronic data interchange system, provides weekly forecasting data to more than 3500 of its 5000 vendors. If vendors know what is happening on the consumer end, as well as what retailers are planning to do, they can do a better job in preparing forecasts.

CHAPTER 2

PRACTICAL GUIDELINES FOR FORECASTERS

N. Carroll Mohn
The Coca-Cola Company

Forecasts are critical inputs to a wide range of business decision-making processes. From letters, teaching forecasting, managing the function and consulting work, I know that many people are striving to get a practitioner's grasp of the subject — some feeling for the applied state of the art and its science.

Unlike the status of affairs a decade or so ago, there now is a considerable body of literature regarding not only the need for forecasting from the organizational viewpoint, but also the available methodology and technique to accomplish the development of forecasts. One area, however, sorely lacking for attention in the published material is forecasting and its role within the organization system: what it is; how it is communicated to users; and generally how the forecaster does the forecasting job beyond preparation of the forecast proper.

To address such issues, several years ago, a group of forecasters in Atlanta organized a "forecasting special interest" group. Under chairmanship of John Reid, then Forecasting Manager at Coca-Cola, and now a Senior Vice President for Planning and Development, the group met monthly over the course of one year. The basic structural format for the group was to provide a forum whereby forecasting practitioners from the Atlanta metropolitan area could meet to discuss and exchange ideas on issues of common interest. Participants in this special interest group numbered 15 and represented organizations of differing sizes, from both the public and private sectors. A basic format for the informal luncheon meetings consisted of an initial 10-15 minute introduction by a member on the specific topic of interest, followed by a group discussion, with the presenter also serving as moderator.

My purpose, then, is to bring to light several of the implementation issues discussed by this group of forecasters at their monthly meetings. I want to touch upon a potpourri of topical interest areas, followed by several concluding remarks on what I see in the future for forecasting.

I have designed the content here somewhat in the manner of a reference document for business forecasters. My comments are intended as a form to which new concepts, viewpoints, and examples can be appended as they arise.

WHY TRY TO FORECAST?

As forecasters, at one time or another, we have to ask ourselves why we should try to forecast in the first place. Our group's discussions focused us on a three-part response to this question:

First, the power of forces such as economics, competition, markets, social concerns and the ecological environment to affect the individual firm is severe and continues growing. Secondly, forecast assessment is a major input in management's evaluation of different strategies at business decision-making levels. Thirdly, the inference of no forecasting is that the future either contains "no significant change" or there is ample time to react "after the fact."

Our collective conclusion is that forecasting is far too important to the organization to have appropriate management and resource backing. Each firm must develop its own explicit forecast system so that alternative courses of action can be identified.

ARGUMENTS AGAINST FORECASTING

But arguments against forecasting abound and, as forecasters, we must understand and address them. Our interest group considered three such arguments. One concerns bad personal experience with forecasts for products, investments, weather, politics, economics, and stock market. This kind of argument is no more than emotional reaction to the notion of forecasting.

Another frequent argument against forecasting is a user's resentment of speculations of loose-cannon journalists; extreme claims of sensation seekers, or ill-informed college or university professors. Such speculations often are prophecies, propaganda, fears or hopes. They rarely are systematic forecasts based on logical forecasting procedure. Nothing I say here is intended to deny that opinions, speculations and fears may be right; indeed, more so possibly than a forecast. The point is that speculation is not a forecast any more than a layman's opinion about next week's weather is a meteorological forecast. Nor do I imply that speculation may not be useful, at times, in drawing attention to matters of future concern.

Finally, we sometimes encounter the flat dismissal of forecasting methodology. For example, "we just simply don't know how to forecast." I believe that such dismissal is largely because of misunderstanding or incomplete knowledge of the state of the art in forecasting.

You may have encountered other arguments, and it follows that we as forecasters should pursue the discipline of formally responding to each of them.

WHAT IS FORECASTING?

You may have noticed some of my comments thus far center on what forecasting is and is not. One of the first steps in our discussions was to define what we mean by forecasting. Wrangling with all the definitions that abound, we settled into defining forecasts as numerical estimates by date of the future that can be achieved with a specified level of support. Furthermore, the prediction is reproducible through a system of logic; i.e., if you apply the system to a given set of data and situation, the results are fairly consistent regardless of the analyst. True forecasts, therefore, rest on logic and not rhetoric.

Notice that this definition is not only a statement of what will occur, but also of what is possible. This latter part is more properly "planning" since it is a conditional statement of possibilities if support is given. So we view the elements common to useful forecasting to include: involvement of future and time; reliance on historical data; and uncertainty.

RATIONALE FOR FORECASTING

Another consideration in forecasting is the rationale for why it actually works. We can see the future coming, if we know what to look for because many things often progress in an astonishingly orderly manner over time. This consistent progress provides a basis for forecasting. At the same time, many things respond to needs, opportunities and support resources. If these driving forces can be identified, we believe future progress can be forecast.

FORECAST TRACKING

Because uncertainty always exists in forecasting, "tracking" is the means of keeping tabs on how well actual observations follow forecasted values. The primary purpose of tracking is to determine if and when forecasts should be revised. This is typically done by members of our group in one or a combination of two ways:

1. **Applying judgment rules.** Several rules used by members of our interest group include revising (a) when forecast errors exceed average period-to-period changes in actual observations, or (b) borrowing from econometrics, when errors are in the same direction for at least two consecutive periods, or (c) even more simply when errors exceed the adjustment capability of the company.

2. **Use of confidence intervals.** Borrowing from the discipline of manufacturing quality assurance, this means revising forecasts when actual observations fall beyond the forecast control band.

USES OF FORECASTS

The manner in which forecasts can be of value to users varies by individual management style. Notwithstanding, there are three basic uses of forecasts: planning, control and communication. In planning, forecasts identify new needs. They highlight opportunities and threats, establish goals, reveal problems, clarify issues needing better information, show timing and help to determine lead-time questions. On the other hand, used as a control mechanism, forecasts establish required performance and timing, and clarify areas needing monitoring. Finally, forecasts are a communication vehicle to management among functional areas of an organization like marketing, finance and production; and among people in divisions of the same firm.

ROLE OF THE FORECASTER

The role of the forecaster: objective analyst versus biased implementer and coordinator. This is an unusual paradox confronting the forecaster. Objective analyst generally is preferred by all of us, but it is idealistic when forecasting is viewed as an interface between art and science in practice. Forecasters must be responsive to organization needs and see that forecasts are used properly by assuming a degree of sales effort to educate users in understanding forecasts. "Biased implementer and coordinator" recognize that most practical forecasting is not done in a vacuum but rather in an environment of interchange between forecaster and forecast user.

To what extent should forecasters measure performance? Implicit in this question is the premise that most forecasters are, at some time or other, expected to give opinions, either formally or informally, concerning the performance of forecast users. Interestingly, this evaluation requirement is viewed as a necessary evil of the forecasting job since the issue is raised as to whom, other than the forecaster, is better equipped to assess certain aspects of user performance as they relate to controllable and non-controllable events. Perhaps the manager of sales analysis is a possible candidate. Yet in many organizations this person and the forecaster are one.

A significant portion of the attention for this issue centers on how our role as forecasters actually undermines the interpersonal relationships upon which we depend to accomplish forecasting tasks effectively. The fact that forecasters frequently need input from users causes concern for the degree to which working interactions would be impaired by the forecaster's evaluation role. In cases where the forecast is dependent on the user's input and the forecaster is faced with evaluating management performance, this task should be pursued to better management's understanding of its decision situation — something in the spirit of the McGregor positive "Theory Y" feedback concept.

HOW TO COMMUNICATE FORECASTS

What methods should and shouldn't be used in communicating forecasts? Basically, in our meetings, we agreed on seven elements that should be communicated in a forecast presentation:

1. Purpose or usefulness of the forecast (including its timeframe)
2. Key underlying assumptions
3. Input data
4. Forecast numbers themselves
5. Graphic display of history with the forecasts
6. Any other comments placing the forecasts in proper perspective
7. Reporting on the past forecasting performance record (This element was considered as an optional, but helpful step to establishing the forecast function, especially when the track record is favorable.)

Equally important are approaches for achieving successful communication. Successful forecast communication factors are: (a) oral, face-to-face delivery, (b) simplicity, (c) progressive dissemination, and (d) forecast ranges. Even though a written document is necessary, oral communication is the most effective means of "getting the forecasts across" to users. Second, simple presentations seem to be a watchword; that is, avoiding undue technical explanations, and keying our presentations to audience sophistication. The third point stresses that the forecast users need to be phased into progressive communication with the forecaster.

The ideal situation is a series of forecast presentations beginning with the most influential audiences and working progressively downward. The typical approach is to first "sell" the boss, then sell the first line subordinates (in a meeting with the boss), next, selling second line subordinates in a meeting (with their bosses), and so on.

Another successful communication element is for the presentation of the forecast to be a team effort which includes both the ranking individual responsible for the forecast (thus, lending credibility) and the technical expert(s) who does the actual preparation of the figures.

If we, forecasters and our customers, maintain continuous communication and interaction, usually no surprises are expected by the users. Consequently, in preliminary predictions, we should supply prediction ranges to prevent our users from latching on to singular numbers. Finally, resource expenditures for forecasts should not be emphasized, to avoid slanting user assessment of the forecasts. One further rather broad issue we encountered was whether to compromise technique to facilitate communication. In general, we agreed that technique must not be compromised to enhance the communication process. Where there is drastic diversity in the complexity of methods associated with different forecasts, we forecasters should select what we perceive as the most accurate forecast, regardless of the related methodology. This position, however, does not exclude the judicious adherence to statistical "parsimony," — that all things being equal, we should use the simplest approach — nor does it suggest that we should not be selective about what technical elements we choose to communicate to a specific audience.

The responsibility of communicating — indeed, educating — the user is an undeniable one for us as forecasters. A possible approach to meeting this responsibility successfully is to find a "rock" in the organization, a person who likely will be around for a while, with and through whom professional understanding can be developed. There are basically two strategies of pursuing the communication process where forecasting technique is concerned. Ideally, but definitely long-term oriented in nature, the first is the process of beginning with simple models for educating users, and then gradually evolving to the more complex methodology (if necessary) for the purpose of enhancing the forecaster's credibility. Alternatively, for the shorter term, the second approach is to take the single best shot, methodologically speaking, to develop the forecast, and then simplify its presentation according to the level of user sophistication.

Another point worthy to mention is that a "quickly generated" forecast sometimes tests a user's actual need for "good" projections. The trick is to find some way to be sure that the forecast user will come back if he really does need more sophistication.

Periodically, we forecasters have been trapped by some of our "quickies." One possible remedial approach is to add at the bottom of a communication something like, "this forecast would be sharpened by doing so and so; I stand ready to provide this refinement if you will just contact me."

Our discussions concluded that too often we are judged as forecasters more on our ability in presentation than on our technical competence. This seems to suggest either (a) the need for some kind of "interface" person; or (b) development of skills to present technical concepts in lay terms. We should avoid adding so many assumptions that users perceive the forecasts as meaningless. As a summary point, there is usually a natural evolution associated with the development of forecasts, i.e., as communication improves, it becomes much easier and more acceptable for organizations to use forecasting techniques of increasing complexity.

DATA HORROR STORIES

Sprinkled throughout the course of our discussions, war stories of data-related problems kept surfacing. Based on actual forecasting experiences, several generalized observations evolved (despite the watchword here being "ad-hoc"). Here are several examples, some you too may have encountered.

1. Frequently data are not kept at a low enough level of aggregation to be useful in the forecasting function.
2. Sometimes there is actually too much data with which to deal, based on the resources allocated to developing forecasts.
3. Many routine data reports generated are obsolete, at least for forecasting purposes.
4. Generated data sets are often incompatible because of timing inconsistencies, and lack common denominator standpoints for the forecasting system.
5. Data retrieval systems many times have not been debugged adequately.
6. Inflexible information system structures frequently inhibit forecasting efforts.
7. A multiplicity of data sources trying to measure the same item often means that we as forecasters must spend much time reconciling data sources rather than actually doing forecasting.
8. Finally, the distinctions between accounting and financial data versus sales or marketing data create a diversity of difficulties for forecasters.

OTHER USEFUL APPLICATION CONCEPTS

There are a variety of other useful applications concepts beyond those already mentioned that surfaced in our series of meetings:

1. The principle of "parsimony" has been mentioned, but deserves re-emphasis: always choose simplicity over complexity, if things are equivalent.
2. Forecasts must be revised periodically as time brings horizons closer and conditions change. This activity includes the need for detection of errors and for incremental corrections to improve understanding of underlying relationships.
3. From the forecaster's perspective, it is desirable to have a centralized source for data within the organization, e.g., a data base administrator, computer programmer, or librarian.
4. The forecaster's quest for the "Holy Grail" is to search for those key factors that are truly sensitive — to search for patterns of experience in one's own company and industry.
5. Finally, forecasting should not be viewed as an "answer" or a "decision," but, rather, as one more input for decision-making in managerial work. It seeks to make the reasoning explicit, again based on logic, not rhetoric.

FUTURE OF FORECASTING

In closing, I would like to shift focus and address the issue of the future of the forecasting profession — the future, meaning what lies before us and what role we should play.

First, we need to achieve agreement on what our forecasting profession is. It has intrigued me that the term 'forecaster' is not altogether well defined. Many people are called forecasters who do very different kinds of things loosely called forecasting. This fact poses the issue about what the relationships are among the types of forecasters and forecasting.

We can identify specifically two groups of forecasting activities. The first is research on forecasting theories, which is the development of models and techniques as done usually in academia. Another is the application of forecasting approaches performed primarily by practitioners. Practitioners work in government, industry, and sometimes in universities, but most often in a capacity as consultants. These two types of forecasting activities, theory and practice are seen by most of us as being related and I think they should be. But the question is are they really?

Our study group concluded that a large gap separates what practitioners consider useful, and what researchers develop. We noted the implementation omissions in research, while still recognizing the rapid progress made in forecasting models and techniques. This difference between the direction of research and the requirements of practitioners is a challenge to the forecasting discipline. It can be observed in other disciplines — for example, statistics, which is closely related to our profession of forecasting.

We forecasters, also, face the problem of a lack of common background. No undergraduate degree exists in forecasting. Before becoming forecasters, we all have had to study something else: statistics, mathematics, engineering, economics, psychology, computer science, business administration or whatever.

We lack an organizational culture — an organizational coherence in how we see ourselves and how we think and sense in relation to problems. Some of us may have a fairly limited perspective of our profession and think that only abstract problems are allowed. This limited perspective may be required for theoretical advancement of our field but certainly cannot be the view of most practicing forecasters. If that ever happened, our profession would run the risk of becoming detached from real problems and, consequently, losing visibility and impact.

There is another dangerous limited perspective of how we are seen by others. In some countries where The Coca-Cola Company does business, predicting the future is actually unlawful. The purpose of such laws or regulations is to protect the public from the exploitation of those who profess to foresee the future.

We should aim to avoid viewing ourselves or being viewed by others from these distorted and limited perspectives. As forecasters, I think our future is in viewing ourselves in a broad context — as members of a profession applying scientific techniques. This maturity, however, can be achieved only through some type of agreement between researchers and practitioners. This agreement should be a consensus that forecasting is both 'art', in the creative sense and 'science', in the sense of the disciplined use of techniques. Most of the art will come from the practitioners. If we can reach such agreement, our different backgrounds will become a key advantage rather than limitation.

We must work hard, however, to realize what should be a primary objective for the International Association of Business Forecasting. The aim is a unification of theorists and practitioners. Unification can be realized only by developing consistent scientific techniques supporting forecasting application. As forecasters we always should make use of scientific techniques, data and concepts. We should avoid blind acceptance of assumptions. Over the past 30 years, new and powerful techniques of forecasting have been developed. These methods have been embellished by improvements in data collection and publications concerning many and varied topical areas.

The most limiting aspect of forecasting, I believe, is the set of underlying assumptions that combines data and scientific techniques. Much of forecasting has led to poor predictions, not because of data deficiencies or inadequate techniques, but due to the absence of realism in the choice — indeed, the recognition — of the fundamental assumptions. This is one of the most basic aspects that all sciences face, and plays an even more critical role for social sciences.

Our business and economic environments are changing extraordinarily fast. The stability of their structures is short-term and is characterized by abrupt evolving changes. To generate good forecasts in these situations requires a major effort if we are to predict with accuracy, the direction and occurrence of these abrupt changes.

A problem with our times is that the future is no longer what it used to be. But the future is made up of our understanding of how things will happen and of our understanding of the coming of identifiable events. In the process of accounting for this coming, it is not enough to apply elaborate techniques to good historical data. There is a more fragile job of how we should represent a future that supports our scientific forecasts.

The professional societies such as International Association of Business Forecasting have a task in developing the forecasting profession. By means of conferences, publications and other activities, they should do all they can to promote forecasting and its application, as well as to foster the unification of practitioners and theorists. The goal is an increased effectiveness among forecasters leading to an improved contribution of forecasting to the well being of our society.

REFERENCES

1. Bright, James R. "Working Outline To Forecasting." (Unpublished) Circ. 1969, pp. 1-5.
2. Dagum, Estela Bee. "The Future of the Forecasting Profession." **International Journal of Forecasting.** Vol. 5, No. 2, 1989, pp. 155-157.
3. Makridakis, Spyros. "The Art and Science of Forecasting: An Assessment and Future Directions." **International Journal of Forecasting.** Vol. 2, No. 1, 1986, pp. 15-39.
4. Mohn, N. Carroll and John C. Reid. "Some Practical Guidelines For The Corporate Forecaster." **Interfaces.** Vol. 7, No. 3, 1977, pp. 70-75.

CHAPTER 3

TEN COMMANDMENTS OF BUSINESS FORECASTING

Chaman L. Jain

St. John's University

1. Thou shall learn to accept the future. The present exists only as a fleeting moment. What is present now will become past in a matter of seconds. Everything that we think and do from this point on will affect the future. It is the future that matters most. This is where we will be spending the rest of our lives.

2. Thou shall never take statistical numbers for granted. They are as flexible as a newborn child. One can mold and shape them in any way to prove ones point. Disraeli once said, "There is a lie, there is a damn lie and there is statistics."

3. Thou shall question forecaster and his/her numbers before accepting them. The more you know about the forecaster, data used, and assumption made in preparing forecasts, the more you will be in a position to evaluate them.

    Each forecaster has a bias of his/her own. Forecasts of a forecaster in New York are likely to be influenced by the ups and down in the stock market; in Detroit, by the ups and downs in the car industry; and in the South, by the ups and downs of the agricultural market. Also, some forecasters are conservative with a tendency to under-forecast, and others are liberal with a tendency to over-forecast. Many forecasters have their own pet models, which they use irrespective of the nature of data.

4. Thou shall need forecasts. Like it or not, you cannot run business without them. It's not uncommon to hear from someone, "we don't need forecasts." Everyone uses forecasts whether one recognizes it or not. They use forecasts to make a production plan, plan for Christmas sales, and develop a strategy for promotion. The only difference is that those who claim they use forecasts have a somewhat formal system in place, and those who claim they don't, use an informal system (seat-of-pants estimates).

FORECAST PREPARER

5. Thou shall never judge a model by its level of sophistication. Judging a model by the level of sophistication is like judging the quality of a product by its price tag. Simple models may work as well or better than the sophisticated ones. In search for a model, start from a simple to more complex one until your requirement for forecasting accuracy is met.

6. Thou shall never trust a model. It may fail you anytime. Keep a close eye on its performance. If and when it stops working, discard it. But before discarding it, make sure it is because of the model and nothing else. A model may not work in one specific period because of an unusual circumstance — the company lost one large customer, shortage of raw material, or tampering of a product (e.g., Tylenol in 1982). Try to understand why it did not work. If it was because of some unusual circumstances, it will start working again when the normal situation resumes.

7. Thou shall recognize that forecasts will be wrong. One thing we can be sure of in forecasting is that they will be wrong, though the size and direction of an error vary. Forecasters often aim for not eliminating the error all together but minimizing it. The error is not a terrible thing either, as long as it is well within the acceptable limits, we don't repeat the same error, we learn from it, and we put it to our own advantage.

8. Thou shall need blessing from the top management to set up a formal forecasting system. Don't even think about building a forecasting system if you don't have the full support from the top management. The system requires a huge sum to start and a huge sum to maintain. Without their support, you, the forecaster, will get nowhere.

9. Thou shall never be emotional if someone adjusts your forecasting numbers. Different functional heads often have an urge to make some judgmental adjustments. But document the original and adjusted forecasts, so that they know in the future who was right and who was wrong.

10. Thou shall never be a good forecaster unless you are a good marketer as well. Preparing just accurate forecasts is not sufficient. You have to know how to sell them to the users. If users don't accept and use your numbers, the forecasts are useless, no matter how accurate they are.

CHAPTER 4

FORECASTING GUIDELINES

D. F. D'Attilio
E. I. Dupont de Nemours & Co.

Forecasting theory is a must, but there is no substitute for hands on experience. Here is what I learned over the period:

1. Best approach is to stay at the forecasting job continuously, always modify the forecast on the basis of fresh information.

2. Thoroughly understand your starting points — what your current level of net income is, what your current capital expenditure rate is, and so on. They will serve as points of reference.

3. Identify assumptions underlying the forecast in a clear, concise manner.

4. Avoid jargon. Present forecast in a logical and easy to understand format.

5. The forecast horizon should rarely be more than a year, and sometimes should be less than that.

6. Never work for more accuracy than needed. Round numbers wherever possible.

7. Use simple, straight-forward forecasting techniques. Sophisticated and complex procedures do not guarantee more accurate results.

8. Where possible, use personal computer, not main-frame system.

9. Always challenge existing forecasting procedures. Cross check results via other approaches such as statistical methods that include trend analysis, regression and exponential smoothing.

10. Periodically, evaluate the overall forecasting system. Conduct an audit.

CHAPTER 5

THE CHANGING ROLE OF SALES FORECASTING WITHIN AN ORGANIZATION

Charles W. Chase, Jr.
Wyeth-Ayerst Pharmaceuticals

The nineties have made information one of the most important commodities in our business environment. The companies with the best information, and who have learned how to manage it effectively have prospered over the competition. This need for accurate information has compelled companies to re-define the responsibilities of Sales Forecasting and Marketing Analysis. To truly understand the implications surrounding these changes one must recognize the evolving roles of the sales forecasting process. During the past several years sales forecasting has become a segmented discipline supporting two separate roles, both not necessarily mutually exclusive of one another. The first can be described as *"Tactical"* or demand forecasting. Demand forecasts are essentially sales forecasts of consumer demand at the customer (account) level utilizing P.O.S. (point-of-sale) data. In turn, those projections are compared to customer inventory resulting in a customer demand order. This is the difference between order forecasting and sales demand forecasting. The primary purpose of sales demand forecasts is to drive manufacturing and replenishment requirements associated with Efficient Consumer Response (E.C.R.). E.C.R. is a pooling of retailers' and manufacturers' resources to obtain knowledge through the use of information and technology to improve marketing decisions and customer service. Together, the retailer and manufacturer increase shelf turns and market share both of which grow the business and improve profitability.

The second role of sales forecasting can be referred to as decision-support forecasting or *"Strategic"* forecasting. Strategic forecasting focuses on producing regional level sales projections that assist management in the development of the financial budget, marketing plan, and long-range strategic business planning. Subsequently, providing management with detailed business analysis (i.e., price sensitivity, media responsiveness, and event analysis) of the business drivers that influence sales demand. In other words, tactical demand forecasting tends to be more short-range sales/logistics based, while strategic sales forecasting is more long-range marketing/finance oriented. Both roles require similar proactive statistical methodologies that integrate those business drivers impacting the business, such as price, advertising, coupon drops, consumer/trade events, and competitor influences. The differences occur as we begin to look at the business in a more finite manner (i.e., regional or account-specific slices). In these particular situations, data requirements change significantly. The need for account specific and/or regional level historical information becomes extremely important depending on the purpose or role of the sales forecast. Furthermore, managing this additional information requires more complex system capabilities, and integration of Field Sales information, as well as customer point-of-sale (P.O.S.) data.

The enabling systems supporting the sales forecasting process should have the ability to interactively gather all the pertinent information required to provide actionable decision-support analysis. Such analyses will ultimately influence the development of the marketing plan, the financial budget, and capacity planning. Furthermore, more sophisticated forecasting software packages need to be embedded as the primary engine allowing practitioners to choose from an array of methodologies. Like a surgeon of medicine they can dissect the information and apply the proper procedure accordingly. Unfortunately, companies in many industries, particularly the consumer packaged goods industry, have found that their forecasting processes and systems have not kept pace with rapid technological advances; and the failure to update them has inhibited their ability to achieve new business advantages. Many companies are aware that improved forecast accuracy can improve cost efficiencies by lowering finished goods inventories, but only few have begun to realize how structural analysis can help increase marketing spend efficiencies, thereby increasing profits. However, they are unwilling to commit resources to develop more sophisticated forecasting applications and redesign processes that eliminate barriers between political agendas and practical needs. Companies who are striving to become more market-driven also recognize that the involvement of a more highly skilled and motivated business forecasting team can help them navigate through these processes and operate the supporting systems. Subsequently, empowering them to continuously improve the processes and systems to meet the evolving needs of the business.

Most companies today have disaggregated sales forecasting process driven by simplistic methods, rather than an integrated sales forecasting process driven by sophisticated methods. Those companies who learn how to design and implement an integrated sales forecasting process that combines both strategic and tactical forecasting will experience the benefits of reduced finished goods inventories and an improved knowledge base. As a result of these changes business forecasters need to become generators of sales forecasts instead of gatherers and processors of sales forecasts. In other words, in these new roles, practitioners must move to a proactive stance providing actionable decision-support analysis that influences executive management decisions.

As companies begin to harness the power of information to better serve their customers, as they reengineer their processes and systems to increase efficiency, and as they train and empower their employees to continuously improve all areas of the business, they need to seriously consider the benefits of business forecasting. Those who begin to increase their ability to anticipate customer demand will also better understand the implications of their actions in the marketplace.

CHAPTER 6

TEN PRESCRIPTIONS FOR FORECASTING SUCCESS

Mark J. Lawless
National Fire Protection Association

Since the demand for forecast services is a derived demand, it is important that forecasters understand and adapt to the changing need of those who create the demand. In order to understand and adapt, it is wise to consider the factors, which are changing the expectations for performance of those who use the forecast. Forecasts are used as a part of the management decision and control processes, which in turn are a part of the larger effort (and responsibility) of the management to create value for the shareholders or other constituent groups. More than ever before, managers are being measured and rewarded based upon their ability to create acceptable business returns for their investors, and continue to add value in a market environment which is becoming more efficient, competitive, and global in scope. Forecasters are expected to provide information, which supports these needs. There are ten prescriptions for the success of a forecaster.

PRESCRIPTION NO. 1

The first prescription for forecasters is to carefully evaluate and consider their future projects in the context of the potential ability of the effort to support the value creation expectations of the shareholder and of the management. Given the value focus of the management and the shareholders, the willingness to support broad level forecasting and market research activities which cannot be directly linked to business operations and value creation is likely to diminish. The ability to demonstrate that the forecasting project will improve operations, support increasing sales efforts, or similar value creation activities will increase the chances of acceptance, and will increase the role of the forecast function in the management of the business. Understand the factors, which create value for the company as well as for the management.

PRESCRIPTION NO. 2

The second prescription is to vigorously incorporate technology into the forecast process and methods. The effects of corporate downsizing and continued pressure of competition will place great stress on support functions throughout the organization, including the forecast function. There will be less time and less human resources with which to develop forecasts. The computer hardware and software has certainly made this feasible, and the prudent forecast function will carefully consider the substitution of technology for personnel. The investment in personnel is like an annuity, while the investment in technology is characterized by bursts of investment (but not the commitment to a recurring fixed cost element). More importantly, the technology integration will make possible the development of forecasts in the shortened time frames which management has available to it. And doing so with higher reliability, expert systems, decision support systems, and neural networks will be increasingly used in the profession.

PRESCRIPTION NO. 3

The third prescription for forecasters is to work carefully with management to make realistic promises. In an environment of changing expectations for management, it is important for forecasters to manage the expectations for the forecast function. Forecasters should work carefully with managers to understand their needs, and to communicate in advance the reliability issues, operational and business issues, and other ramifications to be realized from the projection. It is most important not to make unrealistic promises, since this undermines the credibility of the function and the value of the function to management's long-term value creation responsibilities. Be realistic in managing expectations, and resist the tendency to over promise. (Remember what happened as a result of the over promising of the strategic planning functions — which in many cases are now non-existent or substantially reduced in size and effectiveness.)

PRESCRIPTION NO. 4

The fourth prescription is to understand the nature of the decision to which the forecast is going to be applied. Management may not be asking for the best approach to meet their decision need. Or the design of the forecast model and its reliability characteristics may be affected by the nature of the decision to be made. Get into the management's heads in order to discern the application and need, rather than blindly jumping into a projection process with the tools at hand, which may not be the best tools for the purpose.

PRESCRIPTION NO. 5

The fifth prescription is to carefully characterize the relevant conditions and operative variables on a prospective basis. Given the changing environment in which the forecasts are being applied, it is important to monitor the expected performance of the model or approach over the time horizon for the management decision. Since cycle times, product life cycles, and technology life cycles are all decreasing, it can be dangerous to simply assume that the patterns and operative variables which have characterized the past will continue indefinitely into the future. Patterns and relationships, which may have existed for long periods of time, can be quickly compromised in a global competition and in culturally diverse markets.

PRESCRIPTION NO. 6

The sixth prescription is the use of a band of projections along with scenario development. The very conditions under which businesses and management operate are becoming more volatile in nature. This higher degree of operating risks implies that the development of point projections is increasingly inappropriate to the situation. This is more appropriate to decisions, which face a range of uncertain outcomes, and for which the management must assume the responsibility of making a decision based upon expected values. The use of point projections can be quite misleading and communicate a sense of certainty that is inappropriate to the business condition. Probably, nothing has done more to indict the validity and accuracy of forecasts than the use of point projections where a band of projections should have been used.

PRESCRIPTION NO. 7

The seventh prescription is to ensure that a monitoring process is established to inform management of decisions, which should be revisited as a result of actual conditions observed. The purpose of a projection is generally not to just provide a single estimate, but is quite often to better understand the business considerations which have the most potential for changing a management decision if the associated values were to change. An important decision feature of a projection is to know when its assumptions are no longer valid and to abandon the forecast when actual conditions begin to vary substantially from those postulated in the forecast. Careful identification of operational leverage points and critical variables to the forecast model assist in the development of effective mechanisms which help management in being sensitive to changes in market and competitive conditions. The trick is to stay focused on the variables and conditions, which truly make a difference to the forecast and to the management decision, for which the forecast is targeted. Ultimately, the only true measure of a forecast is its ability to improve the quality and effectiveness of management decisions.

PRESCRIPTION NO. 8

The eighth prescription is to work with the management to develop specific operational models, objectives, business strategies, and a set of business variables, which are critical to their operational goals. Because the use of forecasts tends to be decision oriented, it is important to study and understand the operations (and management culture) of the organizations, which are using the forecast. Forecasters should align their interests and concerns with the management groups to which they are providing forecast information. This informs the forecaster of the issues that are most important to the management group, which assists both in the forecasting and the interpretation of the ramifications of the forecast. This alliance or partnership of management and forecaster is essential to the credibility and effectiveness of both forecast and forecaster. It also creates the basis for adaptation of models and forecasts as the operating environment of the management continues to change.

PRESCRIPTION NO. 9

The ninth prescription is to spend time with the management to ensure that the methods fit the business problems (and management culture), the management conceptually understands the statistical quality and reliability of parameters of the projection, and alternative scenarios or assumptions are clear to the management in its choice of forecast. It is important for the forecaster and the management to have a common base of understanding of capabilities and the limits of the forecast and the methods used. Since management is not interested in forecast methods, but rather is concerned about the effectiveness of their decisions, it is wise for this development of a common frame of reference to minimize technical jargon. This is a difficult undertaking, since it is incumbent upon the forecaster to express technical concepts in a non-technical and intuitive manner to the management. Since a critical part of the forecaster's job is to create realistic expectations (do not over promise), this prescription may actually be the most important, and is supportive of all of the others previously described.

PRESCRIPTION NO. 10

The tenth (and last) prescription is for the forecaster to acquire general management skills and perspective. There is an old saying, "If you can't beat them, join them." This is an advice which may be important for forecasters in every organization or company. In order to be effective as a forecaster, to some degree one has to think like the management. This implies that the forecaster should not consider himself or herself to be a data evaluator outside of the functions for which the projections are being provided. An effective forecaster must understand the business, the markets, the competition, and the operations as well as (or better) than those who are making the management decisions. Technology advances (both hardware and software) will continue to reduce the need for purely technical interpretation of the forecasts. The more important characteristics of a forecaster will be the ability to understand, interpret, and recommend actions appropriate to a management or business situation. It is important for forecasters to expand the horizon of their interests to include all of the facets of operating and managing a business, even if the interest stops at using the information for future forecasting needs. Acquiring such knowledge and skills will increase the credibility of the forecast and the forecaster, while making the forecaster a more effective part of the management team and of the management process. In a world of increasing competition and technology adoption, simply providing statistical, econometric, and technical forecasting skills will not be sufficient. Like the expert systems and artificial intelligence systems that are developing, the forecasters must also adapt their activities and roles to the changing patterns of business and management need.

The environment of business continues to change at an increasing rate, and with it the demands on management to create value is increasing. The role of forecasters is changing as well, and the value created by the forecaster is very much a consideration in the role which forecasting plays in the management decision process.

If management must create value for the shareholder, the forecaster must create value for the shareholder as well. Hence, rather than pining for earlier times when things were better for forecasters, we need to adapt to the changing environment as well. We need to be continuously asking: "How can we create value? How can we enhance value? How can we assist others in creating value?" If forecasters will ask themselves these simple questions, and act upon their answers, the ability of forecast functions to be effective and credible will take care of itself. Looking to the needs of the management decisions, using whatever information is available (imperfect though it may be), and developing the forecasts and recommendations in the context of these management needs are important parts of the forecast function.

To be successful in the future, there are two important ground rules for all forecasters — be relevant and be effective. The ten prescriptions for success are a means of being both.

CHAPTER 7

THE FORECASTING FUNCTION: CRITICAL YET MISUNDERSTOOD

Luis Reyes
i2 Technologies

Let's begin with by stating the obvious. Forecasting is probably one of the most important functions in an organization. It has a direct impact on strategic planning, and acquisition and allocation of resources. Many argue that forecasting is also one of the most misunderstood functions in corporate America. How can such an important business function be misunderstood? This is the question often raised by many practicing forecasters. This paper provides specific points of view on this matter, as well as a road map to make the forecasting function successful.

WHY FORECASTING FUNCTION MISUNDERSTOOD

A part of the answer lies within the forecasting profession itself. The traditional forecaster is a technical individual who can build complex models to determine trends and relationships in the data. This is important in business forecasting but it is only a part of the total equation. The other more important parts are business knowledge, and interpersonal and communication skills.

Sales and Marketing professionals, who collectively play a large role in shaping the demand for a product, generally do not understand the forecasting function, nor do they have any interest in understanding the technical lingo (R square, Durbin Watson, etc.). Therefore, the forecaster must be able to communicate to the management in non-technical terms. The forecaster must describe the specific products and account strategies that are to be used by different functions. This is essential because forecasts that do not account for such strategies (promotions, price structure, competitive activities, etc.) will be of little value. Furthermore, the forecaster must communicate the impact of a strategy on the forecast, given trends, seasonality and other causal variables. If the forecaster does not communicate to the management in simple terms, all the hard work will be mostly wasted and credibility will be lost. It is that simple!

Communication is the cornerstone of successful forecasting. The forecaster obtains information from Sales and Marketing, as well as from models about seasonality, trends and causal relationships. The forecaster then communicates all the information to the management, thereby closing the communication loop. Unfortunately, this loop is the exception rather than the rule in many of today's forecasting functions, especially within the consumer products industry. Often the emphasis is placed on one dimensional "black box" forecasting. This is typified by a system with historical shipment data going in and some sort of forecast report coming out, without any business input. This practice adds little value to the organization, and perpetuates the obscurity surrounding the forecasting function. In fact, the "black box" approach to forecasting is probably the principle cause of this misunderstanding. This has resulted in many failures in forecasting, making management increasingly reluctant to invest in or promote forecasting as a function. Although management as a whole generally agrees on the positive value of developing forecasts based on facts and causal data, only marginal and usually inadequate resources are committed, often ensuring failure from the start.

Although the above comments seem to paint a negative picture of the forecasting profession, don't be discouraged. Forecasting professionals can add enormous value to the business in terms of higher customer service levels, substantial inventory cost reduction, and market-place knowledge. We just need to make some adjustments.

HOW TO STRENGTHEN THE FORECASTING FUNCTION

How can the organization reap tangible benefits from the forecasting function? It requires management's courage to establish the function with necessary resources and training, and then continues with total support as the function matures. It is very important that individuals selected for the forecasting function have the proper training. This does not suggest that they have to be statisticians, but rather they receive as much training as necessary in model development and data analysis. To ensure a full understanding of the drivers and constraints that govern the business, it is crucial that the forecasters are integrated into the business process. In addition, forecasters should be somewhat extrovert and possess good communication skill. Generally, there is no problem with professionals of other disciplines becoming forecasters. In fact, this is often the case. However, it does present a serious problem when these individuals are not trained properly or do not have the necessary interpersonal skill required by the job.

Another essential ingredient of a successful forecasting function is its strategic placement in the organization at large. Since forecasting is primarily concerned with the marketplace, there must be a direct communication line between the forecaster and the Sales and Marketing professionals. Sales and Marketing professionals have vast amounts of knowledge of the marketplace, and can impact the forecasts through promotions, price structures and other strategic initiatives. The forecaster should have first hand knowledge of these plans, because they have the greatest impact on Product Demand. Many believe that the forecasting function should be a part of the Marketing department. In reality, it should not matter to whom the forecasting function reports to as long as it has access to this market information.

One more thought about the forecasting function: forecasting practitioners probably have one of the toughest jobs in the company. The job requires that the practitioner maintains objectivity and does not succumb to political pressure that is so common in forecasting, makes decisions based on hard evidence, challenges those who disagree with facts, raises issues when necessary, regularly measures his or her own performance, and is flexible to change the course when the model or strategy is not working. The forecasting function must have total management support, especially during its infancy. Otherwise, given the nature and complexity of the job, as well as the visibility placed on the "numbers," the process and the individuals are likely to fail.

The forecasting tool-kit is another important component of a successful forecasting function. It has already been established that it should not be a "black box," but rather an interactive tool that can be easily used by the forecasters and to some extent, by the organization as a whole. Key to the tool - box are models that can establish seasonality and trends from data, as well as relationships with causal variables. The tool-kit should provide graphical reporting and error tracking capabilities to facilitate analyses and reporting of the forecast history and causal data.

The supporting database should be multi-dimensional representing product structures, as well as geographical areas where the products are sold. Such a database facilitates the analysis of data and the development of forecasts at levels that make the most sense. For example, it may be more effective to forecast a highly promoted SKU at an account level, and non-promoted SKU at an aggregate level. Likewise, it may be more effective to have the Key Account Managers develop a forecast of a promoted SKU in conjunction with buyers, using a simple smoothing model. The account specific data such as inventory, consumption levels, regional promotions, etc., can be captured and analyzed independently or in aggregate. Finally, consider this example. What is the value of a low forecast error at an aggregate level when key accounts are in backorder because the inventory was deployed in the wrong warehouses. The dimensional database can help to solve such a problem.

SUMMARY

To summarize, "black box" forecasting functions must evolve an interactive approach in order to add value to an organization. In addition, the forecasting practitioners must have a strong analytical skill, as well as good communication and interpersonal skills. The forecasting function is more than just modeling. It requires the forecaster to understand the business drivers, and communicate the results to management in non-technical terms. The forecasting tool must be robust. It must include a dimensional database, forecast error measures, reporting features and causal models. Management must make significant commitments to the forecasting function in terms of support, resources, training, and process execution. With all these, the forecasting profession will gain credibility and dispel obscurity that surrounds it.

The formal forecasting function can improve customer service levels, as well as increase both the bottom and top lines of the P&L. Substantial savings can be realized in inventory carrying cost by improving forecast accuracy. It can reduce loss of business due to stock-outs, and improve top-line sales. In addition, models that incorporate causal variables such as promotions, economic measures and competitive activity can increase top-line sales by identifying the most consumer effective programs in a given period of time or economic condition. An organization that includes this knowledge in their strategic portfolio can reap tangible economic benefits and stay one step ahead of the competition.

CHAPTER 8

STATISTICAL FORECASTING: VOODOO MAGIC OR INTELLECTUAL EXERCISE

David J. Kitska
Rubbermaid, Inc.

Most anyone would be amazed at the rapid development of business forecasting software, a development which parallels the incredible growth of the computer industry as a whole. Certainly no one can deny the positive benefits: complicated data management and statistical analysis can now take place on any executive's desktop. Software companies have been very sensitive to the call for forecasting packages that require no technical expertise and only a few keystrokes to run. Unfortunately, with any positive development there are always potential problems. In particular, while statistics is now a widely used tool in business forecasting, it is also one of the most abused and misunderstood. Statistical analysis often suffers from unrealistic assumptions on the part of management and is therefore often relegated to an improper role within the company's organization. The purpose of this paper is to help situate statistical analysis properly within the entire forecasting scheme. To do this, we must overturn some of the popular perceptions of statistics and achieve a realistic understanding of what it can do and cannot do. This paper, however, is not a scholarly treatise. It largely embodies my own opinions and observations, and so the reader may take it at face value.

THE TWO EXTREMES

Based upon my experiences and conversations with analysts in other companies, I have concluded that many managers and other non-technical people have distorted views of statistical modeling and software. At opposite ends of the spectrum, we have those who dismiss the whole idea of statistical forecasting as some kind of "voodoo" magic and those who have completely unrealistic expectations of the ease and accuracy of such methods.

Admittedly, people usually fall somewhere in between with varying tendencies toward one extreme or the other. However, both of the extreme cases share a common characteristic in that their stereotypical attitudes arise from a lack of experience with statistics. At the risk of over-generalizing, I will deal only with the extremes and allow the reader to contemplate the intermediate types.

THE PESSIMISTS

Individuals tending to the first extreme often treat statistical forecasting as a mere "intellectual exercise." They may look at the software and the formulas as something "dreamed up" by academicians who have no understanding of how the "real world" works. They sometimes do not understand how a simple statistical formula may predict a world, which is full of complication and uncertainty.

Their attitudes, nevertheless, are understandable and, as we will see, not without some merit. Most statistical methods have either been originated or refined by academic people in a scholarly process that often occurs outside the practical business world. Naturally, practitioners will be suspicious of a process in which they do not usually play a part. Many of the mathematical calculations in statistical models often appear very esoteric to anyone without the technical background.

Although the pessimism is understandable, it may still have serious negative consequences. In the worst case, statistical forecasting may be so thoroughly distrusted that it may not even be attempted. This often happens when management harbors the attitude that the only way to make a forecast is to rely on intuition and experience. While these ingredients are certainly indispensable in a forecasting system, they are not the only sources of information, nor are they the only basis for justifying particular forecast numbers. Statistics can be a useful tool among all the other ingredients.

It has also been my experience that whenever statistical analysis is neglected, data management and report writing suffer as well. A significant part of a good forecasting system is organizing the data in the most useful form and persuading people to examine that data periodically. When statistics is a serious pursuit, people have an immediate incentive to capture, store, organize, rationalize, and analyze the data. When statistics has low priority or is neglected entirely, the incentive for data management diminishes.

THE OPTIMISTS

At the other extreme, you will find people almost captivated by modern sophisticated computers and mathematical formulas. They sometimes attribute superior reasoning and limitless power to those electronic brains. I heard perhaps the best expression of this attitude when I once heard someone say, "Anything that a human mind can do, the computer can be programmed to do as well or better." Moreover, these people often mistake statistics as a "cut-and-dry" science, devoid of any human interpretation, judgment or creativity.

NO SUBSTITUTE FOR HUMAN JUDGMENT

These optimistic feelings often lead to two major fallacies. First, it is often believed that a forecasting system can be fully automated where the only user intervention is a few strokes on a keyboard. When this goal is pursued, the forecaster may be forced to abdicate much of his or her analytical function and is reduced to a clerical position. Secondly, the electronically produced forecasts are expected to be consistently accurate since, after all, they were generated by the "all knowing" super machine.

STATISTICS: NO PANACEA

Anyone who has had to forecast hundreds or thousands of items continuously can tell you that forecast accuracy can vary considerably from product to product and from time period to time period. Applying a statistical algorithm to a product's history implicitly assumes that the product is statistically predictable in the first place. Certain products have enough of a repeating pattern in their history that they can be closely approximated by such a method, but others are so volatile that some other non-statistical treatment would be preferable. These are some basic facts of forecasting which no computer or software package, to date, can change.

The common problem with the die-hard pessimists and the extreme optimists is that they are both searching for perfection. The pessimists dismiss statistical forecasting because it isn't perfect, and the optimists soon become disillusioned because their grand expectations must collide with reality. Both types of individuals must learn to accept statistics on a realistic basis.

Statistical methods have been and always will be an important part of forecasting, but they are not a panacea. Forecasters and managers must realize that most statistical algorithms are derived from highly theoretical and often ideal assumptions. Often these assumptions can only be partially met in the real world. A method, which is "best" from a theoretical point of view, may not be best in all applications.

For example, there is a difference between what a forecaster would mean and what a mathematical statistician would mean when they speak of an "optimal" forecasting method. The statistical definition of "optimally," whether it be in classical sampling theory or in stochastic processes, generally refers to several ideal properties resulting from a large number of replications, or in the broadest theoretical sense, from all possible replications. Statisticians often use a measure called the theoretical "mean square error" to compare different forecast methods. Optimality for a forecaster, however, places more emphasis on minimizing the forecast error for specific, finite time periods.

When statisticians advocate a certain method because of its "minimum mean square estimator" property (MMSE), they mean that the method will produce the smallest possible average error across all possible realizations of a stochastic process. But a forecaster only has one realization or time series available for analysis: he cannot go back in time and restart the process over and over to generate all possible realizations. The mathematical formula or method for finding the MMSE of a forecast function can be applied to a single series, but the result will only be an estimate, tainted by a certain level of sampling error. The theoretical forecast function may have the smallest long-run average error for all realizations, but that does not guarantee that the estimated function will yield the smallest forecast error for a particular series and for a particular time period.

Moreover, statistical forecasts are in fact estimates of conditional expectations. In other words, a statistical model technically does not predict the "next value" in a time series; rather, it estimates an expected or mean value for a future time period. Also consider the fact that a recorded time series itself will contain sampling and measurement error and may be only an incomplete record of a product's entire history.

STATISTICAL FORECASTING: MIXTURE OF ART AND SCIENCE

When we recognize all these sources of imprecision, it is clear that statistical forecasting cannot be approached as a "cut-and-dry" science. For reasons cited above, any statistical forecast will contain error: that's why it is always a good policy to examine confidence intervals. But what is even more significant is the fact that statistical modeling will always be a mixture of art and science. The computer may follow its programmed check list and turn out its preferred model, but experienced statisticians know that computers do not always make the best statistical decisions. The theoretical assumptions behind a particular forecast methodology may only be partially reproduced in a practical setting. Therefore, it may be necessary to interpret a given situation using a variety of statistical tests and criteria. Uncertainty requires a certain amount of human intuition, creativity, judgment, and experimentation. In other words, statistics does not always follow a neat flow chart. The computer's "mind," however, makes automatic decisions based on specific "If and then" rules and may easily overlook options or subtleties which are apparent only to the human eye.

These comments should not be misconstrued to imply that imprecision can be used as an excuse for sloppiness in statistical technique. By creativity, I am not advocating that the analyst abandon theory and follow arbitrary feelings, or perform some manipulation just because it "looks good." Every method should have some theoretical motivation or appeal. But those familiar with the theory of statistics know that there will often be room for judgment and for several possible solutions within a general guiding framework.

THE PROPER ROLE FOR STATISTICS

What, then, is the best policy for treating computer-generated forecasts? Such forecasts should always be treated with a certain amount of suspicion and subjected to an extensive evaluation.

When hundreds or thousands of products are involved, the forecaster obviously cannot review the computer's logic and judgment behind every forecast. As a practical compromise, I suggest that the forecaster should identify those products, which are most vital to the company's business and concentrate on them. This can be done, for example, on the basis of sales volume by choosing the twenty, thirty, or so top selling items. The forecaster should perform continuous data analysis on these items, including interactive model building and forecasting as a check against the computer's automatic methods. If a forecaster wishes to understand the company's business patterns with all its trends, cycles, and seasons, the forecaster must keep a close relationship with the data, or at least part of it. That relationship cannot be surrendered entirely to a machine.

When all the statistical forecasts have been finalized, the forecasting process itself must continue through a complex administrative process. This fact bewilders those who believe that the "forecasting system" is in place as soon as the software is loaded. Management must bring together personnel from a variety of areas — product management, inventory control, manufacturing, and sales — to review and evaluate the forecasts because of their practical hands-on experience with the company's day-to-day business, these people will be in the best position to judge the forecasts' credibility. They will have access to information not considered by the statistical models. They will be in the best position to answer questions such as, "Do the forecasts make sense based upon what we know about the business environment, our own business plans, competitive activities, and customer behavior?" In this case, statistics is allowed to play its role among other sources of information: it becomes one tool in a complete arsenal.

STATISTICAL MODEL: SIMPLIFICATION OF REALITY

Keep in mind that a statistical model is a simplification of reality and is therefore inherently imperfect. A time series model only looks at the previous patterns in a product's history, estimates appropriate parameters for the trend, cycles, and seasons, and then projects that pattern into the future. In this way, time series models are naive. Exogenous variables can be introduced to form regression or transfer function models, but even these are only approximations of the real world.

It would be unfair to dismiss statistical models entirely because they are "too simple" or "too naive." They may not process the same amount or the same kinds of information that the human counterpart would, but, in reality, they were never meant to do that. Part of their beauty is their parsimony: their purpose is to use a narrow range of information in the most efficient way. Statistical models are meant to be economical starting points.

Moreover, a distinction should be made between what Barr and Zehna would call a model's accuracy and its utility. Of course, a forecast analyst's primary goal is to produce the most accurate forecasts possible, and so the accuracy criterion is very important when choosing between several different forecasting methods. However, while a model may not be as accurate as desired, it may still offer important information about the particular product in question. In other words, the model may still have a utility or a usefulness that goes beyond the question of accuracy for a specific time period. The model fitting process, with its preliminary data analysis and post-hoc diagnostics and evaluation, can help an analyst discover and measure underlying trends, cycles, and seasons. A model, which indicates that a product may be nearing a peak in its performance or that a shift in trend may be occurring, may have a qualitative value even if the model's quantitative estimates of that peak or trend are questionable.

STATISTICAL MODELS LACK THE ABILITY TO PEER INTO THE FUTURE

Because statistical models are summarization of the past, they often lack the ability to peer into the future or to consider very recent events. Sometimes, additional adjustments are necessary after the model-fitting process is complete. For example, a statistical model typically does not consider any orders, which may already be in-house for those future periods. Thus, it is not unlikely for a statistically sound model to forecast, say, 1,000 pieces of a certain item for next month and for there to be an order already in for 1000 pieces. The model obviously is not structured to consider this "future" demand because it lives only in those months which have passed into the company's official history.

What can be done statistically in a situation such as this? We could go back to the computer printout and examine the forecast's confidence intervals to arrive at a maximum threshold level. Or we could apply additional statistical methodologies to see if we could produce a more realistic forecast. Or perhaps, we could boost the statistical forecast by some percentage based upon what we would normally expect in demand for that particular month and season. For instance, suppose that we wish to forecast an item's total demand for next month and that based on historical patterns, we would expect about 20% of next month's orders already to be in-house. The computer forecasts 1,000 units, but the total demand already is 1,200. About 20% of that 1,200 is ""normal" demand and the other 80% is part of what a statistician would call "white noise." A crude adjustment would involve treating the 1,000 number as an accurate forecast of "normal" demand and then adding to that the 80% of the total demand considered abnormal. The total forecast would then be $1000 + .8 (1200) = 1960$.

Of course, this latter method is imprecise. The 20% is an estimate and therefore contains sampling error. Because the rate of order entry for future months may be highly erratic, the estimate of 20% may have very low efficiency and reliability. We also naively assume that the 1,000 units is an accurate forecast of the "usual" demand.

In the end, we cannot escape the necessity to have statistical forecasts tested by those who have the practical business knowledge. In fact, final responsibility for the forecast should reside with management and not with the technical people. The role of the latter group should be to provide the best possible software and statistical support to the practitioners. The managers are obligated, in turn, to give their technical people the necessary tools and to grant them an active role in the forecasting process. Both groups must develop empathy and respect for each other. Managers should have realistic expectations of statistical forecasts, and the forecasters must appreciate the practical business world. Forecasters must expect and welcome a certain amount of skepticism and should not be offended when managers unscientifically "tweak" or "massage" the forecasts. In the final analysis, what is the ultimate purpose of forecasting? It is not intended to be an intellectual exercise. It is intended to provide the most accurate number possible, using all of the available tools and personnel in a unifying organization.

REFERENCES

1. Barr, Donald, and Peter W. Zehna. **Probability: Modeling Uncertain.** Reading, MA: Addison Wesley Publishing Company, 1983.
2. Box, George, E. P. and Gwilym M. Jenkins, **Time Series Analysis: Forecasting and Control.** 2nd ed. San Francisco: Holden-Day, 1976.
3. Pankratz, Alan. **Forecasting with Univariate Box Jenkins Models: Concepts and Cases.** New York: John Wiley and Sons, 1983.

CHAPTER 9

HOW TO COPE WITH REALITIES OR WHY FORECASTS GO AWRY: GOOD OLD CHARLIE HOLDS THE KEY

Charles W. Gross and Thomas W. Knowles
University of New Hampshire

Almost all of the forecasting literature is devoted to introducing, refining, augmenting, and comparing various mathematical techniques. The methods do differ in complexity, ranging from the "soft" techniques such as Delphi to the more "rigorous" such as Box-Jenkins and econometric models. Nonetheless, the focus is almost exclusively on seeking that "better" technique. Further, advancing computer availability and technology have greatly facilitated diffusion of "scientific" forecasting throughout the ranks of practitioners. In turn, each of these disciplines also tends to develop a love affair with that next "better" technique. The problem is that the resulting forecasts themselves are not necessarily getting that much better. Many offices have a "good-old-Charlie," an analyst who seems always able to beat the most elegant model. Each period "Charlie" doodles a bit on a scratch pad, plays a little with a calculator, scratches his head and adds a fudge factor, and presto. The result is a forecast that is very good, one that management "buys." And in fact, "Charlie's" forecast is as accurate, if not more so than that spit out by the most elegant computer system using the "best" of those "better" techniques. Charlie's success may be credited to E.S.P., or even luck. But it is far more likely that it is due to a deep understanding of his organization's inner working past, present and future. Few people have the artistry of a "Charlie." And the systematic reliability of "Charlie" or his replacement can certainly be questioned.

Thus, there is a great need to develop technique-driven-forecasting systems in most organizations. But equally questionable are the blind-faith following of and "overkill" on technique. No mathematical forecasting technique can capture all of the organizational interactions that lead to the actual sales results. The effectiveness of forecasting systems, and their resulting forecasts, depends on, in large part, whether or not an organization's dynamics are taken into consideration. This paper explores several of these operational issues.

First, the environment of the forecaster we envision is a manufacturing company. The company produces many different products. Forecasts are at the individual product level and are for short and intermediate time periods. Finally, the forecasts themselves are construed to represent estimates of "demand levels" for the products.

DATA BASE DYNAMICS

"Charlie" has a big advantage over a purely technique-driven forecasting system. He probably has a great understanding of what the data mean. Further, he probably has some additional information not contained in even the most complex database.

A major issue involves the adopted definition of "demand." Is demand the number of units of the product that customers will request to be shipped during the period? Or the number of units for which orders will be placed? More specifically, how accurately does the data on which statistical techniques are applied describe the adopted definition of demand?

In the first place, historical data are generally recorded for shipments and orders. But the database generally does not include orders lost or shipments not made because customer requirements, such as for delivery, could not be met. Secondly, unusual events are not generally recorded in the database. Holidays and strikes are two obvious examples. Another is the common reporting of four five-week months in a calendar year. Several other factors are less obvious and far more difficult to adjust for in a formal sense. Some dealers may have had or are planning special promotional efforts, which may affect sales. Competitors may have been or can be expected to be unusually aggressive or weak. Internal or external price policies may have been or may be changed. The product may be moving periodically through successive stages in its life cycle; complementary models of the firm or its competitors may have been introduced, discontinued or changed in some way; interest rates may have fluctuated drastically or may be expected to affect future sales severely; shifts in government spending and resulting dislocations may be important; technology may be evolving; and so on.

There is a multitude of factors, which may be important to consider, some more than others in different time periods. It is virtually always the case that not all of these potentially important factors are contained in the database. Yet "Charlie" may know of them historically and may be able to anticipate them in the future. Further, his special knowledge could be and often is used to crack the credibility of the formal model.

JOB EVALUATION DYNAMICS

Forecasting specialists often treat forecasts as objective "facts," something like deterministic technique driven inanimate "truths" devoid of intra-organizational implication; this is terribly naive. Practically every person in an organization has a vested interest in forecasts because they directly affect operations. Sales forecasts are cornerstones of the entire budgeting and planning process. Each budget, in turn, directly affects the intended activities of a given department. The scope of a department's activities might be expanded, contracted or remain the same, all departments and all functions are affected.

It is useful to consider why forecasts are prepared to begin with. There are many purposes. One is for resource allocation and planning. Resources include the manufacturing facility. Forecasts, as inputs to the material requirements planning (MRP) system, have an impact on decisions involving facility loading, as well as capacity planning such as levels of subcontracts, overtime, shift additions, and facility expansion or contraction. Resources also include funds, as in cash management. Forecasts, as inputs to budgeting, influence decisions concerning investment, borrowing, operating budgets, and the like.

Another forecasting purpose is to help in assessing whether and when to introduce new products. Forecasts for current products signal when new products should be brought "on line" to help achieve goals. Further, the forecasts for the new products themselves are useful in this regard.

RELATIONSHIP BETWEEN FORECASTS AND GOALS

Perhaps the most invidious effect of forecasts is their direct impact on people's job performance evaluation; forecasts tend to be adopted as rigid goals throughout the organization.

In the case of salespeople, forecasts tend to have a major impact either formally or informally. One of the most commonly used criteria for evaluating sales force performance is attained sales volume: forecasts often are formally translated into quotas against which attained sales volume is compared for incentive compensation, promotion and even retention. Even when the forecasts are not formally cast into quotas, they still tend to be used, even if unconsciously, by managers in judging sales force performance.

The same is true in other areas as well: production personnel are evaluated on how well they produce the finished goods which the forecasts anticipated to be required; personnel people are evaluated on how well they hire and train the required workers, and so on. Thus, forecasts are related to job evaluations in most functional activities within organizations, either directly or indirectly.

INTRA-ORGANIZATIONAL CONFLICT

Individuals with different functional responsibilities have different perspectives concerning forecasts. This is because the consequences of forecast errors and the patterns of demand have different effects on the functions. Conflict is the inevitable result.

Production managers favor long and steady production runs. For this reason they prefer that seasonal patterns not be extreme. Forecasts, which are too low, may lead to expediting orders and interrupting long production runs. Consequently, they often prefer that forecasts be a little high rather than too low. If forecasts are substantially too high, however, their reaction depends upon the production implications relative to the capacity of the facility. In periods when the facility is likely to be below capacity, a forecast, which is substantially too high, may level the manufacturing load of the facility and be desirable from the production manager's point of view. Conversely, in some periods, a forecast, which is too high, may overload the capacity, result in unrealistic master production schedules and be undesirable from the same perspective.

Marketing managers, particularly those in sales, prefer that forecasts be on the low side since they are likely to turn into quotas or form the basis for bonus calculations. Salespeople are also eager to push the easiest products to sell despite any manufacturing implications of periodic or seasonal fluctuation.

Purchasing is responsible for the acquisition of raw materials for the manufacturing facility. The lack of raw materials can be very dangerous to job security. Thus, there is an inclination to desire large forecasts so that adequate supplies are more likely to be on hand. Larger forecasts also may result in larger orders and the possibility of quantity discounts, and, hence, decreased average cost per unit. For both reasons, Purchasing prefers forecasts, which are high rather than low.

Financial managers seek steady cash flows. This greatly simplifies their responsibilities concerning cash management. This also greatly reduces difficulties in dealing with capital markets, because it reduces wild swings in working capital. If heavy seasonality does exist in one product, for example, these people are likely to exert heavy pressure on other products to take up the slack. Or, products with highly fluctuating sales may be avoided altogether.

The goal and budget-setting process differs among organizations. However, it is common for the process to begin with each functional unit preparing forecasts from its own perspective. This is true even if a similar set of quantitative techniques is available to the various functional units. Differences are the result of the model selected or the "adjustments" associated with the "other factors" which neither a mathematical forecasting model nor the general database typically incorporates.

Each of the separate forecasts is then amalgamated into a single over-all set of forecasts for the entire organization. Conflict is the rule in this step as it is natural for each functional unit to seek to advance its own interests. Further, accepting a set of forecasts and goals favored by one functional unit often makes it more difficult for the others to attain their objectives. This means, of course, that they perceive a reduction in the likelihood of a favorable job performance evaluation. Accepting a forecast of steady cash flows, for example, means that salespeople will be judged, in part, by their abilities to offset any inherent seasonal influences. Similarly, the acceptance of certain high sales figures might necessitate unsteady production runs, which have a negative impact on future evaluations of production people. In essence, each functional unit within an organization operates at cross-purposes to a degree.

The way in which the conflict becomes resolved depends upon the particular time and setting. External factors might have a bearing such as an expected recession or an anticipated competitor move. Internal factors also play a role: cash flows, profitability, and workforce pressures are among the many internal factors affecting a solution.

As shown in Figure 1, it is useful to think of a matrix of factors separated by whether they are internal or external and whether they are economic or reflect constraints and pressures by groups of constituents. Each of these factors can affect the eventual forecasts and goals adopted by management. Since tradeoffs are inherent, the eventual resolution is a compromise, which is influenced by internal political actions.

MANAGERIAL DYNAMICS

Once overall forecasts and goals are adopted they often become very much like self-fulfilling prophecies. Put simply, outcomes can be managed to a degree, and knowledge of that fact by managers reduces the credibility of forecasts purely derived by even the most elegant of the extrapolative techniques. The ability to manage, which is being forecasted, should be taken into consideration in the design of a forecasting system.

THE SALES FORCE

Perhaps the greatest ability to manage the outcome lies with the sales force. A sales force is generally evaluated periodically, monthly or quarterly. One way in which the outcome can be managed is in the timing of the release of orders.

FIGURE 1 SOME FACTORS AFFECTING EVENTUAL FORECAST RESOLUTION		
	EXTERNAL	**INTERNAL**
Economic Factors	Recession Inflation Interest Rates Competitor Actions Technology	Technology Criteria for Economic Evaluation Internally Generated Cash Flows Market Development and Marketing Strategy Cost Management Profitability
Constituent Pressures	Stockholders Suppliers Customers Political and Legal Environment Distributors	Unions Political Strength of Functional Units Personal Objectives of Senior Management Workforce Skills and Availabilities

The practice takes on a couple of forms: some orders may be "borrowed" from the next period if they will help the salesperson this period (e.g., increased bonus). Actual orders at the end of one period may be postponed until the next one if they can be of greater value in the future.

The holding back of orders is also common at the end of a year. The intent, of course, is to decrease the forecast and associated goals for the next year. Further, it provides a head-start on the new year.

Bonus and commission schemes based on performance during one period can foster such activity. Salespeople adjust the release of orders to their benefit. Such a practice is common, even when salary compensation plans are used. Personal experience with automobile manufacturers, for instance, suggests that real orders can differ from actual orders by as much as five percent over a quarter for a given zone representative. What is more important is that such practices are often tolerated by managers who are under pressure from above.

The sales force can also manage the demand mix of products by aggressively promoting specific products or accounts. In fact, how well a salesperson performs with a particular product or customer group is often used as a criterion in evaluating performance.

Management can and frequently does change the relative reward structure for a particular product. Sales contests and other promotional activities, for example, might be offered to salespeople and dealers. This has an impact on the efforts of the marketing network: customers may be pressured into the "preferred" products. In industrial settings, this might also result in a different pattern of customer sales calls since the mix of products purchased often varies from account to account. Thus, demand may be increased above the forecasted value for the "preferred" product at the expense of other products. Similarly, management can change the relative reward structure for a particular account or type of account: additional credit is given for prospecting new accounts, to illustrate.

OTHER FUNCTIONS

Other functional activities besides sales can also manage outcomes. For example, the financial staff might raise the minimum profit margin acceptable on an order. Similarly, a decision may be made to alter transfer prices within the organization resulting in unanticipated performances by operating units. A side issue is the continuous conflict existing between those judged by sales dollar volumes and those by profits.

Inventories within a physical distribution system can provide the opportunity to manage outcomes: pressure on dealers to carry additional inventory, for example. Similarly, inventories may be transferred between manufacturing plants and warehouses. Even the speed of warranty replacements may be altered to affect inventories and resulting performance measures. The results of many of these decisions may be offset in the long run. Nonetheless, they do have a definite impact on a particular period.

OTHER FACTORS

To be effective, forecasting systems should also take into consideration several other, often ignored, factors. To begin, one should recognize that forecasts are almost always wrong. Consequently, their usefulness is not necessarily derived from exactly anticipating the future. Instead, their prime benefits are to orient management toward systematic thinking about business units and other components, to estimate implications of reasonable future scenarios, and to be prepared for deviations through contingencies. Thus, an important question to ask is "What will be the managerial impact of a more accurate forecast?" A reasonably accurate forecast in a timely fashion is often far better than a much more accurate forecast (but still wrong) which is obtained after long planning or corrective action.

Another factor to consider is the ease of analyzing and understanding of forecasts by those who are to act on the information. A reasonable assumption to make is that most managers have forgotten nearly all that they ever knew about statistics and mathematics. Complex equations, statistics, and so on only lead to disuse of the related forecasts. Forecasts should be simple to understand.

It is also useful to provide confidence intervals. They provide two benefits: (1) they explicitly alert managers that forecasts will always be wrong to a degree and (2) they help to build credibility. Managers quickly learn to distrust over-zealous technicians who promise the "best" answer with the "best" technique, but end up being wrong anyway. Confidence limits acknowledge that techniques are not totally precise, which is recognized intuitively by most managers. Reported confidence limits help to avoid the impression of over promise.

Another factor to consider is the amount of time a forecasting system requires of the decision-maker. A common mistake is to acquire relatively sophisticated interactive software because of their neat techniques. Yet the amount of time required to use the package, ignoring skill level and training difficulties, often exceeds the time available for the forecasting task. A mid-western electronics company, to illustrate, bought such a package so that product managers could forecast more accurately at the individual product level. Only after considerable time and cost for training was it learned that realistically, the system would never be used. A forecast for each product required two to three hours of terminal work. And each product manager had responsibility for 75 to 300 products. At the extreme, it would have taken three person months of time just to prepare each month's forecasts! At best, only a couple of person-days would ever be allotted per month because forecasting was only a small part of a product manager's total responsibilities. As in this example, any incremental accuracy from a complex system often has only a small impact on the overall criteria for evaluating performance (e.g., profitability) and, consequently, may not be worth the effort. A system of automated smoothing models was found to be more useful in this application despite the lower accuracy.

The final factor to consider relates to timeliness and feedback. As indicated above, but worth repeating here, timely information during a forecast period is essential to a successful forecasting system. The prompt reporting of results and forecast updates during the forecast period enables a manager to adjust to less than perfect forecasts as errors become apparent. Such systems help managers since they enable them to manage the outcomes.

CONCLUSION

Many forecasters concentrate their attention solely on developing that next "better" technique which will somehow greatly improve forecast accuracy. However, sales forecasting is not an exact science. Far too many factors affect sales for there ever to be very close precision as captured solely by some quantitative technique.

To begin, databases tend not to contain all of the important information needed to gain a full picture of history. For example, prior as well as anticipated competitive actions are likely to be omitted. Another factor is that forecasts are related to the way job performances are evaluated. There is inevitable conflict, which affects the eventual forecast that management "accepts." A third factor is that sales can be managed. And there are several other factors as well.

A couple of changes seem needed for the development of more effective forecasting systems. One is the development of better data bases. The capturing of many additional factors is essential. For example, careful analysis might reveal there had been significant borrowings of sales from one period to the next. Then, one probably should include in the database progress against goals throughout the periods.

A second change is the development of technique modifications to incorporate these factors. For the borrowing of sales example, to illustrate, adjustment procedures may be developed based on progress versus goals for a particular time horizon. Similar adjustment for other factors might increase the likelihood of generating accepted, useful forecasts.

It is important to focus on technique development. But it is also important to recognize the operational realities of applications. By understanding the operational realities, it may be possible to modify the environment in which the forecasts are made to mitigate the effect of these factors. For example, the sales force's compensation plan might be altered to reduce the incentive for borrowing across periods.

The next major significant improvement in forecasting accuracy may very well come from explicit attention being focused on such operational realities.

REFERENCES

1. Chambers, John C. Satinder Mullick, and Donald D. Smith. "How to Choose the Right Forecasting Technique." **Harvard Business Review.** July-Aug. 1971, pp. 45-74.
2. Gross, Charles W. and Robin T. Peterson. **Business Forecasting.** Boston: Houghton Mifflin, 1976.
3. "Measuring Salesmen's Performance." **Business Policy Study.** No. 114. New York: Conference Board, 1965.
4. Plossl, George W. "Getting the Most From Forecasts." **Production and Inventory Management.** 1st Quarter 1973, pp. 1-15.

CHAPTER 10

ROLE OF THE FORECASTING FUNCTION AT DURACELL USA

Rich Gordon
The Stanley Works

Duracell North Atlantic Group, a division of Gillette, is the world's leading alkaline battery manufacturer with the highest USA market share. Our USA product line includes alkaline major cells, lithium photo batteries, hearing aid batteries, high powered rechargeable pack batteries (e.g., camcorder & wireless phone) and specialty batteries. We are a CPG (consumer packaged goods) company with a component product dependent on the use of devices such as toys, flashlights, pagers and radios.

UPSURGE IN MASS CUSTOMIZATION OF PRODUCTS

Our core business is Alkaline Major Cells. These are Duracell's D, C, AA, 9 volt and AAA batteries you find in stores. The five standard battery sizes are built into thousands of SKUs to ship our customers every month. Consider more than 20 basic pack sizes such as common AA cell 2 packs, 4 packs, 8 packs, 12 packs and special 20 cell size packs for the warehouse club channel. These pack types go into various types of shipping cartons and trays creating over 80 open stock SKUs.

We also produce more than 50 standard types of prepackaged displays, mostly to support incremental retail locations. The displays can ship using a variety of promotions including standard, seasonal and custom consumer marketing messages and offers. Our sales force works with retailers to optimize their return on these incremental displays using customized promotional offers and different product assortments. This creates thousands of different shipping SKUs each month. The compromise reached in our Supply Chain Management system was to forecast packs and components in these prepackaged displays.

Marketing and sales has effectively turned five basic batteries into thousands of skus to meet customer requirements. This has boosted our sales volume. Before this mass customization, our sales were significantly less than the current level. In this article, we will discuss the forecasting of the core five batteries and their thousands of SKUs.

OUR CUSTOMERS

Most of our batteries are sold at the retail outlets. It is difficult to find a retail outlet where batteries are not sold. Our distribution includes grocery stores, drug stores, mass merchants, warehouse clubs, hardware stores, home centers, electronics shops, convenience stores, Variety stores, and many other trade channels. As the market leader since the eighties, we have close to one hundred percent distribution penetration for our product line.

OUR FORECASTERS

Market and sales forecasting at Duracell is a process which entails predicting consumer behavior, understanding channel activities, the competitive environment and, above all, our products. Our forecasters are reasonably comfortable making decisions with limited information. We have found for a forecaster to be successful, the person should have good presentation, analytical and interpersonal skills. Our department currently has six people and reports to Finance. A forecasting background is not necessarily the key to success. Our staff has worked in previous positions as a government economist, product manager, CPA, production engineer and sales analyst.

FORECASTING MISSION

Our official mission is: "To provide a reasonable base, in the form of a forecast, upon which strategies and goals can be established." Basically, we are a decision tool for management. We forecast shipments and quantify factors that affect the marketplace. This includes quantifying promotional activities, competitive actions, price elasticities, changes in retail channels, battery powered devices and impact of economic conditions.

The monthly forecast, called the "LE" (latest estimate), is a base for understanding the status of the current action plan. We forecast the market size, POS, retail inventory changes, and shipments for strategic and tactical planning purposes. We are responsible for producing scenarios based on alternative action proposals and providing weekly support for supply chain issues.

FORECASTING PHILOSOPHY

We work with a four part forecasting philosophy:

1. Consumption drives shipments.
2. The marketplace is dynamic.
3. Forecast assumptions are important.
4. One forecast links all planning activities.

Consumption Drives Shipments

We believe shipments are a function of retail sell through. The formula we use is: Shipments = (Retail Market times Brand Share) plus or minus the Change in Retail Inventories. This simple concept is a key to management acceptance of the forecast. (Backorders rarely enter our calculations due to our high level of customer service.) This consumption view of the market is used as a guide to explain forecasts to management. No matter how complicated the analysis used to build forecasts, we present using this simple format. We include percent change over prior year for market, share, consumption and shipments to guide discussion. Explaining the forecast in these terms is an excellent cross validation. Table 1 is a sample displaying the key elements in our consumption model. Management sees the key factors which influence sales and the assumptions they can manipulate or buy into. It also places reasonable limits on growth expectations by market component.

Market size and growth are important assumptions. They are the bases of any forecast. When one clearly identifies the market size, it is easier to evaluate its effect on forecast error. We currently evaluate six different statistical models to determine our market size. Generally, the end results along with percentage growth and key assumptions are presented to management. Occasionally, we are asked for summary reviews of the market models used.

Marketing generally takes ownership of the next element, share. Management can influence share in number of ways. These are advertising, product enhancements, distribution strategies, pricing, etc. The planning (and spending) to influence share creates many consumption scenarios. Market research and sales analysis often influence the management's acceptance or rejection of share assumptions. It is important to note that marketing shares responsibility for variance in share assumptions. The tough part is to identify the degree of share change realized from each marketing activity, historically and forecasted.

Changes in retail inventories are the most difficult to estimate. Many things can influence them. These could include distribution of pipefills with new products and/or expanded plan-o-grams, both of which can influence the share line. Plan-o-grams refer to how product is displayed and stocked on the retail floor. Inventories are also affected by category management activities and retailer efforts to reduce inventories.

In Table 1, year 2002 could be an example of a market wide one week reduction of inventories. Another explanation could be compensation for a year 2001 product push into retailers during year 2001 to meet the goal, (an activity which will come back to bite you if there is no increase in share as a result). Shipments are the net of consumption after retail inventory change.

We display the market in total as well as in various aggregations, such as trade channels, to understand various business issues. This builds a clear understanding of key business assumptions and leads to discussion on the relevant issues. Presenting forecasts using this framework guides management to educated decision making.

The Marketplace is Dynamic

Customer requirements are constantly changing. We work in a competitive environment of mass customization such as account specific packaging, new display types and anti-theft packaging. Competitors are never static in their efforts to gain share. The marketing mix changes with a change in consumer behavior. In batteries, we experience changes in consumer behavior in such things as pantry loading habits, buying of different pack sizes, responding differently to promotions and new battery powered devices. Retail channels are dynamically changing. Changes resulting from category killers and warehouse clubs may only be a beginning.

TABLE 1 CONSUMPTION MODEL			
Year	2000	2001	2002
Market Size	100,000	110,000	123,000
% Change		10.0%	12.0%
Share	52.0%	53.0%	55.0%
Share Change		1.0%	2.0%
Retail Consumption	52,000	58,300	67,760
% Change		12.1%	16.2%
Retail Inventory		2,000	(1,303)
Change	0	60,300	66,457
Shipments	52,000		
% Change		16.0%	10.2%

Forecast Assumptions Are Important

In many ways forecast assumptions are more important than the numbers themselves. The assumptions driving the forecast are key to management decisions. It is difficult, but very important, that forecasters quantify volume against assumptions. When management approves a forecast using the consumption philosophy, variance becomes a shared issue. Management shares ownership of market size, share and shipment expectations. Each component can be evaluated on its own merits when measured for error. The dynamics of issues such as market growth compenstating for aggressive share goals become simpler to evaluate and understand. Error becomes less important than how the forecast assisted management with decision making.

Statistical models are excellent for generating comparative forecasts, thereby enabling the forecaster to evaluate some sku issues. But pure statistical modeling and/or "black box" approaches add limited value to management decision making. In many ways we take an engineer's approach, that is, to optimize the use of information available to produce a solution which works best for the situation. We live by the expost forecast, using the model that tests most accurate. Simple models often work best for our product lines in tactical forecasts of less than a year. Aggregate level forecasts for more than one year work well with causal models and ARIMAs.

Scenarios regarding action plans and competition are evaluated to provide management with an effective tool for decision making. Without market parameters, one cannot judge the reasonableness of these forecasts. When reviewing assumptions, we explain the factors that are driving forecast change and error. Forecast change refers to direction going forward while forecast error is a measure of forecast compared to actuals.

One Forecast Links All Planning Activities

This means that the same forecast is used for Marketing, Finance and Production planning activities. When all parts of the company work with the same forecast, it insures coordination of resources. This might seem a simple concept, but we know of very few firms which operate this way. We have been working in a one number forecast environment for over a decade now.

FORECASTING CYCLES

We have five different forecasting cycles; Competitive View, Strategic Business Plan, Tactical Plan, Latest Estimate (monthly) and Supply Chain Management (weekly). We start the planning cycle with a market forecast including projections by pack types and channels for our key competitors for the next three years. Our first cycle of competitive view takes four months to complete for management presentation. We then measure how the competition is doing to those forecast assumptions for the remainder of the year.

The competitive view is used as a starting point for our strategic business plan. Marketing approves an updated view of the marketplace and factors driving market growth over the next five years. We work with marketing to explore programs and product innovations which may change the market share. The strategic business planning process takes about four months to complete with all the revisions with different scenarios.

The strategic business plan becomes the base of our tactical business plan. This also takes about four months. We generate sku level monthly estimates for next year and annual sku detail for the next four years. These three long term plan cycles, competitive, strategic and tactical drive our planning process. The "LE" (Latest Estimate) is our monthly review process. This forecast covers the next 12 months concentrating on the current fiscal quarter and year. We do an intense analysis of what happened during the prior month. Issues and assumptions going forward are reviewed with the marketing team. This is presented to senior management (President, VP of Finance, VP of Marketing and VP of Sales) for their approval and direction at aggregate levels by the fourth day of the fiscal month. On the sixth day of each fiscal month, we review the senior management presentation, decisions, and include risks with respect to manufacturing, finance, marketing and sales. We discuss issues in much greater detail while we present a sku level forecast to the managers responsible for making the numbers happen. The monthly LE with our best sales, marketing and forecasting knowledge is split into weekly buckets for our supply chain efforts. We evaluate sku variance on a weekly basis. Those SKUs outside of acceptable variance parameters are researched to determine if mid-month production forecast adjustments are required.

FORECASTING DATA

Forecasting data comes from a multitude of sources. Our internal information includes bookings and shipments. Many retailers will send point-of-sale (POS) census data, often through EDI transfers. Here an account will let us know how our products are going through their cash registers. We also purchase market data including competitive data through Nielsen and IRI for the grocery, drug and mass merchant channels. They provide POS by survey of market place scanner data including competitive information.

The data sets are the best we can get, but it is important to realize they are not pure. Shipments and demand have backorder, order timing, diverted (gray) product and other issues. The account POS census often does not adjust for theft or false scans. False scans can occur when a check out person uses a dummy number or scan one item to represent different products with the same price e.g., using AAA 4 pack for AA 4 pack. Occasionally, account census POS data has an inconsistent population of stores reporting weekly sales. The major weakness of account POS data is that retailers do not release competitive data with the EDI transfers. That is why the Nielsen and IRI data are very important even considering the sampling errors which may occur in their data releases.

There are many other data sets we use. Some retailers share their expectations of what our products will sell in their stores. Economic data and industry data of battery powered devices are helpful in our causal modeling. Our sales team and sales analysts are great resources for account information such as future promotions, competitive actions, plan-o-gram changes and pricing issues. Often a brief conversation with the salesperson can explain the "why" behind the numbers. Our market research team feeds us advertising effectiveness, brand awareness and consumer usage studies. This wide range of data is used differently for each of the forecasting cycles from competitive view to tactical latest estimate.

MIS SUPPORT

We have found that forecasting productivity is interdependent with DSS/MIS support (Decision Support Systems/Management Information Systems). It has proven helpful to keep our database administrators aware of how we use the data. We continually challenge them for expanded system capabilities while explaining its value to our processes. They try to keep us on the leading edge of software availability while keeping us away from bleeding edge technologies. We work together to reach the best compromises throughout all system improvements. They are an integral part of our forecasting team, and continually try to improve our systems.

Optimizing forecasting systems seems a simple concept, but extremely difficult when one considers the adhoc analyses required and inconsistant information flow. An ideal system has yet to be developed, here are some things we would like to see. System should be such which facilitates analysis from multiple sources at multiple levels. Multiple sources include shipments, orders, point-of-sale data received from retailers, retailer inventories, historical forecasts, point-of-sale data received from market research firms, market data by competitor, macro-economic data and other related data sets. Multiple levels mean that the data can be converted into equivalent units, dollars and skus, and /or separated by packaging type, component, account level, geographic territory, and trade class.

Data warehousing should use equivalency tables for products with multiple names. In the data warehouse, one database may identify a product by UPC code and another by a component of a display SKU. (UPC is the standardized bar code used to identify a product for many cash registers).

A good forecasting system should have flexible data analysis including model building with any database and spreadsheet. Flexible manipulation of multiple statistical methodologies are needed to optimize and evaluate data patterns with market based judgment. The dynamic marketplace forces us to continually evaluate data for informed judgments about rarely occurring events. Quick response time is necessary for "on the fly" types of analyses and department productivity. Forecasters do not have the luxury to wait overnight for the results of a preliminary analysis. Graphic capabilities are used for both presentation and analysis. Expost and error reporting with flexible holdout periods and various holdout paradigms are tools the forecaster would desire in the MIS part of the forecasting solution.

An important concept missed by many system designers and DBMs (DataBase Managers) is that the longer the dataset the more opportunities for improved forecasting. Many corporate systems only hold 3 years of history. Ideally a forecasting system should hold five or more years of data at the lower levels. Appropriate levels of aggregated data should never be purged. Longer datasets enable the forecaster to experiment with more sophisticated models. Econometric modeling is a good example. It is difficult to model the effects of recession on product sales with less than one recession in data history. We even store prior forecasts to facilitate error analysis.

FORECASTING MODELS

Our forecasting toolbox has three primary forecasting methodologies: judgmental, time series and causal. We have found no single model that meets all forecasting needs in the corporate environment. We use whatever best suits the situation, depending on the forecast horizon, information available, and the dynamics of the issue. Dynamics can include stage of product life cycle, top down vs bottom up forecasting, shifts in the competitive and market environments, management objectives and most importantly, how the forecast is being used. A wide range of models can be applied to similar situations. We have found certain models that work great for some trade channels but yield horrible results for others. Judgmental forecasting has both qualitative and quantitative methodologies. There are qualitative judgments in the design of most time series and causal methodologies as well. We use the sales force composite, senior management survey and committee forecast review when appropriate. When forecasting new product placement in stores we use quantitative judgmental forecasting by applying Baysian probabilities. The sales staff sends their best estimates of target accounts considering the new products, which month, and quantity of pipefills. In building the model with a significant number of accounts across a fair number of sales people, the probabilities getting placements times pipefulls times the month produces a good idea of initial production requirements. This way optimistics sales projections offset pessimistic sales projections. For this method to work, periodic measurement of actuals to forecast should be shared with the sales managers. Another judgmental approach to this same issue would be to use market research and management judgments to drive diffusion curve equations.

Time series forecasting is based on the historical data. There are simple to very complex time series models. As simple as it sounds, sometimes a Naive 2 model (base plus a percentage growth) can be the best model for forecasting some products when there is good research behind the growth factor. There are a multitude of time series models including multiplicative seasonal decomposition (extremely good for some trade classes), optimized exponential smoothing curves, moving averages, Box-Jenkins and ARIMAs.

Causal models, which also require the forecasts of explanatory variables, often work well with long term assumptions. The challenge is in finding a good forecast of the causal variables going forward. Often the correlation analysis alone will help managerial decisions. We have also used Matrix relationships and explored some non-linear multiple regressions.

We have found presenting forecasts to management using the consumption framework is key to achieving our mission of providing a reasonable base for decision making. We use the Naive 2 model to display aggregate level forecasts. As explained in the section on forecasting philosophy, this model is simple to understand. We rely on the reality check of explaining the forecast using simple methodologies. By reviewing the forecast in this manner, the forecaster is well prepared to explain to the management the changes in the forecasts.

SUMMARY

Management confidence in our forecasting department has been built from a history of reliably explaining market factors as they relate to business decisions. The key to presenting a forecast is understanding your audience. Typically, senior management are not concerned with methodologies used to generate a forecast. Their primary concern is the action plan generated from the forecasting process. They steer the corporate ship using the information given by the forecasting compass, thereby adjusting the forecast to meet objectives.

CHAPTER 11

ROLE OF JUDGMENT IN FORECASTING

Chaman L. Jain
St. John's University

Why do we need judgment in forecasts particularly in this age and time when science is so well developed, forecasting models are so well advanced, computer power is so enormous and fast, and all kinds of data are readily available? Judgment biases forecasts? Biased forecasts are less accurate. These are the complaints I often hear from those who distrust forecasts.

It is a dream of every forecaster to develop a fully mechanized forecasting system. With that, there will be no argument which and whose judgment we should include, forecasts will be generated with a touch of button, and anyone with a little training can replicate numbers. God is great, but He hasn't given the power of perfect foresight even to those who prayed to Him all their life. How could you expect Him to give this power to a man-made machine (system) who doesn't even know there is such thing as God, and can not even spell His name unless so programmed.

Can we do without judgment? One way to answer is to see where judgment is used and how important it is in each use. There are five main areas where human judgment is used in forecasting: (1) where there is no data, or past data are no longer applicable, (2) in analyzing and treating data, (3) in selecting a model, (4) in adjusting final numbers, and (5) in expanding test results to a national level.

Where there is no data, as in the case of a new product, there is no choice except to use judgment. At times, data may exist but they are no longer applicable as in the case of a fashion product. One fashion product often does not follow the pattern of another fashion product. The past data may no longer be relevant where there is a permanent shift in the data pattern. This can result from such things as merger or acquisition. One cannot depend much on the past performance where a large percentage of sales come from a few customers. Here loss or gain of just one customer can make the difference. Also, judgment is the only way to forecast far into the future, say, 20 or 30 years into the future. During that long period, anything can happen — technology may change, new competitors may enter into the market or the existing ones may decide to exit out, and socio-demographic structure may dramatically change.

Judgment is often needed to determine whether there are abnormal values (outliers) or permanent shift in the data pattern (structural change). One forecaster may view a certain value as an outlier and the other, a part of the pattern. Even after such determinations are made, judgment has to be made how to adjust or handle such data since there is no set procedure.

Judgment plays an important role in matching a model with a data set. Each data set has a set pattern, whether we recognize it or not. Each model captures best a certain data pattern. The quality of forecasts depends on how well we can match the data pattern with a model. With all the statistical diagnostics at our command, matching data with a model is still more an art than a science. Also, many forecasters have their own pet models, which they use regardless of the data pattern.

CHAPTER 12

FORECASTS, BUDGETS, AND GOALS: IS THERE A DIFFERENCE?

Larry Lapide
AMR Research

One day I was having lunch with a close colleague of mine who was the forecasting director for his company and asked him how the new promotional forecasting system that he had implemented was going. (He had spent a lot of time and effort insuring that the system met all his company's forecast needs, basing the system on sophisticated multivariate statistics to model promotional effects.) He stated that he was somewhat disillusioned because his Finance organization was routinely driving the system with budget numbers, basically overriding the forecasts and defeating the purpose of numbers generated by relatively sophisticated statistical models.

I mentioned to him that generally whenever I talk about forecast processes, I usually point out that companies need to acknowledge the fact that, at times, there will be a difference among some planning numbers. In particular, sales budgets, goals, and operational forecasts don't necessarily need to be equal. So his Finance organization should not always override operational forecasts with the budget numbers, and should actually feel comfortable with an operational sales forecast that is different than what the budget assumed.

Failure to allow the operational sales forecast to vary from the budget frequently results in what can be called 'hockey stick' forecasts that are heavily loaded on the backend. For example, take a case of a company whose first two fiscal quarterly results are below budget expectations by 15%. If the company fails to recognize or accept these shortfalls as changing business conditions, they might add them into the last quarter's forecast. This would make the last quarter's forecast up to 30% higher than the original forecast, representing an unrealistic 'stretch' by any means. The revised sales forecast numbers would have a drastic uplift on the backend, resembling the end of a hockey stick. Companies that load significant sales shortfalls into the backend of operational forecasts in order to tie them to the budget are typically just fooling themselves – possibly even abrogating their fiscal responsibility! Most companies would do well to learn the value of thinking about budgets, goals, and operational forecasts as separate sets of planning numbers, while still maintaining an understanding of the relationship among them.

WHAT ARE BUDGETS, GOALS, AND OPERATIONAL FORECASTS?

To understand why this is the case, let's first discuss what are these different sets of planning numbers. The definition and purpose of budgets, goals, and operational forecasts are described below:

Budgets: These numbers are typically assembled by financial organizations once, prior to the start of a fiscal year. Some companies do a budget correction within the year if conditions differ substantially from those assumed in the budget. The numbers include revenue, cost, and margin projections. The primarily purpose of budgets is to plan and control financial resources throughout a fiscal year. Budgets are usually time consuming and normally take months to develop, due to the need to negotiate and rework the assumptions. A lot of effort is spent on them because they will be used to drive such activities as hiring, buying, adjusting salaries, expending capital, and promoting products. Anyone who gets involved in these budgeting processes knows they are not fun. But, typically, they are done once a year.

Goals: These are numbers assembled to provide incentives to achieve the objectives or goals of functional organizations, such as Marketing, Sales, and Customer Service. Like budgets they are also typically done once a year. For example, Sales or Marketing goals are tied to the revenue performance of a company, with each individual member responsible for carrying their own set of goals that support the organization's overall goal. Goal-setting processes are less time-consuming than doing budgets, but are usually done once a year. However, if changes in business conditions warrant it, corrections may be made once or more during the year to insure that the goals are reasonably realistic. This insures that individuals do not get unduly penalized during their performance evaluations.

Operational Forecasts: These are numbers assembled to drive the actual operational activities of an organization. In many manufacturing environments, for example, these would drive what raw materials are purchased, what products are made, and what inventories are held. Unlike budgets or goals these numbers essentially drive what is going to happen 'when the rubber meets the road.' By their nature the numbers have to be extremely realistic, based on the best knowledge of what is going to happen. This drives companies towards generating these planning numbers much more often than those for budgets or goals — typically on a monthly or weekly basis.

WHY CAN'T THEY ALWAYS BE EQUAL?

On the face of it most people would take the position that budgets, goals and operational forecasts should be equal. After all, shouldn't everyone in the organization be 'on the same page'? If operational forecasts are different, then how can we insure that resources are applied so that goals and budgets can be met?

Figure 1 represents an illustrative, but realistic process chart for budgeting, goal setting, and operational forecasting for a typical company. As depicted, operational forecasts are updated more often, so by their very nature these planning numbers will be different at certain times of the year. If operational forecasts stay consistent with the budgets and goals, they will not truly represent business conditions that are inconsistent with assumptions made during the budgeting and goal setting processes.

Certainly at the beginning of the year, budgets, forecasts, and goals should be aligned. Sales numbers for budgets and forecasts should be exactly the same, while goals might be higher to provide incentive to certain employees to 'stretch' beyond what is budgeted or forecast. Throughout the year as operational forecasts are updated, the planning numbers will tend to differ. However, during the year, when goal and budget corrections are made, these numbers should once again align to the operational sales forecasts.

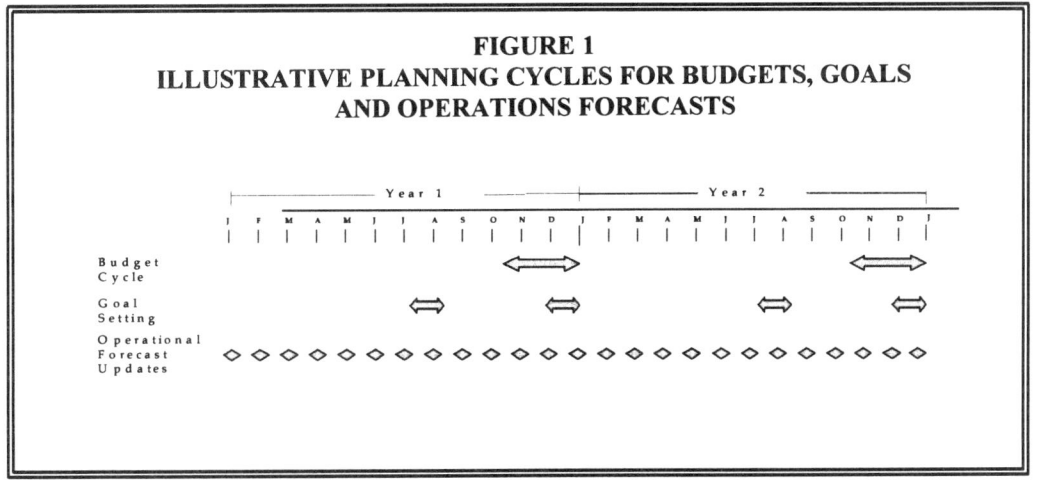

FIGURE 1
ILLUSTRATIVE PLANNING CYCLES FOR BUDGETS, GOALS AND OPERATIONS FORECASTS

BUT WHAT SHOULD WE DO WHEN THEY ARE DIFFERENT?

The primary issue that arises whenever the operational sales forecasts differ from the goal and budget numbers is that it looks like the company is somewhat out of control, especially when there is a revenue shortfall. It gives the appearance that some employees are not performing well. This makes most forecasters reluctant to change the operational sales forecasts, trying to avoid organizational conflict. At times this works and people do 'make' their original planning numbers. However, frequently this just delays the inevitable. Eventually, when it is too late to do anything about it, the operational forecasts are adjusted to be different and the organization is worse off.

A better solution is to keep the operational sales forecasts as realistic as possible and deal with the organizational conflict. If a company is not meeting its budget or goal sales numbers, then the operational forecasts should be changed as soon as possible; immediately followed by an investigation into the causes of the shortfall or surplus. If a problem is identified and a reasonable contingency plan is established to address it, the operational forecasts can be realigned during a future forecast update. For example, take the case where budgeted revenues are not being met because the sales force is understaffed relative to the budget or the marketing organization did not get the promotional resources it was budgeted. 'Sweeping these revenue shortfalls under the rug' by not changing the operational forecast certainly avoids organizational conflict; however, it will not provide executives with the visibility needed to address these resource issues in a timely fashion.

FORCE ACTIONS, WHEN NECESSARY

In conclusion, companies should recognize the difference among operational sales forecasts, sales budgets, and sales goals. These planning numbers could differ throughout a fiscal year. However, when they do differ, it is important to use the information as a signal to take a corrective action, not avoid conflict! Whenever warranted, operational forecasters will have to be brave, changing forecast numbers to reflect reality, in lieu of unrealistic goal and budget-based planning numbers. While this will get them involved in many of the organizational frays that will ensue, they will be helping to insure that their companies stay on a profitable track by following realistic plans.

CHAPTER 13

THE CHANGING ROLE OF ECONOMISTS IN PLANNING

Lawrence Chimerine

WEFA Group/Wharton Econometrics

(Although this article was written in Spring 1988, many of his views about the role of economists still hold. Ed)

In recent years, many companies have decided to scale back or eliminate their internal economics functions. While cost cutting, and mergers and consolidations, have contributed to this phenomenon, the main reason behind this trend is that many corporate executives feel that their economics departments have not played a useful role in the management process. This article will address the issue of how economists can play a more important and effective role in the corporate planning and decision-making process.

I will begin with a brief discussion of the major goals of an organized planning system and then discuss the changes in the environment that are causing many companies to alter their approach to their planning and decision making activities. Finally, I will discuss how the changing economic environment and the new approach to corporate planning are affecting the role of corporate economists, and how in my view, economists can become more effective within their organizations.

WHY PLAN

The 1970's saw explosive growth in the use of strategic planning, but not enough growth to keep pace with the uncertainties of the business environment. The need for systematic, organized planning is greater now than ever before, the reason is that there are more non-certainties and more changes in more business areas than in previous periods.

These changes affect individual sectors differently. For example, past increases in oil prices have hurt the auto industry but have led to booms (temporary) in oil drilling and energy research and development. Large demographic changes, increased defense spending, high interest rates, and volatile exchange rates are also affecting the stability of many industries; frequently, resources need to be redirected from shrinking markets to growing markets. Facility location and other decisions also become more critical, and more difficult. Only within an organized planning system is it possible to address, evaluate, and respond to these issues in a systematic way. Fundamentally, the way to avoid the consequences of adverse developments, or to reap the benefits of favorable changes, is to anticipate them and, in an organized manner, develop strategies to deal with them. This is particularly relevant for developments external to the organization, such as changes in the economic, social, political, technological, or competitive environments.

An understanding of the general economic and government policy environment in which business will be operating is a major starting point for this process, for numerous reasons. First, the levels of demand facing the industry will be determined at least partially (though not wholly) by the behavior of the external economy. Second, shifts in government economic policy can affect the business by impacting both the economy and competitive conditions in their industry. Finally, there are numerous structural and micro type changes taking place which can greatly impact the markets for many products and services.

For these and other reasons, a firm must form judgments about the nature of the economic and government policy environment during the plan period; in many cases alternative sets of environmental assumptions should be considered, and their implications be studied, in order to assess the risks inherent in the environment. This approach also has the advantage of pinpointing those environmental developments which should be watched most closely during the plan period. The need to plan therefore reflects the fact that companies cannot control the markets in which they operate nor many of the factors which influence those markets. Thus, the first ingredient for effective planning is being able to anticipate many of those forces which affect end markets and various business decisions and then, second, to determine their potential impact on the business. This is an essential part of the planning process even though most of those outside forces can be predicted only with some degree of error. Even though it is generally recognized that all forecasts will contain some error, an effective planning system can be operated on the assumption that forecasts will not be perfect so that the ultimate objective of such a system becomes to minimize the cost of forecast errors. In my view, only an organized approach to planning, as will be described below, can offer any hope to accomplish that objective. Furthermore, there are numerous outside forces which affect many markets that can be forecast with little error (i.e., some demographic changes) —these are also best addressed within a systematic process.

In sum, any organization, which must make commitments to resources in the present, automatically builds some type of forecast into the decision-making process. The reasons to formalize this process into a systematic, organized planning system, with a major role for the business economist, are:

1. Some forces in the future, which will in part determine the performance of the business, can be anticipated with a high degree of accuracy — the purpose of planning in this context is to make certain that appropriate implications are drawn and translated into the best possible decisions.

2. For those forces that cannot always be forecast with a high degree of accuracy, an organized planning system can help reduce the costs associated with the forecast errors

that may occur. In effect, such a system becomes a mechanism for dealing with uncertainty.

3. A systematic approach to planning should be one from which new opportunities emerge, both from the changing environment as well as those which result from developments within the industry and within the particular organization.

THE CHANGING EXTERNAL ENVIRONMENT

There are a number of environmental changes that are taking place within our economy that suggest that sole reliance on macroeconomic analysis and forecasting, as important as they are, are not sufficient for effective business planning and decision making — increased reliance on more micro analysis will thus be necessary. This can be contrasted with the situation that existed in previous years at that time, when the economy did well, most businesses shared in it and when the economy did poorly, most businesses were adversely affected (though some more than others). Thus, there was a relatively close pattern of performance across the economy, no matter how the economy was segmented — whether by region, industry, or end markets.

Today, however, there is far more variation in performance across different sectors of the economy, regardless of what might be happening to overall GNP growth. In my view, this reflects the fact that there are more changes taking place beneath the surface of the macro environment than ever before. Some have been building for several years, while others are relatively new; some are relatively permanent, others less so; but all are having a significant impact on business planning. These major structural changes include the following:

Demographic Shift: The U.S. economy is in the early stages of one of the sharpest changes in its demographic structure in history.

First, the age distribution of the population is changing very rapidly, involving a sharp decline in the number of teenagers, and a large increase in the number of individuals in the 35 to 45 age range. This shift will significantly impact the distribution of consumer spending.

Second, the long decline in the birth rate is continuing, although at a slower pace, but the number of births is now beginning to rise because of the increase in the number of women in the major child-bearing-age categories.

Third, a dramatic change is taking place in the distribution of income in the United States. Large reductions in personal income taxes, coupled with recent increases in social security and excise taxes, have shifted the tax burden away from upper income groups toward middle and lower income groups. In addition, cutbacks in Federal spending have reduced income for the poor and near poor — these groups, as well as those in the so called middle class, have been adversely affected by the shift in the job mix in recent years.

Fourth, the strongest component of personal income growth in previous years has been interest income and dividends. These should remain a relatively large share of household income in the years ahead and, of course, they accrue principally to people in upper incomes.

Fifth, the composition of households is also changing significantly — households are now smaller on average and as such any given level of the population is likely to have more households than would have been the case historically; a growing share is now headed by non-married individuals; and a growing share is also characterized by two income earners. Finally, the population is aging rapidly and is growing more slowly. All of these and other demographic shifts will have significant effects on many markets and many industries in the years ahead.

Real Interest Rates: While real interest rates have declined somewhat recently, it is highly likely that interest rates in both nominal and real terms will stay relatively high for the foreseeable future. This reflects: (a) a continued likely cautious attitude by the Federal Reserve toward increasing money growth in order to prevent a new inflationary surge; (b) the prospect of very large Federal deficits which will put continued pressure on financial markets; (c) deregulation and other changes in financial markets, including the availability of new financial instruments, increased competition for funds, and an increased desire for high returns on savings; and (d) the need to continue to attract large amounts of foreign capital to the United States.

Increased World Competition: Increased competition in world markets will stem partly from the fact that the world economy will be characterized by large amounts of excess capacity for many years, as well as by the search of many producers in different countries for new markets to bolster their performance. In addition, an overvalued dollar against many currencies, and the narrowing technology, productivity and quality gaps between the United States and the rest of the world, will also contribute to an increase in competition from foreign sources in the United States.

Deregulation: The decade of the 1970's witnessed deregulation in many parts of the transportation sector— this has in recent years spread to financial institutions as well.

Technology: Despite weak productivity growth in recent years, there is now much new technology, which will ultimately affect productivity in many industries, and also will cause dramatic changes in the way many products and services are marketed. For example, almost every industry will be impacted by the revolution in data processing and micro processing, either in the way its products are produced, the cost at which they are produced, or the way they are distributed.

Defense Buildup: The massive defense buildup (especially in procurement) has had a favorable impact on many industries in recent years — there is now significant evidence to suggest that deficit reduction pressure, possible detente with the USSR, a change in the political climate, etc. will cause significant cutbacks in military spending in the years ahead.

Volatile Exchange Rates: One of the major factors causing the wide variation in sectorial performance in recent years was the overvalued dollar in the early 1980's. This obviously held down export sensitive industries (and their major suppliers), while benefiting the consumer sector and those industries sensitive to interest rates. We are now beginning to see a reversal of these patterns in response to the sharp decline in the dollar, which began in early 1985.

Tax Changes: The tax structure has been changed dramatically in recent years, with a significant effect on the distribution of the tax burden between corporations and individuals, across different income classes. Some of the tax changes have been very narrowly directed (especially some of the base broadening measures) and are having, and will continue to have, significant effects on very specific sectors of the economy. It is likely that there will be more such tax changes in the years ahead.

THE IMPACT OF THE CHANGING ENVIRONMENT

These and other factors appear to have produced several major changes in the U.S. economy:

Increased Volatility: The cyclical patterns of the U.S. economy appear to have changed dramatically in the last 15 years. Gone are the reasonably regular business cycle patterns that the United States experienced in the 1950's and 1960's of three or four years of steady economic growth, followed by a mild recession, followed by more growth, followed by another mild recession, etc. Recessions now sometimes come more quickly, or more slowly, and are often followed by spurts of more rapid growth than we have had before. Furthermore, the potential for much sharper swings (much deeper recessions) also seems to be larger than in the past. This volatile economic environment reflects increased turbulence in financial markets, floating exchange rates, increased internationalization of the economy, and more volatility in interest rates.

Increased Uncertainty: There is more economic uncertainty today than in past years, reflecting the volatile economic patterns, the impact of shifting economic policies, the effect of various structural changes and the increased impact of overseas activity on the U.S. economy. All of these changes have created an environment that contains more uncertainty than before, thereby increasing business risks.

Increased Competitiveness: Competition in the U.S. economy has become stronger, and is likely to stay that way for a long time, reflecting deregulation, the globalization of the economy, and other factors.

IMPLICATIONS FOR PLANNING

For planners and economists, the implications are numerous. First, structural change is having a significant effect on business organizations. Close historical relationships between company sales and specific economic indicators (such as GNP or industrial production) no longer hold in many cases. Industry performance is being affected by a host of factors over and above the pure macro environment. Producers are now seeing different markets for the same product — move in opposite directions. Industry performance relative to the business cycle is diverging from past trends — the same holds for regional performance. There is more variation across industries, regions, and different markets than there has ever been before. The planning process requires that both underlying macroeconomic developments and specific structural changes be factors into the analysis of different markets. It is not only necessary to determine which markets will benefit from these changes and which will be adversely affected, but what new opportunities will be emerging. Second, increased emphasis on marketing and product development strategies are necessary because of the demographic changes. Third, it is likely that regionally-oriented decisions— plant location, store location, finding new regional markets, determining new markets outside the United States, regional based sales forecasting, etc. will become more critical than ever before, rather than the historical tendency to plan predominantly on a national basis. Fourth, increased attention to costs and productivity will be necessary as a result of the shift away from the inflationary environment of the 1970's. Finally, procurement practices may have to be adjusted, reflecting changing delivery schedules, materials availability, and changes in the cost of holding inventories relative to the opportunity costs of having insufficient stocks. These are issues that can and should be addressed by economists.

Another major implication relates to the increased risk in the environment. Planning a business on the assumption that forecasts are always correct has always been risky; this is even more true now. In fact, the cost of a wrong forecast is probably greater now than it has ever been before. Decision makers and planners must ask, before decisions and plans are made: What is the consequence of being wrong? What happens if the assumptions that underlie the plan or decision are incorrect? What does it mean for the business?

An ideal planning system helps to deal with risk and uncertainty. Helping management understand and manage risk should be a more important activity for the business economist — one tool is the use of alternative forecasts. This does not mean giving management 86 different macro outlooks based on 86 different assumptions and saying "One of these will be correct — pick the one you like." The whole purpose of alternative forecast scenarios is to assess the magnitude of risk. It is essential that a mechanism be in place for selecting a few alternative scenarios and then assessing the likely impact on the firm (i.e., How much lower will sales be? How much more will a new plant cost us? What will inventory costs be?). Only in this way alternative forecasts can be useful.

The uncertainty associated with the forecasting and planning process also should be addressed in another way — one of the key objectives of the planning process is to minimize the cost of forecast errors, which combines the potential forecast errors with their likely cost to the organization. In effect, business plans must take into account the potential cost of the forecast being wrong. In most cases, firms should adopt forecasts that minimize the cost of being wrong — this may be very different from the traditional approach of basing plans on the most likely outlook. In most organizations the distribution of forecast errors varies by activity, by division, and possibly across the business cycle. But at any point in time, even if forecast errors are symmetrically distributed, the costs of these errors to a business are not likely to be symmetrically distributed.

In many organizations, by the very nature of their business, the cost of overpredicting business activity may substantially exceed the cost of underpredicting, especially in those businesses in which overprediction results in a commitment of resources that cannot easily be reversed, but in which underpredictions can be corrected by additional resources later. The specific characteristics of the business will frequently determine what the distribution of the cost of forecast errors will look like.

It is extremely important that economists understand the distribution of the cost of forecast errors for their own organizations. If the cost of overpredicting is disproportionately high, economists might well present a forecast to management for use in setting plans that is more conservative than what they believe will happen. Because no economist can be certain what will happen, forecasts should be biased in the direction of reduced risk to their businesses— this requires a clear understanding of how forecast errors will impact the organization. Furthermore, while it is generally believed that one main purpose of forecasts in the planning process is to provide consistency across divisions or operating groups, this may no longer be appropriate. In fact, when the distribution of forecast errors varies greatly across operating units, a different economic forecast for planning purposes should be considered for each— some may require a more optimistic forecast, some less optimistic. The changes taking place in the environment also make it essential to emphasize business monitoring. Too many times companies put plans in place, do not look at them for nine months, and then find they are way off track. By that time it is too late to take action to limit the adverse effects of the planning error — early recognition of errors is the best way to limit their impact. Each business should be regularly monitored on a frequent basis, relative to plan and relative to the economy, to identify if it is off the track, why, and to allow for fast corrective action. With the increased volatility in the environment, monitoring becomes an increasingly important activity. Economists can and should participate in this activity.

CHANGES IN PLANNING ACTIVITIES

The shifting external environment is also producing many changes in the way many companies are structuring their corporate planning activities.

1. Planning is becoming more line oriented. The speed with which the environment is changing can best be recognized by those closet to their own markets.

2. Planning is becoming more strategic, issue oriented. Many companies have concluded that the enormous number crunching in recent years has become too unwieldy. Furthermore, the focus was frequently more on the numbers than on identifying the key issues; this is now being changed.

3. Planning is becoming more continuous. Because of the major business risks and the rapidly shifting environment, companies are planning on a more continuous basis.

4. Companies are striving for more flexibility. Remaining flexible is an increasingly important ingredient to success in today's global environment. This flexibility extends to marketing strategies, production, etc.

5. More emphasis is being placed on understanding the environmental factors that affect the business. Many of the fast growing industries in the past appeared to be immune to environmental impacts — this is no longer the case, and thus there is now increased attention to determining what those effects are.

6. Business planning is becoming more global. Virtually every business in the United States is in some way being affected by the increasingly integrated worldwide economic environment. This cuts across virtually all activities: production, purchasing, identifying best end markets, pricing, etc.

7. Many companies are increasing their focus on competitive analysis. The increased degree of competitiveness, both domestically and internationally, requires more intense focus on competitive analysis and strategizing than was true in many cases in the past.

IMPLICATIONS FOR THE BUSINESS ECONOMIST

I would make the following suggestions to most business economists:

1. **The focus of macro-analysis should be on change and on risk:** Macro economic analysis and forecasting will always be an important input into the business planning and decision making process. However, it is more important to focus on the changes in macroeconomic trends, and on the major risks, than it has been before, rather than simply on more and more numbers. Questions such as "What could go wrong?" and "Will average growth during the planning period be greater or less than it has been historically?" "When will the next recession occur?" should be asked on an increasing basis.

2. **Upgrade micro-analysis and forecasting:** As discussed earlier, the diverging performance within sectors, and the changing sectorial mix, make such analysis far more critical than in the past.

3. **Emphasize research on the impact of the environment on the business:** Companies need to know more about how the changing environment will affect their business — in many cases, these relationships are in the process of changing from what they have been historically. Corporate executives frequently complain that economics is not being made relevant — the only way to make it relevant is to relate what is happening in the environment to as many aspects of the business as possible, and to communicate the implications in the language of business, not economics.

    Economists should consider enhancing typical forecasting work with market research, which, in many cases can supplement economic analysis very effectively, to help understand how conditions are changing and what the implications are. Insights into changing consumption patterns, price performance ratios, product substitutions, changing distribution channels, and industry mixes all can contribute to better modeling and forecasting.

4. **Increase the emphasis on cost forecasting:** The increased competitive environment requires much more focus on cost effectiveness. The economist can play a key role by evaluating the company's wage costs in relation to the competition and to general labor market conditions, by evaluating whether the company is procuring at the lowest possible cost, etc. Costs should be forecast, particularly for substitutable materials, and alternate sources should be evaluated. Personnel and compensation departments should be advised on appropriate salary plans and labor conditions in different labor markets, and similar advice should be provided to other departments.

5. **The economist should play a major role in business monitoring.** On a regular basis, the economist should be helping to monitor sales relative to plan, relative to economic trends, and relative to overall industry performance; frequently, this sales monitoring is best done both on a national and a disaggregated basis. Wage and procurement costs should also be monitored. The corporate economist is the ideal person to coordinate the

analysis of all of the data, to develop seasonal adjustment factors, to put statistical tracking models in place to identify performance variances from plan (either positively or negatively), and to help identify the reasons for variations, all of which are vital for effective business monitoring.

6. **Engage in regular dialogues with management and business units to keep corporate executives aware of what is happening in the economy**: It is increasingly important to keep management informed as to whether economic trends are in line with previous expectations, whether forecasts are being changed, (if so, why), on the major risks in the environment, on the effects of economic conditions on the business, etc. This is not effectively done through memos and reports — it is best accomplished through direct dialogue and a regular presentation schedule. This approach will also help the corporate economist learn what executives feel is important, what decisions they are most concerned about, how they think the environment is affecting their performance, etc. The dialogue during regular meetings helps to directly translate environmental analysis into decision-making needs.

7. **Employ a global orientation:** Even domestically oriented industries are now being affected by international factors.

8. **Be sensitive to changes:** Be sensitive to the changes that many companies have made in the way they plan, and in their planning process.

64

PART II

THE FORECASTING TEAM— MANAGERS AND FORECASTERS

INTRODUCTION

To succeed in the forecasting function, managers (users of forecasts) and forecasters have to work as a team. This section describes what forecasters and managers have to do to accomplish it. To be a good team player, the forecaster has to understand his/her role. He/she is not indispensable. He/she is a provider of input used in decision-making, and not a decision-maker. He/she has to understand that statistical forecasts are nothing more than baseline forecasts. Judgmental overlay by managers often tends to improve forecasts. The forecaster has to learn, among other things, the language and culture of the organization. Managers also have to recognize their role. They should not perceive forecasters as just number crunchers. They should understand that forecasts are just 'maybe' and thus contingency plans are required. To get the most from forecasters, they have to be honest with them. They should know what forecasting is all about, and how numbers are generated, at least, conceptually.

CHAPTER 14

THE YOGI AND THE KOMMISSAR

Robert Brown
Material Management Systems

Al Migliaro
Institute of Business Forecasting

(Upon whom does the burden of effective communication rest? The forecast, technician, herein is referred to as The Yogi or the business manager, user, herein is referred to as The Kommissar. Mr. Brown, a Yogi of long standing, places the onus on his colleagues; Mr. Migliaro, a Kommissar of equally long standing, places the burden on the forecaster. Mr. Brown identifies the jargon as the primary barrier to effective communication and proposed a remedy; Mr. Migliaro points to three other factors as the culprits and offers his own prescription. Ed.)

Robert G. Brown

Some very good work is being done by technicians to improve business forecasting. Often the business manager doesn't realize the full benefit of that work; it's an appalling waste of resources when business does not capitalize on such work. First, it is a waste of time of technician when his results aren't used effectively. Second, business suffers by using less than the best tools, or by using good tools ineffectively.

There are three points to consider: jargon, thought processes, and feedback. Since the technician who develops better forecasting tools is something of an intellectual, what Koestler calls a Yogi, the burden for improving on all three of these points probably is on him. Koestler describes the business executive as a Kommissar, who is prone to getting things done, rather than thinking about them.

JARGON

Bob Thrall, a professor at the University of Michigan, once began a presentation to a room full of admirals by turning to a rickety blackboard. As he wrote down some very precise mathematical symbols, he told the admirals, "it is obvious that we can write down the following covariance matrix." True, but not especially informative to that audience.

The mathematicians and computer programmers who develop better tools for forecasting have an extensive priestly jargon. That jargon serves two purposes: effective communication within the profession, elimination of ambiguity through the use of mathematical symbols and computer acronyms. If the speaker (or writer) uses a term correctly, anyone else in the profession knows exactly what is meant. Jargon is compact. One professional can communicate very complex concepts quickly to another professional.

The other purpose of professional jargon is less admirable: because other members of the same profession understand the jargon, it serves to identify the outsiders, and assures their exclusion from the Priestly inner circle. Economists, doctors, lawyers, preachers, accountants, and sculptors all have their own jargon, both to communicate to the in-group, and to exclude outsiders.

The professional technician who wants to be sure that the professional business manager can use the forecast techniques has to be alert to his own jargon. Further, he has to understand that the business manager has another jargon. It is extremely helpful if the technician has a quick ear for languages, and can use managers' jargon accurately. That makes the listener feel that the technician is one of his in-group. The manager who hears his own jargon being used accurately gives a more sympathetic ear, because the speaker is part of his group. He also understands more readily because the jargon conveys complex concepts efficiently.

Of course, the technician, who can't use the other's jargon accurately, should avoid it. Inaccurate use of jargon merely emphasizes that you are an outsider and don't understand the concepts you are trying to convey.

THOUGHT PROCESSES

It is not sufficient to make a word-for-word translation from the jargon of the technician's profession to the jargon of the manager's profession. Saying "function of" for "$f(x)$," or "plus" for "+" doesn't really help. Neither would "add together" for "plus." The mathematician or computer programmer who develops better forecasting tools has a value system built up over years from his professional associations. A rigorous deductive proof carries immense persuasion to another Yogi. The Kommissar hasn't time to listen to deductive proofs. They don't mean anything.

The Kommissar wants to see results. The nearer the bottom line, the better. Enumeration of special cases where something works turns off the usual scientist. He knows that a single counter example can disprove a theory, but no list of positive examples, however long, will substantiate theory, A long list of successes may increase the probability that the theorem is true. The Yogi tries to prove, in general, why a forecasting procedure has to work simply won't be heard by the Kommissar who has to use it. Show him positive results.

"Yes, but." is a common reaction. Your method works all right on that example, but how about this case. Or, "It won't work on…" Those responses are a marvelous opportunity to get the user to understand. If your method really is so good, quietly demonstrate how it works in those cases, too. Don't prove. Demonstrate.

Of course, that means you have to understand what the user's problems look like, and develop forecasting methods that really do work on the problems that are real to him. For the optimum solution to a problem, the user doesn't think he has much use.

The technician has to understand the jargon, the thought processes, and the operating environment of the user, before starting to develop a better method of forecasting. Then, the results, rigorously obtained, are likely to be relevant to the user's needs. It's easier for the business manager to understand something that he perceives as relevant. He's more likely to perceive the technique as relevant, if it is relevant.

FEEDBACK

Effective communication, whether between Yogi and Kommissar, or between husband and wife, can be greatly enhanced by feedback. Stop frequently to check whether the other understood what you said, whether he heard what you meant.

For a scientist that should be easy. Form a hypothesis about the other's reaction if he understood what you meant. Design an experiment to put that hypothesis in jeopardy. The experiment may be a question, or an observation of the other's body language. If the experiment confirms the hypothesis, go for another sentence assuming that you are being understood. If the observation is contrary to your model of how the other should react, stop right there to clean up the communication. A sermon or a lecture or an article does not allow much in the way of testing whether you are being understood. In a lecture, you can watch to see who is taking notes and whether anyone is smiling or nodding. But the note-taker or nodder may be writing a letter or thinking of something else entirely. In an article you can't even see the audience.

Face-to-face conversation does permit feedback and testing. Too many conversations are really lectures. The listener has ample time to think of what he's going to say when he gets a chance to break in, instead of listening to what you're saying. When a Yogi really wants to get something across to a Kommissar, he will first of all be aware that there are two quite different sets of jargon involved. There are two quite different value systems and habits of thought. Possibly as often after each sentence, and certainly after each paragraph, the Yogi will stop to test whether the Kommissar understands accurately. The Yogi might even think of testing whether he himself understands accurately what the Kommissar is trying to say.

To one who hasn't tried it, that would seem to slow down the conversation, with so many extra tests built into the complicated statement. An expert at conveying the ideas may have found that his conversation is actually shorter, because all of it is productive in conveying an idea accurately and efficiently.

Most of the effective techniques of forecasting for business involve making a prediction, observing the actual sales or interest rate or account balance, and then modifying the forecast because of the difference between what was forecasted and what was observed. The same concept can be transferred to effective techniques for communicating from one culture to the other about forecasting.

Al Migliaro

We've been hearing about the importance of communication for more than a generation. In most discussions, the burden of effective communication is placed on the communicator. It is a heavy burden; not only must the communicator reduce complex issues to simplistic terms, he must cram them into a few entertaining words. Implicit in this view is that the listener has no responsibilities; he needs only to lend an ear.

We are only now beginning to recognize that there can be no communication in the absence of listening. Some people — the iconoclasts — go so far as to insist upon intelligent listening.

After some 40 years of interpreting business, professional and government jargon as a writer, editor and business manager, I have concluded that it is not jargon alone that blocks clear communication. Jargon, as Mr. Brown points out in the accompanying article, has the virtue of precision in communicating a total concept in one or two words or even an acronym when used by members of the same profession. The same cannot be said in defense of the three other barriers to effective communication, which I propose to discuss in this response to the position taken by Mr. Brown in the accompanying article. The three barriers, which I prefer to label prerequisites to intelligent listening or reading, are: a command of the English language and its grammatical structure, some knowledge of the subject matter under discussion, and the ability to know what we don't know.

THE LANGUAGE

Psychologists tell us that some people think in words (verbalize, is their term) and others in pictures (visualize) and still others in both pictures and words. One word or phrase can trigger an idea in the minds of verbalizers; other words gush forth as they develop the idea. Hence, they are restricted in their thinking only by the size of their vocabulary. The visualizers, on the other hand, see a picture of the idea in their mind's eye, followed by a kaleidoscope as the idea develops. The verbalizers usually have a better command of the language and can communicate their ideas to others with greater ease; they can "paint a picture" with words. The visualizers are those who frequently use such terms as: "You know what I mean" or "I know what I want to say, but I can't say it." As a group the visualizers are more creative and less logical. Both groups, whether they are listeners (readers) or communicators, will benefit from an extensive vocabulary and knowledge of the connotation of words as well as their precise meaning.

A good grasp of the rules of grammar is also important. The English language is precise. One can say precisely what one means by the right choice of words, correct punctuation and sentence construction. Unfortunately, this precision in the language is lost by careless writing and careless reading. Ambiguity frequently is the result. Here, for example, is a sentence the meaning of which can be changed radically by a comma:

"The forecast was not accurate, because of the model used."

With the comma placed in front of "because," the sentence means that the forecast was wrong and that the reason for the error was that the wrong model was used. Removal of the comma changes the meaning to: The forecast was right on target but the reason for the accuracy was not the model used, implying that some other element was responsible for the accuracy. Orally, one or the other meaning is conveyed by voice inflection. Misuse of words or terms by the writer or misinterpretation by the reader also can lead to misunderstanding. The terms "market research" and "marketing research" are an example. These terms are used synonymously, even in the professional literature. Each has its own, precise meaning. When a researcher is engaged in "market research," the focus is on the market, its composition, size, definition, etc. When the object of the research is to determine the relative effectiveness of one or more marketing strategies on a specific market, one is engaged in "marketing research" and one uses "test marketing" methods. "Market testing" methods are used to validate "market research" findings resulting from an analysis of existing data.

The intelligent listener has a problem when confronted by either loose writing or precise writing. He doesn't know which of the two he is dealing with — consequently he's confused. The unintelligent reader, not even aware that the problem exists, blithely interprets the words on the basis of his own limited knowledge with the result that there is a 50% chance of misinterpretation.

The careful writer is also in a dilemma: shall he write for the careful reader or succumb to the notion that erroneous grammar is perfectly all right, because usage by the unwashed has made it acceptable? Regardless of which he chooses, he is bound to confound one or the other group.

KNOWLEDGE OF SUBJECT

Experts cannot agree on a definition of intelligence. They do concede that knowledge is one of the elements found in intelligent people. A child who has learned that a stove is hot and that to touch it produces an unpleasant sensation has knowledge. If he continues to touch hot stoves, he is not intelligent (unless he enjoys being burned); he is not using the knowledge to his own benefit or to that of others. Intelligence is thus a function of knowledge, $i(k)$, for the purpose of this discussion. Application of the $i(k)$ function to the Yogi-Kommissar relationship implies that effective communication (EC) can be achieved when each has knowledge of the other's discipline. The degree of effectiveness grows exponentially with the amount of knowledge each has of the other's specialty; $EC = [i(k) * (u)] + [i(k) * (u)^2] ... [i(k) * (u)^n]$, where "u" = units of knowledge. Does this mean that the Kommissar and the Yogi each needs to have an equal number of units of knowledge of each others specialty, especially advanced mathematics in the case of the Kommissar, in order for each to listen intelligently? No!

The Yogi, for example, uses his technical knowledge and skills to construct a model that represents real world events, say, market behavior in response to a certain set of stimuli. While a thorough knowledge of advanced mathematics is required to construct such a model, it does not follow that one needs the same degree of knowledge to understand it and make a judgment about its efficacy. But to say that the Kommissar is not obligated to have any knowledge at all about how the model is constructed and what it purports to show, is to sustain the Peter Principle: a Kommissar who lacks a working knowledge of the work of members of the professional disciplines under his direction has certainly reached his level of incompetence. One should not infer from this that I am suggesting that Kommissars should have sufficient knowledge of advance mathematics to construct a model or to manipulate data like a technician. What is being suggested here is that he recognizes that forecasting is a science (as well as an art form) and that it can help explain certain events and that he, at least, be aware of the various techniques available to the mathematician/ forecaster to help produce a forecast. If a Kommissar has no knowledge of how the specialists under his direction arrive at their recommendations, it is incumbent upon him to learn as much about those methods as is required to make an informed judgment about what he is being told or, to put it another way, to listen intelligently.

KNOWING WHAT WE DON'T KNOW

The person who has the ability to know what he doesn't know is, in my estimation, at the nadir of intelligence. Those who admit their ignorance know the serenity that one derives from confidence in oneself. Such people are a valuable asset; they seldom make an error in judgment. They do not tread where angels fear to go. Those who lack this ability are dangerous to the financial health of an enterprise that employs them. They are the ones who propose simplistic (not simple) solutions to complex problems, the hare-brained scheme that fails. A post-mortem of such a failure reveals that it was due to some element, some piece of information, that was overlooked. The problem solver didn't know that element could have been present.

The Kommissar who hasn't taken the time or made the effort to acquaint himself with the emerging science of forecasting can, for example, assume that forecasting is an easy thing to do: "You just take last year's sales and add "n" dollars for the new customers we got this year and voila, you have the forecast for next year's sales. Who needs all those fancy equations. They're just a lot of theories, anyway. "

Naive models are appropriate in many cases. However, a Kommissar who believes that extrapolation techniques are suitable for all sales forecasting situations, such as the sales manager quoted above, is himself naive — he doesn't know that other methods exist and that one of them may be more appropriate to a situation. Intelligent listening is not his strong suit; he probably takes a similar naive view toward the work of other subordinates.

How does the Yogi deal with such a Kommissar? Will the prescription offered by Mr. Brown work? He says it does, and he should know. But, I suggest that my fellow Kommissars shed the facade of omniscience and freely admit to the next Yogi they meet: "Sir, I don't know what the hell you're talking about; talk to me in words of one syllable, because I know that what you're saying is important to me." Then ask him to suggest a book on the subject suitable for novices. The Yogi will number you among the most brilliant personages of the ages.

CHAPTER 15

WINNING MANAGERS' TRUST IS FORECASTERS' OTHER JOB

Arnold B. Maltz
Ross Laboratories

As a practicing forecaster, I have been amazed and disappointed at how organizations have used my projections. In one case, management accepted every monthly forecast, and refused to believe the long-term downward trend. In another case, forecasts were simply declared irrelevant during each new rescue meeting. Conversely, I have seen top management use projections as if they were certainties; the results were equally disastrous, since we did not make backup plans. I have also put together the typical "forecast for the banker," which must be rosy enough to justify the loan.

A good forecaster possesses significant insights about his/her subject. But this unique viewpoint is often ignored by the forecaster's audience, whether they believe the actual predictions or not. Not only have I consistently experienced this sense of being viewed as a technician, but the literature indicates that this problem is common to many forecasters.

I contend that this tendency to evaluate the forecast while ignoring the forecaster stems from a lack of credibility in the person doing the forecasting. When the planner lacks credibility, the abuses occur which led Drucker to say that "forecasting is not a respectable human activity." In my experience, projections are either overvalued or ignored unless the source of the forecasts is explicitly included in the discussion. Even then, people often take what they want from the forecast to support their own positions.

I consider the optimum case to be when the forecaster and his/her forecast are not only looked at, but also used as a significant factor in decision-making. Such participation and influence indicate to me that a forecaster has credibility within the organization. I would further argue that it is the forecaster's job to change his status from a tolerated (and dismissed) outsider to a valued member of the management group. At least three issues must be addressed: (1) Translation— the forecaster must make his/her ideas intelligible to everyone who might use the projections. (2) Accuracy—the various audiences must believe that the forecasts are either accurate, or that the possible inaccuracies are clearly marked. (3) Organizational fit—the forecaster must convince decision makers that his/her aim is to improve organizational performance, not to solve problems in the abstract.

THE TRANSLATOR

Forecasters spend much of their time with mathematical models and methods, trying to separate and identify various trends. As the organization grows, the problems become more complex. More powerful and more complicated methods are usually required. Computer manipulation emerges as the only easy way to deal with the huge mass of data, make sense of it, and project the effects of various actions. Even in small to medium size companies, a corporate model must embrace all aspects of the business, while seasonal, secular and other trends can be delineated only with statistical methods. The forecaster must translate this abstract framework into a managerial setting. Managers deal with people and concrete events; they must obtain measurable results and ask employees to perform specific acts. Forecasters must reflect this action point of view as they communicate the main point of their projections. This means using familiar terms and ideas from the user's world, rather than structures from the technology of forecasting.

At the same time, the responsible forecaster has to convey the uncertainty that goes with any projection. Managers live in a world of events, where something either happens or does not. Forecasters should use the concrete language of that world, but make it clear that forecasts are maybe, not certainties. A properly translated forecast indicates not only what is likely to happen, but why it might not.

"To translate" means "To put into the words of a different language." Every organization has its own culture and worldview. In fact, each functional area within an organization has its own language. Each is specialized, based on that area's day to-day concerns. It is the forecaster's job to provide information to each in a way with which its customer is comfortable. To insure common ground between forecaster and operating area, the two should work together to develop the first model for the area. The users specify key factors affecting the forecast, and the mechanisms for changing them. The modeler translates these specifications into an abstract simulation of the operation. The result of this simulation should be projections in the same format as current reports. This allows immediate checks by the user for "reasonableness." Handing a report written in a familiar format makes the whole idea of forecasting more comfortable to the forecast user.

NO ROAD MAP

As the forecaster and user work together, the user will begin to see forecasting as a tool, not a road map. The forecaster ought to act as a technical consultant. He/she should encourage the user to test the model(s) every step of the way. Both should ask all the questions they can think of. This questioning process will help refine the model, and also will demonstrate that no simulation is based on complete, perfect knowledge.

The user should also backtrack the model, seeing how well the model would have done in the past. All of these efforts will convince the user that no model is better than its assumptions, and that these assumptions come from limited human experience. The forecaster has translated his/her forecast successfully if the user understands the terms of the forecast, and its limits. Both of these objectives can be achieved through the user's involvement and respect for the user's viewpoint.

USER NEEDS

To illustrate, consider a decision on fleet replacement in a trucking company. Three groups want forecasts: (1) The operations group needs to know how the fleet upgrade will affect equipment and driver utilization. The relevant variables are current and projected weight per load, current and projected miles per driver per day, and current/projected miles/tractor/day. The maintenance group requires projections of fuel efficiency, breakdown frequency, and maintenance hours per vehicle per year. The finance group must have cash flow and depreciation projections, balance sheet analyses, and maintenance expense protection.

BASIC INFORMATION

Certain information is basic to all three forecasts: sales volumes, network structure and service levels. But this information must be combined with input from each area to answer each group's questions. For operations purposes, the forecaster must relate total sales with load average to calculate trips. Then trips, equipment speed, distance, and safety rules are employed to find staffing requirements.

For maintenance purposes, miles and hours of service are added to miles per gallon, repair frequency per hour, preventive maintenance schedules, etc. to determine maintenance staffing, fuel requirements, parts inventories, etc.

For financial purposes, the treasurer uses purchase price, estimated life, government tax regulations, sales volumes, and many other items to determine if the company can afford to replace equipment and how to finance the replacement. The forecaster must work with each group to satisfy its special needs. He/she must be sure that the sales can forecast into tonnage and miles for operations, into miles for maintenance, and into revenue and cost per mile for finance.

LINK AREAS

As translator, the forecaster must ensure that the miles maintenance needs, the miles operations uses, and the miles finance requires are all compatible. The forecaster also must link areas, so that the change in cost per mile projected by maintenance shows up correctly in finance savings estimates.

All of these project jobs are part of the translation process. Each group depends on the forecast for key information; the forecaster must be sure the specific information is usable by the group. Each group supplies specialized information to the forecast; the forecaster must make clear how that information critically affects the forecast. Once this two-way flow of information has been established, translation has taken place. The various users know what the forecast has to say about their area, and they have helped to define the forecast's terms. At the same time these users understand that the forecast rests on assumptions and outside input, and that no forecast will produce a perfect projection of the future.

When users realize both what the forecast says, and the limits of the forecast, the forecaster has also taken the first step to credibility within the organization.

ACCURACY

If a forecast is to be useful and credible, it must pass two tests of accuracy. The forecast must be technically correct, judged by objective criteria (usually mathematical). And, the forecast must pass the users' test of accuracy. This section discusses some strategies a forecaster can use to convince users about forecast accuracy. The discussion assumes the forecaster has done the statistical tests and convinced himself of the forecast's validity. How does a non-forecaster convince him/herself that a projection is right? He asks, "Does the forecast make sense?" Any forecast should appear internally consistent. Columns should add up and cross-foot with appropriate rows. Round off errors should be allocated. Most important, the forecaster should continually check with users for obvious mistakes. These users can point out results that are counter-intuitive. The forecaster can then re-check these suspect projections. Either the forecast methodology is incorrect, or some major shift in the business is being predicted. If the forecaster insists that a hard-to-believe change is on the way, he/she should try to restate and support that conclusion so that the users can accept it. Otherwise the forecast will remain suspect (and probably unused).

PREDICT THE PAST

Another approach involves showing how well the model predicts the past. Since the audience has lived through the events, this approach can be especially effective. For example, I was once requested to project the effect of a change in customer mix for my (then) employer, a large trucking company. I displayed profit margin and percent less-than truckload (LTL) weight on the same graph. The striking relation "sold" my projection of improvement through better LTL mix.

A variation is to forecast aggregate quantities in the short term. Usually I predict company wide sales 1-3 months out. Success with this easy problem gives management information, and builds confidence in the forecaster's accuracy and competence.

Finally, the forecaster must address the issue of "useful accuracy." Various forecasting problems demand different levels of accuracy. A 5-Year Plan for the outside bankers does not have to be highly precise in the later years. The bankers are concerned that some organized planning is going on, and that business projections and financing requests are coordinated. Probably, they will never compare fifth year projections to actual results.

REAL CHOICES

On the other hand, an operating forecast is only useful when its accuracy gives management real choices. If a manager has five people working on the same job, the forecast must predict work available to well within 20%. If the projection is not that close, it contributes nothing to the daily staffing decision.

A forecaster must prove that forecasts are accurate enough for the organization's needs. First, the various technical questions must be settled to the best of the forecaster's ability and knowledge.

Second, the users must be convinced that the projections are reasonable, likely and informative. In this effort, the various non-technical suggestions in this section may be helpful. Once the forecaster has convinced the organization that the projections can be believed, he/she has taken another step toward credibility and effectiveness.

FORECASTERS IGNORED

Professional forecasters function as staff. Even when they are understood and believed, their input may be ignored. For me, this has been the most frustrating experience of my career. No matter how clear is the forecast and no matter how good his/her track record is, management may refuse to believe straightforward projections.

In one instance, I had been projecting revenue within 2% for eighteen consecutive months. I predicted a drop of 20% over the next six months. The president, the chairman of the board, and an outside consultant, refused to credit my projection. As it turned out, I was too optimistic. The literature indicates many forecasters could tell similar stories.

By necessity, forecasters have an overview of the entire corporation. They are mostly bright, analytical people. But management often ignores the forecaster's recommendation; sometimes management even ignores the forecaster's interpretation of his/her own forecast.

CLOSE THE GAP

"The preparers (of forecasts) again rated their own ability to work within the organization and to understand management problems much more highly than the users (of forecasts) did." In other words, management does not believe that forecasters see management problems clearly. Management also mistrusts forecasters' perceptions of how a corporation solves problems. Forecasters are simply not part of the management team. Why does this situation exist? To quote from Wheelwright and Clarke; "Perhaps basic to the gap between users and preparers is the technical emphasis of the preparers and the managerial emphasis of the users." As I have argued throughout this paper, it is the forecaster's job to close this gap. Previously, I discussed ways to make the forecast understandable and believable. Another step is required if the forecasters are to influence decisions consistently: they must show that they appreciate management's circumstances. Forecasters must be sensitive to the organization's structure, priorities, and limitations. Otherwise, users will perceive forecasters as "outsiders." Management may use some of their projections but will ignore personal input from the forecaster.

INPUT FOR ACTION

Forecasting always has a context, and it is one of the forecaster's tasks to work within that context. Forecasters should realize that managers use input (such as projections) for action. Therefore, the forecaster should try to see the implications of his predictions. If a major change is being evaluated, it should be recognized that change in an organization takes time and has costs. All should agree on how to build in these costs and time lags. Possible reactions to the forecast should be explored before the presentation to management. If revenues are predicted to fall sharply, for example, the forecaster should model various ways to cut costs. Attention to forecast implications will save management time and show the forecaster's non-technical side. Also, users are more likely to ask questions if possible actions accompany a forecast. After all, action is their stock in trade. The behavior I have suggested should bring managers and forecasters closer to each other. Beyond behavior, though, is the question of outlook. Managers try to control situations, and mold organizations to obtain results. Good managers see themselves initiating and structuring change, "Making things happen."

STEREOTYPES

By contrast, the forecaster is perceived as a researcher and observer who takes pride in finding the hidden obstacle, the next change in trend. Besides, the forecaster deals in abstract, quantitative descriptions of reality. The forecaster's usual role is finished, according to this perception, when the cover memo for the latest quarterly projections is finished; all that remains is to defend the projection.

If the organization and its people accept these stereotypes, the forecaster's other possible contributions are discounted. Indeed, if the forecaster himself accepts the stereotype, he makes no other contribution. Instead, the forecasting group becomes associated with problems and idealized, abstract visions, not solutions and action.

Consider the general manager who notes that volume is down and costs are edging up. The manager of forecasting asks for a few minutes. He rushes in, eager to share that he has found the answer. Sales will be down 15% because product "A" has fallen drastically. The chances are 80% that A's plant will have to be closed but there are a few more tests to run. Then the forecaster leaves, thinking he has addressed the problem.

ONLY A 'NUMBER CRUNCHER'

In fact, the general manager is probably wondering how to turn product "A" around, and cut plant costs. As general manager, and former "A" plant manager, he knows that the unfunded pension liability and increased overhead on other products makes closing plant "A" impractical. The general manager has again seen the manager of forecasting as a "number cruncher" with no feel for the "real world." If the presentation is understandable and believable, managers will accept the forecaster's finding that a trend exists. But forecasters must demonstrate awareness of management's situation, or their personal input will be ignored. They must show users that they do not believe that closing a plant is as easy as deleting a line in a program, or by simply asking the salesmen to push something new that will increase sales. Also, forecasters must accept the proposition that the course an organization takes is usually a compromise. Rarely does the action work out as neatly as a computer model.

INSIGHT

A good forecaster has a tremendous insight into the needs and possible problems of an organization. He/she is one of the few in a position to see the whole picture. But this asset will be wasted unless others accept her/him as part of the management group. Technical competence in a manager of forecasting is a given. But the holder of the job has to prove her/his practicality as well. Otherwise, the organization will never fully utilize the manager's talents.

CHAPTER 16

THE FORECASTER AS A KEY MEMBER OF THE STRATEGIC PLANNING TEAM

Robert Altabet
Duracell North Atlantic Group
Division of The Gillette Company

As a forecaster, I may be just a bit biased, but I strongly believe that our unique skills, as professional forecasters or as managers with forecasting training and experience, enable us to be significant contributors to the strategic direction of our companies. I hope I can share a few lessons from my own experience that will help some of you step further into such a role. I was fortunate during my career to have had early exposure to forecasting as a strategic tool. Duracell, in the mid 1970s, was still a relatively small company, giving us all the opportunity to work on a wide variety of projects, well outside our functional specialization. As Duracell grew, I had the particular good fortune to be reporting to that rarest of Marketing Vice Presidents, one whose early career was also in forecasting and sales analysis. He helped me make that transition from being a master technician at forecasting sales to using forecasting as a tool for managing the business. His two favorite questions still resonate in my ears: "Is the news good or bad?" and "What would you do about it?"

ROLE OF FORECASTING SHIFTS LIKE A PENDULUM

During the last 25 years, I have seen forecasting from a variety of functional environments, ranging from finance, to distribution and logistics, to the world of marketing and sales. Forecasting plays a key role in all these functions. But its emphasis shifts back and forth like a pendulum, one time on one function, another time on another function, and then back again. The latest emphasis of forecasting has been in the areas of scheduling and logistics, renamed "Supply Chain Management." This goes back to the operations management issues that I saw when I entered the workforce in the early 1970s. This is certainly an important area, and comes, as did prior waves, from tidal shifts in computer capabilities that have enabled us to use techniques, which were once considered highly sophisticated and complex, efficiently and economically in a business operating environment.

These are, of course, valuable tools for business, and, during their implementation phase, will make noticeable contributions to a new, more efficient inventory and operating environment. But the operating departments are like a wheel that no one pays attention to until it squeaks. When things are running smoothly, the end customers and the departments with a customer focus do not pay attention to the intense work that goes into keeping things on track. But, in the midst of the intense work that is needed to integrate forecasting systems as a part of the weekly or even daily operating environment, the forecaster should not lose sight of the fact that he or she can make a significant contribution in strategic discussions also.

FORECASTS PROVIDE STRATEGIC DIRECTIONS

And, perhaps we can all be just a little selfish and career oriented. The movers and shakers of a company are those with responsibilities for change, for the new ideas in managing and implementing adjustments in strategic directions. For different companies, this may come from various departments ranging from sales, to marketing, to R&D, to finance. But they all have a need for quantitative and forecasting skills. They rarely have training in forecasting. They know little of the mathematical tools at our disposal for understanding the business. While they are experienced and smart businessmen, sophisticated techniques can give them a glassy eye look. But they desperately need the insights available from a good forecast manager, the guidance that can tell them which business issues to focus on for the greatest effect. They need it with a translation to the normal argot of sales and marketing terminology such as competitive advantage and product portfolio management.

EVOLUTION OF FORECASTING AT DURACELL

Let me digress for a moment and talk about the evolution of forecasting at Duracell which may provide some guidance to others on how to balance the forecasting needs for an operating environment with the requirements for a strategic direction. Like many other companies, when I joined Duracell in 1974, there was no dedicated forecasting department. Forecasting was a sideline activity of departments that needed the input and had no forecasting department to turn to. The Marketing Department did its forecasting, with the work done by entry level Assistant Product Managers. The Logistics Department ran time series and exponential smoothing models to forecast for warehouse replenishment and production scheduling. These models were developed by operations researchers but were managed by lower level inventory coordinators, with little understanding of alternative techniques or approaches. Our Finance Department did a third forecast, guided more by corporate financial requirements than by any analysis of business trends or cause and effect relationships. None of these forecasts were linked. The Sales Department set quotas completely independently of other departments.

We made two important changes in 1979. First, we instituted a dedicated forecasting group. This did more to upgrade the quality of the forecast and its utility than anything else could have. A Conference Board study of forecasting accuracy in that same period highlighted a dedicated forecasting department as the single most important variable impacting forecast accuracy, well ahead of any methodological variables. The independence from other groups created a more professional and objective model. Skill training was truly focused on forecasting rather than numerous other skills required for a different primary function. The departmental status made forecasting a recognized contributor to the company's business discussions. Management recognized the independence of the forecast and the analysis behind it. The second step was a single number linked system for all forecast users in all departments. But one number system has its own pitfalls. For example, a conservative forecast may seem to make good sense to manage risk in planning financial goals. This may be difficult to reconcile with forecast whose objective is to use in a sales quota system where stretch, hard to achieve targets, can provide the motivation to the sales department to deliver a stronger sales result. But, having lived through both alternatives at more than one company, the cohesion and unity of response to issues with a single number system outweighs any other issues. When any one of us has a problem, we all share the same motivation to fix it, since we are all committed to the same plan. For any strategic overview, the forecaster is then speaking the same language to everyone in the company. As we look at the 1990s, Duracell has begun a new transition to manage the increased workloads that resulted from integration into the operating modes of a supply chain management project. While all forecast activity must continue to be linked and is managed by experienced forecast specialists, operating divisions now have a forecasting group that manages the regular marketing and sales updates and supports logistics, scheduling and budget management. But the long-term forecast view, which is adjusted in tandem with strategic shifts, is managed by a true strategic forecasting group. This restores their ability to focus on the long-term issues that would have been otherwise squeezed by time pressures. And we are now even bringing some of the benefits of our North American dedicated forecasting approach to our European businesses that could not previously justify dedicated forecast groups. With this strategic focus, our forecast team can look at long-term trends that affect our business such as new electronic technologies and can plan strategic market research to understand key variables that will affect us.

WHAT MANAGEMENT WANTS

What are the goals of a forecast? Accuracy? Accuracy with the right lead-time? Accuracy at the monthly level? At the SKU level? The operations team certainly wants all of those. The more accurate the forecast with more lead-time, the happier they are. That simplifies their job. And we certainly need to provide that, but management has other priorities as well. What does management want? Not accuracy, but usefulness; utility as a management and decision tool. They are not asking us to tell them what will happen, an answer that the operations folk would be quite happy with. They want to know what can happen and what they can do to change what will happen. They want you to give them control.

Throughout history, great kings and generals have used seers to help see into the future. But we all know the "shoot the messenger" syndrome. We may have more scientific methods for prognosticating, and maybe we are even more accurate, but the people equation has not changed. We must go beyond delivering the news to be effective; we must deliver the commentary and make it actionable. My favorite example, of about three thousand years vintage, comes from the story of Joseph in the Bible. He forecasted Egypt's seven years of plenty to be followed by seven years of famine to Pharaoh, possibly the first historical record of a long-range economic forecast. He could easily have stopped right there; he had accomplished the mission set before him. As we now know, he was even accurate. But his step into the strategic planning team is what set him apart. He defined a problem, the risk of famine. He answered the question, "Is this news good or bad?" And most importantly, he offered solutions. He answered the second question, "What would you do about it?" He pointed out the opportunity for Pharaoh to profit from this by storing the crops from the good years and selling them when the years of poor crops would finally come. For Egypt, the famine never caused a problem because Joseph made a suggestion about what to do.

These are the steps that the forecaster must take to make the transition from technical advisor to being a key member of the strategic planning team.

CAUSAL MODELS PROVIDE INSIGHT INTO THE BUSINESS

So, how do we get there? Some key messages: getting close on the forecast may be good enough. Incomplete but timely forecasts are better than perfect but late forecasts. Insight on causation is better than accuracy. As forecasters we frequently look at trends in some sort of time series mode. These are tools that can often provide the basis for quite accurate forecasting. And in the short term, they may be better than many causal models, because we do not always understand the reasons why, and even when we do, the data may not be timely. Sometimes, even when we know the value of causal models, we are concerned about a host of technical issues. Missing data points, data quality and integrity issues are all good technical reasons for potentially flawed analyses. And, in a world of infinite time, I might wait for resolution of these concerns.

But business moves very quickly and decisions must be made whether the available information and analysis are complete or incomplete. If we, the forecasters, do not provide answers to those causative questions such as which variables really drive sales, management will make decisions without that information. The decisions will be based on back of the envelope analysis with less rigor than a forecaster could bring and less understanding of a dynamic market place. How often have you voiced the query, "Why would they do that, it did not work the last three times?" Product mangers will keep on recycling old solutions if no one keeps a track of what happened when those solutions were used in the past. As such, we should maintain records of what we do. Learning from history, research and experiment should be built into the way we think.

I had one awakening over a dozen years ago when I told our Vice-president of Marketing that we should not change the forecast in spite of this glorious photographic battery marketing plan that had been put together. I explained that he could not expect "marketing magic" to change some very solid underlying trends. I may have been right, but it was clearly the wrong way to say it politically. What I should have been highlighting were the controllable and uncontrollable factors that could make a difference. In our case, at least for the short term, camera sales, camera features and technology and consumer photographic usage factors were in the uncontrollable category. Pricing, channels, distribution, advertising, merchandising and promotions were controllable. Analysis of the sensitivity of each of these variables led to some specific recommendations for influencing sales. The right focus turned out to be a merchandising effort rather than advertising or promotion. Merchandising may not be as exciting and sexy as an advertising program for a product manager who wants to advance to the big league products where advertising makes greater difference. The forecaster must provide the systematic analysis that can lead us to a right conclusion. I am not even fussy about the models, whether we identify key variables with linear multiple regression analyses, with or without dummy variables or with nonlinear models. In my experience, I have seen first class analysts come to the same conclusions from simple matrix and cross-tabular analysis as those who used sophisticated techniques.

And there is no single comprehensive model that works for everything, even within a single industry. The models and statistical tools may change from product line to product line, and may change over time as the market structure changes as a result of new product entries, new competitors and/or changing consumer behavior. We must be flexible enough to keep reinvestigating the answers. And we must be brave enough to offer solutions, not just to describe the results. We also make many assumptions about the market, about trends, or a host of other things. These ceteris paribus, all things being equal assumptions, are critical. These are necessary or else our models would be too complex, too incomprehensible and/or have autocorrelated variables. We would suffer from the "Moon Shot" problem, where a change of one degree could mean million of miles. Keep the models as simple as you can to solve the problem at hand; additional complexity will get you in trouble.

But do not lose sight of those assumptions. Chart them, both the explicit and the implicit ones. The explicit ones are usually easy. They come from the variables we have chosen not to use in the model for the sake of simplicity. The implicit ones are a bit harder, they come from understanding your frame of reference as well as "what everybody already knows." You and management need to monitor these assumptions for future impact. Sudden changes are the indicator that a model or an approach is in need of revision. The implicit assumptions can be a good input to generate some really "out of the box" thinking that can lead to radical changes in approach. For example, as noted earlier, camera technology and features were treated as an uncontrollable variable at one point. But in the early 1980s, Duracell began a program to work closely with the original equipment manufacturers (OEMs) of cameras to influence designs, rather than just sell product. We were able to launch a new lithium photo battery that did not just deliver longer battery life, but rather provided faster recycle time for the flash. The ready light could come on in 4 to 5 seconds rather than 10 to 20 seconds. The discussions began with a review of implicit forecast assumptions that led someone to ask what we, Duracell, could do to take a greater control over the future of the battery category rather than to accept it as it is. Today, partnership with OEMs is a major part of our strategic platform.

SPEAK THEIR LANGUAGE WHEN PRESENTING

Finally, the presentation must be converted to terms that our top management can easily relate to and lead to buy in and acceptance. Save the impressive methodology for presentation at forecasting conferences. That may mean simplifying a model or abstracting only the key data. Once you know the answer, it can frequently be presented in a much simpler analytic framework. If more advertising is the key variable, present a chart showing only the relationship between advertisement and sales or advertisement and market share. Painful as it is when we have done good work that we might like to share, top management is usually not interested in the gory details or even the creative use of statistical techniques that got you there, no matter how proud you are of your work. Definitely turn your work into graphic presentations whenever you can, particularly when data show cause and effect relationship, not just the broad trends. Simple arrows, identifying the period when a variable changed will be more powerful than any review of the rigorous use of dummy variables that originally led you to that conclusion. Studies have shown that management is more likely to believe you with a presentation that used graphics. Speak their language of distribution, shares, and competitive advantage.

Develop alternative scenarios with varying assumptions. It may be more work, but seeing the consequences on paper of a poor decision can be a more powerful motivator than just the positives of a good decision. Keep it brief. Whenever possible, get buy in to one idea at a time. Like everyone else, top managers need time to adjust to a change, especially if they had a hand in setting the original direction.

SUMMARY

As forecasters you have the knowledge and skills to be a part of the strategic planning team. In fact, you can move into top management if you want to. We cannot view forecasting as an end in itself, but as a tool for management for decision making. It is our compass during the fiscal year, telling us whether we are on or off course. It is also our sextant and charts telling us which star to steer by to stay on course, the course being your own company's mission. Remember that the ship's captain usually apprentices as a navigator using compass, sextant and charts. And you, the forecaster, can move into that top management role with the right attitude and career development.

You can begin this transition by developing a track record for useful insights and objective recommendations, for gently demonstrating in post audit mode the reliability of your forecasts. You advance by making forecasting a tool for key management decisions, and you win by making the recommendations that are grounded in logic and facts rather than in emotions and gut feelings. After a little while, your management team may begin to wonder how they ever did without you.

CHAPTER 17

MANAGER'S ROLE IN FORECASTING

Gary F. Wilkinson
GTE, Midwestern Telephone Operations

The manager's role in the forecast process is to bring a broad perspective to decision-making. It is necessary to insure that the process does not become isolated from users and that it is used to the fullest potential for helping management adapt to change.

Many conversations with users of forecasts start with the phrase "if only we could get accurate forecasts. . . " These users normally then explain the difficulties faced by their respective function due to poor forecasts. What is the real problem? Are forecasters not doing their jobs well? Have the theoreticians let us down? Perhaps, the forecasters are doing as well as can be expected, but the users of the forecasts have unrealistic expectations.

Managers of forecasting groups are often placed in a difficult position of wanting to improve the process but not being sure what needs fixing. How can they decide what changes are necessary when users are dissatisfied and the forecasters respond that they are using the latest techniques and demonstrate this by displaying extremely complex mathematics. In this article I will suggest some general principles for managers to help them work through this predicament.

FORECASTING: A COMPONENT OF DECISION-MAKING PROCESS

The first principle is that the forecasting process must be viewed as only one function within the overall decision-making process. It is not possible to view forecasting in isolation. For example, in telecommunications, forecasting is one stage in the total process of deciding upon the amount and deployment of equipment and manpower to provide service. The experience we had in GTE Midwestern Telephone Operations was that when we viewed the entire decision-making process for capital and manpower deployment, some problems, which initially had been attributed to "bad forecasts," really had other causes.

One instance involved a problem with central office switching equipment where additional line cards had to be ordered during the installation of a new digital switch. Without these line cards, the office could not be cut into service. These last minute activities resulted in wasted effort and increased cost. The problem had been attributed to forecast inaccuracy since the engineers said they followed the forecast in calculating the equipment needed. However, in digging a little deeper, the problem really resulted from engineering decisions specifying the amount of test and administrative lines needed in a central office. Only customer lines had been included in the forecast and therefore additional capacity for administrative and test lines needed to be added to the forecast to provide adequate equipment.

Numerous other examples from other industries are available. The key lesson is that the manager must bring a broad perspective and understanding of how decisions are made in the company and to assure the forecasting process is satisfying the information needs.

DIALOGUE IMPROVES FORECASTS

The second general principle is that it is necessary to insure considerable dialogue between users and the developers of the forecast. If managers find that forecast users have little idea of how the forecast was developed and the forecasters cannot explain in some detail how the forecasts are used, then fundamental discussions between these groups are necessary. All participants in the decision-making process should understand the purpose of the forecasts, data and techniques used to develop the forecast, expected accuracy, and the way the forecast is used.

UNDERSTAND LIMITATIONS

The third principle is to understand the inherent limitations of the forecasting process. Although forecasters are generally optimistic about their ability to provide accurate forecasts, managers need to probe deeper. Graphs of older forecasts compared with actuals provide three indicators for the manger on forecast limitations.

The first is simply the comparison of the various forecasts with the actuals. Naturally, large deviations indicate that a great deal of uncertainty exists in the forecasting process and unless there is a major flaw in technique, this uncertainty can generally be expected to continue.

A second indicator is the spread of forecasts made at different points in time. Ideally, the forecasts made at different points should be fairly consistent. If they vary greatly, probably the process is not well understood, either because of its complexity or because it has a large random component.

A final test in understanding forecast limitations is to inspect whether the forecasts have picked up turning points. No forecasting process is perfect at predicting turning points, but greater confidence can be placed in the forecasting process if it has demonstrated that it can predict changes in trend. What is the value of understanding forecast limitations? In many cases users want a single number without equivocations.

However, the key to building an adequate decision-making process is to understand the risk in the forecast and build greater flexibility in the system as risk increases. A highly flexible system, which can react quickly, requires less accurate forecasts. In circumstances where forecasts have a great deal of uncertainty, the manager must attempt to build as much flexibility as practical in the system.

SIMPLE MODELS

The fourth principle is to force the forecasters to simplify the process. Too many forecasting processes have become so complex that even those who built the models are not sure how they behave. Simple models are preferred to complex. Complexity, which adds little to expected accuracy, should be eliminated and managers should constantly question the need for complexity. Also, presentation of the forecasts to management should use simple illustrations and explanations. Forecasters tend to enjoy complex mathematics, but all forecasting processes should be able to be explained in laymen's terms. If the process cannot be explained to management without resorting to complex jargon, it should probably be discarded.

FALL IN LOVE WITH DATA, NOT MODELS

The fifth principle is to guard against the tendency for forecasters to become enamored with technique. Clearly, technical expertise in building forecasting models is extremely important. However, applying a particular forecasting method follows the hard work of understanding the requirements of the decision-making process and the data used in developing the forecast. Gwilym Jenkins often said in his lectures that analysts should fall in love with their data not with their forecasting models. In fact, forecasting models should never be trusted and should constantly be tested, and, if found inadequate, easily discarded. It is unfortunate that a number of forecasters keep using a particular technique because they have become comfortable with it.

SIMULATE POSSIBLE OUTCOMES

The final principle is to fully use the forecasting process to simulate a number of possible outcomes. This forces management to consider a range of possible conditions in their planning. Clearly, businesses which have planned for a number of potential conditions are better able to adapt and profit from a change than those companies who are unprepared for conditions other than those of a single forecast.

CHAPTER 18

THE ROLE OF A FORECASTER

Adam M. Pilarski
McDonnell Douglas Corporation

Nichols Filippello in his Presidential address of the National Association of Business Economists (NABE) in 1984 said that a plethora of articles had recently appeared in publications such as The Wall Street Journal, The New York Times and Time Magazine, questioning not only the forecasting as a profession but also the need for its existence. The situation has not improved since then. The press is often just as negative as the person on the street who sees forecasters as nothing more than a creator of numbers with a crystal ball. Even our sophisticated critics, who refrain from slapstick comedy attacks, believe that our forecasts are ridiculous at best, and possibly quite dangerous. All these developments are detrimental to the psychological well-being of all of us as forecasters. The damage to our psyche is only the beginning. An attack on our material well-being has begun. Numerous large manufacturing concerns and banks have either drastically cut down their planning, forecasting and economic staffs or altogether abolished them.

KNOW YOUR PLACE

As a forecaster you must know your place. There are many roles you can play as a forecaster. You can be useful in getting the customers listening to your sales people. You can be quoted favorably in the press enhancing the name of the company. You can also be a "high priest," blessing the ground where a new project is to be initiated. The forecaster may be highly skilled and educated, well paid and well respected, has a good exposure to the top management and provides necessary input to the company's most important decisions, but he/she is not the boss. The acceptance of this fact will help forecasters tremendously in their job, though it is not easy to do.

Quite often we forecasters do not realize our position vis-a-vis the decision maker. Decision makers and forecaster possess very different characteristics. To judge a decision maker by the criteria of evaluating forecasters is the crux of the problem. The mistake commonly made by a forecaster is to believe that he/she is smarter than the decision maker. Therefore, the forecaster should be making decisions. This kind of thinking is not only wrong but also can lead to the unemployment line.

A major error that forecasters make is that we do not understand characteristics that make a good CEO are not necessarily the same as of a good forecaster. The fact that the CEO cannot explain a decision scientifically does not mean that the decisions are wrong. Total understanding of forecasting methods is not a prerequisite for a good CEO. Rather the necessary characteristics of a CEO are courage to take risks at the right time, vision, boldness and political instinct to get the job done. The CEO can make the right decision with or without the help of a forecaster.

Sometime the forecaster is called "professor." This is not a compliment particularly when coming from a decision maker. I recall a comment of this sort when a sales vice-president in our organization said to his new director, a former forecaster: "So, Bill, how many forecasts did you sell to our customers today?" The forecaster, on the other hand, often sees the decision maker as the one who makes decisions without fully understanding their impact. The impact of such a thinking on the part of both forecaster and management (forecast user) is quite damaging. Think of a fascinating experiment in physics. Take a balloon and a stick with a nail sticking out. Hit the balloon with a stick. Repeat the experiment a hundred times. Such an experiment will damage the balloon more so than the stick. The result will be significant at any level of statistical significance you might desire. We (the forecasters) are the balloon. In the case of open conflict, we are the first ones to pop. Luckily, however, in majority of the cases, the relationship between forecaster and decision maker is not one of open conflict.

NOT INDISPENSABLE

A common mistake many forecasters make is that they believe they are indispensable. The President cannot make annual presentations without their forecasts. Without them, business plans cannot be made. This is clearly a mistaken notion. The president can do without them. Business plans can be prepared with other people's forecasts. Remember, there is not one single individual in an organization which is irreplaceable. Forecasters, who feel that decision makers will be sorry if they leave, often find to their surprise that they are not missed at all after they are gone. All of this leads me to emphasize once again that forecasters should know their place. Moses should have brought this down from Mount Sinai as the Eleventh Commandment: "Forecaster, thou shall know thy position." You may be very smart and educated but you are not the decision-maker. You are simply a helper. Do not judge the real decision maker by the wrong criteria. Know who the boss is. You are there only to provide the support.

ROLE OF FORECASTER

Let us now examine what role a forecaster should play. To begin with, you must be useful. There is a great danger to your economic health as a forecaster when you are highly respected by the management but your input is not used in the decision making process.

For a forecaster to be useful, the information you provide must be relevant. The relevance can be measured by observing the degree to which your information affects decisions. Affecting decision is what counts. Producing beautiful and professional documents do not do the job. They can bring you fame and esteem among fellow forecasters. But forecasters are not the ones who sign the paychecks. Think about it for a while. If asked about the job, what is the first thing you, as a forecaster, are likely to describe. You may say, "we produce an Outlook Book which is considered to be best in the industry and distributed worldwide. We prepare a quarterly briefing on the economy for the management. The briefing is used by the Chairman of Board of Directors in his remarks to the Board." All this is lovely. The moment the Outlook Book becomes your most significant achievement, you should start worrying about your job tenure. There is a great danger of being highly respected as an intellectual (or forecaster) but ignored by the decision makers. Thus, our major responsibility is to realize which issues are important to the management and which ones are not.

FINDING RELEVANT ISSUES

How should one go about finding out which issues are relevant? One way is to simply ask. Sometimes it works, other times it does not. There are times when management does not know what forecasters can do. Finding ways how the company can save money is always a good way to start. In our organization, people in the purchasing department spend hundreds of millions of dollars in buying parts from subcontractors. They did not know that my group forecasted exchange rates and inflation rates of different countries. When they learned about the availability of such forecasts and started using them, they saved the company millions of dollars by obtaining better contracts. The purchasing people were not interested in fancy presentations or in understanding how these forecasts were prepared. Just by quoting our numbers to the subcontractors they managed to get better deals. All we had to do was to find out where we could be of use. Foreign exchange was one area where we could be of use. So try to think what decision-makers need and direct your efforts to fulfill them. Also, it is important how productive, not how impressive, you are. Forecaster should not attempt to impress the decision-makers, they are already impressed with our education, fancy vocabulary and sophisticated models. Since we understand fancy models, it is not necessary that management should do so too. Try to be as simple as possible in explaining models to the management. Some forecasters try to become very technical for the wrong reasons, that is, to impress the management. The decision maker is the judge. If the decision maker doesn't understand your presentation, it will prove counterproductive. Your presentation will be ignored. We cannot snow the decision makers. They have to be convinced. If they are not convinced, we, the forecasters, are not doing our job.

BE HONEST TO YOURSELF

Be honest to yourself as well as to the users of forecasts. It is entirely proper to say that our forecast will materialize only if the past relationships hold. Or, our forecast is as good as the independent variables used in the model. In the past we experienced "X" percent of error which created "Y" amount of risk. If we make any assumption, we should state it clearly even if we have doubts about its validity. I always find management surprisingly sympathetic. They understand that forecasting is difficult, and at times very crude approximations have to be used. Without us they will make assumptions themselves, which might be even more crude than ours. So there is no problem here. The only problem is when we get too technical. So, try to be as explicit as possible.

Humor always helps, but caution is advised. If you have only a few minutes to brief your president, it might be advisable to skip the joking part. Try to be believable. Sometimes you know the future and no one else in the industry does. The management does not believe you. In that situation the best thing to do is to convince the management to use scenario analysis.

Finally, be sure to have the support of your management. Do not surprise them with a total novel approach to do business. Let them know what you want to work on. Get their approval. This way they may decide to support your project wholeheartedly. Also, they may provide some helpful suggestions.

CHAPTER 19

THE NEED FOR A FORECASTING CHAMPION

John T. Mentzer, Mark A. Moon and Carlo D. Smith
University of Tennessee

John L. Kent
Southwest Missouri State University

Outstanding performance in sales forecasting is a difficult, yet worthy goal for any company. However, there is more to achieving outstanding performance than selecting the right piece of forecasting software or choosing the optimum statistical technique. Forecasting must be viewed as a fundamental business process.

Over the past three years, our research team has undertaken a data collection effort aimed at identifying those factors that contribute to a company's ability to be successful in sales forecasting. This data collection took the form of in-depth analysis of the sales forecasting management practices at 25 companies. The purpose of this paper is to present one of the key findings from this research. Specifically, our intent is to discuss the important role that a *forecasting champion* can play in the critical business process of sales forecasting.

First, we will briefly describe the data collection effort that serves as the foundation for our ideas about the roles and importance of a forecasting champion. Second, based upon our findings from the 25 companies we have studied, we will describe the general characteristics of a sales forecasting champion. Next, we will discuss the roles that sales forecasting champions can play in companies that take different approaches to the sales forecasting process. The paper will end with a discussion of the potential benefits that a company can realize from putting a sales forecasting champion in place.

THE DATA COLLECTION EFFORT

This research began with the selection of companies with histories as leading financial and/or market share performers, though not necessarily top performers in sales forecasting. In fact, to understand the variations in sales forecasting management performance in successful companies, the selection process was intended to include companies that have achieved varying degrees of success in forecasting sales. In addition, companies at different levels within the supply chain were included. This selection process resulted in site visits with 20 manufacturers, three distribution firms, and two retailers: Allied-Signal, Anheuser-Busch, Becton-Dickinson, Coca Cola, Colgate Palmolive, DuPont, Eastman Chemical, Federal Express, Hershey Foods, Kimberly Clark, Lykes Pasco, Michelin, Nabisco, J.C. Penney, Pillsbury, ProSource, Reckitt and Colman, Red Lobster, RJR Tobacco, Sandoz, Schering Plough, Sysco, Tropicana, Warner Lambert, and Westwood Squibb.

Company analysis began with a request for any documentation of the sales forecasting management process. This documentation included reports, documentation of systems and/or management procedures, and informal protocols. Once this information was analyzed, an interview schedule was arranged with anyone in the company affiliated with sales forecasting, including developers and users of the sales forecasts. Before visiting the company to conduct the interviews, a detailed 8-page protocol was sent to each person to be interviewed. The interviews were conducted on-site by the research team, with two members of the research team in each interview to ensure inter-judge reliability. Interviews were tape recorded and the transcripts from these interviews were analyzed for sales forecasting management content. The purpose of this analysis was to identify those key factors that support the successful management of the sales forecasting function.

One factor that consistently had a strong impact on the level of sales forecasting success was the existence of a sales forecasting champion. The following section describes the characteristics of forecasting champions at those companies that are particularly successful with sales forecasting.

GENERAL CHARACTERISTICS OF A SALES FORECASTING CHAMPION

Whether the head of a recognized forecasting group, part of a loose collection of forecasters within different departments, or a user of the sales forecasts who does not actually develop them, we found that sales forecasting champions have several characteristics in common. These characteristics are:

- Appreciation of Sales Forecasting Role for Planning
- Recognition of Cross-Functional Role
- A Leader, Not a Clerk
- A Sales Forecast Developer and User
- A Good Understanding of Forecasting Techniques
- A Full Awareness of the Role of Forecasting Systems
- Mentor/Trainer
- On-going Training

APPRECIATION OF SALES FORECASTING ROLE FOR PLANNING

Successful sales forecasting champions have an appreciation of the managerial/planning role that sales forecasting plays within the corporation. This encompasses an appreciation of the iterative role of sales forecasting and business planning. For example, one company in our study begins their planning process by developing a market-based sales forecast. From this base, the annual business plan is developed. If the market-based sales forecast does not generate sufficient revenue for the business plan, the sales forecast is sent back to the champion with instructions on how much sales must increase in each market over the original forecast to meet the plan. The champion in this company then works with marketing and sales to determine how much additional resources need to be budgeted for marketing efforts that will help to increase sales to the desired level. This revised sales forecast goes back to planning and continues to iterate until a realistic plan is finalized. The key to this iterative, forecast-to-plan-to-forecast-to-plan, process is a sales forecasting champion who understands and guides each step so that a realistic, market-based forecast and plan are developed.

RECOGNITION OF CROSS-FUNCTIONAL ROLE

To manage the process just described, the sales forecasting champion cannot have his/her business orientation planted in one functional area. Rather, the sales forecasting champion must understand the planning purposes for which the sales forecasts will be used by the various business functions (e.g., marketing, sales, finance/accounting, production/purchasing, and logistics). Each of these areas has unique planning needs to which the sales forecasts are an input. Marketing plans usually consider projected product changes, promotional efforts, channel placement, and pricing — all these have an effect on demand. Sales management is typically concerned with setting goals for the sales force and motivating salespeople to exceed these goals. Both these concerns require accurate demand forecasts. Finance and accounting are charged with the job of projecting cost and profit levels and capital needs, all based upon a given sales forecast. Production must concern itself with two very different sales forecasts — a long-term forecast for planning capital requirements such as future plant and equipment, and a short term forecast for the production planning and raw material purchasing schedules. Since logistics is responsible for moving products to specific locations, sales forecasts are needed at the product level by location. To be effective, and regardless of where they are located in an organizational chart, the sales forecasting champion must understand these divergent functional needs and deliver a sales forecast that meets them.

A LEADER, NOT A CLERK

To accomplish these cross-functional, managerial roles for the sales forecasts, the sales forecasting champion must be a leader and an advocate who recognizes the importance of sales forecasting as a critical, company-wide management function. As we will discuss in a later section, this role can take different forms depending upon the way sales forecasting is organized in the company. However, regardless of the form, the sales forecasting leader and advocate should possess two core characteristics. First, the sales forecasting champion must be able to clearly explain the role of the sales forecast in the planning processes of the various functional areas. Not only must the sales forecasts be credible (i.e., accurate and believable) over time, but the sales forecasting champion must be seen as a credible representative of these forecasts.

Second, this credibility must extend to all company areas and levels. The effective sales forecasting champion has the organizational clout (either through authority or persuasive ability) to be taken seriously by top management and the management of all the business functions.

A SALES FORECAST DEVELOPER AND USER

The establishment of this credibility, advocacy, and understanding comes largely from the same source. The sales forecasting champion must be seen as someone who has experience not only in developing sales forecasts, but also in putting them to use in the business planning functions. Experience in developing sales forecasts lends a technical and market-based credibility to the sales forecasting champion. Whether in marketing, sales, production, or logistics, experience in using the sales forecast lends an element of "they are really one of us." They understand the planning needs to which the sales forecast will be put, and the implications of inaccurate forecasts on the users. This dual experiential background for sales forecasting champions gives them credibility with their constituents and provides the information necessary to develop quantitative forecasts and adjust them qualitatively when necessary.

A GOOD UNDERSTANDING OF FORECASTING TECHNIQUES

The dual experiential background just discussed also dictates that the sales forecasting champion *understand* the use of quantitative and qualitative sales forecasting techniques. The champion may or may not have strong statistical training, but he or she always has a strong understanding of the environment in which the company operates and is aware of the advantages and disadvantages of different statistical approaches. We call this latter trait *quantitative analysis strength*, rather than statistical strength, because it means much more than just the ability to analyze a stream of numbers with statistics. Rather, it is an understanding of where certain statistical techniques do and do not work, and when qualitative (informed business environment) analysis is superior to, or can augment, statistics.

FULL AWARENESS OF THE ROLE OF FORECASTING SYSTEMS

Similarly, the effective sales forecasting champion is not necessarily a "systems person," but has a clear understanding of the role systems play in the development of accurate and timely sales forecasts. It is surprising how many companies have no clear definition of the sales forecasting process or the systems which bind that process together. In effective companies, these processes and systems are well defined and are clearly understood and explicated by the sales forecasting champion.

Without such clear communication of how the process and systems interact, islands of analysis will develop within the forecasting process. Islands of analysis are systems phenomena where one individual or group develops a sales forecast based upon their own information and needs, and does not share that information or forecast with others in the company. The resultant sales forecasts may be significantly different than forecasts developed elsewhere in the company (other islands) and these differences lead to conflicting plans.

MENTOR/TRAINER

Effective sales forecasting champions spend much of their time developing sales forecasting skills in others. The mentoring dimension of this characteristic is aimed at developing a similar appreciation in others of the role of the sales forecasts in the planning and management of various functional areas. Fostering an appreciation in each functional area for the forecasting needs of other functions within the organization is often a long and difficult process, one that requires considerable mentoring skills on the part of the sales forecasting champion. Many companies have staunchly ingrained planning processes that start with income estimates that will meet the expectations of external financial analysts and work backward to a "sales forecast." It is not an easy task to change this process to one that starts with a market-based sales forecast, develops the financial plan from this base, and iterates back and forth between sales forecast and business plan until a plan has been reached that takes into account marketplace and financial realities. Again, the sales forecasting champion role as a mentor is an integral part of bringing such a change to fruition.

The sales forecasting champion as a trainer recognizes the need for input to the sales forecast from multiple sources and the training requirements needed by each of those sources to ensure forecasting improvement. Sales forecasting analysts need training in the use of statistical techniques and the advantages and disadvantages of each technique (i.e., when and where each technique should and should not be used). Marketing personnel need training in how to use their market-based knowledge to make qualitative adjustments to the sales forecast. Similarly, salespeople need training in how to use their customer-based knowledge to make qualitative adjustments to the sales forecast.

Production and logistics personnel need training in how to bring their capacity planning perspectives into the sales forecasts. It is not necessarily the job of the sales forecasting champion to conduct all of this training, but it is their job to identify these training needs and help each group obtain the proper training.

ON-GOING TRAINING

Finally, sales forecasting champions as mentors/trainers recognize their own on-going training needs. The state of the art of sales forecasting changes every year, and the effective sales forecasting champion attempts to stay current in these changes. Attendance and participation at conferences and seminars, as well as staying current in the sales forecasting journals and books, are all characteristics of effective sales forecasting champions.

VARYING ROLES

Although effective sales forecasting champions possess all the characteristics just discussed, these characteristics take on different manifestations depending upon how the sales forecasting function is organized in a company. Mentzer and Kahn presented a typology for sales forecasting organizations, which is quite useful when examining the changing role of the sales forecasting champion. This typology places sales forecasting organizations into one of four categories:

1. The **Independent** approach, where each functional department involved in the sales forecasting process develops its own forecasts for its own internal uses, independent of all other departments.
2. The **Concentrated** approach, where one department is assigned the responsibility for developing the sales forecasts and all other departments must use the resultant forecasts.

3. The **Negotiated** approach, where each functional area makes its own independent forecasts, but representatives from each functional area get together each forecasting period to reach negotiated final forecasts.

4. The **Consensus** approach, where a committee — with representatives from various functional areas and one person in charge — develops the sales forecasts, based upon information input from all the functional areas.

In the independent approach, considerable islands of analysis exist and, in fact, little of the management planning, cross-functional, or systems perspectives discussed previously exist in the organization. In this approach, the role of the sales forecasting champion is that of the most fundamental of change agents. Understanding and documenting the forecasting process, plus building credibility for the forecasts and their role as champion is the first responsibility. Through persuasion (as opposed to any formal authority), the sales forecasting champion gradually builds an appreciation for the advantages of the coordinated sales forecast that is used by all the functional areas of the company.

If successful, the sales forecasting champion will be instrumental in moving the company to a concentrated approach. Since this approach places the sales forecasting function within one functional area, the background of the sales forecasting champion becomes important. However, it is the role of the champion in this approach to raise the sales forecast above a parochial perspective. In a sense, the champion must become an advocate for the functional areas where sales forecasting is not located, so that a truly cross-functional approach to sales forecasting begins to develop. Similarly, in the negotiated approach, the role of the sales forecasting champion is to move the culture in which sales forecasts are created from one of reconciling different functional forecasts to one in which the various functional areas provide input to develop a consensus forecast.

In the negotiated and consensus approaches, the existence of a separate sales forecasting function — with the champion heading the function — becomes more prevalent. This function typically reports to upper management, rather than being subsumed under a specific functional area. At this point, the sales forecasting champion moves from a primarily persuasive role to one in which formal authority exists. It is with this formal responsibility, and the authority for the sales forecasting function that accompanies it, that the champion can fully realize all of the characteristics previously discussed.

BENEFITS OF A SALES FORECASTING CHAMPION

The benefits that accrue to a company with an effective sales forecasting champion are considerable. First, the advocacy/leader role of the sales forecasting champion inevitably leads the company to the higher (negotiated or consensus) stages of the Mentzer and Kahn typology. These higher stages typically result in greater coordination of the sales forecasts and forecasts that are the result of informational input from all business functions.

Second, the forecasting champion provides a focal point for the discussion of sales forecasts and their use. This leads the organization away from "finger-pointing" by each functional area to a greater understanding the role of sales forecasts in business planning.

Third, the existence of a forecasting champion embodies one entity with the responsibility to examine sales forecasting performance. Such responsibility eventually results in the implementation of a consistent and equitable performance evaluation system that rewards all parties involved in developing the sales forecasts based upon sales forecasting effectiveness. This benefit of tying rewards to performance, alone, greatly improves the quality of sales forecasts available.

The company-wide combination of these benefits will result in improved customer service, lower supply chain costs, and reduced risk for the company. Although the first of these is obvious, the supply chain cost savings come in the form of lower inventory levels, lower production costs, lower raw material purchasing costs, lower incidence of trans-shipment (which occurs when product is originally shipped to one location and demanded at another), and lower incidence of product obsolescence (because the shelf-life expired). Finally, any time a company improves its ability to accurately anticipate future demand levels, less money can be committed to plant and equipment, production, and forward staging of inventory — all of which reduce the level of risk the company is carrying.

CONCLUSIONS

Continuous improvement of any business function will not happen if it is not part of someone's job. The same is true of sales forecasting. It must be someone's primary responsibility. This is the role of the sales forecasting champion. We have observed sales forecasting champions in numerous companies and, as a result, tried here to describe the characteristics they need to be effective in this role.

In a sense, the role of the sales forecasting champion is to bring focus and attention to a critical business function that often does not receive sufficient upper management consideration. Understanding the role of sales forecasting in business planning, eliminating the inherent biases from the various business functions, and creating a cogent and reasonable sales forecasting process and accompanying systems are all critical functions for any company. The elevation of the sales forecasting champion, and his/her function, on a par with the other business functions is a critical element in the future success of any company. The job of creating this elevation, in the final analysis, falls to the sales forecasting champions themselves.

REFERENCES

1. Mentzer, John T. and Kenneth B. Kahn. "The State of Sales Forecasting Systems in Corporate America," **Journal of Business Forecasting**. Vol. 16, Spring 1997, pp. 6-13.

CHAPTER 20

BRIDGING THE COMMUNICATIONS GAP BETWEEN MANAGERS AND FORECASTERS

Charles W. Gross
University of New Hampshire

In 20 years we have come a long way, or have we? While at Ford, I prepared my first professional sales forecast in 1967. Management wanted accurate sales projections so that four European assembly plants could be cited. For this we used very "sophisticated" methods: a simple index of auto sales based upon the number of miles of paved roads, the size and age of the "car park" (the total stock of autos on the road) and the age of that "car park." Little attention was paid to issues such as minimizing error, multicollinearity, autocorrelation, and economic theory. Management was not ready for such esoteric topics, and neither were we. While we developed models, there was "Old Bert," the mystic. Bert would caustically and occasionally ask, "How's it coming guys?" Then he tuned his radio to a station reporting stock news, placed a few phone calls to various people within the company, cleaned his nails and sharpened his desk load of pencils — an ironic feat by itself, as no one ever saw him actually use the pencils for anything other than to clean his ears and write down a few stock tips— and ate a sack lunch at his desk while reading the sports section. But Bert would out-forecast everybody.

Much has changed in the interim, and the future looks even more demanding. We now have Box Jenkins (models which no one understands, but all are afraid to admit), state-space models (which are even worse), enhanced smoothing models, vector regressions, and so many other models and other mysticisms that Alcharnedes himself would nod approval. Bert is no longer with Ford. He now cleans up on small wagers made with retirees in St. Petersburg by forecasting winter baseball scores. Instead, Ford has Ralph; who tunes his radio to a CBS all news station, places a few phone calls to various people in his company, cleans his ears with his pencils, and uses his PC to calculate his personal net-worth twelve times a day. He, too, out-forecasts everybody. Why? One lesson that I learned from my experiences with many companies over the years from the Berts and Ralphs of the world is that managers often know many things that forecasters do not know and will never know if they follow any formal forecasting model with blind faith.

OPERATING PROBLEMS IN FORECASTING PRACTICES

A promising note is that sales forecasting offers a bright future. An increasing number of companies are recognizing the field as being extremely critical. And there are an increasing number of bright people focusing their attention to the field, in both the academic and the applied worlds. But there are also several problems which require attention; problems which, if left unaddressed, will negate the efforts of the dedicated, and cause the field to become relegated to an idea scrap yard, much like that which threatened the field of operations research. Perhaps in that case it was caused by initially over promising what could be delivered, perhaps by lack of application. In the case of sales forecasting, the risks are of both being blinded to the dimensions of applications, and, at the same time, with the incompetently applied. Both are partially the result of a communications gap between forecasters and managers. Here is where the Berts and Ralphs excel. They understand the pulse of their organizations and use this knowledge to shape their forecasts. Let us first consider the role of managers and then that of forecasters in causing the communications gap.

MANAGERS

Managers contribute to a sales forecasting communications gap in several ways. That they do not know about the models, both their nature and their assumptions, is one problem. Another is that they believe they can "force" the numbers and manage the models to give them what they would like to hear.

Don't Know About the Models: Most managers do not know very much about forecasting models themselves. This causes several problems including misapplication, faulty model testing, unintentional withholding of key information, and "forcing" forecasts to match expectations.

One of the major difficulties is in misapplication. To illustrate a common experience, a manager of a mid-western railroad company recently told me his attempts to use single exponential smoothing to forecast grain shipments so that his company could make an adequate number of grain cars available. Because the series contained considerable trend, plus the fact that there was significant seasonality present, the model selected was simply inadequate. The assumption of single smoothing did not match the conditions in the series. This plus the fact that a weight of alpha = 0.4 was selected solely because "That was the weight used in the text book at a prestigious business school's MBA program." This, of course, led to the model's poor performance. A poor initial model selection is not always a major difficulty. But in this case, it caused him not to try any other smoothing model. "We tried smoothing, and it didn't work," was his response. Since one smoothing model did not work, he discarded the entire family, much like throwing out the baby with the bath water.

A closely related problem is that managers, being a competitive, challenging breed, want to test a forecaster's ability to forecast. This is the way that it should be. Yet, forecasters often deliver an hour-long oration to managers about why there is a need for a reasonable amount of data and that a forecasting system is going to "hit" some series quite accurately, and miss some, but on balance, will do a better job than is currently being done. Further, that the models should be tested over several series so as to give them an accurate trial. In turn, managers proceed to supply a history of 12, perhaps 24, of the trickiest, most unusual, worst case data that man has ever detected. The test series contains erroneous sales entries, negative sales in some periods due to adjustments, huge one-time orders from some oil emirate country that never occurred before and will never occur again, the worst blizzard in history, and other things so "screwy" that God would have a tough time keeping track of them. Then, with a straight face, the manager says, "I got you this test data. We're anxious to see how your forecasting package will work." Then, he might add: "We were only able to get 24 months of data because our records only go back that far and we were too busy to get information any further back because we would have to dig them out of storage somewhere. By the way, we didn't have time to get you those 15 other series that we talked about. Good luck." Lots of luck, indeed!

A third problem stemming from managers not knowing about various models is that they do not know what information to provide forecasters to enable them to build adequate models. Forecasting work is tough enough when critical information is provided, when it is not, the work becomes impossible. For example, when working with a high-tech electronics company a few years ago, I recall being asked to develop a system to forecast sales at the individual product level. Weeks had passed by, models were built, and the tests were finished. The result looked promising, but when we met to examine them, come to find out that the data furnished consisted of orders, affectionately called "bookings." What management really wanted to forecast was sales deliveries, called "shipments." In between, there was another category of sales called "releases," which represented orders that were "released" to operations for production. There were also considerable time lags between bookings, releases, and shipments, and a backlog of orders in each category.

Of course, in such a system, I should have captured the interrelationships of all of these categories within the models. But despite several queries about the nature of the business before hand, I did not learn about them until later, when we were examining the model's results. Fortunately for me I had good working relations with the company. I then changed directions and captured what was required, but there was a lot of wasted time and effort in the process.

Managers know many things which may have an important effect on sales and their forecasting, such as the introduction of new products by competitors during the forecast period, aggressive marketing promotional programs at various time periods, supply shortages, and so on. Yet, many times these vital pieces of information are not mentioned. Here again the Berts and Ralphs excel over other forecasters, they intuitively use this information when they make their forecasts.

Still another problem is that management frequently "cheats" when it evaluates a forecasting system. It is not uncommon for management to test the accuracy of a new forecasting system by holding out the most recent 6 to 12 months of data, have the new system forecast sales for those periods, compare the forecasts to the actual values, then measure the forecasts with the forecasts generated with the old system. Such a test sounds fair, does it not?

Well, the way it often happens is that forecasts generated in the old way were not prepared 6 or 12 months ahead of time at all, they were prepared a month ahead of time in a "rolling forecast." Of course, only the final numbers entered under the old system, the one month ahead numbers, are used by management to compare "their" results with "your" results. In fact, sometimes the old forecasts were not prepared until a few days or a week before the end of the month, when almost all of the sales for that month were already known. The only way that a new forecasting system can be adequately judged is on a comparable basis with what is currently being done.

Forcing Numbers: Another big problem is that managers believe that they can "force" the numbers. Plans are often developed in an almost vacuum. The numbers represent what management would like to see from a financial perspective. When forecasts do not meet top management's planned volumes, the plans are seldom changed. Instead, the marching orders are to generate new forecasts. Then, when results do not meet plans, there is a deafening scream cascading down the halls "Why the He … can't we forecast this ahead of time?" Many senior managers do not want forecasts as such. What they really want is numbers that match what they would like to see, and then somehow for the results to match those numbers. Forecasting will never be able to do this job.

FORECASTERS

Many forecasters are also blinded to reality. They live inside their computer's CRT and their models, instead of within the real world that their simulations represent. Worse yet is that they begin to worship the models by following them with "blind faith," believing that they are the reality. Forecasters have taken a narrow view of sales forecasting; focusing on mathematical techniques, rather than on organizational complexities. There are at least two types of such myopic visionaries, the technical zealots and the incompetent.

Technical zealots: The goal of this group has been to develop that "next better algorithm"—one that, in all its mathematical splendor, will unlock the mysteries of the universe, and will be suitable for forecasting in all situations. They regal in mathematical complexity, despite the fact that simpler models might work just as well. Their rhetoric argues the merits of time series extrapolations versus regression models, despite the fact that both are good, depending upon the situation. Perhaps more significant is that models are developed, for the sake of mathematical elegance, that require 80 or more months of sales history; despite the fact that companies seldom have that many data points available for any product, even for old ones. Most historical disaggregated data over a couple of years old have typically been stored in the deepest recesses of low rent warehousing. Further, little attention is given to the nature of the reporting systems. That "bad data" are usually present but are seldom considered. The non-quantitative aspects that must be accounted for are ignored. Forecasters also fail to recognize that a business is a system of interacting components that must be considered. New mathematical techniques alone are not likely to generate much better results. This does not mean that there is no longer a need for technique development. Future inroads will indeed increase forecasting accuracy. But the great strides forward in increasing forecasting accuracy are most likely to be made in the area of building forecasting models within a more meaningful context; namely, management information systems.

Incompetents: An irony is that technique does matter. Using competently selected models from among those currently available, or even from new and evolving ones, is critical. A problem is that there are also technically incompetent practitioners within the profession. All fields have them, and sales forecasting is no exception. They are the ones who believe that one model will fit all circumstances because either they developed it in the first place, briefly learned about it in school, or perhaps got lucky and were able to forecast a few series accurately at some point in the past. After all, even a broken watch is right two times a day.

To illustrate, consider the hypothetical time series: 5, 10, 15, 20, 25, 30, 35, 40. How many forecasting packages can predict 45 as the next number? Not too many. Then, for those packages that pass this first test, impose a set of known seasonals on the series, such as 0.8, 0.9, 1.1, 1.2 to represent quarters. Multiply them together to yield the new series: 4.0, 9.0, 16.5, 24.0, 20.0, 27.0, 38.5, 48.0.

How many packages will forecast that the next number is 36.0, and do so without error? The problem is a simple one, yet most forecasting software cannot solve this problem or its kind, despite the fact that any analyst or manager can solve it by hand in just a few minutes.

The standard answer has been "let's have more data." Or, let's use "real numbers," ones conveniently containing high degrees of error—so much error that it obscures the ways in which the models work altogether. Further, the literature contains many papers that claim to examine forecasting packages. But what do they focus on? The wrong things! — pretty graphs, easy-to-use commands, and whether or not the numbers can be loaded easily. Frequently some series are tested for which correct answers are unknown.

Seldom are packages tested on whether they can actually forecast a known theoretical series, such as the above example of 5, 10, 15, and so on. There are many similar series possible, and a solid forecasting package would be able to forecast them. At least one would know that the models work as they were intended. The first step in model selection, then, would be to identify the conditions found in a given application and pick the model whose assumptions most closely match those conditions. Similarly, some forecasters hold a "management is stupid" belief. Some writers, software developers, and seminar presenters believe that management will never grasp anything more mathematically rigorous than a simple average or simple exponential smoothing. So they pre-judge what management should be exposed to and that is all that management gets.

Managers are also responsible for this by demanding topics that are simple to grasp. Whatever the reason, the effect is that management does not know that there are many more models available. Even disclaimers such as, "interested users should do further research," does not limit the responsibility, as further research is almost never done. The problem is that management then tries to use the overly-simple models, which do not work very well.

NEED TO BRIDGE THE KNOWLEDGE GAP

Clearly, progress has been made over the past decade or so. And the accomplishments are probably much more than are implied by my intentionally overstated comments. But there is also room for considerable improvement. And this improvement will not likely come until the communications gap between forecasters and managers is successfully bridged. Several directions seem in order.

Managers

Managers need to be more open and honest. They are not experts in techniques, probably have only limited exposure to models, and probably need considerable help from experts in developing successful applications within their organizations. At the minimum, they must be as open as possible about explaining the relationships among variables, whether or not they eventually become incorporated into a forecasting system, so that set of procedures can be customized to fit the particular application.

But they must also use common sense in judging any forecasting system. If a forecasting packages produces "garbage," meaning wrong solutions to models, then the package is probably a poor one. Make the tests fair and meaningful. Do not load tests with exceptional cases, but make them rigorous.

Forecasters

Forecasters also need to be honest. A pet model or approach is never the best alternative in all, or even in most cases. Sales forecasting is complex, and the ability to adapt models to many different situations is the key to successful application. No one model or approach is best in all cases. And a comprehensive systems approach is probably needed.

A "Systems Approach" is Needed: In fact, managers do know many things about the operations of their companies—things that affect sales. The next generation of significant improvements in forecasting methodologies will likely come from advances in the design of information systems, which incorporate this knowledge into the forecasting process.

Far too many factors affect sales of organizations. Organizations are complex systems which involve many components. Future development is most likely to come from forecasters leaving their comfortable surroundings of computer CRTs and programs, and entering the operating reality of managers; not as managers, but as students of the "real" world. Here is where the "old Berts" and "Ralphs" are able to beat many modern forecasters. They simply understand their organizations and their environments much better than many mathematical model builders.

These systems will contain many features, such as the routine capturing of abnormal events into the data base. They will also incorporate other peculiarities, such as the fact that sales are indeed manageable—at least to an extent. When results are below quota, for example, managers exert pressure, which often translates into improved sales. They will also allow for capturing "slack orders" that the sales force "carries in its pockets" at the end of most periods. In slow periods, these are "bogus" orders, sales which are expected early in the next periods, but are reported ahead of time to maintain quota. In boom periods, these are current sales which are deferred into the next period so as to avoid spiraling quotas. Future systems will also look at the systematic interaction between sales and other components of a business, such as planned marketing campaigns, competitive actions and customer intentions.

Learn about the organization: Forecasters also need to roll-up their sleeves, get into the trenches with management, and learn about the organizations with which they work. Forecasts are but one input into the decision-making process, and forecasters know very little about the entire process.

Systems will have to be developed which capture this process within an organization, yet remain within the time and accuracy constraints of managers. Many questions must be answered for this to happen. The mark of genius is knowing which questions to ask, not in knowing the answers without asking those key questions.

PART III

FORECASTING
AND
MARKETING RESEARCH

INTRODUCTION

Forecasting and marketing research in many ways go hand in hand — one complements the other. Marketing research is often used to answer questions such as: Whether or not a new product will succeed? What kind of technological breakthroughs are expected and how they would affect us? What drives the consumer demand? How sensitive is sales to price? How much lift promotion provides? How to detect competitive activities? How to determine plans and forecasts of customers who are reluctant to provide such information? How to estimate lag effect of advertisement? How to track performance of forecasts provided by outside agencies such as A. C. Nielsen, Audits & Survey and Data Bank? This section shows how marketing research can be used to get answers to such questions. In some cases, however, marketing research is used as a sanity check.

CHAPTER 21

ELICITING ACCURATE SALES FORECASTS FROM MARKET EXPERTS

Mark Barash
Nabisco Foods Group

As developers of sales forecasts, the basis of what we do is often focused around statistical models, be they simple models or sophisticated models, incorporating such factors as seasonality, trends, trade promotions, and pricing. However, there are situations when there is nothing in our models that can adequately predict our sales, such as in the cases of new types of trade or consumer events, large one-time orders, new items, and special items such as holiday or commemorative items. In these cases, we need information from people who are much closer to the market, whom we will call for the purpose of this paper, the "market experts."

A market expert can be a member of the sales force, either internal or broker-based, a product manager from Marketing, or a distributor, dealer or customer. Building a process that elicits accurate information from the market experts is an important part of effective sales forecasting.

CHALLENGES IN ELICITING FORECASTS

The primary responsibility of a market expert is usually something other than effective forecasting. In that case, forecasting is secondary to him/her. For some market experts, best forecasts may not be the best for them. Here are some of the situations where this is the case:

1. Where forecasts are used as an input to sales quota.
2. Where forecasts drive production and distribution.
3. Where forecasts don't determine success.
4. Where customer does not wish to reveal his/her plans.

WHERE FORECASTS ARE USED AS AN INPUT TO SALES QUOTA

Market experts under-forecast where forecasts are used as an input to their sales objectives or quotas. Lower forecasts mean lower sales quotas. If sales quotas are maintained at low levels, they can be easily achieved. But this distorts the reported forecasts. Distortion occurs because here market experts intentionally under-forecast.

108

WHERE FORECASTS DRIVE PRODUCTION AND DISTRIBUTION

Market experts tend to over-forecast where forecasts drive production and distribution because they suffer if supplies of products are inadequate. Market experts who suffer from under-forecasting but not from over-forecasting will over-forecast. Marketing brand managers want to be certain that their brand products are available in sufficient quantities so that they can achieve their volume goals. They are often not accountable for the cost resulting from holding inventory in excess of demand. The sales force wants adequate distribution in the local warehouse that supplies to their customers. In this way, the salesperson or sales manager can ensure achievement of his/her sales quota. The Operations Department usually absorbs the cost of wasted or misdirected products, so over-forecasting satisfies the salespeople's goals. This phenomenon is often reported.

WHERE FORECASTS DON'T DETERMINE SUCCESS

A member of the sales force has a primary accountability to sell, and his/her compensation structure reflects that. A marketing person is similarly oriented. Dealers, distributors and customers are often not accountable for poor forecasts. In all these cases, the market experts dedicate their time to those tasks that determine most their success. Distortion in such cases occurs because forecasting is not high on their priority list.

WHERE CUSTOMER DOES NOT WANT TO REVEAL HIS/HER PLANS

The distortion also results where a vendor's customer is reluctant to reveal his/her plans. The retailer (the vendor's customer) is often unwilling to reveal its plans for a sale on the vendor's products, thinking if its competitors find out they may retaliate. Another common secret that impacts forecasting is diversion. Diversion occurs when a customer purchases merchandise at a reduced price during a trade promotion, and resells it to other customers of the vendor at a profit when the trade promotion is no longer in effect. In this case, neither the salesperson nor the customer would reveal the plans to the vendor. Here, of course, the forecast inaccuracy is not the main problem. Here the main issue is the loss of revenue to the vendor. In both of the above cases, forecasts are distorted, and can occur independent of each other.

So the question is, under the circumstances, what we can do so that we can elicit reliable market information, necessary for preparing good forecasts? Here are some of the solutions. The ideal solution, of course, is to create an environment in which the market experts have the desire to provide well thought-out and unbiased sales forecast information.

PROVIDING AN INCENTIVE

Elicited forecast information can improve if compensation or performance evaluation of market experts is based on their forecast accuracy. A number of companies make Marketing Product Managers accountable for accurate forecasting on their annual appraisals. One consumer product company offers a monetary reward to field salespeople for their accurate forecasts. Furthermore, good forecasts can be used as one of the criteria in the annual sales contests of field salespeople. This can help some, but the incentive is not strong enough if faced with inventory shortages. In that case, one still has an incentive to over-forecast. We see one extreme situation at a company in the health care industry in which the dealer is responsible for placing orders for new items with a large lead time. Here, in essence, dealer provides a forecast with a high degree of commitment behind it. He/she is responsible for carrying costs resulting from optimistic forecasts in which case merchandise has to be returned. Of course, with low forecasts dealers will run short. In that case, both the vendor and the dealer will have the same objective, that is, to forecast accurately, which is ideal for any company.

TEAM FORECASTING

A team forecasting approach has been reported in two companies in the health care industry. This does not provide a formal incentive to forecast accurately, but senior management has mandated that accurate forecasting is the entire team's responsibility, not just that of the Forecasting Group. This high level management support makes it possible for these companies to get accurate judgmental forecasts. This is a very positive approach and should be tried whenever possible.

MAKING A GAME OUT OF IT

Creating competition in forecasting among peer market experts can also generate some positive results. The Forecasting Group at one consumer products company publishes reports comparing forecasting accuracy across brands (for Marketing) and across sales districts (for Sales). These contests bring out pride in individuals who like to be the best in every area and dislike losing, even if they don't perceive forecasting to be particularly important. This approach probably works best with internal market experts, rather than distributors or customers. The Forecasting Group at another consumer products company publishes reports that compare Marketing or Sales accuracy measures with the Forecasting Group's statistical model numbers. The report produces a challenge in Marketing and Sales to "beat" the Forecasting Group's forecasts. In that case, the Forecasting Group may seek advice from those who do better than their statistical model numbers on a consistent basis. They may ask them what is missing in their statistical models? What can they do to improve their forecasts? This interchange can lead to improvement in statistical models and perhaps reduce the time needed to prepare forecasts.

ADJUSTING INPUT

Calibration of a consistently biased forecast is another solution. At one manufacturing company, dealers provide sales forecasts well ahead of time of orders. For the dealers, there is no harm in forecasting high, but unavailability of merchandise ordered is possible if the forecasts they provide are low. Accordingly, forecasts are biased on the high side. The Forecast Group may find a consistent upward bias in the dealers' forecasts. In that case, the forecaster can arrive at reasonable forecasts by adjusting downward the dealers' numbers by a constant factor. This type of approach will work as long as the dealer does not know that he/she is being calibrated. The Modified Delphi approach, as presented in Ken Goldfisher's paper in the Winter 92-93 issue of the *Journal of Business Forecasting*, is a more sophisticated variant of this approach.

USING OTHER FORECASTS

The process of arriving at forecasts by combining (or reconciling) forecasts prepared by different departments can also improve the quality of forecasts. In a number of companies, different functional heads prepare their own forecasts. Account managers, for example, are becoming more responsible for thorough sales planning. A forecast is a by-product of this plan.

To make the forecasting process work, the Forecasting Group should make sure that it has a well thought-out process which can enable it to obtain sufficiently accurate forecasts from different market experts. This process can be as simple as just using the market experts' numbers, as in the calibration example, or as sweeping as involving senior management to tell the market experts that their devotion to forecasting is as important as that of the forecasters. In any case, significant time and efforts are needed to build a strong base of qualitative forecasting.

CHAPTER 22

MARKETING RESEARCH AND SALES FORECASTING AT SCHLEGEL CORPORATION

George F. Meyer
Schlegel Corporation

The Schlegel Corporation sells weather stripping, hardware, and related components to the manufacturers of residential windows and doors such as Andersen, Pella, and Season-all as well as to the distributors who pre-hang exterior doors for installation at the job site. In this environment, the contribution of marketing research to the forecasting process depends largely on the stage of the product life cycle. Prior to the introduction of new products, marketing research determines overall sales potential. Most products are application-specific. Therefore, they require an initial market segmentation study and estimates of the annual production of relevant window and door units. For example, marketing research might be asked to answer such questions as: "How many wood and clad-wood casement windows are used in new residential construction and remodeling?" To provide these numbers, we maintain an extensive construction industry database, including a use-factor model based on F. W. Dodge Residential Statistics.

CONCEPT STUDIES TO TEST CUSTOMER ACCEPTANCE

Marketing research also conducts concept studies to test customer acceptance and provide estimates of initial sales volumes. Typical concept studies include interviews with potential customers to determine their opinions about the product. Although such studies are qualitative rather than quantitative, the results often can be quantified. For instance, a respondent might say, "I would use this product only with prime entry doors, i.e., 'front' doors." We can then estimate the annual production of prime entry doors using the market model described earlier.

PRIMARY AND SECONDARY RESEARCH NECESSARY FOR NEW PRODUCTS

At best, new product sales forecasts have "order-of-magnitude" accuracy. The issue is whether or not sales of the products are likely to be large enough to cover the associated overheads and meet minimum profitability targets. Assuming that the results of the primary and secondary research are favorable, the next step is to put the product on the market. As products mature and the customer base stabilizes, we use Census II to determine seasonal adjustment factors. The seasonal adjustment factors are used to allocate estimated annual sales to specific months and to interpret monthly sales results.

For established products, we prepare shipment forecasts covering periods ranging from a few months to the year-and-a-half span that is incorporated in our annual Profit Plan. The basis for these forecasts is the model we have developed based on regional window and door usage factors for new residential construction and residential remodeling supplied by F. W. Dodge. We use the housing starts forecasts provided by the National Association of Home Builders as input for the new construction segment of the model.

However, roughly 60% of all residential windows and doors are used in replacement and remodeling projects. This means that housing start forecasts provide only a partial indicator of future product demand. We use the dollar value of permits issued for residential additions and alterations as the input for the replacement and remodeling segment of the model. We forecast these series on a regional basis using the Winters algorithm. Except for the Northeast Census Region, the mean percentage error is in single digits over 18-month horizons.

MARKETING RESEARCH PROVIDES SANITY CHECK FOR MATURED PRODUCTS

For maturing products, the role of marketing research is to provide a "sanity check" on forecasts. Marketing research monitors the market to detect and assess changes in competitive activity that might affect the forecasts. An equally important role is the assessment of external factors on the dynamics of the market. For example, we are currently studying the combined effects of higher lumber prices, the proposed BTU tax, and energy-conservation regulations on the types and numbers of residential windows to be made over the next four years.

In addition to forecasts for in-house use, we use regression models to prepare shipment estimates for some of our larger customers, based on housing starts and remodeling activity in their primary trading areas. This is a new service and we do not have extensive data on accuracy. However, the initial models have a mean percentage of error of less than 5% on a quarterly basis — without managerial adjustment for such things as the impact of weather and special promotions.

At Schlegel, marketing research and forecasting are both done by the same organization. Although their roles change as products mature, they are — and will remain — complementary disciplines.

CHAPTER 23

INTEGRATING MARKET RESPONSE MODELS IN SALES FORECASTING

Charles W. Chase, Jr.
Wyeth-Ayerst Pharmaceuticals

Most practitioners believe their primary responsibility, as a forecaster, is to provide senior management with accurate point estimates of the future. This is a misconception. The chances of management, or anyone for that matter, using your forecasts at face value is almost zero. At best, we can only hope to influence the sales forecast. In fact, by providing management with only accurate point estimates forecasters are doing a disservice to their company. Particularly, if the product(s) they are forecasting appear to be in a state of decline. As forecasters it is our responsibility to provide senior management with "actionable decision support analysis" influencing policy changes that result in improved profitability and growth. In other words, we need to identify and establish relationships for the elements that drive demand so management can optimize those factors to expand the business.

Accurate point estimates are a result of in-depth causal analysis that measures the effects of the marketing mix on retail sell through on shelf. Using retail syndicated scanning data provided by A. C. Nielsen or Information Resources, Inc. (IRI), internal marketing expense data from product P&I's, advertising spending information (i.e., TV media, cable, and print dollars) and external market information, we can develop market response models that determine the push/pull relationship associated with our business activities. The underlying premise is if we can adequately understand what drives consumer demand or sell through on shelf, we can then determine what needs to be shipped to our customers (i.e., Wal-Mart, K-Mart, Walgreens) and who distribute our products through the various channels of distribution (i.e., Grocery Stores, Drug Stores, and Mass Merchandisers).

CONSUMPTION MODEL

Classical multiple regression methods can be utilized to model marketing activities incorporating retail price, sales promotion, advertising, merchandising (%AVC — All Commodity Volume) features and displays, store distribution, FSIs (Free Standing Inserts or Coupons), product rebates and seasonality to predict retail sell through. Once we can determine consumer demand, we can construct a second model using retail sell through as the primary driver along with trade promotions, gross dealer price, factory dealer rebates, cash discounts (or off-invoice allowances), co-op advertising and seasonality to predict factory shipments. The basic equation can be written using the general notation:

$$Y_i \quad = \quad B_o + B_1 X_1 + B_2 X_2 + \dots B_n X_n + e_i$$

If the retail take-away of product A is:

Retail Take-Away = B_0 Constant + B_1 Price + B_2 Advertising + B_3 Sales Promotion + B_4 %ACV Feature + B_5 FSI + B_6 Store Distribution + B_7 Seasonality

Then its factory shipments will be:

Factory Shipments = B_0Constant + B_1Gross Dealer Price + B_2Factory Rebates + B_3Cash Discounts + B_4Co-op Advertising + B_5Trade Promotions + B_6 Seasonality

MEASURING FSI AND TRADE PROMOTION LIFT

Dummy variables can be used to measure the unit lift associated with qualitative drivers such as FSI and factory trade promotions. For example, in the case of FSI, we can use the circulation quantity (i.e., 55 million FSIs) instead of one's in the period(s) they are dropped and zeros in the period(s) when they are not dropped. This will not only give you the ability to measure the average lift, but also the magnitude associated with each million dropped (or circulation). In the case of factory trade promotions, traditional methods of ones (turned on) and zeros (turned off) can be used. However, you need to create three separate dummy variables for each trade promotion to measure the lift associated with forward buy, sell through, and post shipments. In other words, trade promotions require three separate lift variables to properly predict the quarterly spike associated with a trade promotion. For example, customers (i.e., Walmart, K-Mart, and Walgreens) will want product shipped one month prior to the trade promotion to pre-stock their shelves for the promotion. This is called forward buying. Then the promotion usually lasts four to six weeks requiring a second variable to calculate the actual sell-through and restocking of the product. Finally, many manufacturers offer tiered trade promotions with multiple offerings giving the channel distributors (i.e., Walmart, K-Mart, and Walgreens) opportunities to back fill their inventories after the promotional period to bring inventories back to original levels. These activities usually occur in the third month requiring a third variable.

MEASURING THE LAG EFFECT OF ADVERTISING

Most recently, polynomial distributed lags have been utilized to model the cumulative affects of advertising at retail over time (t). The general notion of a distributed lag model is that the dependent variable, Y_t, responds not only to changes in an input variable X at time t, but also on the past history of the X_t series. If for example, we stopped all advertising on Product A, its share of the market would not drop to its ultimate point overnight. Rather, we would expect a gradual erosion of its market share as consumer's perception of the product dims as memory fades. This technique is extremely effective in helping forecasters better understand the dynamics of advertising awareness which has helped marketing managers maximize their advertising spend. The general linear distributed lag equation can be written as:

$$Y_t = \quad + B_0X_t + B_1X_{t-1} + \dots B_nX_{t-n} + e_i$$

This method used to build market response models, known as ordinary least squares, has some very attractive statistical properties that have made it one of the most popular methods of regression analysis. Ordinary least squares regression may be a linear modeling approach, however, many times it works in situations that you would think it normally would not. Many have found that sales forecasts using regression models are generally superior to those based on simple extrapolation techniques. They provide a useful starting place for formulating a sales forecast; identifying factors for which judgmental decisions can be made; and provide a framework to insure consistency of the sales forecast process. Subsequently, it has been found that sales forecasts with subjective adjustments generally are more accurate than those obtained from the "purely" mechanical application of the regression model. In other words, a combination of model building and subjective market expertise are required for the successful prediction of the future.

CHAPTER 24

FORECAST PERFORMANCE OF AN AUDIT SERVICE – COCA-COLA'S EXPERIENCE

N. Corroll Mohn
The Coca-Cola Company

How do managers and marketing research analysts measure forecast performance of an outside auditing system to which they subscribe? A scoring scheme is outlined to grade forecasting performance of a purchased audit service. An example of real store sales data is used. The issue is how to track the forecast performance of outside audit estimation. Its importance is reflected in the size of marketing research subscription budgets for audit estimates (e.g., sales volumes, market shares) from such companies as A. C. Nielsen, Audits & Surveys, Data Bank, and Maritz Marketing Research. Moreover, frequently managers and research analysts do not know how to tackle proper evaluation of an outside audit system. Objective means have been developed and refined over multiple applications. Even though the approach described here has proven useful, it can be adapted or modified to meet particular requirements. The goal is to provide a mechanism for ensuring that optimal quality audit estimates are obtained for the research dollars invested. Certainly, no company subscribing to an audit service should be without a performance tracking system. The proposed approach defines a grading scheme with four different, equally weighted measures:

1. Direction Change
2. Randomness
3. Explained Variation
4. Slope

Each measure is now illustrated with store audit and actual sales data.

DIRECTION CHANGE

How effective are the directional changes predicted by an audit service? Measuring ability to correctly estimate movement of a time series (e.g., sales) up or down from period to period usually is the single most important audit performance component for managers. The measurement criterion is: Percent of direction changes for actual (sales) from period to period correctly estimated by the audit service.

Example: From inspection of the graph in Figure 1, there are 2 of 11 cases where lines for actual sales and for audited sales move in opposite directions. Hence, percent of correctly predicted direction movement is 82% [(11-2)/11].

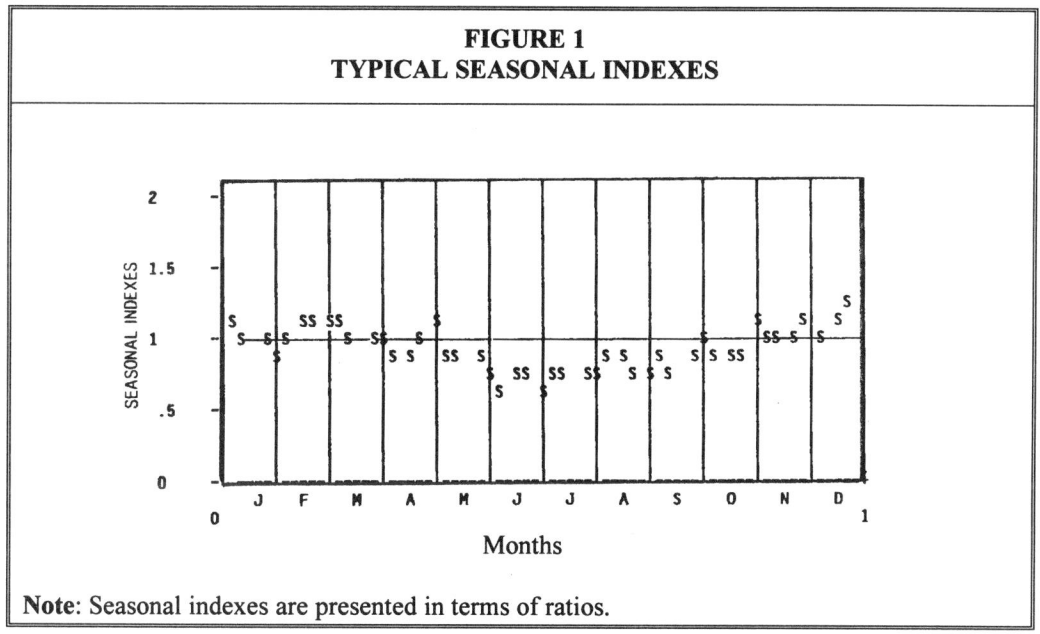

FIGURE 1
TYPICAL SEASONAL INDEXES

Months

Note: Seasonal indexes are presented in terms of ratios.

RANDOMNESS

Do the audit deviations from actual have a pattern? If so, the service data have a problem of diverging from the actual figures. The measurement criterion is: Percent of audit variances from actual (sales) with at least three successive deviations, positive/negative, from prior periods.

Example: From inspection of the 11 variance change signs computed in Table 1, a rule of thumb of at least three successive increases/decreases suggests randomness of errors. This indicates that the store audit service is performing well for the randomness criterion. Percent of acceptable pattern in the audit estimate variances from actual sales is 100% [(11 – 0) / 11].

EXPLAINED VARIANCE

What percent of actual is explained by the audit estimates? The measurement criterion is: Coefficient of determination, R^2, for simple linear regression of actual on audit estimates.

Example: From fitting a linear model to explain actual sales with audit estimates (Table 2), the percent of actual explained by audit (adjusted for degrees of freedom) is 84% (R^2 — adjusted).

	1987						1988					
	Jun	Jul	Aug	Sep	Oct	Nov	Dec	Jan	Feb	Mar	Apr	May
Audit Estimate	5.2	5.5	5.1	5.3	5.9	6.3	8.9	6.9	6.4	7.1	5.7	6.2
Actual Sales	5.3	5.8	4.3	5.2	6.2	6.1	9.5	6.9	5.5	7.1	5.6	4.9
%	98	95	117	101	95	103	93	100	115	100	105	126
Change Sign		-	+	-	-	+	-	+	+	-	+	+

TABLE 1
COCA-COLA
STORE AUDIT EVALUATION: RANDOMNESS
(Millions)

TABLE 2
COCA-COLA
STORE AUDIT EVALUATION EXPLAINED VARIANCE
(SLOPE)

Regression Output	
Constant	-98617.8
Standard Error of Y Estimate	54313.19
R Squared Adjusted	0.842781
No. of Observations	12
Degrees of Freedom	10
X Coefficient	1.130102
Standard Error of Coefficient	0.154351

SLOPE

On average, how much do actual (or conversely, estimated) data change when estimated (actual) data change either one unit or one percent? The slope of the line in Table 2 is key. There are three cases for this measurement criterion:

1. Positive slope between 0 and 1. Use face value of the slope.
   Example: When the slope equals 0.91, the score is 91%.
2. Positive slope greater than 1. Use the reciprocal of the slope (i.e., 1/slope).
   Example: For the store audit example introduced, the slope equals 1.13. The score, therefore, is 88% (1/1.13).
3. Negative slope, less than 1. Use the reciprocal of 1 plus the absolute value of the slope.
   Example: When the slope is -0.66, the score is 60% (1/1.66).

THE REPORT CARD

When the four criteria outlined above are averaged, the result is summary performance where:

A = 90 - 100 = Excellent
B = 80 - 89 = Good
C = 70 - 79 = Average
D = 60 - 69 = Poor
F = 50 - 59 = Failure

TABLE 3 STORE AUDIT REPORT CARD						
Product	Direction Change	Randomness	Explained Variance	Slope	Avg.	Grade
Coca-Cola	82	100	84	88	88	B+
Fanta	91	100	94	69	88	B+
All Products Combined	100	100	88	84	93	A

Over the period for which data are available, the store audit service in the example has had "good" performance in tracking sales for Coca-Cola.

Mean = (82 + 100 + 84 + 88)/4
= 88%

Grade = B+

A store audit report card for Coca-Cola, Fanta, and all combined products for a market are summarized in Table 3. Clearly, performance for this particular store audit service is satisfactory and requires no corrective action. If a report card were unsatisfactory, however, the grading scheme enables the focus on the specific area(s) requiring improvement in forecasts furnished by the outside audit service.

CHAPTER 25

RESEARCH IN FORECASTING NEW TELECOMMUNICATIONS SERVICES

Bruce R. Sokol
Sprint Corporation

Two general predictions echoed by telecommunications futurists are listed below:

1. The next decade will be associated with personal communications services, where one telephone number will allow you to be reached in the office, in the car, at a mall, or at home, anytime of the day.
2. The next decade will be associated with a new level of video services to the home with two-way communications. This will allow such services as customized home shopping, movie rentals without the VCR tape, the video telephone, and interactive video games between people miles apart.

These predictions assume two technological breakthroughs: One, technological development related to personal communications services (PCS) and the other related to fiber optic technology in local telephone infrastructures. The net effect of these technologies could result in the appearance of these services even sooner than expected.

With this sort of eminent change in potential lifestyle, industry players such as long distance companies, equipment manufacturers, local telephone companies, cable TV companies, and cellular companies, to name a few, are jockeying for a position to take advantage of the ensuing opportunities. As expected, though, this makes life very interesting for product forecasters at these companies.

DILEMMA

As one would figure, historical data related to these products is hard to come by. As such, forecasters around the industry must rely exclusively on primary research, secondary research, and the observations of market trials. This sector of forecasting which I refer to as new product forecasting (NPF), or "forecasting without a safety net," entails a strong background in market research techniques, resources, and applications. In some ways, the NPF discipline requires more of a background in market research than in traditional forecasting techniques. In this article, I will describe a market research technique adopted at Sprint for the purpose of forecasting personnel communications services and other new product concepts.

CONJOINT ANALYSIS

Conjoint analysis is a statistical research tool, which attempts to simulate customer choice based on a given set of market conditions (i.e., price and product selection). Using the PCS example, the following describes the data collection process of a conjoint study. Although several forms of Conjoint analysis and software exist, most will ask a series of questions with the objective of determining the utilities of various attributes of a product such as price and quality. Conjoint questioning may entail various formats including ranking several products with different attribute mixes, asking the respondent to indicate the likelihood (0 to 100) to purchase a product with specific attributes, or choices between paired product profiles. An example of this is given below:

DELUXE WIRELESS TELEPHONE SERVICE	BASIC WIRELESS TELEPHONE SERVICE
You can make both outbound and inbound calls from a wireless phone booth while in a car or at home. Price: $29.95 per month	You can make both outbound and inbound calls from a wireless phone in your home, but only outbound calls in the car. Price: $19.95 per month

How likely are you to choose one service or the other?

Definitely Deluxe   **Definitely Basic**

1	2	3	4	5	6	7	8	9	10

Based on the information from several iterations of these questions, utilities for each service/price combination are derived for each respondent. By regressing these utilities across the full sample and assuming certain attribute levels, a conjoint model can simulate the expected long-run penetration of each service based on specific price points and service options. Assume that this Conjoint study and identified price points revealed the following three-year penetration for PCS.

Simulations such as this allow one to estimate market penetration based on the expected price and other product attributes. This allows not only quantifiable product forecasts, but also a tool for management to test the success of different marketing strategies.

The PCS example is shown in order to illustrate the process of using primary research to predict the future adoption of product concepts. However, an actual forecast model derived from a PCS Conjoint study would involve many other variables such as substitution for local "wireline" telephone service and cellular service, population growth in the service area, market share of PCS competitors, price of the actual portable phones and service quality. While the task of predicting the sales of new technology will never reach the comfort level that some executives would like to have for investment decisions, market research applications such as Conjoint analysis are available for the purpose of minimizing that uncertainty.

TABLE 1			
	Share	Customers	Revenue
Deluxe Service ($29.95/Mo.)	10%	10,000	$3,594,000
Basic Service ($19.95/Mo.)	18%	18,000	$4,309,200
No Service	72%	72,000	$0
Total of the 3rd Year Revenue			$7,903,200

* Service area contains 100,000 households

PART IV

FORECASTING APPROACH

INTRODUCTION

Before deciding on the forecasting process and/or system, one has to decide on the forecasting approach because forecasting approach can affect the forecasting process and consequently the forecasting system. Should we use top-down approach or bottom-up approach? Should we categorize products by the stage of life cycle the product is in and develop a separate model for products of each stage? Should we categorize products into highly promoted and least promoted and then develop a model for each? This section describes not only various approaches the forecaster can opt for but also when and where each one is appropriate.

CHAPTER 26

WHAT IS THE BEST APPROACH TO FORECASTING?

Chaman L. Jain
St. John's University

There is no single approach that works in every situation. Each situation calls for a different approach. The best approach, of course, is the one which is cost effective, fits well into the philosophy and the culture of a company, involves different functional heads in the process, and yields most accurate forecasts in a timely manner. Here are the approaches often used in business:

1. Bottom up and top down
2. Product life cycle
3. Products highly and least promoted
4. Large and small customers
5. Product categories
6. Combination of different approaches

BOTTOM UP AND TOP DOWN

With the bottom-up approach, forecaster first prepares forecasts of each and every SKU (item) in each and every region, and then aggregate them to arrive at category and aggregate level forecasts. In some companies, the forecaster obtains SKU level forecasts from salespeople in different regions which are then summed up to arrive at aggregate forecasts. In the case of top-down approach, the forecaster prepares first the overall forecast and then disaggregates it into regions, categories and SKUs. The overall forecast is prepared by the forecaster or mandated by upper management.

PRODUCT LIFE CYCLE

The product life cycle approach is most appropriate where products have a distinct life cycle pattern. Here products are first categorized into different stages of their development, and then forecasts are prepared by selecting the best model for each category. Howmedica, Division of the Pfizer Hospital Products Group, for example, uses such an approach. It categorizes products into four stages: (a) newly introduced products, (b) mature products, (c) products with a declining demand,

and (d) obsolescent products. It defines mature products as the ones which have a demand history of at least two years. Products with declining sales are those that are still viable yet their demand is declining. Obsolescent products are those which are almost at the very end of their life cycle.

PRODUCTS HIGHLY AND LEAST PROMOTED

Generally speaking, products that are highly promoted are more difficult to forecast than those that are least promoted or not promoted at all. Some companies classify their products into these two categories and then use one set of models to forecast the sales of highly promoted products and another for other products. For example, Caterpillar Inc. does not promote tractors that have been discontinued, but it receives regularly orders for their parts. For those parts, says Larry M. Newbanks, Inventory Systems Research Manager, the company does not develop a forecasting model to generate their forecasts. Their forecasts are intuitively driven. A certain number of their orders come in every week and every month. The forecaster assumes that the same number of orders will continue in the future, which works very well for the company.

LARGE AND SMALL CUSTOMERS

If large customers are involved, the company will be better off to prepare their forecasts separate from others. The large customers do not behave the same way as other customers. The loss and gain of just one customer can make a big difference. Furthermore, if in any given month, a large customer such as Wal-Mart decides to promote one of your products, the sale of that product in that month will sharply increase. Therefore, it is better to prepare a separate forecast for each large customer.

PRODUCT CATEGORIES

It is very costly and time consuming to find the best model for each and every SKU. If a company has 25000 SKUs, which is not unusual, it means that it has to find the best model for each one of them. To overcome this problem, very often companies divide their products into categories and then determine the best model for each category. Once the category level forecasts are made, they are disaggregated into SKUs by using their ratios to the categories experienced during the last 6-12 month period. If the ratio of one SKU to its category is 0.05 (5%), then that ratio will be used to the category level forecast to obtain its SKU forecast. In classifying products by category, one should make sure that all the SKUs of that category move up and down together. That is, if the sales of one SKU go up, the sales of other SKUs of the same category also go up. In some situations, one may find two SKUs of the same category do not move together because one tends to cannibalize the other.

For example, Easy Off Oven Cleaner comes with two SKUs, heavy duty and fume free. When the sales of one go up, sales of the other go down. In that case, their forecasts have to be prepared separately.

COMBINATION OF DIFFERENT APPROACHES

The forecaster does not have to stick with just one approach. He or she can combine different approaches. In fact, the forecaster may improve the quality of forecasts if he or she prepares forecasts by using both bottom-up and top-down approaches and then reconcile them to arrive at one set of numbers. The forecasts of both these approaches are expected to be different. But if the difference between them is too big, it means that something has gone wrong. In that case, further scrutiny of their forecasts may be needed to identify the problem.

Sooner or later, the forecaster has to decide on the forecasting approach. It is a pre-requisite for establishing a forecasting process. Of course, the forecasting system cannot be set up until the forecasting process is in place.

CHAPTER 27

A SIMPLE VIEW OF TOP-DOWN VERSUS BOTTOM-UP FORECASTING

Larry Lapide
Advanced Manufacturing Research

Over time I have noted a few published papers that dealt with the topic of whether top-down or bottom-up forecasting was preferable and when. None of them seems to provide simple guidelines that forecast practitioners can understand and use on an everyday basis. When asked about which approach works best, my simple answer had always been to use a combination: start with bottom-up forecasting followed by top-down; with sometimes even middle-up-and-down forecasting.

This is especially the case in operational demand forecasting where having to forecast tens or hundreds of thousands of elements much of the forecasting has to be automated. One does not have the luxury to spend a lot of time worrying about or investigating whether and when each approach should be used. Also, since operational forecasts will invariably be adjusted by different participants during the forecasting process, the forecasts have a good chance of being adjusted top-to-bottom and in-between anyway!

WHAT ARE TOP-DOWN AND BOTTOM-UP FORECASTING?

Figure 1 depicts the difference between bottom-up and top-down forecasting using an example where an item group is composed of three items. In top-down forecasting, a forecast is made for the group, which is then broken down into the lower-level item forecasts. In bottom-up forecasting, each of the lower-level items is separately forecast and the forecasts are then summed up to provide a forecast for the group. These forecast approaches are useful when forecasting based on hierarchical levels along specific dimensions; where higher-level aggregated variables along a dimension are the sum of lower-level disaggregated variables, within the same dimension. Examples of these dimensions and levels are:

- *Business unit dimension*: company comprised of business divisions or units
- *Product dimension*: brand or product group comprised of items, products or stock-keeping-units

- *Geographic dimension*: country comprised of sales regions, districts or territories
- *Operational dimension*: plant/distribution center comprised of customer ship-to locations
- *Time dimension*: year comprised of quarters, months, weeks and days

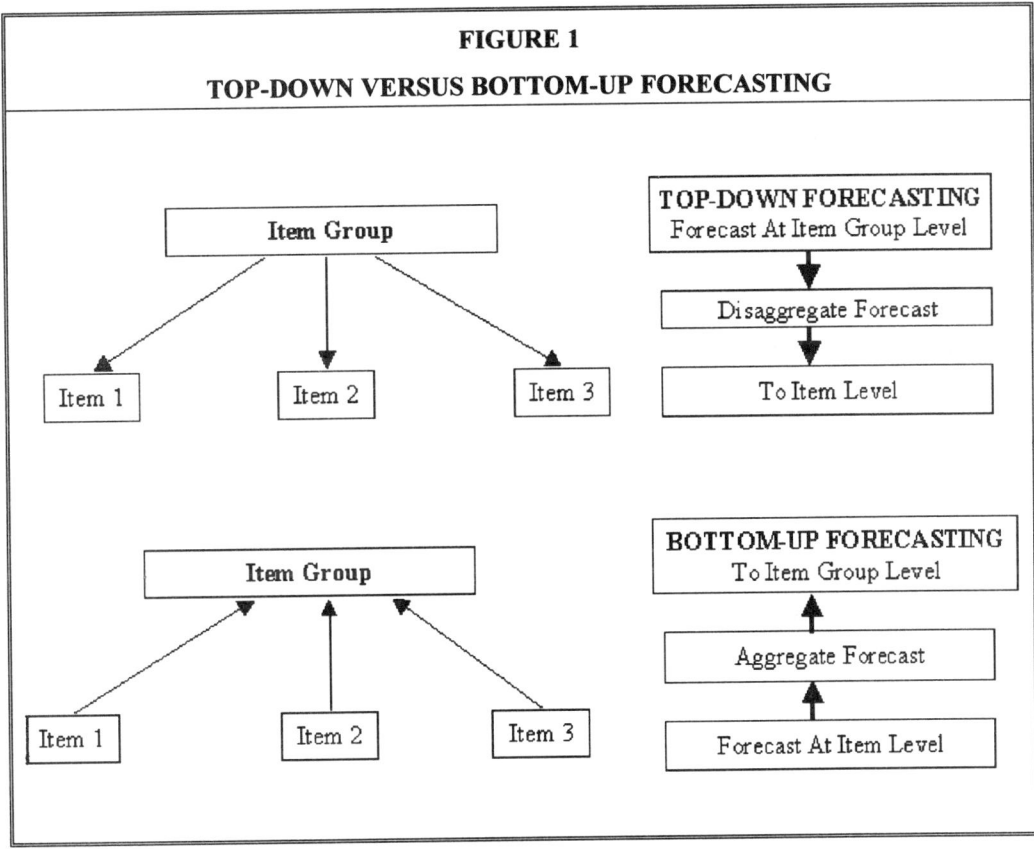

FIGURE 1

TOP-DOWN VERSUS BOTTOM-UP FORECASTING

In top-down forecasting several methods can be used to break down the top-level forecast to allocate it to each of its components. These methods include:

- An equal share across all components
- Component shares based on historical demand represented by each of the components
- Component shares based on forecast demand represented by each of the components

Obviously, for the last method, a forecast for each component is needed. Hence, it is really bottom-up forecasting since a lower-level forecast would have to precede the top-down allocation.

WHY IS TOP-DOWN APPEALING?

The top-down approach to demand forecasting is appealing because it is generally believed that the percentage variations for demand made up of components will be lower than those of the individual items. This is predicated on what is taught in statistics courses about the standard deviation of a mathematical sum of equally distributed independent variables. The standard deviation of the sum of independent variables is the square root of the sum of the variances. Thus, the relative standard deviation of the sum turns out to be less than the relative standard deviation of the variables. This can also be explained as being the result of compensating errors. The random variations of the individual components tend to cancel each other out when aggregated together — resulting in a 'smoother' aggregate variable.

BOTTOM-UP IS USUALLY PREFERABLE TO TOP-DOWN

While it is generally true that the relative forecast error for a sum of demand components will be less than the relative forecast errors of the individual components, this does not lead to top-down being better — especially in operational forecasting. This is primarily due to the fact that one is usually interested in planning for each of the components, not in planning for their sum. For example, in production and inventory planning stock-keeping-unit forecasts (SKU), not product group forecasts are needed to schedule resources and determine replenishment requirements. Figure 2 represents an illustrative case where it would be inappropriate to use a top-down forecasting approach. In this case each of the three components has a different trend: one is increasing, one is flat and one is decreasing. The sum of the three components, however, is relatively flat. Using a top-down approach, one would forecast the sum to be flat.

Allocating down to the components based on either 'equal shares' or 'historical shares' would yield a flat forecast for each of the components — contrary to what is happening. In this case only a bottom-up forecasting approach would work. To insure that the lower-level trends are maintained one needs to allocate the top-level forecast based on the lower-level forecasts.

As a general rule, the top-down forecasting approach only makes sense if and only if, the demand patterns of the lower-level components are the same. That is, all demand components are increasing, decreasing or remaining flat. Otherwise, the bottom-up forecasting approach is preferable. Frequently an aggregated set of products is composed of competing items that potentially cannibalize each other's demand — for example, a product group made of new and old formulations of the same product. For these types of products, the demand patterns are quite dissimilar since some products grow at the expense of the others. Therefore, bottom-up forecasting is preferable in most cases.

WHEN DOES TOP-DOWN MAKE SENSE?

Top-down forecasting only makes sense when a top-level group is made up of components that have similar demand patterns. Even then, it is only useful if a forecaster is trying to speed up computations by avoiding having to forecast each of the lower-level items. Some cases where top-down can be used include:

- Allocating a forecast at a retail chain to individual stores, assuming store-level sales patterns are similar
- Breaking down a national forecast to regional levels, assuming regional-level demand patterns are similar.

- Breaking down a product category forecast into components, assuming that the components either support each other or are frequently purchased together.

Based on the discussion above, my simple view is that forecasters should always use a combination of top-down and bottom-up forecasting. They should start with a forecast of the lower-level components first. Then adjustments should be made to the middle and top levels. These adjusted higher-level forecasts should then be allocated based on the lower-level forecasts — not based on historical or equal shares. After all, why take a chance that all the lower level components have similar demand patterns; especially if you don't have to!

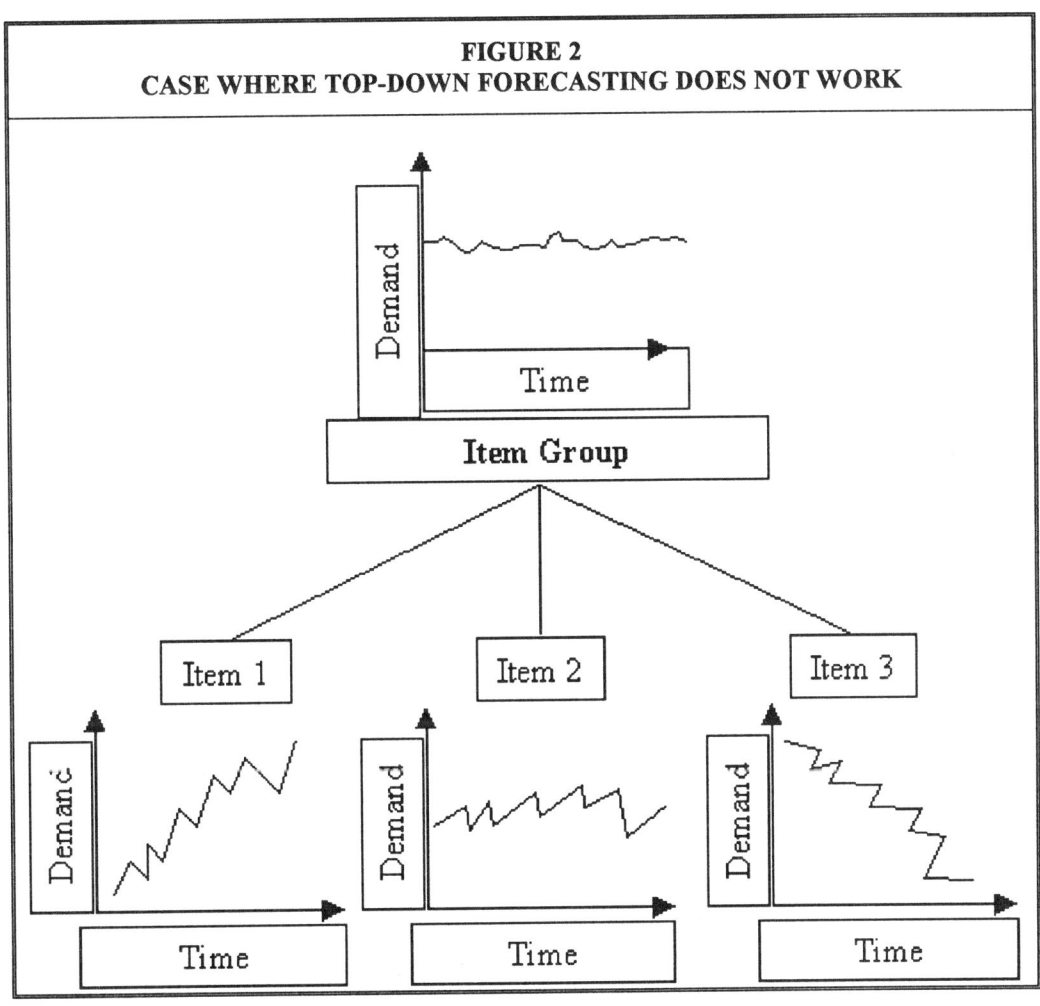

FIGURE 2
CASE WHERE TOP-DOWN FORECASTING DOES NOT WORK

CHAPTER 28

MANAGING BOTTOM-UP AND TOP-DOWN APPROACHES: OCEAN SPRAY'S EXPERIENCE

Paul Gelly
Ocean Spray Cranberries, Inc

During the design and implementation of a sales demand forecasting process, one of the fundamental questions which often comes up is which approach to use — Bottom-Up or Top-Down. This determination is a pre-requisite of several downstream decisions, including: (1) Sales and Marketing involvement in the process, (2) hierarchy and reconciliation procedures within software design, (3) organizational structure of the forecasting team, (4) data inputs into the forecasting process, (5) optimal statistical algorithms and parameter settings, and (6) Sales and Operations Planning (S&OP) process design. Therefore, it is very important that all these factors are considered before any decision is made. Later on, if the process has to be changed, it will not only be difficult to implement but also very time consuming and expensive. The change may call for alternations in the structure of the software design, as well as in the organization of the company.

TOP DOWN APPROACH

The Top-Down approach to forecasting is very common and simple. In this approach, generally, fewer people are involved, even though all the functions (Sales, Marketing, and Finance) can play some role. Furthermore, we can use multiple data inputs including history of consumer data, advertising effects and national promotions, provided they are on an aggregate level. Any regional or customer specific promotions will be difficult to factor in. Therefore, the Top-Down approach is better suited to products that are not heavily promoted and have shown predictable sales patterns over time at a regional level. Another limitation of this approach is that the "political" pressure within the organization may influence forecast decisions. This is particularly true when sales management is trying to drive the organization to meet a quota.

BOTTOM UP APPROACH

Bottom up approach, on the other hand, has its own limitations. In this approach Demand Planners forecast at lower levels (usually by customer or region), and is often done with the assistance of field personnel. For this approach to be effective, there have to be involvement of a large number of planners and sales representatives, which add complexity to the process. This approach allows an organization to focus at a localized level. This is critical if you are allowing customer specific promotional activity as is often the case in the Consumer Products Industry. The Bottom Up approach enables you to use sales forecasts quite effectively for devising plans for warehousing, manufacturing and transportation, as you will be working at a very detailed level. However, there are various problems with this approach. One, you may not effectively utilize the national market intelligence pertaining to consumer insight and advertisement. Two, the lower level historical data are generally more sporadic. Careful attention to statistical parameters will be necessary for managing the data. Three, you will need to develop reporting mechanisms to aggregate forecasts to national or category levels so that they can be used by other functions within the organization.

OCEAN SPRAY'S EXPERIENCE

In the summer of 1997, Ocean Spray Cranberries began a series of supply chain improvement initiatives. The cornerstone of the improvement projects was a re-engineered forecasting process. One of the first issues we evaluated was the Top Down/Bottom Up alternative. As we reviewed all of our product distribution channels, and customer buying habits, we found that in many instances both the approaches could be used. After debating the alternatives for several weeks, we decided to combine the apparently conflicting approaches as the basis for a company wide S&OP planning discipline. We eventually designed a system and organization to support it. Two years later, we have a fully functioning forecasting process, which is working out well.

What we have implemented at Ocean Spray is two distinct approaches, Bottom Up and Top Down, which complement each other. We begin each month with a customer level forecast. Demand Planners work closely with field sales managers to develop a six-month rolling monthly forecast for our top 75 customers. These customers account for 70% of our revenue, and the remaining 30% is handled primarily with statistical modeling.

At the end of first week in each month, we aggregate the Bottom Up forecasts to a national level by category. The Top Down process begins in the second week. During this week we have a series of consensus meetings with managers and directors of Sales, Marketing and Trade Marketing. In these meetings, we review forecast error metrics and the new field forecast. We make adjustments to account for promotions that field sales were not aware of. At the end of this week, Sales, Marketing, Trade Marketing, and Demand Planning finalize the monthly forecasts for the next six months. These are the only forecasts utilized within the organization. But they are reconciled back down to a customer level based upon the customer level inputs.

Exhibit A summarizes the monthly S&OP process and displays how the Bottom Up and Top Down approaches fit and complement each other. Implementing the new forecast process at Ocean Spray was fairly difficult since no formal process existed before. The forecast analysts worked independently to produce one of many forecasts in use throughout the organization. As such, we chose to stagger the implementation. In Phase I, the Top Down consensus process with Sales, Marketing, and Trade Marketing was initiated. We refined this process for six months prior to Phase II. This allowed us to focus the organization on "one number" forecast concept. In Phase II, we implemented the customer level forecast process, which was extremely complex and involved many people. During this time the consensus process evolved into a review of customer level forecasts. This resulted in a shift in focus from opinions to fact based decisions.

EXHIBIT A				
Day 1	**Day 2**	**Day 3**	**Day 4**	**Day 5**
		All forecast reports received from field sales Managers		Final forecast Entered into Manugistics Distribute divisional Rollups (include regional totals)
<-------------- DEVELOP CUSTOMER LEVEL FORECAST ----------------->				
Day 6	**Day 7**	**Day 8**	**Day 9**	**Day 10**
Distribute aggregated forecast	Division changes finalized	Pre-alignment meetings (2) Final alignment Meeting packet distributed	Alignment team reviews packet	Forecast alignment Meeting (Monthly 1-6) (Quarterly 1-18)
<----------------------------- FORECAST CONSENSUS ---------------------------->				
Day 11	**Day 12**	**Day 13**	**Day 14**	**Day 15**
				Supply alignment mtg. (2 - 6 months) Formalize and Communicate Supply issues
<----- DEVELOP SUPPLY PLANS & OPTIONS ----->			<----- SUPPLY ALIGNMENT ----->	
Day 16	**Day 17**	**Day 18**	**Day 19**	**Day 20**
Generate S&OP Pre-read packet and review			**S & OP** Meeting (Monthly 2-6) (Quarterly 2-18)	
<--------------------- SALES & OPERATIONS PLANNING ---------------------->				

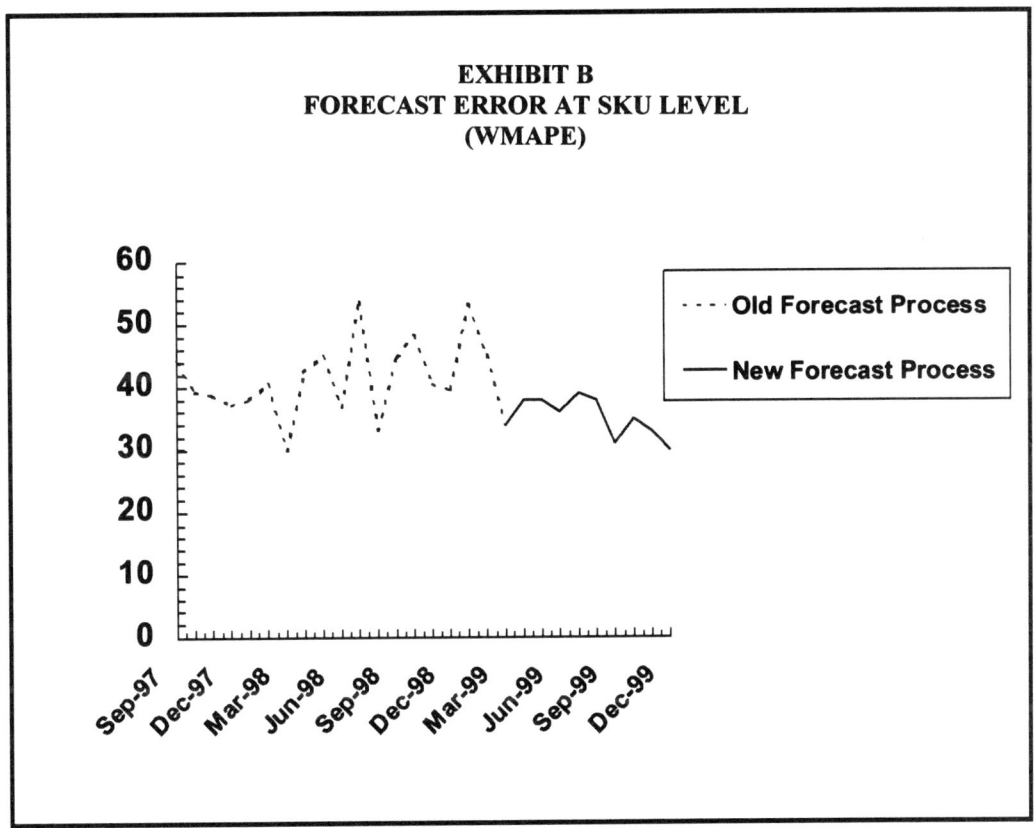

EXHIBIT B
FORECAST ERROR AT SKU LEVEL
(WMAPE)

In the first year of the new process, we have seen improved forecast accuracy. Exhibit B shows the forecast errors at the SKU level. As can be seen, we have not made a tremendous improvement in accuracy yet, but the trend is headed in the right direction. Equally important, the monthly fluctuations in forecast errors have stabilized significantly – we don't experience wild fluctuations as was the case with our old process. This is evident in the ten most recent data points (March through December). If your organization is faced with an opportunity to design a forecast process, give a thought to both Bottom-Up and Top-Down approaches. If you feel that a combination of both approaches can be effectively used, consider the design in use at Ocean Spray as a viable alternative.

PART V

FORECASTING PROCESS

INTRODUCTION

Very often terms forecasting process and forecasting system are used interchangeably, but they are not the same. The forecasting process deals with issues such as: What kind of data/information will be used to prepare forecasts? Where it will come from? What type of forecasts will be prepared? Where will the forecasting function reside? What will be the forecasting philosophy, one number forecast, for example? What kind of forecasting approach will be used? Who will participate in the process? Who will have the authority to override forecasts? How will forecasts be monitored and revised? Forecasting system, on the other hand, deals with issues of mechanizing/automating the forecasting process. This section discusses not only how to set up a forecasting process but also what kind of forecasting processes are in place at different companies.

CHAPTER 29

FORECASTING PROCESS AT RUBBERMAID

Richard B. Barrett and David J. Kitska
Rubbermaid, Inc.

Forecasting at Rubbermaid Home Products Division (HPD) in Wooster, Ohio is a routinized but flexible system that incorporates several major advantages. Forecasting is not confined to a single individual working feverishly behind a PC. The Group Product Managers have final authority over all numbers, but personnel from all functional areas participate. Thus, responsibility for input is widely distributed horizontally and vertically. State-of-the-art statistical modeling and practical business knowledge and experience are synthesized in the process. Constant monitoring of forecast accuracies serves as an impetus for reducing error. Most important of all, the forecasts are not just "show" numbers; they are incorporated into the short-term and long-term business plans to which people willingly react.

THE FORECASTS

All products at HPD are presently partitioned into ten distinct product lines which are in turn subdivided into various product groups. Because items are often marketed in several different packaging schemes to facilitate customer preferences, the 30-, 60-, 90-day and annual forecasts are performed on approximately 600 item-packs. Forecasts are initially done in units, but forecasted average selling prices subsequently translate unit quantities into total dollars for each item, group, and line. The computer system then distributes each item-pack forecast between colors and raw material requirements in three manufacturing sites.

THE PLAYERS

Each product line is assigned to a Group Product Manager (GPM) who reports directly to the Vice President of Marketing and who is also in charge of one or more Product Managers (PM). The GPMs are the general managers of their assigned lines with responsibility for business plans, profit and loss statements, product and accessory inventories, and forecasts. The Marketing Department also employs a Manager of Marketing Information (MMI) who supervises a forecast analyst and reports to the Manager of Inventory Planning and Forecasting (MIPF). This latter position, also directly responsible to the Vice President, provides a critical link between marketing and manufacturing. One primary goal of the MMI, MIPF, and the forecast analyst is to provide GPMs and PMs with the best possible forecasting tools and information. Higher on the ladder is the divisional Operating Committee (OC), which includes the Vice Presidents of Marketing, Sales, Finance, Research and Development, Management Information Systems, and Manufacturing. Naturally, these individuals are not as concerned with specific item-pack forecasts as they are with the overall dollar picture for each product line and how the dollars affect profit issues and shipment goals.

THE ANNUAL FORECAST

About mid-way in the current year, an annual forecast is produced for the following year. The GPMs and PMs review shipments of the current year, current and future economic conditions, activities of competitors, and input from our customers. Accordingly, they produce forecasts of all item-packs, including new items planned for introduction in the current year and next year. They provide, for each item-pack, a forecasted average selling price which is usually historically based and which dollarizes the unit forecast. The forecasts also include policy statements about price changes, item deletions, new colors, product improvements, and promotional activities such as ads, rebates, and special pricing. These forecasts are then totaled to produce "bottom-up" numbers for all lines.

Independently, the OC considers the same kinds of business factors as the GPMs and PMs, reviews the policy statements, and formulates product line forecasts. These forecasts and the GPM/PM "bottom-up" numbers are eventually reconciled. Once the annual numbers have been chosen, the GPMs and PMs are asked to forecast the seasonality of their lines in terms of monthly percentages. Recommended percentages, based on historical analysis, are provided by the MMI and the forecast analyst. Monthly totals for each line are estimated by multiplying the final percentages by the corresponding annual totals. These monthly figures are handed back to the OC for review, revision, and final approval. The finalized numbers are then transmitted to manufacturing so that machine capacity and raw material requirements may be assessed. The annual plan is reviewed again later in the year. The GPMs and PMs are asked to give any revisions to the "first pass" which again are compared and reconciled with any OC revisions. The forecasting process can thus be seen incorporating a certain amount of repetition. The various players and their overlapping responsibilities and inputs act as a checks- and- balance system. The players challenge each other's assumptions about market conditions, competition, product popularity, and the life-cycle of various products. This repetition becomes even more apparent in the 30-, 60-, and 90-day forecast.

THE 30-, 60-, 90-DAY FORECAST

One week out of every month is set aside as "forecast week" although for some personnel, such as the forecast analyst and production schedulers, the 30-, 60-, 90-day forecast is a daily pre-occupation. In the first week of each month, the analyst applies a battery of statistical forecast methods to the demand history of each item-pack. These methods range from the most sophisticated such as state space models and Box-Jenkins to the simplest such as exponential smoothing.

FIGURE 1 FORECAST INPUT/OUTPUT REPORT				
01 Sinkware				
01 Drainboard Mats & Trays				
1195-00	3-Mos. ASP = $1.86		Fcst ASP = $1.90	
Unit	January	February	March	April
1984 Demand	10,000	10,000	12,000	12,000
1985 Demand	12,000	12,000	13,000	13,000
1986 Demand	12,000	10,000	12,000	13,000
1987 Demand	6,000	12,000	500	15
1986 Dollars				
3-Mos. ASP[1]	22,320	18,600	22,320	24,180
Fcst ASP[2]	22,800	19,000	22,800	24,700
1987 Dollars				
3-Mos. ASP[1]	11,160	22,320	930	
Fcst ASP[2]	11,400	22,800	950	
Stat Fcst (Units)				
30 Day	12,000			
60 Day		10,500		
90 Day			12,000	
Error (30)				
PM Fcst (Units)				
30 Day	13,000			
60 Day		11,500		
90 Day			12,000	
Error (30)				
PM Revision Units)	---			
30 Day		20,000		
60 Day			---	
90 Day				
Error (30)				
Dollar Forecast				
3-Mos ASP[1]				
30 Day	24,180			
60 Day		37,200		
90 Day			22,320	
Fcst ASP[2]				
30 Day	24,700			
60 Day		38,000		
90 Day			22,800	

1. Rolling 3-month average selling price based on previous months of demand history.
2. Forecasted average selling price, provided by GPMs and PMs as part of their annual forecasts.

A number of statistical criteria (e.g., goodness-of-fit statistics) are employed to select the "best" statistical forecast for each 30-, 60-, and 90-day period. These forecasts are then reviewed jointly by the analyst and the MMI, and where questionable forecasts appear, further statistical tests are applied.

The final version of the statistical forecast is archived in the computer system and printed in a special report. A sample page from the report, as it may have appeared in January 1987, is reconstructed in Figure 1. At the top appears a two-part identification code which identifies the unique product (four digits before the hyphen) and the particular packaging scheme (two digits after the hyphen). Also appearing are the Product Line and Product Group numbers and description. In this case we have the information for the "1195" in the "00" pack, and this item is classed in our Drainboard Mats and Trays Group under the Sinkware Line. The report displays the unit demand history for the past three years (1984-1986) and any future orders which are time-phased by their requested shipment dates ("1987 Demand"). The unit demand for 1986 and the open orders for 1987 are dollarized two ways: by a historical moving three-month average selling price ("3-Mos. ASP") and by a forecasted average selling price ("FCST ASP") which is part of the annual plan. The Product Manager's "first-pass" forecasts appear in the section marked "PM FCST," his/her final revisions appear under "PM REVISION," and the statistical forecasts are under "STAT FCST." The final section, "DOLLAR FORECAST," dollarizes the most recent PM forecasts by the two average selling prices.

As we move past each month during the current year, the open order numbers become actual demand history. Error percentages for the PM's "first-pass" and final forecasts and for the statistical forecasts are calculated and displayed. Several days prior to forecast week when all statistical forecasts for the new 30-, 60-, 90-day period have been completed, the PMs and GPMs receive complete copies of the report. This schedule gives the GPMs and PMs time to relay comments about the statistical forecasts to the analyst and to formulate their revisions.

On Monday of forecast week (Figure 2), the 30-, 60-, 90-day forecast is entered into the computer and dollarized. On Tuesday, a rigorous review of this "first pass" occurs. This meeting includes the MMI, MIPF, GPMs, and PMs, and the analyst, as well as production schedulers and managers and representatives from sales customer service. Any revisions are entered by Wednesday afternoon. On Thursday, GPMs and PMs meet with the Vice Presidents of Marketing and Sales to compare the dollar forecasts for each line with the monthly business plan targets. Wherever discrepancies occur, the group discusses current and known future business plans and reaches agreement on final action plans and dollar totals.

On Thursday afternoon, the "final" forecasts are entered into the computer and are reflected in all manufacturing plans by the next day.

CONTINUOUS MONITORING

Review of the current 30-, 60-, 90-day forecast does not end on Thursday of forecast week. Several mechanisms ensure a weekly reevaluation. Every Monday morning, the Vice Presidents of Marketing, Sales, and Manufacturing meet with the MIPF to discuss month-to-date order entry, shipments, backlog, and inventory. These statistics are compared with the forecasted monthly totals and the current business plans. On every Monday afternoon, the GPMs, PMs, the MIPF, the MMI, production schedulers and managers, and customer service personnel meet to identify any major problems relevant to their functional areas, including issues that affect item forecasts. Every Friday morning, a new forecast/demand history report is printed and distributed to all GPMs and PMs. They are encouraged to scrutinize the report, but the forecast analyst also reviews each item-pack and questions any forecast in the 60- and/or 90-day period that seems too high or too low. Any revisions are input into the manufacturing computer system on the very same day.

FIGURE 2
30-, 60-, 90-DAY
FORECASTING WEEK SCHEDULE

Monday	2:00 PM	Input Initial Forecast
Tuesday	10:00 AM - 10:45 AM	Review Forecast vs. Demand
	10:45 AM - 11:15 AM	PM/GPM Sinkware, Space Organization, Bathware, Home Office
		PM Schedulers, Customer Service join Group
	1:15 PM - 1:45 PM	PM/GPM Food Preparation, Food Storage, Microwave Schedulers, Customer Service join Group
	2:30 PM - 3:15 PM	PM/GPM Household Container, Refuse Container, Furniture, Schedulers, Customer Service
	3:15 PM - 3:45 PM	PM/GPM Household Container, Refuse Container, Furniture
Wednesday	2:00 PM	Input Forecast Revisions
Thursday	10:30 AM - 11:00 AM	PM/GPM Review Forecast
	11:00 AM - 12:00 PM	V. P. Sales and V. P. Marketing join Group Review Business Plans
	2:00 PM	Input Final Forecast Revisions

CHAPTER 30

THE STRATEGIC POWER OF CONSENSUS FORECASTING: SETTING YOUR ORGANIZATION UP TO WIN

Katy Fosnaught
Borden Foods Corporation

Your annual strategic planning and budgeting process will be significantly enhanced if you use the power of a monthly, one-number consensus forecasting process within your organization as the cornerstone of the strategic plan. Having one number to which the organization commits will enable you to limit the "surprises" that tend to plague the business and add costs to delivering product or service to customers.

There are four basic steps that will enable you to move to a consensus approach for your strategic planning:

1. Develop and ensure a strong, inclusive one-number monthly forecasting process.
2. Support your process with appropriate tools and measurement techniques and capabilities.
3. Support your process with the right organizational infrastructure.
4. Recognize and overcome the change management challenges that will weave throughout all of the above.

STRONG, INCLUSIVE, ONE-NUMBER MONTHLY FORECASTING PROCESS

In order to develop a strong, inclusive one-number monthly forecasting process, you must first begin with the end in mind: what is your vision? You will need to evaluate, based upon your unique business needs, why you are forecasting. Be able to articulate that you forecast to provide a look into the future that will ensure that you are able to match the demand that you are forecasting with the supply that your organization provides.

As a first step in the one-number process, you must begin with a sound baseline forecast of demand volume. This can be at the product level or at an aggregate family level, depending upon your business and the complexity of your product or services mix. The baseline forecast can be driven from historical demand data, using available information within your legacy systems. This baseline forecast can be as simple as a statistical time-series estimate, or as complex as your data and modeling capabilities will allow. In creating a complex baseline forecast, you should remember that the time spent creating the models will yield a high return on investment, and provide significantly higher forecast accuracy than the cost of developing them.

The second step in your one-number process should be the inclusion of Marketing information on top of the baseline forecast. Marketing information, depending upon your business, may include new product introductions into the marketplace. Such information can be incorporated by using a "placeholder" or "dummy" product number within your data set. This "placeholder" is for planning purposes only, and can be given an alpha or numeric designation, as long as the organization knows it is not a product that will be introduced into the marketplace under this number. This "placeholder" can have assigned corporate volume estimates, based upon the new product/service rollout, and can be dollarized later using estimated costs and revenue. In addition, Marketing information may include a consumption forecast using POS syndicated data provided by IRI and AC Neilsen for consumer goods, or other external consumption estimates developed by the Marketing group on existing products/services. The effect of advertising plans and their predicted lifts associated with those activities should also be overlaid over your baseline forecast. Marketing spends a significant amount of time in researching and estimating the lift of different promotions. As such they can tell what you should be adding to the baseline forecast for a given promotion. Finally, the impact of new ways of going to market should be quantified and laid on top of the baseline number. The new ways might include global expansions of your current mix, new segments of business in your existing markets, and/or new ways of reaching your current customers, like E-commerce (the Internet).

Next in the process you should be able to incorporate Sales information into the forecast. As sales is your front line with your customer, they are in an unique position to possess information about those customers, their buying habits, their future promotional plans, their long-range corporate strategies, etc. With continuous global changes in terms of mergers and acquisitions, downsizing, and gaining focus and clarity within the marketplace, many of our customers are changing the way they go to market as well. This can have a significant impact upon your forecast in the future. Interaction with your sales force can be as simple or as complex as your needs require. Interaction can range from phone calls with each sales manager, simply asking, "what do you see are the upcoming changes in your customers in the next 12-36 months?" to the use of E-mail and spreadsheet exchanges, to the most sophisticated Revenue Management systems with optimization capabilities to predict customer activity and forward plan with our customers. (Revenue Management is "an integrated set of business processes that combine people and systems with the goal of understanding the market, predicting customer behavior, and responding quickly to exploit opportunities.")

The final and most important step of your one-number forecasting process is holding a Consensus Meeting. This meeting is critical to ensure that your organization is in step with a single number going forward. Your goal should be to have wide involvement across your organization. This model can take many forms, but as a starting point it should include the Forecasting department, or the department responsible for generating the baseline and assimilating the Sales and Marketing information, as the chair of the meeting, and Senior executives from Sales, Marketing and Finance. Any other function that has a specific impact on the forecast numbers should also be included. In this meeting, the starting point can be the Forecaster's presentation of all pertinent information that led him or her to the ultimate recommendation.

During the consensus meeting all significant future plans that affect the baseline forecast should be reviewed and their implications discussed. The final output of the meeting should be a single number for the organization that all team members agree upon. Every one may not be in full agreement on each bit of information provided, but they agree to support the number that is established as the one-number forecast. This number should include all volume targets, "go-find" volumes, new products, visionary business direction and its impact, and any other information that may be specific to your organization.

Once the consensus forecast has been developed, it is fed downstream to other planning systems, and people throughout the organization. The forecasted demand turns into a production and/or distribution plan where the team can perform "what-if" analyses on the forecast. This can, and often does, raise footprint and capacity issues, technical capability issues, warehousing and distribution issues, and opportunities for increased cost-effectiveness. As soon as all issues are clearly identified with the forecast, sales and operations planning meeting should occur. In this meeting, the original consensus team, in addition to Supply Chain and operations functions, should review all the issues identified by the forecast. The team will determine the course of action. This action may be as simple as securing another warehouse in eighteen months to account for additional demand and the required inventory investment, to more complex action, which could be a recommendation to build another production facility in thirty-six months to meet the new demand for products.

At this point, the consensus forecast may be revised to account for timing issues and supply limitations (it takes forty-two months to build a new plant, so we need to delay the introduction of some new products). The new forecast is now ready to be dollarized. The demand should be dollarized based upon each product or service projected selling price. The operational forecast is dollarized in the form of conversion and distribution costs given the new product mix and estimates, capital investments needed to meet the demand, SG&A expenses to mirror new activity, purchasing estimates for long range contractual buying, etc. All of these estimates are assimilated into a strategic financial forecast that can be widely communicated to your stakeholders.

SUPPORT YOUR APPROPRIATE TOOLS

In order to support your process with the appropriate tools and measurement capabilities, you must first determine what is the right technology for your needs. Does your current system support a five-year planning horizon, if this is the length that your strategic plan requires? If you have not yet selected a tool, I would recommend reading "What Forecast Application is Right for You?" by Dr. Larry Lapide. Once you have selected a tool, you need to support that tool with the right data and data structure. Are you going to forecast true, unconstrained demand? If so, then you will need "untouched" orders from your customers, before the dates have been changed or modified to reflect your current supply issues. Are you going to use actual shipments? If only shipment data are available in your legacy systems, then you need to understand that it will be difficult for you to predict true, unconstrained demand, as that history is unavailable. If the data of unconstrained demand is really what you need, then you have to develop a plan to capture such data in your new system on an ongoing basis.

What other data do you need, besides internal demand history, to improve your forecast accuracy? The information available today is overwhelming. This can include POS syndicated data for your products and/or services, CPFR data (collaborative planning, forecasting and replenishment), VMI data (Vendor Managed Inventory), Global economic outlooks, Corporate earnings estimates, Demographic data and Revenue Management/Sales data. You can use this information effectively, but first ensure that you know how you can capture it, and why you are going after these data in the first place.

It is equally important to be clear on the structure of your data. You need to consider who your audience is. It is imperative to use a one-number approach for strategic planning with a capability to slice and dice the data against multiple dimensions to meet one's divergent audience's needs and expertise. A common product view, or hierarchy, for your data is necessary to provide a common point for a corporate roll-up. Sales looks at the business much differently than Marketing, and you, as a Forecaster, need to be able to communicate effectively to both functions. In addition to a product view, you must also have a common geographic view shared throughout your organization. Sales may be looking at a customer market/region area, while Supply Chain may be looking at a distribution center area. Finally, you must be able to meet your organization's needs on a time horizon. Does Supply Chain need the forecast in monthly buckets to determine capacity needs, while Finance needs only a yearly total? Make sure that you meet the minimum requirements of your audience.

Once you have developed your data structure and data set, it is imperative that you validate your information with your key stakeholders prior to using it. This will save many frustrating hours on the back-end once you discover that you need to go back to the drawing board. Remember, to be successful in leading a one-number forecasting process you must be all things to all people. You must be able to support inclusion in the process and consensus decision-making throughout your organization. Furthermore, make sure that you have a way to measure the accuracy of your forecast once developed. You should be routinely reporting this accuracy back to your consensus team because continuous improvement is part of the process. There are many benchmarking efforts available from the Institute of Business Forecasting, and articles in the Journal of Business Forecasting that will assist you in developing your specific measurement criteria and needs. Remember, the objective of measurements is to drive improvements in your process. Each business and each process is different, with different dynamics that drive demand and supply. Be sure to capture all necessary information to fit your organization's needs.

PROCESS WITH AN APPROPRIATE ORGANIZATIONAL INFRASTRUCTURE

The Forecasting function within many businesses reports to many functional areas, including Supply Chain, Sales Marketing and Finance. The one common characteristic, however, successful consensus forecasting organizations share is that their Forecasting personnel remain neutral and unbiased in the consensus process. One of the critical success factor for a consensus forecasting group is a strong leader or champion of the one-number process. This champion, along with

Forecasters, needs to possess a strong influence management skill. Forecasters should be able to get information from many different groups throughout the organization to build an accurate forecast. Each Forecaster should possess not only statistical/mathematical capability but also strong interpersonal and conflict resolution skill because he or she may be called upon any time during a consensus meeting.

RECOGNIZE AND OVERCOME THE CHANGE MANAGEMENT CHALLENGES

The change management factor is perhaps most critical to your success in moving your organization to a true one-number consensus forecast. The first question you should ask yourself is "what is in our current forecasting process that is not in our annual strategic business planning process?" and second, "what is in our annual business planning process that is not in our operational (short-term) forecasting process?" You need to test for dissatisfaction with the current process. If dissatisfaction is present around any part of the current process, you can begin to improve upon the process, make changes and drive benefits.

First, begin by reviewing the benefits of a one-number process with your senior executives. You need to enlist their support by being able to articulate the benefits that your organization will reap. You need to meet and work with each functional leader within your organization to understand the concerns of each of them about moving to a one-number strategic planning process. Their concerns may include the perceived loss of power in making long-range business decisions for their functional interests. Be empathetic to their concerns, and be able to reassure them that this is not a loss of power, but a stronger support network for their long-term plans. As you work with each of the team members, you should listen closely what they have to say and try to modify your proposed process or data set in light of their concerns. It is critical to remember that your role as a Forecaster is one of support.

Once you have engaged all of the consensus team members in the development of your process and data validation, you need to provide specific training and detailed plans for responsibilities, format, and timing of the interaction. This will ensure accountability.

You should always strive to create a climate of trust around your consensus process. Each team member needs to feel that his or her opinion mattered, and you will look closely the comments they have made. Remember, you can teach an old dog new tricks, but it takes twice as long and will require ten times more patience.

In the end, how does your organization win with a one-number consensus strategic plan that does not engage in a one-off, limited participation/ communication process that happens once a year? You increase involvement across the organization. Involvement creates commitment.

You increase communication – all actions are aligned with a consensus driven direction, thus increasing the likelihood of including all pertinent information. You identify problems with the strategic plan early in the game, and act proactively to head them off. You decrease the resource strain of a once-a-year event that causes many sleepless nights and weekends, and finally, you increase the "do-ability" of your plan. You avoid unachievable timelines and volume go-finds that are typically forced into a strategic plan.

REFERENCES

1. Chase, Charles. "Revenue Management: A Review." **Journal of Business Forecasting**. Spring 1999, pp. 2, 28-30.
2. Lapide, Larry. "What Forecast Application is Right for You?" **Journal of Business Forecasting.** Spring 1999, pp. 12-14.

CHAPTER 31

FORECASTING PROCESS AT CABLE AND WIRELESS BARTEL COMPANY

Gwenocia Chandler
CWBARTEL, Barbados

Cable & Wireless BARTEL Limited (CWBARTEL) was incorporated in the year 1903. It is a regulated organization with assets of Bds $231m (US $115.5m) as at the end of the financial period 1997. Expressed demand (connected mainlines plus requests in hand) for the same period was about 100,000 lines. The telephone system is totally digital and the network infrastructure is currently being upgraded from copper to fiber optic in some areas. This upgrade enables us to keep up with international standards. The company has received high praise in recent times for the level of service provided at international conferences held in this country. CWBARTEL, together with CWBET (The International Telecommunications Carrier), played a key role at the United Nations Global Conference held here in 1994. The most recently held Caricom Heads of Government conference attended by the President of the United States of America, Mr. Bill Clinton, saw BARTEL again excelling and meeting international standards.

The challenge for CWBARTEL, however, is not only to keep pace with technology. Our country's commitment to the informatics industry (data processing for international companies such as Airlines); the pending deregulation of Customer Premises Equipment and the introduction of the Internet have created new opportunities and threats in the market place. The need to respond quickly to change therefore is important. CWBARTEL has thus embarked on a structured approach to forecasting as a way of ascertaining and dealing with future challenges.

THE FORECAST SYSTEM

The forecasting system within CWBARTEL operates at three levels: (1) Corporate strategy level (2) Departmental level and (3) Marketing level.

Corporate Strategy Level

At this level forecasting is carried out by the Corporate Strategy Unit in consultation with the Chief Executive Officer and the Regional Business Office. These forecasts are in line with the mission and scope of the organization, as well as with the mission of the Cable and Wireless group of companies, which according to the vision statement is, *"To lead the world in integrated communications."*

Factors influencing this mission include the company's culture and resources, the environmental opportunities and threats provided by policies, regulations, and changing customer expectations. These forecasts are usually qualitative, using such techniques as Scenario and Delphi. Scenario technique refers to the construction of several set of circumstances that could arise in the future and which form the boundaries within which contingency planning can take place. Delphi technique, on the other hand, is based on panel members producing independent forecasts, but the final forecast is a distillation of the views of the entire group of participants. The outcome of this is to formulate specific objectives that are disseminated to the functional departments.

Departmental Level

Forecasts at this level are formulated with a view to meeting targets set at the corporate level, e.g., promoting growth and adding customer value while optimizing the use of resources. The forecasts seek to answer such questions as:

- What market segments should be targeted?
- What customers' needs CWBARTEL can satisfy?
- What level of infrastructural development should be undertaken?
- In which geographical areas and in what time frame should this take place?
- What level of resource deployment is necessary by each department, e.g., manpower and capital?
- What level of training is required?
- What teams need to be set up to accomplish these goals?
- At what level will these teams interact?

Forecasting at this level is both qualitative and quantitative. The outcome of this is to develop market strategy and formulate objectives that will guide activity at the product and service level (marketing level).

Marketing level

At this level, forecasting is mainly quantitative and seeks to answer questions such as:

- What is the demand for each specific product and service?
- What pricing strategy should be used?
- How can the customers' interest be stimulated?
- What are the competitive conditions in the market for each particular product or service?
- How can resource deployment be optimized for a given product or service?
- What is the return on investment for each product or service?
- At what phase are existing products in the product life cycle?

- Can further growth be stimulated and at what cost?
- What new products can be successfully launched?

In former years the process of forecasting was part of the departmental manager's (also decision maker) function with some input from consultants in specific areas. In recent times, the planning and forecasting functions have been separated. Market Research and Forecast department was set up to provide the necessary forecasting expertise and marketing information necessary for decision-making. With the advent of this new forecasting approach, the first decision-making system identified to be served was related to network infra-structural development. Given that, the basic telephone allows access to most telecommunication products and services, the subscriber demand for this service was identified as the forecast variable.

The need for a subscriber line demand forecast was paramount. Such a forecast enabled decision makers to determine how, when, where and in what quantities with respect to wire center capacity, and adequate distribution (by geographical area) of cable and line plant to capture demand at a source, subject to the budgetary and resource constrains of the company. This activity therefore identified and analyzed CWBARTEL's subscriber base and provided the foundation for revenue forecasting, sales forecasting, inventory forecasting, and resource allocation.

SUBSCRIBER LINE DEMAND FORECAST

Based mainly on the users' requirements it was decided that:

- The demand variable would be subdivided into residential and business line demand.
- This process would involve micro-forecasting and macro-forecasting methods.
- The macro-forecast would relate demand to some socio-economic factors using a causal model.
- The micro-forecast though intuitively related to factors in the environment should seek to provide spatial data necessary for network distribution and involve both qualitative and quantitative assessments.
- The output should be quantified where possible.
- The forecast horizons are: (1) A 'five year' demand forecast to determine the provisioning of plant on the exchange side, that is, distribution of cable plant between the exchange and the cabinet (an intermediary distribution point). (2) A 'twenty year' demand forecast to determine provisioning of plant on the distribution side, that is, the distribution of cable and line plant from the cabinet to the subscribers' premises.
- It was agreed that the building block for data acquisition was the development of a complete and accurate inventory of the network which currently existed.

THE CONCEPTUAL MODEL

In formulating the conceptual model, the factors identified as most likely to impact on the demand were:

- Population growth (POP)
- Housing starts (HS)

- Housing completions (HC)
- Tariff rates (TR)
- Technology (T)
- Probability of getting a line (PROB)
- Relative prices (RP)
- Industrial production (IP)
- Growth in retail sales (as it relates to new business establishment) (RS)
- Non-residential construction (NRC)
- Quality of service (Q)
- Long term disposable income (Y)

Symbolically the demand function for the two variables was given as follows:

Residential Demand => RD = f (POP, HS/HC, Y, RP, Q, PROB)
                                    +   +   + -   +   +

Business Demand   => BD = h (IP, RS, NRC, RP)
                                    +   +   +   -

(Where + and - signs under the variable indicate the direction of influence of a variable has on dependent variables, RD and BD; + sign indicates if an independent variable, say, POP increases, the dependant variable (RD) is likely to increase; and - sign indicates that if RP increases, RD is likely to decrease).

DATA AVAILABILITY

The availability of information for most of the variables identified above has been a problem. However, some of the sources identified were:

- Internal sources — Equipment and technological data
- Town and Country Planning — New developments, change in use of a building (e.g., a warehouse being converted to an office complex would increase line demand)
- Lands and Surveys — Planned land development
- Government Electrical Engineers office — Applications for electrical inspection of new residential and business tenancies
- The Central Bank of Barbados — Economic and financial statistics
- Ministry of Public Works, Transport and Housing — Housing statistics
- Barbados Water Authority — Water connections and zoning as it relates to land use
- Barbados Light and Power — Electrical connections
- Barbados Statistical Department — Demographic data
- Media (television, newspapers, official gazette, radio — Political, social and economic activities

In the initial stages, the forecasting methods were developed with the help of consultants such as Dr. Andrew Downes, who produced the first set of models for estimating the demand for applications for main telephone lines. Mr. Ron Head, a British consultant, assisted in the development of a framework for micro-forecasting. Over the years however persons such as the author have been trained in the techniques of forecasting and marketing research. Today this activity is mainly an in-house function. Software such as Forecast Pro, Econometric Views and SPSS Trends are used in the development of forecasting models.

MACRO-FORECAST MODELS

The models produced initially were based on techniques such as exponential smoothing, ARIMA (Box-Jenkins methodology) and regression. Of these, the linear exponential smoothing methods provided the "Best" forecast. The recent use of the Vector-Autoregression (VAR) technique in forecasting the demand for residential telephone mainlines have produced a model which seems likely to outperform the smoothing techniques.

MICRO-FORECASTING MODEL

A sectional forecasting technique was developed to provide the spatial information necessary for network planning. The island was subdivided into geographical blocks, called forecast sections. For each section, field surveys were undertaken to ascertain the existing level of residential and business tenancies — units irrespective of construct (e.g., wood and wall), or proposed (e.g., residential, business and recreational) which can reasonably be expected to give rise to a demand for telephone service.

This sectional forecasting approach consisted of the following procedures:

- The forecast sections were developed by grouping tenancies within a particular geographical location into homogenous groups determined by housing type (wood, wall or mixed); perceived income type (low, medium, upper, etc.), topography, level of urbanization, usage or function (with respect to businesses), etc. These sections were numbered.
- For each section a count was made of the number of existing residential and business tenancies, the number of vacant lots, buildings under construction or renovation. This information was recorded on photogrammetric maps acquired from Lands and Surveys.
- Data relating to the number of connected lines was collected internally and classified by distribution point (DP) and section. The classification was based on the address of the DP ascertained during the field surveys.
- The residential penetration factor for each section was computed as follows:

$$\text{Re sidential Penetration Factor} = \frac{\text{Number of existing residential lines}}{\text{Number of exisitng residential tenancies}}$$

- Residential sections with similar characteristics were compared and the highest penetration factor used as the short-term potential penetration of telephones for sections within the group.
- Business information listed included function, size, number of persons employed by the organization, connected lines and equipment data (collected internally). From this

information, profiles were developed and the highest penetration level for each category of business was used as the short-term standard for like businesses.

- In some cases where historical data existed, moving averages were used to predict short-term demand growth.
- Data relating to planned development was collected from sources such as building contractors, land developers and The Ministry of Housing, and used for preparing medium to long term forecasts. Other demographic data and information relating to the Government land use policy was also used in the forecast at this level.
- For sections where the information described above was not available, a growth percentage was determined through consultation with the sales department and other users.
- Generally, the forecasting of tenancy growth is based on Government's land use policy and the use of formulas obtained from Town and Country Planning relating to the subdivision of land in certain areas (e.g., one household per 4 acres of agricultural land).
- The exchange and thus the Country's forecast is built up from the sectional forecasts.

Forecasts built up in this manner are compared with the results of the macro-forecast and discrepancies noted with possible explanation. These two types of forecasts are done to complement each other.

JUDGEMENTAL INPUT

As noted before, information is collected from the immediate users and their judgements included in the forecast where necessary. This cooperation has resulted in improvements in forecasts produced, especially the sectional forecasts. In recent years, for example, inputs by the Engineering and Sales departments allowed us to capture the change of business lines demand from a POTS (Plain Old Telephone Service) to a COMNET (Communication Network) System.

The COMNET System requires the use of more mainlines and fewer extensions. According to the Sales Department, the initial requests of businesses switching to this system were equivalent to 110% of the existing level of POTS lines plus extensions. This new development created a level of mainline growth which bore no relationship to the historical data patterns and was in fact a reflection of technological change. If this information were not forthcoming from the sales department and were not used in the forecast, CWBARTEL would have made very inadequate provision for the equipment necessary to support this quantum leap in mainline demand.

IMPLEMENTATION AND MONITORING

Initially the output of the quantitative forecasts was challenged continually by the users. However, occurrences in the past have emphasized the benefits of these forecasts. The forecast errors at the business unit level (constituting connected mainlines and applications) for the past three years have been between 1% and 5%. Today the demand forecast is more widely accepted and is being used either as a point of reference or a variable in other forecasting models and activities such as:

- Sales forecasting and planning

- Revenue forecasting and planning
- Inventory forecasting and planning
- Manpower and other resource deployment planning

Over the years we have devised creative ways to present our information to the users. We present information in the form of geographical maps which give forecast by geographical block as well as other information such as Fault areas and pockets of known unsatisfied demand. The users can, therefore, compare, analyze and visualize the impact of proposed activity in any geographical area.

With the help of the Engineers and Finance personnel, we have structured models in a way that allow the users to perform "what if" scenarios. Such models help to determine the viability of a project either from a financial or socio-economic perspective.

CONCLUSION

CWBARTEL not only strives to embrace advanced telecommunications technology but also to improve all the processes, which help it to achieve its goal of 'total customer satisfaction.' This process is an uphill task, given its level of resources and the age and composition of its outside plant. Through the process of Marketing Research and Forecasting we have created a high degree of awareness, which will help us to overcome the pitfalls and embrace the opportunities.

PART VI

FORECASTING SYSTEM

INTRODUCTION

There are various issues to be resolved before setting up a forecasting system or updating the existing one. This section describes what those issues are and how they should be handled. The issues pertain to infrastructure (hardware, software, and connectware); data management (how to normalize historical data? how to slice and dice data? and where to archive forecasts and forecast errors?); forecast generation (how to adjust data for trading days? how to store and edit parameters used in each forecast model?); forecast adjustment (how forecasts are to be revised and updated?); forecast reporting; and decision support system (what to do if such and such happens?).

CHAPTER 32

THE KEY TO UNDERSTANDING THE FORECASTING SYSTEM

Gary S. LeVee
Information Advantage, Inc.

Forecasting, for most companies, is the central process from which Finance, Marketing, Sales, Logistics and Senior Management direct and coordinate their efforts. Over the past 15 years, I have had the opportunity to review and participate in the forecasting process and forecasting activities within various Fortune 500 companies. What I have discovered is that forecasting within most companies is a disaggregated function that results in key personnel directing themselves in an uncoordinated effort to achieve the company's sales and operating plan.

WHY FORECAST SALES

Recently, on a flight from New York to Chicago, I found myself sitting next to the Chairman of a large Fortune 500 consumer goods manufacturer. I questioned him regarding his company's greatest assets. One key asset he stressed was information. In asking him why information is of such great value, he said, "If I understand what has happened and why it has happened, I can then successfully predict what will happen. If I know where I am going and can affect that, my company will enjoy a significant competitive advantage." In discussing his company's effectiveness to create information from their huge data investment and realize the desired competitive advantage, he admitted their inability to accomplish this consistently.

The experience conveyed to me by this Fortune 500 Executive is not different from what I have discovered to be typical of most Fortune 500 companies. The question I continue to ponder is, "Why have the vast majority of forecasting systems implemented within various corporations over the last several years fallen short of providing the value and return on investment that was expected of them."

When I discuss forecasting with forecasting professionals, invariably the conversation focuses on the accuracy and capabilities of the forecasting techniques that they employ. They seem almost obsessed with what I have come to call "The Magic Model." Forecasting projects a picture in most peoples' minds similar to that illustrated in Figure 1. Figure 1 graphically displays actual demand, predicted demand (based on the utilized or chosen forecasting model) and residual values, which quantify the difference between actual and predicted demand. The end product of the graph is a forecast, which is generated based on the model utilized to calculate predicted demand (the historical forecast). I have seen dozens of forecasting models and systems that do an excellent job of predicting historical demand and create a future forecast accordingly. However, even with the variety of different forecasting techniques, and various computer technologies available today, for the most part, forecast error remains significant, and effective forecasting within major corporations is seldom realized. The result of these experiences raises questions regarding the real importance of the forecasting technique(s) and its contribution to establishing an effective sales forecasting system.

Most forecasting professionals agree that the goal of forecasting is to consistently predict future sales. This results in improved planning and more efficient utilization of corporate resources, including raw materials, production scheduling, logistics planning, inventory management, capital expenditures, promotion spending, and the overall budget requirements necessary to support the forecast. To accomplish this, most companies set out to develop a forecasting system consisting of three major components: a forecast algorithm(s), forecast data/database, and an easy to use system interface for generating the forecast. As depicted in Figure 2, to create a forecast, the end-user, generally through some graphical users interface, retrieves the required data from a forecasting database, streams the data through some forecasting algorithm(s) and then reports the data in both tabular as well as graphic format. The result is a graphic display similar to that illustrated in Figure 1. Following development of the system, a process of installation, testing, training, and phased system rollout is undertaken to support successful system implementation.

FORECAST ERROR IS SIGNIFICANT

Unfortunately, the results of this development and implementation efforts often do not significantly improve an organization's ability to accurately forecast and, most importantly, improve their planning activities. As displayed in Figure 3 and from my experience with several Fortune 500 companies, forecast error versus actual sales for a $100 million brand within a typical consumer goods organization averages 10 percent on an annual basis, 25 percent on a monthly basis, and 40 percent or more on a Distribution Center basis. However, organizations manufacture products on an item/SKU basis and the forecast error at the SKU level balloons to an average of 20 percent on an annual basis, 40 percent on a monthly basis and 50 percent or more at the Distribution Center level. Exacerbating this situation is the fact that the forecast error is consistently inconsistent, often varying from positive (under-estimation) values to negative (over-estimation) values.

Another question I continue to struggle with is, "Why are companies who have implemented a sales forecasting system, similar to that displayed in Figure 2, still not able to successfully affect the accurate, consistent prediction of future sales and ultimately improve planning for the corporation?"

When I query forecasting professionals as to why they are unable to accomplish their anticipated forecasting objectives, I experience a variety of answers. They generally can be grouped into two major categories, the first dealing with forecast accuracy. Probably the most common answer that I receive is that the statistical technique(s) available (The Magic Model) is not applicable to the company's particular products and marketplace. Second, they claim that the system does not have all the necessary features (i.e., forecasts are not generated at the appropriate level of detail), and/or the system needs to provide a bottom up as well as a top down forecasting capability. Next, they explain that the historical data is incomplete, inaccurate or not reflective of the current business environment. And, finally, comments such as the impact of special events (i.e., promotional activities) are not effectively factored into the forecast. While there are many others, these are some of the more common "lacks accuracy" issues.

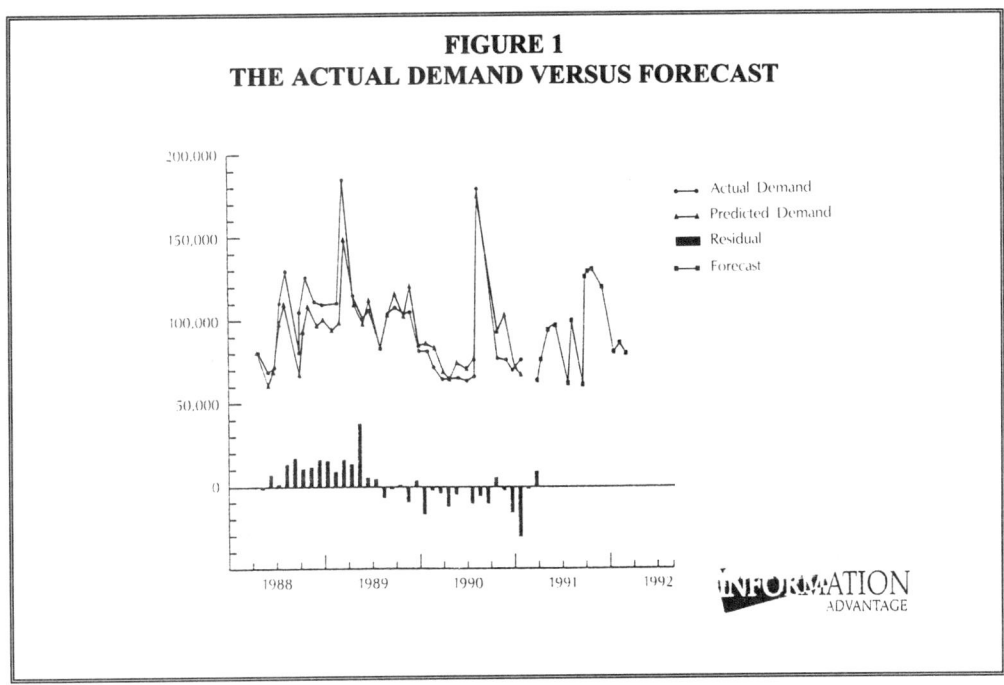

FIGURE 1
THE ACTUAL DEMAND VERSUS FORECAST

The second group of answers I receive can be summarized around the issue of system usability. Typically, I hear that the system, first, is not user friendly; second, is burdensome to use; third, requires significant manual input; and finally, is oriented towards a specific functional area (i.e., Marketing, Planning, and Finance.). While I must agree that any one of these particular issues can certainly contribute to the overall success or failure of a sales forecasting system, from my experience, I have found these problems to be the primary reasons for the inability of most companies to successfully forecast sales.

THE FORECASTING PROCESS

Forecasting is a process, which interacts with multiple business functions. As depicted in Figure 4, accurate and effective forecasts require information from Marketing, such as special events, pricing changes, and various other market factors. The Sales organization must provide competitive information and information about key account strategies and special event incentives. Finance must provide information regarding budgets, the amount available to support the forecasting function, the capital expenditures necessary to support the forecast and a series of other control measurements. And finally, Planning and Operations must provide information regarding raw materials availability, production scheduling, inventory management, and logistics planning. Forecasting in the 90's is a real time iterative process, which requires the interactive exchange of information on a continuing basis throughout the forecasting process. To realize the value and return on investment from implementing a sales forecasting system, the system must be developed and implemented in a manner that will support the corporation's sales forecasting process.

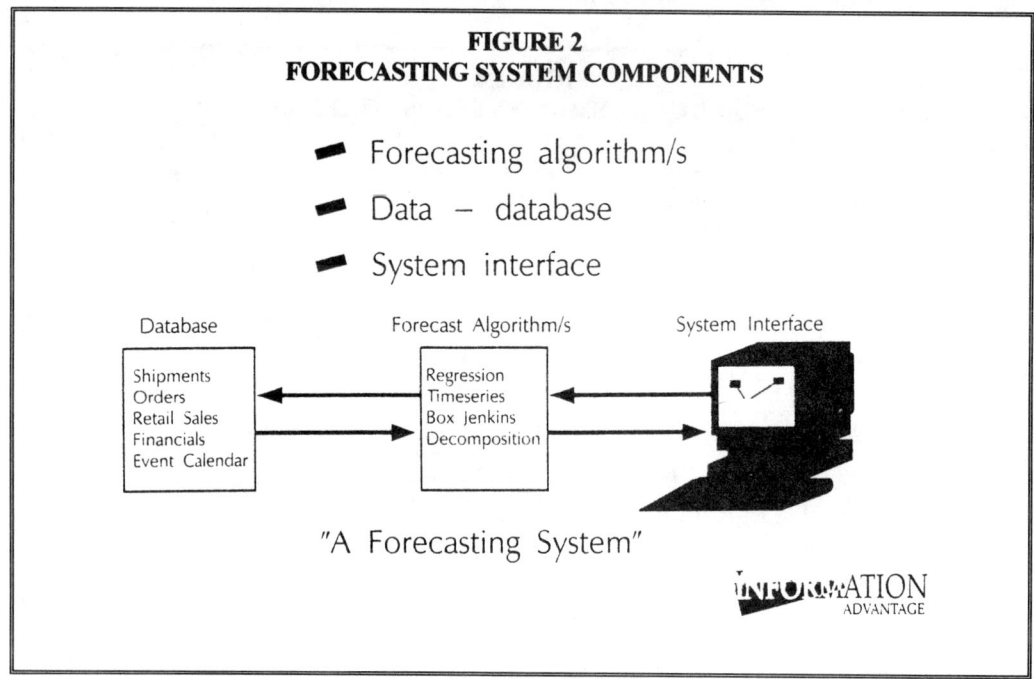

FIGURE 2
FORECASTING SYSTEM COMPONENTS

The typical forecasting process in most Fortune 500 companies today is one in which the forecasting system is isolated and only provides a supporting function. Typically, forecasting is the responsibility of Marketing, who creates a forecast utilizing a variety of manual and computer assisted procedures. If a formalized forecasting system exists, its data/reports are usually utilized as confirmation to support Marketing's forecast and assumptions. On a monthly basis, a forecast review meeting is held, generally with participants from Marketing, Sales, Forecasting, Planning and Finance. It is within this meeting that Marketing generally reviews their forecast and receives input from representatives of the other functional areas, eventually resulting in a consensus forecast. The forecast is then presented, usually in hard copy form, to Planning who manually inputs it into the MRP/DRP planning system.

FORECASTING PROCESS ISSUES

This type of forecasting process results in a variety of different forecasting issues for the corporation. In virtually every forecasting meeting that I have attended, the first 20 minutes are spent understanding/arguing over the data, its validity and its origin. Next, questions regarding the input of special knowledge/market factors, such as promotional activities and events, are discussed and questioned. Third, issues surrounding the forecasting technique or lack of formal techniques utilized are addressed. Because there exists no methodology for the communication and exchange of information between the different business functions prior to or after the meeting, each functional area enters the meeting with a different view of the forecast (future) based solely on their specific knowledge of particular factors. Further, different versions of the forecast, Marketing vs. Sales vs. Planning vs. the consensus forecast, are not saved, and therefore provide no database of information (foundation) for future evaluation and analysis. Finally, there is usually a lack of consistency in the methods utilized by different Marketing professionals. In conclusion, implementing a forecasting system that does not effectively support the forecasting process virtually ensures that the corporation will be unable to effectively and consistently achieve their forecasting objectives.

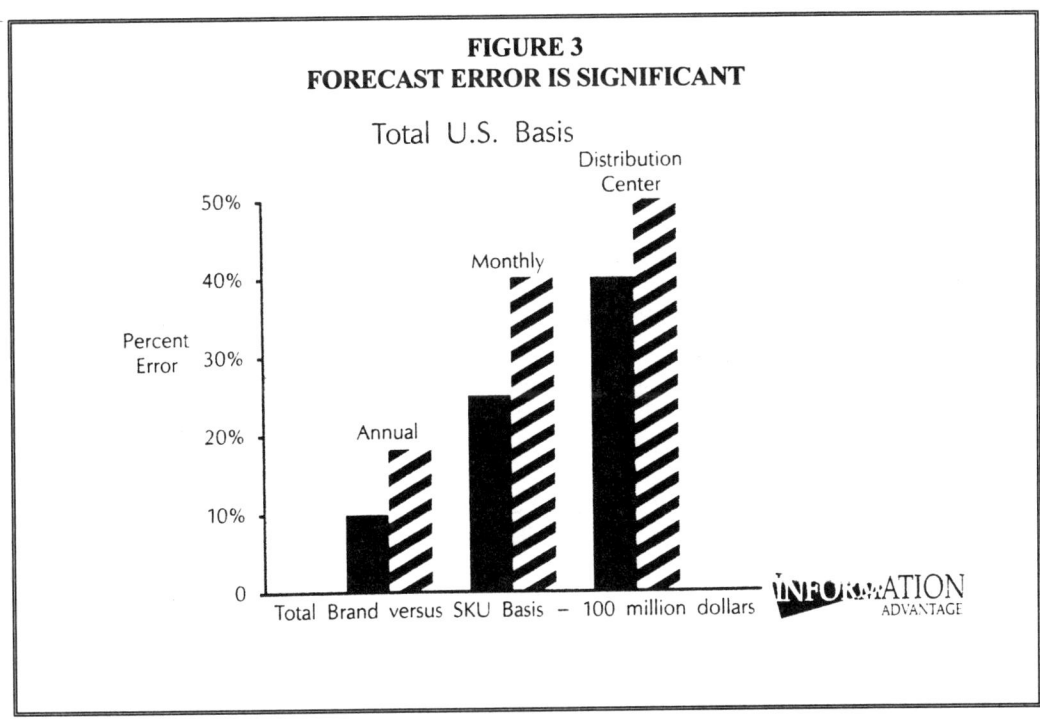

FIGURE 3
FORECAST ERROR IS SIGNIFICANT

A PLAN FOR SUCCESSFUL FORECASTING

It has been my experience that an organization must undergo a series of activities in order to ensure the development and implementation of an effective sales forecasting system. Those activities include:

- **System Analysis:** Identify and review problems and/or difficulties with the current forecasting system. A tremendous amount of information can be gained by studying current and past efforts pertaining to forecasting.
- **Data Analysis:** Identify and review availability of key forecasting data.
- **Process Analysis:** Study and review the current forecasting process, including specific roles and responsibilities.

- **Joint Application Design (JAD):** Define the forecasting objectives and the type of input and level of participation needed from the representatives of each functional area (Marketing, Sales, Planning, Forecasting and Finance).
- **System Administration:** Establish and agree on the forecasting process to utilize within the corporation and agree on specific roles and responsibilities of each functional area for each component of that process.
- **Phased Development/Implementation Plan:** Develop a detailed phased development and implementation plan that defines roles and responsibilities of each participant for each component of that plan. This will facilitate the integration of each system module into the forecasting process.
- **Management Approval:** Present the forecasting system implementation plan and expected dollar value. Then obtain management support from each company functional area.
- **Design By Prototype:** Utilize the information collected from the JAD process to prototype each component of the forecasting system. If a particular system component or components are already available, purchase those accordingly.
- **Demonstrate Prototype Components:** Install and demonstrate each prototype component for end-user evaluation prior to final implementation.
- **Installation:** Install and test each component thoroughly. Then, verify data/database for accuracy.
- **Training The Support Staff:** Provide detailed training for designated support staff.
- **Training The End User:** Provide customized training for each user group about each system component throughout the phased implementation process.
- **On-Going Training:** Plan and schedule on-going training for each end-user group and new end-users.

Companies that follow the approach outlined above will greatly enhance the sales forecasting system. The system will support the corporation's defined forecasting process and ultimately, provide the desired expected return on investment.

Following implementation, there is a continuing need to fine-tune the forecasting system and the forecasting process. This includes automating the system to report brand/SKU's that are performing above and below average and/or acceptable forecast levels, reviewing and evaluating the historical data, forecasting methods and "special events" factors utilized to produce the forecast, adjusting problem forecasts and providing new features and capabilities as needed. To enhance system usability, it is important to review the system interface with end-users and refine it when necessary. In addition, it is important to review the overall system integration into the forecasting process. Effective communication of forecast reports and data must be reviewed and modified as necessary. Roles/responsibilities of each participant with respect to changes and/or adjustments in the forecasting system must be understood and fully agreed upon. Finally, system response and timelines must be analyzed on a continuing basis.

THE VALUE OF FORECASTING

When I enter discussions with forecasting professionals regarding the many forecasting issues within their companies, inevitably one of the key issues we discuss centers on the value of sales forecasting. Often forecasting professionals share with me a level of frustration regarding the corporation's real support and commitment to forecasting. Forecasting and the forecasting function within major corporations often receive a lot of lip service from Senior Management. While everyone agrees on the importance of sales forecasting, especially with the advent of "Quick Response" and other new key customer forecasting demands, most Senior Executives will admit that forecasting is somewhat of an activity with which they have little or no exposure. This creates a certain level of discomfort and distrust for numbers, which are generated through a series of techniques or algorithms (The Black Box) they seldom understand. And quite frankly, the forecast represents a report card that few executives truly like to commit to. It is a scorecard that can quantify success or failure.

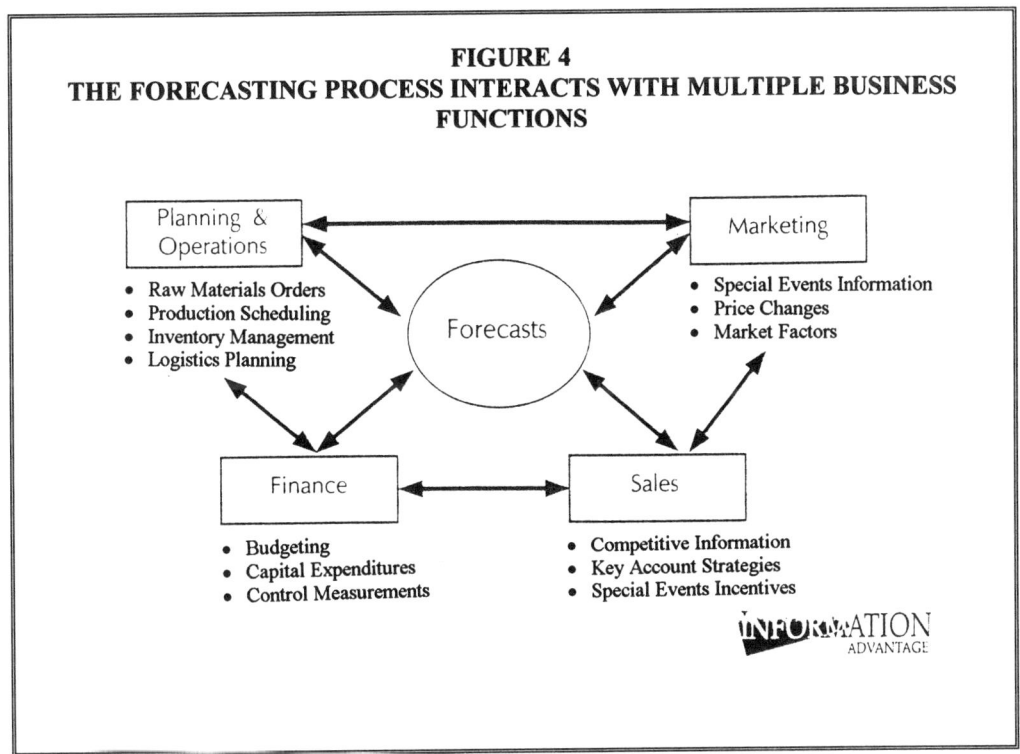

FIGURE 4
THE FORECASTING PROCESS INTERACTS WITH MULTIPLE BUSINESS FUNCTIONS

However, I am always astounded when I ask the question to forecasting professionals, "What is the value of sales forecasting to your organization?" and receive a variety of non-definitive answers. To set up an effective sales forecasting system and process within any organization, requires significant resources, both financial and personnel. It is absolutely unrealistic to expect Senior Management to support the forecasting process and the resource requirements necessary to accomplish effective forecasting if a definitive understanding of the value that will result from it is not completely understood.

Fortunately, companies that have implemented effective sales forecasting systems have experienced dollar savings totaling millions of dollars on an annual basis. These significant savings can result even from modest improvements in forecast accuracy and the planning process outlined earlier. For this reason, it is critical that Senior Management understands the true value of an effective forecasting process to receive the financial commitment necessary.

Further, it is imperative that Senior Management be educated, and has at least a general knowledge of the forecasting system and the process implemented. Knowledge of the process, together with an understanding of the value of forecasting, is essential to receive its fair share of corporate resources and support for the forecasting function.

FINAL COMMENTS

Over time, I have learned that for an effective forecasting process/system, it's imperative that people involved fully understand it. This process/system includes the direct use, input and exchange of key forecasting data, issues and plans among all participants and functional areas responsible for the creation and on-going maintenance of the forecast (Figure 4). Then and only then, the corporation will realize the full benefit that results from consistently accurate forecasts, improved planning, and more effective utilization of their corporate resources. Ultimately, as the Chairman of the Fortune 500 company I flew with recently stated, "Improved forecasting (knowing where you are going) is one of a company's greatest competitive advantages."

CHAPTER 33

CHOOSING THE RIGHT FORECASTING SOFTWARE AND SYSTEM

Alex Safavi
Emerchandise

With an increasing recognition of the forecasting function, more and more companies are searching for a forecasting software or system. In an effort to find the right software or system, the question often comes up what I should be looking at in making a selection, which is the topic of this article.

MULTI-DIMENSIONAL MODELING

Businesses often operate along at least three hierarchies: customer, geography and product. For example, a PC manufacturer can group its customers into two channels: direct and indirect. The direct channel includes selling directly to Corporate, Government and Educational clients. The indirect channel, on the other hand, includes selling to distributors and value-added-resellers. As such, a hierarchy can easily run into four to six levels. The business is becoming more and more dynamic. Every day new developments are occurring in different market segments. The business can respond quickly and effectively only if it can forecast these developments ahead of time. Consider two regions: Western and Eastern. The sales forecast of the Western region is usually lower than the Eastern region. If forecasts are tracked at the country level, the unique developments of each region will be overlooked. If you include suppliers, demographics and other dimensions in the model, you'll quickly run into six to eight business dimensions. Therefore, to determine and analyze the development in each dimension, the forecasting software/system must have a multidimensional modeling and forecasting capability. Furthermore, these dimensions are interconnected. Each combination of customer, geography and product identifies a unique market segment which needs to be forecast separately. The forecast that is uniquely created for each market segment reveals the emerging trends, thereby allowing a company to respond right away.

This is not the be all and end all of the multidimensional forecasting. Within each dimension, a hierarchical model is required to align the forecast that is generated by different teams at different levels of the organization. For example strategic planning tends to generate long-range forecasts at the region, product line and channel levels. Tactical planning, on the other hand, calls for short-term forecasts by product groups and territory. The question one has to ask is: "Does the software/system offer a flexible framework to model, forecast and reconcile the forecast of all the relevant market segments?"

SYSTEM FLEXIBILITY

Have you ever lost a customer? If you have, you need a system that enables you to update the information easily so that it reflects the change. On the other hand, if you gain a new customer you should be able to add to your system. Furthermore, the system should allow you to add or remove an exhaustive list of products and territories that correspond to a customer that you are adding or dropping. If the system does not have that kind of flexibility but you have hundreds of products sold in dozens of territories, you may wind up spending a good portion of your time in adding products, removing customers, and realigning territories and sales reps.

If a forecasting system is flexible and easy to maintain, it will be a snap to update the information. Data driven and configurable forecasting system enhances team productivity, lowers the cost of maintenance, and improves the responsiveness to business changes.

MULTIPLE DATA SOURCES

Access to relevant historical data is the key to generate accurate forecasts. It is not uncommon for the data to reside on multiple databases. Databases, documents and web sites, all serve as potential sources of forecasting input. Does the forecasting system provide an infrastructure to retrieve and manage data from a myriad of sources at the same time? Very often the data can change at the source without any advance notice. For example, a market research firm might publish a new report or a competitor might announce a new promotion on its web site. Does the forecasting software store a link to the data (as opposed to copying the data from the source)? Instead of physically copying a static view of the data, a good forecasting system maintains a separate link to each data source. The link can be executed at any time. Once executed, the forecasting system will retrieve and display the latest copy of the data.

UNIFIED WORKSPACE

How is the data presented to you after it has been retrieved from disparate data sources? A good forecasting system displays the series that have been retrieved on a single spreadsheet. The user can view and manipulate sales history as well as different versions of forecasts and promotion data without any need to go back and forth between different spreadsheets and user interfaces. The data can be displayed numerically as well as graphically.

COLLABORATION

The premise of collaboration is that more information, the better, because it leads to more accurate forecasts. This is equally true if you leave out some key people from the process. The people, who are not in the loop, will be less cooperative in providing input and have less respect for your forecast numbers. Furthermore, if each department works with its own forecasts, the overall alignment of the operations will be compromised.

There is no single right way to collaborate. Collaboration can manifest itself in different stages of the forecasting process and involve different departments. To achieve proper collaboration within your organization, you can begin by mapping how your team collaborates in the forecasting process in general, and in supporting the forecasting system in particular. Regardless of your specific collaboration needs, the following set of system functions and features can facilitate collaboration:

1. The system enables you to send and receive email from those who are involved in forecasting either as a user or as a developer
2. If it is not possible to meet frequently all the players in person, meeting on-line will bridge the gap. The system allows you to do that.
3. It allows you to view the information in a way it can be helpful to you. For example, you want to see the sales data in dollars, even though it has been entered in pounds. Furthermore, the system consolidates the information by customer or product group automatically.
4. It can annotate the numeric data. Very often a word about a number is worth much more than the number itself. If the system allows you to attach a picture, comments, or a link to a document to the forecast, your partner will be able to understand better why that figure is unusually large or small. Imagine that you choose not to change the forecast for November, but would like to make your partner aware of an event that might have an impact on the sales. You just attach a comment to the projected sales for November.
5. It enables you to create a discussion thread on a subject, such as how one new customer is expected to influence sales. The discussion thread enables the team to share opinions in a structured way. If you can attach the discussion to the forecast for November, the recipient does not have to spend a long time searching for that information which supports it.
6. Different team members may develop different forecasts for the same market. In that case, it will be better if you can observe the differences among different forecasts, as well as display them graphically in a single worksheet.
7. The system allows you to assign a set of rights to a forecast. One person may be allowed to just view the forecasts and other may be allowed to override it if necessary.
8. If your forecasting process is well structured, workflow design and automation support will facilitate the collaboration. For example, a well structured process can make it possible to send forecasts directly to the management for approval, and inform the appropriate stakeholders when an unexpected event requires the forecast to be reviewed and adjusted. If you have a formal sale and operations planning process, workflow automation can be used to enforce the process policies.

FORECAST RECONCILIATION

A myriad number of statistical methods are used to reconcile multiple sets of forecasts, including simple average, weighted average, and time-based and sequential adjustment. (For more information on this topic, see Larry Lapide's article in the Spring 2000 issue of Journal of

Business Forecasting.) You can ask the vendor to show how his/her software is used to reconcile demand forecasted by different models.

FORECAST ADJUSTMENT AND ALLOCATION

One of the challenges of the forecasting process is to aggregate forecast from different territories and business units, present the results to the management and then allocate the management adjusted aggregate forecast back to the same territories and business units. Allocation strategies vary primarily on the level at which the allocation starts and type of algorithm used. From a forecasting software standpoint, the following functions pertain to the allocation process:

1. Does the system start allocation from the middle of a hierarchy? Since there is generally too much noise at the SKU/Location level and promotions are offered at the territory level, it is better to forecast middle-out as opposed to either top-down or bottom-up. In that case, the allocation will also start from the middle of a hierarchy.
2. Does the system account for the interaction among different business hierarchies? If the system first allocates down the customer hierarchy and then down the geography hierarchy, it will overlook the fact that the dimensions are interconnected. Often the allocation algorithms that account for interaction are very tricky.
3. Does it support different business rules used to drive the allocation? Typical business rules include allocation based on: (a) the same period last year (b) moving average (c) and customer/product ratios.

Thus, the forecasting system should be such which can allocate the adjusted aggregate forecast at any level and across all the business hierarchies using different business rules.

DRIVERS OF THE DEMAND

If you plan to use the historical data to generate a forecast, it is critical to understand the drivers of demand in each market segment. The software should allow you to identify the drivers and then link them to the market. Furthermore, it should let you define each event and specify a quantitative model applicable to that event in a specific period, so that you can determine the effect of each driver on the demand. For example, a model may describe how a new product can be cannibalized over time by your existing products and what a competitor's promotion might do to your sales just when you are launching a new product.

The events can be best forecasted and utilized if the software represents each event independent of each other. This will allow you to simulate the outcome of a specific event in the future as well as the interaction between different events. If your business is dynamic, which is mostly the case, you'll need to manage tens, if not hundreds, of different events. Thus, the software should be such which not only identifies and deals with each event individually but also has a capability of dealing with a large number of events. The software should also be able to help in planning an event. For example, when a given promotion should be made in the future.

The software should allow you to control the occurrence of an event over time. For example, a back-to-school event might occur about the same time every year. If the software allows you to account for the occurrence of an event independent of other events, then you'll be able to understand why that event does not always have the same impact. An event, such as promotion, is likely to produce different results based on where and when it is offered.

If the software enables you to define and manage events independent of each other, then question arises whether or not it allows user-defined event models. If the business user has to call a consultant each time he/she needs to adjust the model, the modeling framework will be of limited use.

It will be a plus if the software can determine on its own when a given event was present or not. Unless the forecaster understands and agrees with the business logic used to identify when an event took place and how it interacted with other events, automatic detection and profiling of events would not work well.

Another benefit of modeling the key events is to determine how they might impact the future. It is usually not enough to know when an event took place in the past and when the same event will occur again in the future. It makes a difference if you know the circumstances in which an event occurred. For example, if a major promotion was launched when the weather was too cold for many shoppers, the results are tainted by the weather factor. So, the software needs to provide a framework to model not just the event but also the circumstances in which an event is likely to occur.

BASE-LINE DEMAND

Once you understand what drove the demand in the past, you will be in a position to calculate the base demand. Base-line demand is a measure of demand excluding events, data problems, etc. Just as the user-defined quantitative model can be used to project demand after events, a good forecasting systems will calculate the base-line demand by filtering out the events and data problems that have tainted the historical data.

STATISTICAL FORECASTING

Statistical forecasting is an unbiased way of generating base forecasts. To achieve the best results, one has to filter out all the noise from historical data prior to using any statistical model. Most statistical forecasting software automatically first find out sources of noise inherent in the data and then filter them out. This solution is adequate when there are few easily identifiable sources of noise. So, the best software is that which allows the user to first define independent events and then apply the event information to filter out the noise. The software should also be able identify trends and seasonality, and then account for them in the forecasts.

A variety of forecasting techniques have been developed to deal with different behaviors of demand. The models mostly used predict the behavior of a high volume mature product with a stable demand. New, slow moving, highly volatile and sporadically ordered products require special techniques. Dependencies and cannibalization among products complicate further the statistical forecasting. In that case, it is important to know whether the software offers a large variety of statistical techniques that can meet the forecasting needs of your business. Most forecasting software offer a built in technique, which automatically selects the best from a host of techniques.

NEW PRODUCTS

If you introduce new products frequently, you might need forecasting techniques that can work with little or no historical data. If the demand for a new product is expected to be similar to that of an existing product, the forecasting will be a simple matter. If the demand for a new product resembles the weighted average of certain existing products, the software should be able to handle it. Often a new product is launched in multiple markets. In that case, software should be able to disaggregate forecast into different levels — region, channel, etc.

LIFE CYCLE SUPPORT

The lifecycle of a product varies anywhere from 3 months to a lifetime. Forecasting products with a short lifecycle require the use of special techniques. The software can save you a great deal of time if it can forecast a product by the phase of the cycle it is in.

ANALYSIS

Analysis produces information that can improve forecasts. The best way to improve the quality of forecasts is to identify where the process fell apart in the past, and then try to fix it. Historical analysis highlights the forecasting errors. If your forecast has been consistently above or below the actuals, you may need to upgrade or dampen the forecasts depending on the situation. If the analysis reveals a significant error, but you fail to determine why, then you may have to reengineer the forecasting process and the techniques as well.

Historical analysis also helps to identify what worked best in the past. For example, your volume forecast might have been poor but your dollar forecast was accurate. The analysis may also reveal that the customer forecast was more accurate than the internal forecast. In sum, the forecasting software should enable you:

- To develop and manage forecast by volume, dollar, or any other format.
- To generate and maintain your own forecasts. Some departments and business partners may like to develop their own forecasts.
- To define a threshold, and flag it when the forecast error violates the threshold.
- To compute error by the error measure of your choice.
- To measure and report error by each market segment rather than as a whole.
- To graph the data in any way you want.
- To understand how sales is performing against its targets. If the actual sales are significantly below or above the forecast, there is a need for a quick response. For example, marketing is notified to deal with the poor demand.

In order to communicate and collaborate effectively, all the functions including sales, marketing and planning should use the same analysis software. The forecasting software is that which provides an analysis tool that meets the needs of all the functions.

INVOLVEMENT OF OTHER FUNCTIONS IN THE PROCESS

Most forecasting systems are developed for the use of a forecaster, yet best practices require the involvement of customers, sales, marketing and other business functions in the forecasting process. If sales and marketing do not understand how forecasts are prepared and are not directly involved in the process, they are less likely to trust and use the forecasts. You want to involve the customers because they know more about their business than you do. You want to involve the salespeople because they are the eyes and ears of the market. The forecasting system should support such a process. Furthermore, to have a true collaboration, the forecasting system should provide an easy-to-use framework that addresses the needs of all the business partners including customers, sales and marketing.

INTERNET ENABLED

It's very important to know whether the software under consideration is internet enabled. Internet means different things to different vendors. To some vendors, it is just a means of exchanging emails about the forecast.

My suggestion is to first identify what your business requirements are and then evaluate the software based on those requirements. Let me put it bluntly: if you do all the forecasting, rarely travel, all the historical data you need are on your desktop, and have access to email, then you probably don't need a software which is internet enabled.

Let us say that salespeople as well as your customers participate in the business forecasting process at your company. Then, unless they all are under one roof, you need the Internet as a medium to communicate and share information. Access to email is sufficient if the remote users do not need to interact with each other. The sales team can email you periodically its own forecasting spreadsheet. Where the sales and customers have to query the database and interact each other (e.g., what was your last month forecast, what comment did you make about a customer 3 months ago, and how many pieces were returned?), the email solution will fall apart. The user can't personalize and interact with static spreadsheets. Therefore, a full fledge browser based, user interface solution is required to involve sales and customers in the forecasting process. The software must provide a full-featured browser-based interface for analysis and forecasting.

INTEROPERATIBILITY

A forecasting system needs to support integration with a variety of other systems in an enterprise including Supply Chain and Customer Relation Management. If you already have implemented some of these systems in your organization, you might want to ask whether your forecasting software vendor offers the appropriate interface. If a functional interface is not available, the vendor has to do something about it.

To determine whether forecasting software can be integrated with other systems, use this simple test. Ask the vendor to select a subset of markets, and schedule the job of preparing forecasts at a designated time, and then put the results in a database such as Oracle or SQL Server. This test will show whether the software can automate the generation and transfer of forecasts to an open database. A similar test can be designed to validate linkage to a source database, access and display the sales history of a market. A business user should be able to develop and execute the link.

If your company adheres to 'best practices' of supply chain and customer relation management programs, the forecasting software needs to support them. Vendor Managed Inventory (VMI), Replenishment Program (CRP) and Collaborative Planning, Forecasting and Replenishment (CPFR) are some of the examples of these programs.

SCALABILITY

Scalability is a requirement that must be looked at in evaluating forecasting software. The number of forecasts that have to be made determine the scale. If you have 10 customer groupings, 1000 items and 100 locations across 12 periods, the software has to generate 12,000,000 forecasts. Forecasting at the retail store level and service part level can further explode the number. One has to make sure that the software can handle not only the current scale but also what you expect to be in the future.

GOLDEN RULES

Here are some of the golden rules one should keep in mind while evaluating a forecasting software/system.

1. Don't underestimate the need for a rich and flexible modeling framework. If the foundation is strong, you can add another story to the building. If the architecture is flexible, it can be configured to your specific needs. Otherwise, you will have to constantly work around the limitations of the software and spend your time on non-value added work.
2. Think long-term. Don't buy software just for the next twelve months. Ask whether the software is flexible enough to meet your evolving needs at least over the next thirty months.
3. Make sure that the software/system supports the entire forecasting process. Outline your present and future processes, and create a complete scenario around each process. Let each vendor show you how they will support the process.
4. Make certain that the software has a good analysis capability and can track forecast accuracy by market segment and by the user-defined error measure.
5. Maker sure that the software allows the user to adjust forecast results. The software should identify who the user is and only permits the user to adjust the forecast for a given product at a location.
6. The software/system involves and tailors to sales, customers and other business partners in the forecasting process.

CHAPTER 34

HOW TO CREATE AN ENTERPRISE FORECASTING SYSTEM

Anthony M. Power
SHL Systemhouse

The key application of forecasting is to monitor the health and welfare of a company. Requests for access to the forecast information increase throughout a company as managers want to understand the impact of potential courses of action. As a result, while their technical creation may reside in the hands of a few select professionals, forecasts are the property of everyone.

The development of any large scale application requires a procedure or methodology to ensure end-results meet the needs of the organization. This article discusses the forecasting process required to build an enterprise forecasting system.

FORECASTING PROCESS

To create an enterprise forecasting system four things are needed: First, understand the clients of the forecast — who are going to use it and what they expect to receive. Second, understand the users' requirements. Third, determine data availability. Fourth, evaluate the infrastructure in place, that is, what types of technology and/or systems are in use.

UNDERSTAND THE CLIENTS OF THE FORECAST

In most organizations, line business managers use the forecast as an input to the decision making process. Since forecasts affect the decisions in the entire organization, managers come from all functional areas — sales, marketing, finance, and operations. In addition, the need for forecasts is recognized by all levels of managers — from Assistant Brand Managers to Vice Presidents to CEOs.

From a system design perspective, this diversity of clients assures a range of computer literacy across the entire spectrum of skills. At one end, some users exhibit sufficient skills to create and write their own "programs." At the other end are those whose computer skills are summed in three words — ask somebody else. In between are the vast number of users who need to access corporate reports as well as create their own ad hoc templates.

Companies pay managers to solve problems. As a result, they rarely care about the tools and techniques used to create a forecast. They view the forecast as a guide in the decision making process. It provides a vehicle to play what if games with potential decisions. In order to use the forecast as a sounding board, users place several tacit requirements on a forecast.

First, managers require forecasts, which are robust. Robustness refers to the degree to which users need to think about the numbers. They generally do not like forecasts, which are laden with assumptions, especially technical ones. They do like forecasts, which include a potential range of outcomes and are consistent. Consistency is often more important than truth since most business decisions, particularly in marketing and sales, are based on relative changes over time, e.g. volume is up, flat, or down versus last year. Care should be taken in changing forecast techniques over time, especially between time series and causal models. Changing between techniques with different assumptions can produce sheer frustration among users because a better mousetrap (in terms of an enhanced model) may invalidate historic forecasts and decisions.

Second, users demand a forecasting system, which is flexible and easy to use. Clients of the forecast often define flexibility in terms of ad hoc aggregations, flexible time periods, etc. Easy to use means "standard reports," "works like my other applications," "simple to learn — no training or documentation," etc. This often represents a quandary for system developers — these demands are at the ends of a continuum. Often it is advisable to build different user interfaces for different groups of users.

Finally, users want forecasts that match with their beliefs. Forecasts generated in units or cases for operational purposes fail to meet the needs of other clients. For instance, marketing may make decisions more easily when forecasts are expressed in equivalized units, such as pounds. Sales and Finance often appreciate dollarized forecasts. These can be even further converted into either gross or net depending on their use in decision making. Enterprise forecast systems should provide a means to convert forecasts from the created basis to the reported basis.

Understanding the clients of the forecasts can be best accomplished by talking to them. Interviews or focus groups with a small number of potential users often bring out the real issues surrounding a forecast system. The attendees should be from the same level within the organization and from different functional areas. Here the first suggestion is to prevent senior managers from dominating the process. The second suggestion is to create a team approach to build a consensus forecast system. A common technique for eliciting core information is the use of structured questions. For example, "If you couldn't do (blank), what would you do?" or "When you present to your boss' boss, what do you want to say?"

UNDERSTAND THE USERS' REQUIREMENTS

Once the users of forecasts are identified, the next step is to understand what specifically they want from a forecasting system. Since forecasting rarely stands alone as an independent application in an enterprise, the requirements process may extend well beyond the original scope of the project. Companies often spend months in creating Request for Information (RFI) which detail the expectations for a forecasting system. As a word of warning, these documents (RFIs) often contain wish lists. It is important not to take them 100% literally. One should separate "must have" from "nice to have." The following outlines a composite Request for Information from a variety of manufacturers and retailers. It illustrates that enterprise forecasting system extends well beyond the black box envisioned by many managers. The forecasting system should consist of five main groups of functions revolving around users' activities. They are: System Administration, Data Management, Forecast Generation, Forecast Adjustment, and Reporting.

System Administration

This module governs the access to and visibility of forecasting data and activities as well as the administrative functions dealing with the release of forecast information. It consists of three sub-systems:

1. **Portfolio Management:** It clusters products into similar groups. Groupings are often based on how business decisions are made about such things as promotion and manufacturing.
2. **User Control and Access:** It assigns users to groups and defines what elements these groups can access. Users may like to have access to items beyond those in the group.
3. **Forecast Groups:** It maps products and markets to a series of mutually exclusive and exhaustive groups. In forecasting, each product market combination must be accounted for once and only once. Putting a product or market in two forecast groups would overstate the volume by double counting. Failure to include a product would understate the forecast.

Data Management

This module provides the capability to prepare and manage the forecast data. The first two sub-systems are normally done infrequently once the system is set up. The remaining activities happen every forecast cycle.

1. **History Normalization:** This sub-system allows historic data to be massaged for the purposes of forecasting. This includes smoothing and the removal of outliers.
2. **Product Join**: This provides a mechanism for merging products or discontinuing products.
3. **Archive Forecast:** This stores a particular forecast cycle for use in computing error.
4. **Forecast Error:** This generates in a batch process the forecast errors based on actual and archived forecasts and develops MAD, MAPE, and range of error over time. Variance should be derived by forecast version and type. It also computes safety stock based on forecast error, and supports both forecast and budgeting variance calculations.
5. **Copy Versions:** At the start of each month, it creates versions of the forecast for each functional area — Marketing, Sales, Operations — by copying the statistical forecast to their work area. Changes are applied to these copies of the statistical forecast. Thus, accuracy can be reported for both computer-generated forecast as well as those with management judgment applied.
6. **Create Report Data:** This creates a fully populated table for reporting. Thus, while the forecast may be created at one level in the product hierarchy, this module allows forecasts to be created at any level — from SKU to Total Manufacturer.
7. **Outload:** This sub-system moves and formats consensus forecasts for use in other applications, e.g. for DRP and MPS. It also provides Annual Budget conversions into pounds, units, net and gross dollars, and standard costs.

Forecast Generation

This module deals with the actual creation of a forecast. Five sub-systems are required to deliver the required functionality.

1. **Trading Days:** This sub-system adjusts the data stream based on the number of business days in a period.
2. **Seasonality:** This deseasonalizes the data; stores both the indexes and values; handles moving holidays, e.g. Easter; and adds category specific holidays, such as Halloween for candy or Super Bowl for beer and salty snacks.
3. **Baseline:** This smoothes the data and stores both the indexes and values.
4. **Forecast Engine:** This deals with the actual forecast creation. Time series performs a tournament for various techniques. Among the causal models regression is used to create a predictive model of the volume.
5. **Model Parameters:** It stores and provides edit capabilities for the parameters used in each model.

Forecast Adjustment

This module allows the user to manipulate the forecast and adjust the mixes used in preparing forecasts at various levels in the hierarchy.

1. **Adjust Mixes:** These are the splits that allocate or prorate volume across members of the set. They can be for any dimension, e.g. for period, product, or market.
2. **Adjust Cannibalization:** This provides a means to assign source of business for a new product as well for existing ones. It addresses both the target product issue as well as the time duration.
3. **Adjust Growth Rates:** This allows the users to manipulate the expected growth rate for each product over the forecast horizon.
4. **Adjust Forecast:** This enables the users to apply their expertise and override a forecast. Changes are spread throughout the data to maintain integrity in aggregate values. It provides the capability to capture the users' comments which are stored with the forecast. Reviewers of the forecast need to know which numbers were changed, why they were changed, and by whom.
5. **Maintain Event Grid:** This updates promotion grid for use in regression models; and allows users to create "What if" scenarios.
6. **Maintain Price Grid:** This provides conversion from a volume measure, such as units, to a dollar measure. Time phased pricing allows users to adjust prices across the forecast horizon. Thus the financial impact of a price increase can be simulated.

Reporting

These modules provide access to standard reports and ad hoc query capabilities:

1. **View Statistical Forecast**: Standard forecast reports.

2. **Standard Reports:** This accesses standard report templates for the display of common reports using both forecast and actual information.

3. **Ad Hoc Analysis:** This accesses an ad hoc tool for the creation of custom templates and reports; integrates forecast data with the data warehouse for decision support; and provides capability to report the forecast at any level of the hierarchy. Examples might include:

Time Periods:	Fiscal and Calendar Year
	Weekly, Monthly, and Quarters
	Match to Sales Compensation Periods
Item:	Category
	Segment
	Brand
	SKU
	Distribution mode
Class of Trade:	Division
	Region
	Account

Understanding the user requirements can be best accomplished by working as a team with the end-user community. Many companies create a bridge position between software engineers and end-users, thereby combining skills from both information services and business. This provides a link between desires and deliverables. The purpose is to assure that expectations on both sides are managed. One successful tactic is to use iterative prototypes to get feedback. This provides a solution to the age old problem that users cannot fully specify the application on a priori basis. Finally, software engineers should participate in at least one forecast cycle to understand better the process and the feedback loop.

DETERMINE DATA AVAILABILITY

The third step in building a forecasting system requires documenting the availability of the data to be used. Historically systems have been developed to handle business transactions. As a result they are for fast retrieval and updating of single records. Forecasting represents a key application that views data from another perspective — large quantities of data are reduced to key information. To handle the new requirements of decision support, companies create a data warehouse. Data warehouses store the operational, historical, and syndicated data for the specific purpose of feeding decision support applications. Decision support represents the coordinated collection of data, systems, and tools by which an organization turns data into a basis for action. The four basic decision support applications are:

1. **Reporting:** The distribution of corporate reports to answer the How's business questions.
2. **Analysis:** Ad hoc query tools for answering the Why or how come questions?
3. **Forecast:** Quantifies the 'What if' questions.
4. **Budget:** Defines the financial impact of the proposed action.

The data warehouse for forecasting consists of a variety of information sources throughout the organization. Sales history may contain both orders and shipments. Marketing often supplies promotion and other event calendars as well as any changes in price. Finance provides standard costs and rates as well as the conversion factors for converting data from one basis to another. Finally, syndicated data for industries, lucky enough to have it, offer insight into competitive sales and in-market merchandising. Data warehouses contain vast quantities of information. The following two examples illustrate representative data warehouses for decision support.

1. **Retailer:**   600 stores, 120,000 SKUs, 135 time periods — 108 gigabytes
2. **Manufacturer:** 1,500 accounts, 4,000 SKUs, 76 time periods — 12 gigabytes

The growth in data continues. By the end of the decade it is not unreasonable to encounter data warehouses with terabytes or pentabytes of data. Those working in the area on multi-media applications are concerned that the speed of light may not be fast enough to distribute this quantity of data across current network technology.

Understanding what is available requires a data audit. This process documents the elements available to users. It includes the data source, any changes or transformations, and frequency of update. Ideally, this information should be on line so that the users have access to it at all times. For forecasting, a map should be created which links the source transaction data to that used by the application. This includes extraction, scaling, and projection or coverage routines. Finally, test, test, test. From a quality perspective, the data are what they should be. From a performance perspective, the data are available when needed. Both of these benchmarks assure that user expectations are met or at a minimum managed.

EVALUATE THE INFRASTRUCTURE

The final step is to understand the technological environment that forecasting will use. The New Computer is here. It represents hardware, software and connectware in which the company has invested in. In most companies there exist standards for technology purchases, that is, what types of machines they can buy or cannot buy. Unfortunately these standards tend to be departmental and ephemeral. The changing infrastructure presents unique challenges for the designers of enterprise application systems.

A proto-typical environment might look something like this:

> Historical data in SYBASE.
> Syndicated data in Red Brick.
> Financial information in Oracle.
> Marketing uses Windows.
> Finance uses Macintoshes.
> Sales use laptops with remote access.
> Manufacturing uses UNIX workstations.

The infrastructure is most easily understood by drawing a picture. It should include hardware, software, and network information. In order to provide the most value it should contain model numbers, version numbers, etc. The most difficult thing is to provide the discipline for keeping the map up to date. In the end, for a successful enterprise forecasting system, it must deal with four unique issues, which are: (1) Large number of users with different skills and expectations; (2)

complex application logic; (3) vast quantities of data; and (4) heterogeneous technology environment.

CHAPTER 35

ARCHITECTURE OF THE ENTERPRISE FORECASTING SYSTEM

Anthony M. Power
SHL Systemhouse, Inc.

The chapter before it describes an enterprise forecasting system from a functional point of view. This chapter turns our attention to the technical side, that is, how to build such a system. Before developing the architecture of an enterprise forecasting system, one must first get a handle on the different parts of an application. Decision support applications consist of three main parts, which are:

1. Presentation or control layer
2. Business rules and application logic
3. Database

PRESENTATION OR CONTROL LAYER

The presentation (control) layer collects the choices made by the user and displays the desired results. For instance, a user may want to see the forecasts of a particular group of products as well as their prices, displayed in a worksheet. Alternatively, he or she may wish to view forecast error by geography on a map. The impressions and judgments users make about an application come solely from this layer. They care about the "what," not the "how." An analogy from everyday life illustrates this point. The light switch possesses the characteristics of an ideal user interface — instantaneous, predictable, easy to use, and requires no documentation. Users do not care how the electricity is generated — coal, hydro, or nuclear — but how they can use it to solve a problem — illumination. The earlier chapter outlined various functions in a forecasting system, e.g. system administration, data management, and forecast generation. Developers should build interfaces around the expectations of each work group. Each group will have requirements of their own. The reporting aspect of forecasting represents the biggest challenge for designers.

Some guidelines include:

1. Go over the prototypes a number of times with the users.

2. Present the interface in the language of users.
3. Be ready for constant change.

Given the wide variety of people who need access to the forecast, the goal is to support different skill sets with the same information. A strategy of isolating the business logic and data warehouse from the interface achieves this goal.

BUSINESS RULES AND APPLICATION LOGIC

The second layer of an application (business rules and logic), processes user requests, and transforms the raw data into information. With the large amount of data being processed by forecasting systems, in megabytes if not in gigabytes, the selection of the tools and location for this part of the application becomes paramount for performance reasons. Forecasting requires a significant amount of number crunching because the business rules are enormous — consider the forecast engine which produces information, often through a round robin tournament approach. In the round robin the same data are subjected to multiple forecasting techniques, e.g. naive extrapolation, single- double- or triple exponential smoothing and s-curve, in order to reduce forecast error. As a result, forecast tournaments multiply the actual workload on the computer often by a large factor. This section discusses some of the advances in system architecture that benefit forecasting and enterprise decision support.

Traditional 2 Tier Client Server Architecture

Client server architecture has evolved over the past two decades. In the beginning, there were mainframes. All the work was done on the "big iron." While the mainframe was appropriate for transaction systems, it proved inflexible and expensive for decision support applications such as forecasting. Mainframes are very good at doing high volumes of repetitive and structured tasks — order entry, general ledger, etc. Dynamic or ad hoc activities like decision support do not work as well in this environment because of their lack of predictability. Given the large capital outlay for mainframes, costs need to be spread over a vast number of transactions. Operational systems produce millions of activities required to reduce the per transaction cost. Decision support consists of relatively few queries, which raise per query cost to prohibitive levels. To overcome these problems, departmental computing introduced the file server architecture, which enabled MIS (Management Information Systems) to move data files from the repository to the workstation where they could be processed by the user. The use of a file server and a workstation created a 2-tier system. This early 2-tier system also ran into problems due to the rapid increase in data. It simply could not keep up with the demands of users. The problem of data explosion was overcome at first by the introduction of client server systems. In this architecture, small extracts are performed, processed, and delivered to the user rather than trying to move the whole file. This divide and conquer approach allows the workload to be distributed between various machines. In forecasting, client server provides the ability to retrieve sales history for the products of interest rather than the entire sales history file.

Like any system design, 2-tier client server rests on a set of assumptions. First, there is no explicit way to standardize business logic across the enterprise — as a result end users become end doers. This class of application often delivers data extracts to spreadsheets or other personal productivity tools where forecasts are created. Unfortunately, end users are rarely trained programmers. As a result, undocumented and untested forecast 'programs' abound. This creates meetings where people argue over who has the right number rather than discuss business issues. Forecasting and budgeting applications simply cannot allow this situation to exist.

The 2-tier solutions often assume that decision support is a one way street, i.e. a read only environment. This attitude grew out of the mind set that users should never update operational systems. Companies have generally been good in providing data to users but they have been much poorer in retrieving the user information or decisions made based on the information. This antiquated attitude is shifting with the advent of data warehouses where some update capability is seen as an advantage. The lack of write capability would be a fatal limitation for forecasting where management overrides are a critical part of the process.

The assumptions of the 2-tier client server architecture pose severe limitations for large scale decision support applications such as forecasting. First, how do you manage the Mongolian horde? This issue deals with access and security, from a system point of view for a large number of users. Since different users have different computer skills, it becomes a real problem if business logic ties to the user interface. Second, how do you do two things at once? A 2-tier solution forces the users to "wait for completion" while the job executes. For forecasting, this can take a considerable amount of time for some modules, e.g. forecast generation and override update. Finally, how do we meet management expectations? Management often views system development as a silver bullet that will provide solutions even for difficult process issues.

The 2-tier architecture provides an excellent data transport mechanism. However, it is rare to assume that the answers are in the data as they are stored — they can't be in forecasting since the future hasn't occurred yet. If the goal is simple extraction of simple numbers then 2-tier solutions suffice. However, if the goal is something more than that, then another route must be taken.

3 Tier Client Server Architecture

To overcome the limitations of the 2-tier solution, one can add an application server as the middle tier. The application server sits between the client workstations and the database server to provide the following features:

1. Security and visibility controls which are not built into PCs or databases. Here it assigns responsibility to specific individuals for accessing data from a central repository and preparing forecasts.
2. Background services for scheduling, queuing, and processing of complex application logic. In forecasting, batch processing the standard reports or applying management overrides up and down the product hierarchy frees users to continue their work.
3. Making available substantially more CPU power by minimizing network traffic of vast quantities of data (reduce wait states due to I/O). In forecasting this reduces the time required to create a plan which lets users work through more alternative scenarios.
4. A centralized application engine to which different databases and user interfaces can be attached. For example, sales history can be in one place and prices in another. Also, different

presentation layers can be built for senior managers and analysts — each tailored to their needs but using the same components.

5. Application deployment is simplified because the code is managed centrally. This minimizes the need to upgrade every PC to a common denominator to run forecasting.

6. Application access can be made from a variety of client workstations. This assures that the answer to a question is the same whether it is asked from a Windows, Macintosh, or OS/2 interface.

7. Application development is simplified because the server provides a suitable platform for assembling an integrated suite of applications. The goal of many companies is to integrate forecasting with the planning and budgeting processes. Thus, when the forecast is changed the budget is automatically updated.

At present, the application server is fast becoming a standard for a large scale decision support system. Both Microsoft and Novell have announced support and products for the application server. Hardware vendors position their mid-range machines for use as application servers. Information Advantage has been building advanced decision support applications such as forecasting for four years. Though not for forecasting products per se, both Micro-strategy and Stanford Technology Group provide decision support tools in a 3-tier architecture.

Component Software

Another major advance in the technology arena is the emergence of component software. Large systems such as forecasting reap the benefits of modularity, code reuse, and shortened development time. These are accomplished through the encapsulation of business logic into objects than can be linked together to mirror business processes. Component software offers the benefits of faster deployment, higher quality, and lower costs. For an introduction to object technology, the interested reader is referred to *Object Oriented Technology - a Manager's Guide* by David Taylor.

The application server and object technology provides a means to build a world class forecasting system. The remaining part of the triad is the data warehouse. The last section discusses some of the issues associated with designing databases for decision support and forecasting.

DATA WAREHOUSE

The data warehouse fills the final hole in the puzzle. Decision Support, and forecasting in particular, requires a data store separate and distinct from the operational side of the business. Adapted from Software Magazine, the following table highlights the key differences between operational systems and decision support. The last column in the table shows how forecasting fits between the two classes of systems. The design of a good forecast system will take components from each domain. As a result, the team should consist of individuals with skills from both arenas.

As Table 1 illustrates, the data warehouse for forecasting blends operational aspects with those of decision support. Historically, two approaches have been used for database design. Operational or transaction systems (OLTP) use Entity/ Relationship (E/R) modeling to define the data structures and flow. The goal is to remove as much redundancy in the data as possible. This improves response time for static applications by eliminating the overhead associated with duplicate data. On the other hand, dimensional modeling supports the needs of decision support system (DSS) — dynamic and ad hoc queries. This approach depicts the data in a way that mimics the business — products, markets, time periods, etc. This format allows users to navigate through the data much faster.

TABLE 1 **OPERATIONAL SYSTEMS VS. DECISION SUPPORT**			
Topic/Function	**Operational Systems**	**Decision Support**	**Forecasting**
What Data are Stored	Current data	Historic, Summarized	History and Future
Data Organization	By Application - G/L, Order Entry	By Subject Area – Sales, Finance	By Subject Area and Application
Nature of Data	Dynamic – always changing	Static – history is fixed	Mixed mode - history is fixed, future is dynamic
Data Update	Update continuously	No updates allowed	Update certain data
How Data is Used	Structured and repetitive	Unstructured and analytical	All types
User Response Time	Fast	Medium	Medium

As noted above, forecasting possesses attributes of both operational systems and decision support. As a result, the data design should blend the two. For instance, a bridge from English descriptions (DSS) to manufacturing codes (OLTP) will be needed if forecasting is going to feed DRP/MRP systems. Another blending occurs in the access and control aspects of forecasting. OLTP systems have much more structured access than decision support. Forecasting needs the control of OLTP, e.g. each item is forecast once and only once, and the flexibility of DSS. An example of flexibility can be seen in the following two questions: What items have a forecast variance of more than 10%? What markets are expected to have surplus stock for Product XYZ? In the first case, the system must poll every item to determine the answer. In the second, all markets will be searched for the answer.

The data warehouse is most often built in a relational database management system. Relational database store data according to the association between various attributes. For instance an SKU number might have links to Brand, Vendor, and Category information. These associations, or relationships, provide a high degree of flexibility in application design. The relational database technology is at the heart of client server and is quite adequate for forecasting. Starting from a sales reporting system consisting of sales history and reference tables describing the contents, one can add the required elements and tables for forecasting. In addition to the sales history, the additional tables required by forecasting include:

1. **Forecasts:** The results of the statistical and override process. Full-featured systems store forecasts by version as well as the base forecast. This allows 'best case' scenarios to be plotted against 'most likely' and 'worse case' estimates.
2. **Archives:** Error computation requires the saving of previous forecast cycles because one needs to wait until actual sales come in. When done on a leading basis, e.g. computing error for April based on the forecast made in January, archives are essential for multiple periods. This method of computing forecast error accounts for the lead-time required by the decisions

being made, e.g. packaging, distribution and material sourcing. The window may range from 4 to 12 weeks for common items and up to a year for specialty technical items.

3. **Price Files:** The conversion of forecasts to dollars, or any other currency, requires a stream of prices or exchange rates to be stored as a vector over time. Not only can past dollarized forecasts be generated, but users can assess the financial impact of alternative pricing scenarios — aggressive versus conservative — by manipulating future prices.

4. **Event Calendar:** In consumer packaged goods and retail segments marketing, activities often whipsaw the production and shipment schedule. A good way to anticipate the peaks and valleys, as well as incorporate them into the forecast, is to integrate this data with the forecast data.

5. **Forecast Groups:** This information assigns certain products to a specific group for forecasting.

6. **Security:** The final set of tables defines visibility and edit capabilities to forecast groups by individual user. Visibility controls not only who can view the forecast but also what part of the forecast, e.g. specific brands or markets. Edit tables define the override privileges by forecast group. Thus, it is possible to see the forecast but not to change it. These provide a modicum of control to an often chaotic environment.

Once built, the data warehouse administers and manages the access, and performs maintenance and periodic update activities for forecasting information. Given the importance of these topics, commercial database management systems should be employed.

The user interface, application logic, and data warehouse provide the foundations for a corporate forecasting system. When designed and put together well, not only do they serve the forecast community but also form the foundation for a good enterprise information system.

CHAPTER 36

UPDATING YOUR FORECASTING SYSTEM: WISCONSIN TISSUE'S EXPERIENCE

Shahbaz Alibaig
Wisconsin Tissue

Bryan Lilly
University of Wisconsin Oshkosh

How should you evaluate your forecasting system to make corrective changes? Wisconsin Tissue implemented a formal forecasting system in 1997 and set forth specific objectives which were to be achieved. During the early part of 1999, Wisconsin Tissue evaluated its forecasting system and identified certain corrective actions for further enhancement, which are: (1) know your company, (2) articulate your specific forecasting goals, (3) assess the current forecasting system, (4) identify weaknesses in the forecasting system, and (5) list and prioritize corrective actions

KNOW YOUR COMPANY

Similar to an archeologist studying how a civilization is evolved, the first step in evaluating and revising your forecasting procedure involves unearthing some company footprints. Company footprints or history provide key insights that will help you build and/or enhance the forecasting system. For example, how does the company compete, and to what extent is forecasting an integral part of the company's competitiveness? Wisconsin Tissue is a leading manufacturer in the away-from-home tissue market, a mature market in the paper industry. Wisconsin Tissue designs, manufactures, and sells napkins, placemats, paper towels, bath and facial tissue, and other tissue products to a wide range of business customers such as restaurants, eldercare facilities, hospitals, and convenience stores.

Wisconsin Tissue's need for forecasting grew with its size and diversification. For example, during 1995 Wisconsin Tissue acquired plants in Arizona, New York, and Chicago. In 1996, Wisconsin Tissue entered the international arena when it opened its first facility in Mexico. Today, Wisconsin Tissue also sells its products in Canada. During the time of this growth, Wisconsin Tissue senior management envisioned having a competitive edge over other companies because of its customer focus, emphasis on manufacturing efficiency, and strong use of technology. For example, Wisconsin Tissue has embraced the technology of EDI (Electronic Data Interchange) and VMI (Vendor Managed Inventory). Over 100 Wisconsin Tissue customers currently do business with Wisconsin Tissue through electronic commerce. Because forecasting is part of Wisconsin Tissue's technology architecture, the ability to use the forecasting system is recognized as being strategically important, suggesting that the most beneficial forecasting changes may involve issues well beyond data analysis.

After assessing general company information, understanding technical issues behind how and why the current forecasting system was developed are also important. How does the current forecasting system work, what is forecasted, and what objectives prompted the development of the current forecasting system (perhaps specific objectives not even articulated)?

Wisconsin Tissue started a formal forecasting process in early 1997. Prior to 1997, Wisconsin Tissue did not have a structured forecasting system. To create a formalized forecasting process, a forecasting manager was hired. This forecasting manager reports directly to the director of marketing, and hence the flow of information is funneled through marketing. In 1998, a cross-functional forecasting consensus team was created. The role of this team is to review and approve forecasts. Additionally, this team facilitates information sharing to non-marketing departments. "The philosophy used at Wisconsin Tissue is to use the forecasting tool as a method to provide feedback to various departments in the company," according to Bob Harrington, CFO, Wisconsin Tissue.

Wisconsin Tissue conducts sales forecast on a monthly basis because its Sales Tracker Software only allows for 'monthly' views of the information (a technology constraint). Wisconsin Tissue has hundreds of SKUs and 3 facilities, and forecasting is conducted on an item (SKU) level within each facility. Item forecasts are then aggregated to the product category level. The reason for having a bottom-up forecasting process is because Wisconsin Tissue is interested in planning production and distribution schedules for each of the items, not in planning for their sum.

ARTICULATE YOUR SPECIFIC FORECASTING GOALS

Information about forecasting goals was gathered through informal interviews of Wisconsin Tissue employees who are either involved in the forecasting process at Wisconsin Tissue or are affected by it. These interviews revealed that the development of the forecasting system was guided by several broad manufacturing and customer oriented goals. For example, Wisconsin Tissue management wanted the forecasting system to be used in developing production and procurement plans, and sales and marketing activities. As an example of how forecasting is used to develop marketing activities, promotional programs may have to be activated when a forecast predicts a sales level below the desired one. Another broad goal of the forecasting process was to provide an early customer warning system, and forecasts are used to gain insight into changes in customer trends and competitive positioning. Discussions with managers and reviewing notes of various meetings also revealed that managers had hoped to use the forecasting system to develop strategic business plans.

The forecasting system was also designed to improve three specific areas in which performance was regularly measured. First, to improve asset utilization, forecasting data is used to make equipment purchase and maintenance decisions. Second, to reduce inventory, forecasting data is used to determine safety stock. And third, Wisconsin Tissue uses forecasted information for creating financial statements that are sent to its parent company.

ASSESS THE CURRENT FORECASTING SYSTEM

Forecasting goal analysis should be completed prior to assessing the current system so that valid comparisons can be made between the desired and actual systems. In assessing the actual forecasting system, several questions must be addressed to understand how and why the actual system achieves (or fails to achieve) the desired results. Technical questions must be answered, such as "What quantitative information is used as input to forecasts?" and "What type of hardware/software is used?" Soft-issue questions are equally important to answer and include "What chain of events occurs in developing forecasts?," and "How knowledgeable and involved are the people who use the forecasted information?"

In terms of quantitative input used by the forecasting system, the sole information used at Wisconsin Tissue is the prior two years of shipment records because this data is immediately available (limitation because of a desire for convenience in operating the system). When the formal forecasting process started in 1997, Wisconsin Tissue had historical information going back to 1995. Since 1997, only 2 years of historical data have been used for forecasting, even though the amount of historical information available has been growing. Based on the historical data, an AS-400 based forecasting engine uses regression models to predict future sales (see Table 1). The legacy (old) system has the ability to use five forecasting regression models that vary in their use of trends and seasonal patterns. The forecast user may decide to use a particular regression model, or the user may allow the system to examine all five models and use the model that explains the most variation in the historical data. For example, if the historical pattern of orders for a product is rising steadily, a model that recognizes this rising trend will produce a better forecast than a model that ignores the trend. The choice of using different regression models can be made for each SKU. As such, some SKUs are forecasted with a model that accounts for seasonal patterns while others with a model that does not.

TABLE 1
WISCONSIN TISSUE'S LEGACY FORECASTING PROCESS

Quantitative Input and Processing	Qualitative Input and Processing
• Historical sales data for the last two years is sole quantitative input	• Consensus meeting assesses and revises quantitative forecast
• Sales data is loaded into BPCS forecasting engine	• Sales force gain/loss business provides information for revising the forecast
• Initial forecast is derived by legacy system (AS-400) using regression models such as: i. Least squares analysis ii. Trend analysis iii. Seasonal patterns	• Other business information from product, marketing and senior managers are used to finalize the forecast

The quantitative forecasts are then updated to include qualitative input. A Monthly Forecast Consensus Meeting is held after the forecasting engine generates the initial forecasts. In preparation of this Consensus Meeting, the forecasting manager develops initial forecasts based on quantitative analysis and sales force feedback of the market. Department managers from finance, marketing, sales and production, all participate in the Consensus Meeting. The meeting involves the presentation of the initial forecasts, making adjustments based on qualitative information. The meeting is also viewed as a business forum where variables such as pricing, production capacity and competitive information are discussed. Besides offering unique insights, the meeting promotes acceptance of the forecasts by ensuring that the final forecasts represent managerial forecasts. After the consensus meeting, additional input from the sales department may be used, if, for example, unusual orders are expected. As a last step, judgments are made at an executive level to finalize the forecasts.

The Wisconsin Tissue's legacy system does not include a mechanism for allowing users such as marketing and production staff members to directly interact with the data to achieve actionable decision support analysis. In other words, users are not connected with the data. Instead, the flow of information is unidirectional, from the Sales Tracker to users, and only the consensus team members can directly interact with Sales Tracker. Non-consensus team users are provided with end-result forecasts but are essentially prevented from adapting the forecast assumptions to derive revised forecasts that would meet their specific information needs. For example, individual managers may wish to make contingency plans based on different forecast scenarios — different assumptions of prices and demands. Interactive scenario testing is not possible within the legacy system. This lack of interactivity from the users side mirrors a general lack of training aimed at helping users understand how to interact meaningfully with the data.

IDENTIFY WEAKNESSES IN THE FORECASTING SYSTEM

Several formal and informal meetings were held at Wisconsin Tissue during spring of 1999 to identify possible ways to improve the current forecasting system. Discussions focused primarily on how well the forecasting system was meeting its goals, and whether there is a need to revise it. Notably, a key strength of these discussions was that solutions were not discussed at this point. Identifying weaknesses was made easier by divorcing the weaknesses from possible solutions.

Further, we note that quantitative/technical weaknesses were relatively easy to identify. Less technically grounded weaknesses surfaced only after in-depth probing. Below are ten weaknesses that emerged, starting with technical issues:

1. **Historical shipment data may misrepresent demand.** Historical shipments may misrepresent past demand because what was shipped may not be what was demanded. For example, products may occasionally be shipped later than planned due to order processing delays, manufacturing disruptions, or inventory stockouts. In such cases, shipment data would under-represent demand because the demand was not fully recognized. By the same token it would over-represent demand at other times, for example, when large shipments were consolidated and shipped in any period.

2. **Other predictive variables should be included in projecting sales:** Beyond historical shipments, other variables such as price and sales promotions affect demand. Omitting

these variables can deteriorate the accuracy of the forecasts, and, at the same time, may give the impression to managers that they have no bearing on the demand. In the tissue market, price is an important variable. Because the tissue market is mature, demand is very sensitive to price.

3. **Limited amount of data is used.** Using only two years of data makes it difficult to estimate whether prior shipment fluctuations were truly due to trends. Although Wisconsin Tissue's legacy system contains historical data of five years, at any given time only two years of historical data is used in the forecasting process.

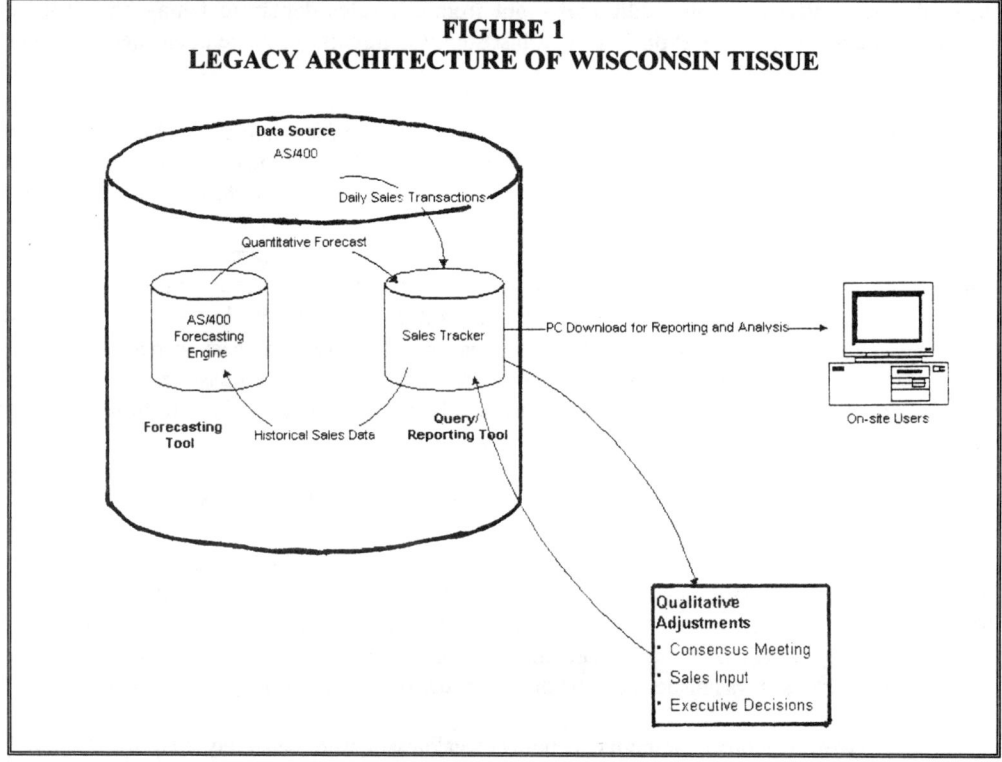

FIGURE 1
LEGACY ARCHITECTURE OF WISCONSIN TISSUE

4. **Limited forecasting models are tested.** The AS-400 model has a limited number of forecasting models. But a more sophisticated engine would allow many other types of regression models including a cross product sales model. In the case of Wisconsin Tissue, some products, such as cocktail napkins and dinner napkins, tend to be sold together.

5. **The software provides users with limited graphic views.** The forecasting output is tabled, and graphic representations are limited to rows of numbers on an AS-400 "green screen." The graphic capability of this software limits the user's ability to visually assess trends and seasonal effects. Lacking a visual interface makes it difficult for users to fully interpret the information.

6. **Forecast results are presented in a static format.** Another problem is that forecasts are presented to forecast-users in a non-interactive manner. If a production manager wishes to understand how asset utilization varies across a range of possible order quantities and

across multiple SKUs, he or she needs to conduct multiple data queries, which is not possible with the current system. Nor does it allow what-if scenarios.

7. **Two-tier hardware architecture imposes problems.** The AS-400 system also functions as a data warehouse. To make it easier for the users of forecast to view and analyze data, the IT department designed a file server architecture that enables users to move data files from the data warehouse to the user's workstation for further analysis. This approach to information flow is called a two-tier architecture (warehouse and workstation).

A major weakness with two-tier system is that end users lack the programming knowledge needed to extract data. Due to the two-tier system, forecast consensus team members often spend time discussing who has the right numbers rather than discussing business issues.

8. **Potential users of forecast information lack training.** Forecast users are not expected to be statisticians. Nevertheless, a moderate amount of knowledge is needed to interpret the forecast output. For example, if users want the final forecast to reflect slowly diminishing competition for a product, they need to know whether or not the regression model has already accounted for that trend. At the time of this review, many users expressed a lack of knowledge about forecasting.

9. **Forecast results are often not used.** Forecasting was designed for specific uses. However, many employees indicated that they are not fully utilizing forecasts. This lack of use may be partly due to lack of knowledge regarding the forecasting system as well as lack of knowledge about forecasts.

10. **Questions lingered regarding whether forecast should equal budgets and/or plans.** Even though a forecasting system is in place, planning or budget numbers are routinely used to drive final forecasts. The budget-driven final forecasts can defeat the purpose of numbers generated by statistical models. Across different managers at Wisconsin Tissue, two different types of forecasts are desired, one for operational plans, and another for budgeting. The current forecast system does not accommodate both uses.

LIST AND PRIORITIZE CORRECTIVE ACTIONS

After identifying weaknesses in the forecasting system, interviews were conducted with various middle managers to determine the severity of the weaknesses in the current forecasting system and to arrive at possible solutions. For simplicity sake, only key problems and plausible solutions are presented here (see Table 2).

The first solution is to improve the quantitative inputs used by the forecasting system. The revised system will use orders instead of shipments, and a further refinement is to use the customer's desired receipt date instead of the actual order date. Using the customer's desired receipt date avoids misrepresenting shipments ordered earlier, which occurs, for example, when customers want to expense an order on a profitable current fiscal period and thus charge a future demand to a current period.

Further, Wisconsin Tissue is currently considering several other quantitative variables to be used in the forecast engine. Given the high overall computer-related competence of Wisconsin Tissue's employees, the data related changes will be fairly easy to implement.

A second solution is to formally detail how forecast output could be used in making various decisions. For example, forecast output was intended to support procurement decisions. Thus, recommendations are being made to indicate how forecast output should be used in procurement decisions. The recommendations are developed with an eye toward training users so that they feel comfortable in using forecast output. Further, individuals are asked to suggest any changes they wish to make in the suggested recommendations.

TABLE 2
SUMMARY OF FORECASTING WEAKNESSES

Forecasting Weaknesses	Severity	Solution
• Historical shipment data may mis-represent demand	3	• Improve quantitative inputs to generate forecasts
• Forecast results are often not used	5	• Clear documentation of how forecast results can be used in decision making
• Potential users of forecast information lack training	4	• Provide in-house training
• Questions linger regarding whether the forecast should equal budgets and/or plans	4	• The final forecast numbers could be adjusted for different users as needed
• The two-tier hardware imposes problems	4	• Reengineered architecture for the company's forecasting system

A third solution is to provide in-house training about regression and other forecast models. Users will be shown not only how to prepare forecasts but also how to use them. The emphasis will be not on understanding formulas but on interpreting output. Users will also be instructed how to conduct what-if simulation or scenario tests. The goal is to develop people who can eventually conduct in-house training programs. But much of the initial training can be outsourced.

A fourth solution is to generate different forecast reports for different users. The production manager, for example, may require a detailed monthly report at SKU level. On the other hand, the marketing manager may need to see a report that shows how different marketing promotions affect the sales. Finally, senior managers should receive an executive summary report that highlights issues that needs to be addressed.

A fifth solution is to update the legacy architecture. A main problem with Wisconsin Tissue's AS400 system is that the data resides in various databases that do not interact easily and are not linked to the forecasting engine. Achieving smooth interactions between hardware and users is recognized as being critically important in a forecasting system.

The importance of interactivity has motivated many companies to move towards relational database management systems to support forecasting efforts. For example, a SKU number might have a link with Product, Brand, Customer, and Product Category information. And as the company integrates the forecasting system with its broader business planning and resource information systems, interactivity is important in terms of linking forecasting information to a general enterprise information system.

A new forecasting architecture is being implemented at Wisconsin Tissue. It adopts Oracle servers that link users to data, and includes Business Objects and SPSS as analysis tools. Before arriving at a recommended system, Wisconsin Tissue's culture was assessed. A company's culture is a primary consideration because people may resist using the system if it does not appear to support their decision process and communication styles. Building consensus and positive evaluations before adopting a new system also increases buy-in. The key features of the new system are:

- A three-tier client server. Oracle servers provide data marts that handle large amounts of data and make this data easy for managers to access. With a three-tier system, the users of the system don't have to be programmers.
- User-friendly data mining and analysis tools that access external data. Business Objects and SPSS share information easily. SPSS is window based and is easy to use.
- Fully integrated business and statistical graphs. Business Objects and SPSS have a wide selection of graphical views including 2-D and 3-D charts, pie charts, and scatter plots.
- Flexible dynamic output. Printed output will be supplemented or replaced by interactive digital output that allows the forecaster/manager to slice and dice the data any way he or she wants. Slice and dice technology allows one to see one 'slice' of a cube of data at a time.
- Internet and Intranet compatibility. Business Objects and SPSS have front-end tools, which can be integrated with the Web. This integration has several advantages such as allowing a user in Wisconsin to immediately share analysis results/intuitions with a colleague in Arizona.
- Ad hoc queries. Good forecasting requires more than predetermined regression analysis; follow up queries and scenario testing are critical. The new system will allow users to answer follow-up questions easily and quickly by running additional analyses.
- A more strategic benefit offered by the new system will be that it will facilitate e-commerce. Wisconsin Tissue conducts Electronic Data Interchange (EDI) with over one third of its customers. The new system will allow Wisconsin Tissue and its customers to share forecasting numbers, improving the ability to coordinate efforts through the business value chain.

LESSONS LEARNED

Many lessons were learned while working on this project at Wisconsin Tissue. The most important among them are:

1. Don't treat the forecasting system as an isolated system. Wisconsin Tissue couldn't have made all the changes effectively without the input from various forecast users.
2. Know your company as well as the role forecasts play before embarking on changing your forecasting system. One should know before hand what kinds of forecasts are needed, and how, when and where they will be used.
3. Scrutinize the goals and actual operation of the existing forecasting system before revising it. You may find some of the goals currently pursued are no longer needed and at the same time

some new goals may surface.
4. Any change in software, hardware, forecasting process and forecast training should be reviewed in unison so that they don't conflict with each other.

REFERENCES

1. Chase, Charles. "Many Plans, One Reality; Which is the Real Forecast?" **Journal of Business Forecasting.** Volume 15, Fall 1996, pp. 22-23.
2. Kahn, Kenneth B. "Revisiting Top-Down Versus Bottom-Up Forecasting." **Journal of Business Forecasting.** Volume 17, Summer 1998, pp.14-19.
3. Lapide, Larry. "Forecast Shipment or Demand?" **Journal of Business Forecasting.** Volume 17, Spring 1998, pp. 28-29.
4. Powers, Anthony. "Architecture of the Enterprise Forecasting System." **Journal of Business Forecasting.** Volume 14, Summer 1995, pp. 6-9.

CHAPTER 37

WHAT YOU NEED TO KNOW WHEN
BUILDING A SALES FORECASTING SYSTEM

Charles W. Chase Jr.
Wyeth-Ayerst Pharmaceuticals

As companies begin to harness the power of information to better serve their customers, re-engineer their processes and systems to increase efficiency, and train and empower their employees to continuously improve all areas of the business, they need to seriously consider the benefits of a fully integrated sales forecasting system. The systems, supporting most sales forecasting processes today, lack the ability to interactively gather all the pertinent information required to provide actionable decision-support analysis, as well as accurate point estimates. Unfortunately, companies in many industries, particularly the consumer packaged goods industry, have found that their forecasting processes and systems have not kept pace with rapid technological advances; and the failure to update them has inhibited their ability to achieve new business advantages. Those who have kept pace with the new technology are experiencing the benefits of improved marketing intelligence, increased forecast accuracy, lower finished goods inventories, and higher customer satisfaction.

Current benchmarking surveys define the best sales forecasting system as the one that provides easy access; reviews and modifies sales forecast results across all corporate disciplines; provides alternative modeling capabilities; has the ability to create a knowledge base by which future forecasts can be redefined; provides timely and accurate ad hoc reporting capabilities; and supports automated link/feed interfaces with other system databases, such as A. C. Nielsen syndicated data, corporate marketing expense information and shipment history, where vital information resides. Over the past decade, the advent of the PC has made it possible for businesses to use advanced statistical software packages that were previously privileged only to academics at major universities who had access to shared mainframe technology. As a result, mainframes have become obsolete processors, and for the most part are now utilized as giant storage bins. These advanced statistical PC applications are nothing more than forecasting engines that interact with the data via a cumbersome interface that utilizes spreadsheet programs such as Excel for data analysis. Meanwhile, PC based client server applications have been gaining wide acceptance throughout the industry as a viable solution to solving the integration issues. Unfortunately, there are only a few vendors who can provide a fully integrated sales forecasting solution that takes advantage of the flexibility that client server technology offers. In fact, only one of those client

198

server solutions has a truly open architecture while the others have primarily closed proprietary architectures.

THE SYSTEM IS NOT A PROCESS

When designing, developing and implementing a sales forecasting system, or any system for that matter, one must realize that the system itself is not a process. On the contrary, it is a supporting tool that facilitates the process. In other words, the system must be built around the sales forecasting process, "*not*" the sales forecasting process around the system. Unfortunately, most integrated proprietary system solutions, particularly those off-the-shelf, assume that your process was designed around the system. Companies who purchase such systems for sales forecasting have two choices either re-engineer the process they just re-engineered to fit the system, or redesign and program the system to accommodate their process. In almost every case the company ends up doing a combination of the two, costing thousands of dollars in additional resources and consulting fees.

The additional time, costs and resources could have been avoided if companies took the time to understand that all system designs require some level of customization. Furthermore, closed proprietary architectures leave little room for company-specific customization. As a result, reporting capabilities are limited; hierarchical override functionality is not existent due to the restricted environment; singular, one dimensional quantitative methods, usually a time series method, such as Winter's Three Parameter Exponential Smoothing, are deployed because they are easier to systematize and require less database maintenance; and finally, most companies think an integrated supply chain solution should include a sales forecasting module when in fact sales forecasting should be part of a sales/marketing analysis and reporting integrated solution. There is no fully integrated supply chain solution that contains an adequate sales forecasting module to meet the requirements of providing actionable decision support analysis in addition to multiple quantitative applications. All the supply chain solutions focus on Master Planning Scheduling (MPS) and Distribution Requirements Planning (DRP) with little attention toward sales forecasting.

Simply put, the system should be made up of a combination of off-the-shelf and customized hardware/software. There is "no" integrated off-the-shelf solution that can solve all the sales forecasting issues surrounding every situation. Some customization is always required, especially, given the complexities of today's marketplace.

THE IMPORTANCE OF A DATA WAREHOUSE

To succeed in implementing a new sales forecasting system the forecast practitioner must have the right information to uncover seasonal patterns, trends, predict market changes, analyze customer level trade promotion performance, measure sales promotion impact, advertising effectiveness, and much more. Most companies have all the necessary data. However, it resides in various fragmented system databases that are unable to interact easily with one another. Furthermore, these systems were never built to handle complex queries in a timely manner. Data queries made through the Management Information Systems (MIS) department may take weeks or even months to be completed. As a result, decision support analysis is not readily available forcing critical sales forecasts to be made on gut or intuitive feelings.

This is why it is important to develop a corporate data warehouse that fits your business needs. The job of a corporate data warehouse (CDW) is to untangle and consolidate the maze of sales, marketing, financial, and external information needed to manage the sales forecast. It archives the data by extracting and clearing (or filtering) the information, and storing it away from operational systems. Subsequently, it allows easy access and analysis by the end users (i.e., sales, marketing, finance, sales forecasters, and executive management) who are business decision makers.

RECOMMENDED SYSTEM DESIGN

Like any other systems design and implementation project, the quality of the upfront planning, the level of understanding of the process by the development team, and most of all, the support of senior management, have a far greater impact on the success of the sales forecasting system implementation than anything else. Sales forecast practitioners contemplating to implement a sales forecasting system should recognize that for many users this will involve a major cultural change. The most obvious change is that data analysis tasks will be shifted from management information systems staff and/or forecast practitioners to users at all levels of the organization. Consequently, getting started does not mean trying to design the perfect system solution. The sales forecasting system should be designed to grow and expand as your needs and abilities grow. This is why the system should be interactive, multi-dimentional, and PC based that has an open architecture. Also, it should be object oriented with a relational database.

Interactive means the system should be interactive with the entire user community. For example, all the disciplines such as marketing, field sales, finance, finished goods planning, and senior management have access to the sales forecast system. In fact, the marketing and field sales organizations must be able to interactively participate in the sales forecasting process and, if necessary, override at various levels in the product hierarchy. If finished goods planning, finance, and senior management have access to various reports, they can query the database to conduct basic ad hoc analysis, such as viewing year ago actuals versus current sales forecast.

Multi-dimentional PC based means the system should ensure that both time series and causal modeling methods are available with the touch and feel that a PC software engine offers. It should also provide forecast model capability at the brand aggregate, sub-brand aggregate, and Stock Keeping Unit (SKU) levels. Complete drill down, up, and around functionality should be available when reviewing reports. Finally, the system must have on-the-fly ad hoc reporting capabilities with private and public viewing authorization.

Open and object oriented architecture implies that the system is built like a lego set. Each object linked to one another by a common element. In other words, it should have the capabilities to combine multiple off-the-shelf software applications, such as sales forecast engines and Excel spreadsheets to create an integrated solution. Furthermore, those objects can be customized to fit the sales forecasting process and modified as the process changes without disrupting the integrity of the information flow. For example, user requests for enhancements should be implemented by simply taking a copy of the current object, customizing it, and then overwriting it with the new object without shutting down the entire system.

A relational database is a software tool to store and manage data in a corporate data warehouse. Such tools offer superior performance and manageability of the data by linking disparate data tables through common references, such as product codes, customer names, UPC (unique product code) numbers. These database engines could well be the catalyst for the success of a system design.

Only a handful of companies have experienced such systems. However many others are adopting these architectures to solve their common sales forecasting needs. As the price and performance costs for data processing continue to fall, the middle-tiered companies, who do not have the same deep financial pockets as their larger competitors but have similar needs for finding efficient ways to control costs, will be able to improve their sales forecast accuracy.

PART VII

DATA, DATA SOURCES, AND DATA ANALYSIS

INTRODUCTION

Forecasts are as good as data used in preparing them. With the development in technology and willingness of supply chain partners to share information with vendors, forecasters have now access to more data than ever before — POS data, warehouse movement data, customers' forecasts, etc. But mere availability of data is not enough for preparing good forecasts. One has to understand the data before using it. Because, which data to use and how much, and which model to use, depend very much on the nature of data. This section describes not only what kinds of data are available — internally and externally — but also how to study the data, that is, what to look for in analyzing the data.

CHAPTER 38

SYNCHRONIZING SUPPLY CHAIN OPERATIONS WITH CONSUMER DEMAND USING CUSTOMER DATA

Daniel A. Kiely

Wyeth-Ayerst Pharmaceuticals

For many years, monthly factory shipment data was the only type of non-syndicated demand information available to vendors for forecasting product consumption. Although factory shipment data does not provide the best consumption forecasts, vendors were left with few alternatives. Other demand data, better suited for forecasting consumption, was either difficult or expensive to acquire.

However, since the late 1980s, developments in systems technology and improvements in supply chain management have enabled retail customers to provide their vendors with better data. Two key technological developments that have enabled customers to transfer and vendors to process consumption data are Electronic Data Interchange (EDI) and high-speed, batch-processing forecasting software. Coincident with the advent of these innovations was the evolution of cooperative customer-vendor business programs including Vendor Managed Inventory (VMI), Continuous Replenishment Planning (CRP), and Collaborative Planning, Forecasting and Replenishment (CPFAR), which became the hallmarks of 1990s supply chain management. The combination of new information technology and cooperative supply chain partnerships has made possible the sharing of consumption-based forecasting information in near real time. The results of these developments have been dramatic: improvements in product-forecast accuracy, reductions in supply chain inventories, and efficiencies in product distribution. This chapter reviews demand data streams that are transmitted by customers to their vendors. Throughout, a customer is defined as a retailer that sells finished goods to the end-users, consumers. A vendor is defined as a manufacturer that produces, distributes and sells a finished good to a customer.

DIFFERENT CUSTOMER DEMAND DATA STREAMS

At present,, instead of monthly factory shipment information, vendors have begun to use four other types of demand data to drive demand planning systems. These alternative data streams are (1) customer forecasts, (2) consumer purchases, (3) customer warehouse withdrawals, and (4) customer orders. Collectively, these customer-supplied data can be used to form the basis for bottom-up product forecasts which, when aggregated and rolled back up the supply chain, more accurately predict independent demand than do factory shipment-based forecasts. Independent demand is the requirement for items that is influenced by factors that are external to the firms that comprise the supply chain. These external factors bring about random variation in demand for such items. Consequently, independent demand forecasts are typically projections of historical demand patterns. As such, it is assumed here that independent demand is derived from point-of-sale (POS) based consumption data, since consumption is outside of the control of suppliers, vendors, and retail customers. The primary reason for using customer-supplied POS information, as opposed to factory shipment data, is to drive the demand planning system with independent demand. Demand planning systems driven by POS-based forecasts are best suited for synchronizing supply chain plans with consumer demand.

Dependent demand, on the other hand, is directly related to, or derived from the bill of material structure of other items (e.g., raw materials, component parts and manufacturing inventories) or distribution requirements (e.g. warehouse inventories). As such, demand for these items is directly dependent upon internal factors that are within control of the firms that comprise the supply chain. It is important to note that dependent demand need not be forecasted, since it can be calculated with certainty through Material Requirements Planning (MRP) or Distribution Requirements Planning (DRP) logic. Dependent demand for products is typically calculated by customers' Order Management Systems (OMS), vendors' Manufacturing Planning Systems (MPS), or their Distribution Requirement Planning (DRP) software. Such demand obtained from the output of these systems takes the form of purchase orders, factory shipments, and customer warehouse withdrawals.

CUSTOMER-SUPPLIED FORECASTS

The first type of customer-supplied information is demand forecasts. Some large retailers, instead of supplying raw demand data, provide ready-made forecasts to their own vendors. Wal-Mart and Target, for example, have established collaborative forecasting and replenishment programs whereby simple four-week moving averages of sales data output from their IBM INFOREM inventory reorder point systems are sent to vendors via EDI. Vendors then compare their forecasts with their own to arrive at consensus forecasts. Proponents of CPFAR are typically large retail customers who argue that their close proximity to consumer activities make them best qualified to forecast consumer demand for finished goods. Customer-supplied forecasts that are based upon POS data are derived directly from the retailers' checkout counters. Consequently, POS-based forecasts of consumption produced by customers are typically more accurate than those produced by vendors that do not use POS data.

POINT OF SALE DATA STREAMS

Landvater and others have shown that statistical forecast models based upon POS time series data are the best for predicting consumption. Vendors most commonly capture POS data in one of two ways — either directly from customers or through syndicated data providers. Vendors typically receive customer-supplied POS information in the form of weekly EDI 852 transactions through the VMI or CPFAR processes. The major benefit of using customer POS is that it captures consumer take away; as such, it reflects true independent demand. Customers often transmit POS data at 24-hour intervals, permitting vendors to analyze consumption in near real time. Real time, high frequency data can be extremely useful for examining performance of new product launches. By comparison, syndicated consumption data suffers from lag effects. Syndicated data providers require long lead times to collect, process, and transmit consumption data to their subscribers. Consequently, it can take anywhere from 14 to 21 days for syndicated POS data to reach vendors.

Another great advantage of using POS data to forecast consumption is that, by nature, POS data is less variable than other types of customer demand information. Captured at the lowest level of aggregation, POS data reflects the way in which inventory is steadily `consumed at the retail store level, on a daily or weekly basis and at the lowest saleable unit of measure. Low variability is particularly emblematic of POS data transmitted by retailers who sell by the 'everyday low price (EDLP) regimen.' The EDLP based POS data signature is characterized by gradual, step-wise changes in consumer take away, free from promotional noise. As such, POS data generally does not contain erratic fluctuations, which are typical of demand patterns that occur at points further upstream in the supply chain. Customer demand data captured further upstream exhibits more variations since that is where noise, due to special promotions and trade deals, originates. The lower variability and greater stability that is inherent in POS data, therefore, can provide better fitting statistical models and more accurate forecasts.

One disadvantage of POS data is that it sometimes can be unreliable due to inaccurate scanning at the check out counter. Improperly scanned POS data must be cleaned before loading into historical demand database tables. But perhaps the greatest disadvantage is the extreme granularity of the data. Retail store POS data contains high level of details, which renders it unusable for most MRP and DRP software applications. For use in vendor demand planning systems, retail store POS data needs to be aggregated. In response to vendor requests, customers have rolled up store level point-of-sale information to the customer warehouse level. (Target Stores, for example, aggregate POS data up to the customer DC level before transmitting to vendors.) Where POS-based customer forecast information is not available, aggregated POS information is the next best data stream, which can be used to forecast consumption.

CUSTOMER WAREHOUSE MOVEMENT DATA

Where even aggregated POS data is not available, customer warehouse movement (WM) data is the next best alternative for forecasting consumption. WM information is the standard data stream of EDI 852-based VMI transaction systems. An added bonus for using customer EDI 852 WM data is that it comes neatly packaged with daily on hand inventory balances, which, when aggregated across all customers, provides insight into daily trade inventory levels.

The major disadvantage of using WM data to forecast independent demand is that it reflects dependent demand. Technically, WM should be calculated using DRP logic if POS forecasts are available. Another disadvantage of using WM data to forecast independent demand is that some VMI customers transmit warehouse withdrawal data in higher units of measure (cases or pallets). As such, there is often more variations in the WM data than in POS data that is transmitted in lower saleable units of measure (eaches or pieces). This is because WM demand data is one step away from the final point of consumption, and the higher variation reflects the way in which retailers pull from warehouse racks case or pallet quantities for store replenishment. For example, if the number of eaches per case for a particular SKU is twelve, WM data may be stratified in multiples of twelve eaches. Most statistical models that are fitted to stratified data produce lower coefficients of determination and, consequently, poorer forecast accuracy.

CUSTOMER ORDER DATA

When a vendor cannot obtain POS or WM data, either directly through customers' systems or indirectly through third parties, customer order history can be used as a proxy for independent demand. A major advantage of using customer order data is that it is easily obtained; it is typically captured daily or weekly through corporate Order Management Systems. Despite its disadvantages, order data is still preferred to factory shipment data for predicting consumer demand because it is closer to final point of sale.

There are primarily three disadvantages of using order history to predict consumer demand. First, like WM data, customer order data reflects dependent demand and does not capture consumer take away in the current period. Rather, order data reflects what the customer believes their product stocking requirements will be to adequately meet consumer demand in future periods. Consequently, customer order quantities include safety stock requirements as well as expected sales. Order history, therefore, is more useful if the forecasting objective is to predict customers' warehouse replenishment quantities. Second, order data is typically transmitted in customer units of measure, such as cases or pallets which increases variation. Consequently, order data-based forecasts that are intended to predict consumer take away are more likely to have larger errors than those that are based on POS data.

The third disadvantage of using purchase order history pertains to customer order behavior in the presence of stock-outs in a no backorder environment. In a no backorder environment, order quantities that cannot be filled during the current order cycle are cut from the purchase order. Empirical evidence collected at Johnson & Johnson Sale and Logistics Company (JJSLC) has shown that customers often tend to over compensate for poor product supply by adding the current cycle's cut order quantity to the next cycle's purchase order. If product supply problems continue for many weeks, customers tend to continue reordering accumulated quantities in an attempt to replenish depleted inventories.

Supply chain simulations developed at MIT have modeled other types of customer order behavior that are similar to those observed at JJSLC. The simulation reveals that, when stock-outs occur, order and inventory patterns at various echelons in the supply chain exhibit large variations that grow in magnitude from retail store to customer warehouse and from customer warehouse to vendor distribution center. In explaining this phenomena, Towill writes, "by the time the original stepwise increase in customer orders reaches the factory, it typically leads to an expansion of production relative to the marketplace, by a factor of more than six. A second characteristic of the simulation is the wavelike increase in orders, which propagates up the chain and depletes all inventories in turn. This is best exemplified at the factory, as the large surplus of orders placed during the out-of-stock period is eventually produced." Forecasters using order history must be aware of this "bullwhip effect." It corrupts natural order patterns by artificially inflating demand and inventory requirements. If left uncorrected, a statistical model will project the inflated demand forward; consumption forecasts based on accumulated reordering will be misinterpreted as natural surges in demand. It becomes necessary, therefore, to clean order history that is captured during stock-out periods. The forecast analyst can correct inflated order history and align the statistical forecast with natural order patterns by using various techniques. Masking as outliers, data points collected during stock-outs, is one method of correcting for inflated orders. Another technique is to substitute inflated data points with the mean of the time series if the product is non-seasonal, or the average of the two data points immediately preceding and following the inflated data point if the product is seasonal.

FACTORY SHIPMENT DATA

Factory shipment data has two advantages when used for purposes other than forecasting consumption. The first advantage is that it does a good job of forecasting financial cash flows. Once shipments are released, one can estimate the timing and quantity of account receivables. The other advantage of using factory shipment information is that it is inexpensive and easy to obtain. Factory shipment data is easily collected from financial transactions found in invoicing systems.

However, when used to forecast independent demand, factory shipments suffer from three disadvantages. First, factory shipments represent movements in product supply, not changes in demand. By forecasting shipments, demand plans ignore what is actually demanded and considers the vendor's ability to fulfill demand. Second, shipment data is very volatile for vendors that have not synchronized production to consumption; it is often characterized by high peaks and low troughs.

The factors that create fluctuations in the demand patterns are erratic customer inventory levels, irregular customer orders quantities, highly variable replenishment lead times, and rapid inventory building at the customer distribution centers (in anticipation of promotions, for example). These factors are very difficult, if not impossible to decompose, isolate and remove from shipment history. Third, the underlying seasonality of shipment data may not be the true representative of pattern of consumer purchases, but rather created artificially by the "pipeline push strategies" that some vendors employ to meet corporate financial targets.

If any of these factors are present, shipment-based forecasts rarely provide a true indication of what will happen in the marketplace. As a result, large errors are often associated with consumption forecasts that are based on factory shipment data. The traditional approach for compensating for such errors has been to carry enough safety stock, the cost of which far outweighs the savings incurred by accessing and storing shipment information. In short, shipment-based forecasts are the best used as a last resort to forecast consumption and drive production plans when other types of customer demand data is not available. Some vendors have used factory shipment data to forecast international demand for products where POS, WM, or purchase order information for foreign customers is not available.

BLENDING DIFFERENT CUSTOMER DATA STREAMS

In the future, consumer-driven demand planning systems will require the use of all types of customer-supplied data. This is because not all retail customers possess the capability to collect,

208

process, and transmit consumer data to their vendors. Smaller, less sophisticated retailers often do not own and operate the POS collection equipment or EDI systems that link their warehouse inventory control systems to their vendor's manufacturing and distribution planning systems. (However, a recent development in the demand data market is the appearance of third party data providers such as EMS. Third party data providers specialize in installing EDI systems for retailers who wish to supply their vendors with WM or POS data, but either lack the expertise or do not want to incur the system implementation or maintenance costs.) Therefore, it is necessary for vendors to blend multiple data streams if their customer base exhibits a wide range of technical competency. This is particularly true for large multinational corporations that sell products internationally to customers located in less developed markets. Vendor demand planning systems that use a mixture of customer forecasts, POS, WM, order history, or even factory shipment data, will become commonplace as more firms aspire to capture one hundred percent of their market-based consumption demand.

When aggregating forecasts based on different types of demand streams, it must be noted that each type must be time phased before loading into the forecast system. Time phasing insures the data streams, upon which the aggregated forecasts are derived, are properly synchronized, and the resultant forecast quantities fall within the correct time buckets. The amount of time displacement for a given type of data is dependent upon (1) purpose of the forecast, (2) periodicity of the data, (3) transportation lead time between each successive link in the supply chain and (4) source of the data (supply chain location of origin). The purpose of the forecast, which is, to predict vendor warehouse movement; the periodicity of the data, which is one week; and the lead time between each successive link in the supply chain, which again is one week. If the source of the data is at the point of sale, the POS history must be lagged two periods before loading into the demand planning data base since it represents demand two weeks after shipment from the vendor's warehouse. Similarly, if the source of the data is the Customer's warehouse, the WM history must be lagged one week before loading since it represents demand one week after shipment from the vendor's warehouse. Order history, on the other hand, needs not be time phased before loading. Customer orders are usually placed one period in advance of anticipated customer warehouse withdrawals and already reflect the current week's shipments from the vendor's warehouse.

REFERENCES

1. German, W. E. **Problems in Industrial Dynamics.** Cambridge Mass.: MIT Press, 1968.
2. Landvater, D. **World Class Production & Inventory Management**. 2nd ed. New York: John Wiley and Sons, 1997.
3. Mentzer, John, Kenneth B. Kahn and C. Bienstock. **Sales Forecasting Benchmarking Study: Executive Summary.** Knoxville, Ten: University of Tennessee Press. 1996.
4. Towill, Dennis R. "Managing Effective Supply Chains." **Value Adding Systems.** 1966.

CHAPTER 39

DATA ANALYSIS

Chaman L. Jain
St. John's University

For good and effective forecasting it is necessary to study the data. If there is any problem in the data, you may know it. If you know the problem, you may know what to do with it. If nothing can be done, you may know at least how much trust you should put in your forecasts. Data study, says Hans Levenbach, is a numerical detective work. It can tell you how much data to use, when and where adjustment is needed, what pattern the data forms, and so on. All this information can help you in improving the quality of forecasts. Preparing forecasts without examining the data is like enlisting a person into the army without a physical checkup.

CHECKLIST

Next question is what to look for in the data. Here is a checklist:

How much data do you have? The selection of a model depends, among other things, on the size of data. Some models need more data than the others. Box Jenkins, for example, needs a minimum of 50 observations.

How reliable is the data? Reliability of a forecast depends, among other things, upon the reliability of data. If the data are not reliable, so would be your forecasts. To determine the reliability of data, check the source of data (some sources are more reliable than others). Also check the basis of data, that is, whether data are based on actual enumeration of the universe or sample test. Data based on enumeration of the universe are generally more reliable than sample test.

Are we missing any data? It is necessary to know whether or not any data are missing. Missing data may very well be a missing piece in a puzzle. They can distort the true pattern of data. When adjustments are made for the missing data the pattern may become clearer. Particularly, in time series models, one has to interpolate the value for the missing period.

Is there any change in the definition of data? The data become incomparable when the definition changes. Therefore, it is necessary to make sure that all the data you are working on are comparable.

If you are using the sales data based on shipment, make sure all the data are based on the same definition; and if based on payment, make sure all the data are based on the same parameter.

Are the data aggregated or disaggregated? Sales of a company as a whole is aggregated sales. The data become disaggregated when broken down, say, by division, territory, line of merchandise or customers. Often one gets a much better picture about a series from disaggregated data. Disaggregated data may reveal that most of the sales come from a certain segment — a certain territory, a certain line of merchandise and/or a certain customer. If a large portion of the sales comes from a certain segment, the forecaster has to watch very closely the activities of that segment in preparing forecasts because a change in that segment can make the difference. Forecaster may have to prepare separate forecasts of those segments. Disaggregated data can also tell the forecaster which segments are stable and which ones are not. Such information can be helpful not only in preparing forecasts but also in determining their reliability. Sales forecasts will be highly unreliable if a bulk of the sales comes from segments which are highly unstable. Because any change in them can affect the forecasts.

Is there a structural change in the data? The structural change (shift) is an abrupt change in data pattern and/or data relationships. The change is permanent. Structural change can occur because of merger or acquisition, change in the line of merchandise, introduction of new products or abandonment of old ones, exit or entry of a major competitor, regulatory changes, major product recall, and loss or gain of one or more of large customers. Regulatory changes in banking, trucking, airline and telecommunication industries have caused structural changes by distorting the old relationships. In the banking industry, for example, permitting banks to expand beyond state boundaries, giving more flexibility in types of services offered, phasing out of interest rate ceilings (maximum interest rates to be paid on CDs) and allowing banks to offer accounts such as a NOW account have caused significant changes in monetary and financial relationships.

The sales data pattern of Johnson and Johnson's product, Extra-Strength Tylenol, changed in 1982 when someone tampered with its capsule. The sales data pattern of the oral contraceptive, Ortho, changed in 1975 over the FDA concern about the reduced levels of estrogen. The structural change tells us that the data prior to the change are not comparable to the ones that follow. Therefore, in preparing forecasts, you may have to exclude certain data.

Is there outlier(s) in the data? An outlier is an unusual (abnormal) value, the value that deviates significantly from the norm. The value may be extremely low or extremely high. In one particular year, the sales went down sharply because of the shortage of a key raw material. In other year, sales went up sharply because of one big order from Saudi Arabia. The values of both these periods are unusual. They are unusual because they are far from the norm. So, if you discover an outlier, the first thing you want to do is to account for, that is, why it happened. If you know what contributed to the outlier, then you may know whether that element is likely to recur particularly in the period you are forecasting.

How many are working days in each month/week of the historical data? The number of working days differs from one month to another, from one week to another. One month may have more Saturdays, Sundays and holidays than the other. Sales of department stores, for example, are very much affected by the number of Saturdays, Sundays and holidays in a month.

Are there seasonal variations in the data? Seasonal variations are those which occur regularly and periodically. The length of a seasonal cycle is always less than one year. For example, sales of department stores reach peak in the months of November and December because of Christmas. This happens regularly (because it occurs every year) and periodically (because it occurs every year at the same time). The length of a cycle can be measured either from peak to peak or from trough to trough. The period covering from one peak to the next (or from one trough to the next) has to be less than one year. In other words, if we are preparing annual forecasts, we should not be concerned about seasonal variations because annualized data do not contain seasonality. But, if we are preparing forecasts for a period less than one year, say, for months and quarters, we have to make adjustments for seasonal variations.

Whether or not to make adjustments for seasonal variations depends on a model. Some models like classical decomposition have a built-in-mechanism for making adjustments for seasonal variations.

What phase of the cycle the product is in? The forecaster needs to know whether a given product is in an introductory phase, mature phase, declining demand phase or obsolescent phase. The product in each phase of a cycle requires a different model for forecasting.

Is there abnormal distribution in the data? Often it is assumed that the data are normally distributed, that is, data form a bell-shaped distribution (normal curve). If not, one has to look for a model which is unique to that situation.

Do data form a linear or curvilinear trend? Since each type of trend requires a different model of forecasting, the knowledge of a linear or curvilinear trend can help in selecting the right one.

PART VIII

TIME SERIES MODELS

INTRODUCTION

The time series models are one of the three types of models, which are most often used in business forecasting. The other two types are cause-and-effect and judgmental models. In this type of forecasting, forecasts are prepared by rolling forward the numbers by using one method or the other. Here it is assumed that the past data pattern will continue into the future. Although there are a number of time series models, we will discuss only the ones which are most frequently used in business. A recent survey of practicing forecasters conducted by the IBF shows that about 60% of them use time series models. Among the time series models, the ones most often used are averages, exponential smoothing and simple trend. The reasons for using times series models are three fold: One, they are easy to understand and use. Two, most of the forecasting done in business is short term, and times series models are generally more suitable for this type of forecasting. Three, forecasting in business became popular only in the last 15 years or so. As such, most of the forecasters are fairly newcomers in the field. Newcomers normally start out with time series models.

CHAPTER 40

AVERAGE AND WEIGHTED AVERAGE CHANGE MODELS

Chaman L. Jain
St. John's University

Time series models are univariate models. They require only the data of a series to be forecasted. If you wish to forecast sales, you need only the data of sales. If you wish to forecast cash flow, you need only the data of cash flow. Forecasts are prepared by extrapolating the data using one technique or another. In so doing, an assumption is made that whatever pattern existed in the past will continue in the future. Such models are, by and large, easy to understand, easy to use, and less expensive. Their simplicity, however, should not be construed as less effective. In some situations, time series models may work even better than other models.

As we know:

Forecast   =   Pattern + Error

The more a given model captures the pattern in a data set, the less will be error. Each data set forms a certain pattern and each model captures a specific pattern. If we marry the right model to a right data set, error will be the lowest. The right model may very well be the time series model. Generally speaking, time series models are most appropriate for forecasting the overall sales of a company, sales of established products or non-promoted products (products which sell themselves), and for short-term forecasting. Such models are good for short-term forecasting because in the short period data pattern does not change significantly from one period to the next. However, some people view forecasting with a time series model as driving a car with windshield glass completely blacked out, and the driver drives it looking at the rearview mirror. It is fine if you are driving in the Mojave desert. It won't matter which direction the car goes. But, if you are driving on a highway full of curves, this will be a prescription for disaster.

There is a long list of time series models, but the ones that are often used are:

1. Average Level Change
2. Average Percent Change
3. Weighted Average Percent Change

4. Moving Average Level Change
5. Single Moving Average Percent Change
6. Double Moving Average Level Change
7. Double Moving Average Percent Change
8. Single Exponential Smoothing
9. Double Exponential Smoothing
10. Trend Line
11. Classical Decomposition
12. Cumulative Sales Index
13. Family Member Forecasting

AVERAGE LEVEL CHANGE

Each model is based on certain assumptions. The average level change model assumes that the sales change from one period to the next by the average of previous changes. Here is a step-by-step procedure for computing forecast with the average level change model using the sales data of City Stores given in Table 1:

Step 1: Compute the level change in sales from one period to the next. Level changes are given in Col. 3. The level change in period 2 from period 1 is $15.6 mil. ($371.6 - $356.0); in period 3 from period 2 is $2.1 mil. ($373.7 - $371.6); and so on.

Step 2: Compute the average of level changes. This comes to $2.7 mil. ($24.1 ÷ 9). This implies that the sales on the average increase from one period to the next by $2.7 mil.

Step 3: Prepare the forecast. The forecast of period 11 will be the current value of period 10 plus the average level change, which comes to $382.8 mil. ($380.1 + $2.7). Incidentally, the actual sale was $393.5 mil. This means that the forecast error for this period was $10.7 mil. or 2.7%.

AVERAGE PERCENT CHANGE

The average percent change model works the same way as the average level change model, except it assumes that the next period sales will increase (decrease) by the average percentage change. Here again we use the data of City Stores to demonstrate its procedure. (See Table 2) Here forecast is prepared as follows:

Step 1: Compute the level change in sales from one period to the next, the same way as before. The level changes are given in Table 2, Col. 3.

Step 2: Convert the level change, given in Col. 3, into percent. The percent change in sales in period 2 over period 1 is 4.38% [($15.6 ÷ $356.0) × (100)], in period 3 over period 2 is 0.57% [($2.1 ÷ $371.6) × (100)], and so on. These values are given in Table 2, Col. 4.

Step 3: Compute the average percentage change. This comes to 0.76% (6.81 ÷ 9). This means that the sale, on the average, is increasing at the rate of 0.76% from one period to the next.

TABLE 1		
AVERAGE LEVEL CHANGE		
Period **(1)**	**Sales of City Stores (Mil. of $)** **(2)**	**Level Change (Mil. of $)** **(3)**
1	356.0	----
2	371.6	15.6
3	373.7	2.1
4	380.4	6.7
5	364.8	-15.6
6	373.1	8.3
7	367.4	-5.7
8	373.4	5.9
9	374.1	0.8
10	380.1	6.0
Total		**24.1**

$$\text{Average Change} = \frac{\$24.1}{9}$$

$$= \$2.7 \text{ mil.}$$

$$\hat{Y}_{11} \quad = \$380.1 + \$2.7$$

$$= \$382.8 \text{ mil.}$$

Step 4: Forecast the sales of period 11. This will be the actual of period 10 plus 0.76% of it, which comes to $383.0 mil. [($380.1) + ($380.1 × .0076)]. As mentioned above, the actual sales for this period was $393.5 mil. This means that the forecast error of this period is $10.5 mil. ($393.5 - $383.0) or 2.7%.

WEIGHTED AVERAGE PERCENT CHANGE

The above two models assume that all the periods are equally important, and thus give an equal amount of weight to the value of each period which is one. However, in some situations, the forecaster may feel that the most recent periods are more representative of what will happen tomorrow than the older periods. Thus, he or she may like to give more weight to the most recent periods and less to the others.

There is no hard and fast rule for assigning weights. It all depends upon which weighting scheme captures best the data pattern. In one situation, the weighting scheme of 1, 2 and 3 may be most appropriate, while in other, of 2, 4 and 6. The weighting scheme of 1, 2 and 3 implies to give weight of 1 to the first change, 2 to the second change, 3 to the third change, and so on. Here is a

218

step-by-step procedure to prepare a forecast, using the weighted average percent change model and the sales data of K-Mart Stores (Table 3).

Step 1: Calculate level change in sales from one period to the next, the same way as we did in the case of level change model. The level changes are given in Table 3, Col. 3.

Step 2: Convert the level change into percent, the same way as we did in the case of average percent change model. The percent changes are given in Table 3, Col. 4.

Step 3: Col. 5 in Table 3 gives weights we have assigned to each percent change. We have assigned a weight of 1 to the first percent change, 2 to the second percent change, and so on. Multiply the percent change (Y) with its weight (W), that is, Col. 4 × Col. 5. Their products are given in Col. 6.

TABLE 2
AVERAGE PERCENT CHANGE

Period	Sales of City Stores (Mil. of $)	Level Change (Mil. of $)	Percent Change
(1)	(2)	(3)	(4)
1	356.0	---	----
2	371.6	15.6	4.38
3	373.7	2.1	0.57
4	380.4	6.7	1.79
5	364.8	-15.6	-4.10
6	373.1	8.3	2.28
7	367.4	-5.7	-1.53
8	373.4	5.9	1.61
9	374.1	0.8	0.21
10	380.1	6.0	1.60
Total			6.81

Average % Change $= \dfrac{6.81}{9}$

$= 0.76\%$

$\hat{Y}_{11} = (\$380.1) + (\$380.1 \times .0076)$

$= \$383.0$ mil.

Step 4: Calculate the weighted average percent change. Using the formula given below, the weighted average percent change comes to:

$$\text{Wtd. Avg. \% Change} = \frac{\Sigma YW}{\Sigma W}$$

$$= \frac{741.48}{45}$$

$$= 16.48\%$$

This means that the sales on the average increase at the rate of 16.48% from one period to the next.

TABLE 3
WEIGHTED AVERAGE PERCENTAGE CHANGE

Period	Sales of K-Mart Stores (Mil. of $)	Level Change (Mil. of $)	% Change (Y)	Weight (W)	Col. 4 × Col.5 (YW)
(1)	(2)	(3)	(4)	(5)	(6)
1	3,101	----	----	----	----
2	3,837	736	23.73	1	23.73
3	4,633	796	20.75	2	41.50
4	5,536	903	19.49	3	58.47
5	6,798	1,262	22.80	4	91.20
6	8,382	1,584	23.30	5	116.50
7	9,941	1,559	18.60	6	111.60
8	11,696	1,755	17.65	7	123.55
9	12,731	1,035	8.85	8	70.80
10	14,204	1,473	11.57	9	104.13
Total				45	741.48
				ΣW	ΣYW

Weighted Average % Change = (741.48) / (45) = 16.48%
$\hat{Y}_{11}$ = (14,204) + (14,204)(.1648) = $16,545 mil.

Step 5: Prepare forecast for period 11. This will be equal to the actual of the current period plus 16.48% of it. This comes to $16,545 mil. [($14,204) + ($14,204) × (.1648)]. This compares with the actual value of $16,527, an error of $18 mil. or 0.1%.

CHAPTER 41

MOVING AVERAGE

Chaman L. Jain
St. John's University

Moving average is another time series model. Unlike average percent change and weighted average percent change models, it assumes that the data of most recent periods, not all of the periods, are appropriate for the next period forecast. When we use 3-period moving average, we assume that the average of the last 3 periods is appropriate for the next period forecast. When we use 4-period moving average, we assume that the average of the last 4 periods is appropriate for the next period forecast. The data of most recent periods are more appropriate because data pattern changes over time. What will happen next period depends much more so on the pattern of most recent periods than of all the periods.

Moving average models come in all shapes and colors. It can be a moving average of levels, called moving average level model; moving average of level changes, called moving average level change model; and moving average of percent changes, called moving average percent change model. Moving average can be single and double. In single moving average, the moving average is computed once, whereas in double moving average, it is computed twice.

SINGLE MOVING AVERAGE

In single moving average, we will discuss two models: (1) moving average change and (2) moving average percent change.

Single Moving Average Level Change Model

In a single moving average change model, we use an average of a certain number of changes for making a forecast for the next period. To illustrate it, we will use the sales data of Jewel Company, given in Table 1. Here is a step-by-step procedure:

Step 1: Decide on the period of moving average. That is, of how many periods of moving average (2, 3, or any other number) we wish to use. This depends on how quickly the pattern changes. If the data pattern seems to change significantly over 2 periods, we will use 2-period moving average, if it changes over 3 periods, we will use 3-period moving average.

In the case of Jewel Company, we decide to use 3-period moving average.

Step 2: Compute the change in sales from one period to the next. The change can be negative or positive. The change in sales in period 2 from period 1 is $210.3 mil. ($2219.6 - $2009.3); and so on. The level changes are given in Col. 3.

Step 3: Compute 3-period moving total of changes given in Col. 3. The moving total is computed by adding the first three changes (i.e. of periods 2, 3 and 4), which comes to $808.5 mil. ($210.3 + $379.3 + $218.9). The value is entered next to the period 4 in Col. 4. Then drop one change from the top (i.e., of period 2) and add one change from the bottom (i.e., of period 5). The moving total of period 5 comes to $761.8 mil. ($379.3 + $218.9 + $163.6), which is entered next to the period 5 in Col. 4. Again, drop one change from the top (i.e., of period 3) and add one change from the bottom (i.e., of period 6). The moving total comes to $678.8 mil. ($218.9 + $163.6 + $296.3). The value is entered next to the period 6. Similarly, compute moving total of changes of other periods.

TABLE 1 SINGLE MOVING AVERAGE LEVEL CHANGE				
Period (1)	Sales of Jewel Company (Mil. of $) (2)	Level Change (Mil. of $) (3)	3-Period Moving Total of Changes (Mil. of $) (4)	3-Period Moving Avg. of Changes (Mil. of $) (5)
1	2009.3	---	---	---
2	2219.6	210.3	---	---
3	2598.9	379.3	---	---
4	2817.8	218.9	808.5	269.5
5	2981.4	163.6	761.8	253.9
6	3277.7	296.3	678.8	226.3
7	3516.4	238.7	698.6	232.9
8	3764.3	247.9	782.9	261.0
9	4267.9	503.6	990.2	330.1
10	5107.6	839.7	1591.2	530.4

$$\hat{Y}_{11} = \$5107.6 + \$530.4 \, \text{mil}.$$
$$= \$5638.0 \, \text{mil}.$$

Step 4: Compute moving average level change. Since each moving total is a sum-total of three changes, moving average will be the total divided by three. Moving average of period 4 is $269.5 ($808.5 ÷ 3); the moving average of period 5, $253.9 ($761.8 ÷ 3); and so on. Moving averages are given in Col. 5.

Note here that the moving average value is not entered the way it is done in statistics. If we do it the way it is done in statistics, we cannot prepare a forecast of the next period. So, we adapt it to the forecasting need. In statistics, the value of moving average is placed at the center of periods to be averaged. In the above example, the moving average is of 3 periods. This means that the first moving average ($269.5 in the above example) should be placed next to the period 3 (center of periods 2-4) instead of next to period 4. But the moving average of period 3 cannot be used to make a forecast of period 5. To prepare a forecast of period 5, we need a moving average of period 4. Plus, we will have a problem if the period of moving average is even, say, 4. Here the center will be the midway between periods 3 and 4. If we place the value between these periods, we will have the same problem. The forecast of period 5 cannot be made using the moving average, which lies between periods 3 and 4.

Step 5: Prepare a forecast. In the above example, we want to prepare a forecast of period 11. This means we are in period 10, making a forecast of period 11. The forecast of this period will be the actual sales of period 10 plus the moving average level change of the same period. This comes to $5638.0 mil. ($5107.6 + $530.4).

How accurate is this value? This can be determined by comparing the forecast value with the actual. The actual sale of this period is $5650 mil. This means that the forecast error is $12 mil. ($5650 - $5638) or 0.2%.

Single Moving Average Percent Change Model

The moving average percent change model works the same way as the moving average level change model except it assumes that the next period value will increase (decrease) by the moving average percent change instead of by the moving average level change. Here again we use the sales data of Jewel Company to illustrate the procedure. (See Table 2) Steps to be followed are:

Step 1: Compute level change from one period to the next, the same way we did in case of single moving average level change. Level changes here are given in Table 2, Col. 3.

Step 2: Compute percent change from one period to the next. The percent change of period 2 is 10.47% [(210.3 ÷ 2009.3) × (100)]. The percent change of period 3 is 17.09% [(379.3 ÷ 2219.6) × (100)], and so on. All the percent changes are given in Col. 4.

Step 3: Decide on the period of moving average to be used. Here again we use 3-period moving average.

Step 4: Compute 3-period moving total of percent changes. This is done by adding the first three changes (i.e. of period 2, 3 and 4), and entering the total next to the period 4 in Col. 5. The first moving total of percent changes comes to 35.98% (10.47% + 17.09% + 8.42%). (See Col. 5) Then drop one change from the top (i.e. of period 2) and add one change from the bottom (i.e. of period 5). This moving total of percent changes comes to 31.32% (17.09% + 8.42% + 5.81%), which is entered next to the period 5. Again, drop one change from the top (i.e. of period 3) and add one change from the bottom (i.e. of period 6). This value comes to

24.17% (8.42% + 5.81% + 9.94%). This is entered next to the period 6. Similarly, compute moving total of percent changes of all other periods.

Step 5: Compute moving average percent change. Since each moving total of percent changes is a total of three changes, the average will be the total divided by three. The moving average percent change of period 4 is 11.99% (35.98 ÷ 3), and moving average percent change of period 5 is 10.44 % (31.32 ÷ 3). Moving average % changes are given in Col. 6.

Step 6: Prepare a forecast. Forecast of period 11 will be the actual of period 10 plus 13.37% of it. The forecast of that period comes to $5790.5 mil. [($5107.6) + ($5107.6 × 0.1337)].

Since the actual value of this period is $5650.0 mil., the forecast error comes to $140.5 mil. ($5650.0 - $5790.5), or -2.5%.

DOUBLE MOVING AVERAGE

As described earlier, in a double moving average model, the moving average is computed twice. Here again we will explain double moving average level change and double moving percent change models.

Double Moving Average Level Change Model

Here again we will demonstrate this model by the sales data of Jewel Company. A step-by-step procedure for preparing a forecast with this model is as follows:

Steps 1-4: The first four steps are the same as in single moving average level change model. Thus, Cols. 1-5 in Table 3 are the same as in Table 1. Here again we use moving average of 3 periods.

Step 5: Compute 3-period double moving total of level changes given in Col. 5. This is done by adding first three single moving average level changes given in Col. 5 (i.e. of periods 4, 5 and 6.). Their total comes to $749.7 mil. ($269.5 + $253.9 + $226.3). Enter the total next to the period 6 in Col. 6. Then, drop one change from the top (i.e. of period 4) and add one change from the bottom (i.e. of period 7). This total comes to $713.1 mil. ($253.9 + $226.3 + $232.9). Enter this total next to the period 7. Similarly, compute double moving total of level changes of other periods.

Step 6: Compute 3-period double moving average of level changes. Since each number in Col. 6 is a total of 3 changes, the average will be the total divided by three. Double moving average level change of period 6 is $249.9 ($749.7 ÷ 3); double moving average level change of period 7 is $237.7 ($713.1 ÷ 3); and so on. All the double moving average level changes are given in Table 3, Col. 7.

Step 7: Prepare a forecast. In the above example, we will prepare a forecast of period 11. This will be the actual sale of period 10, plus double moving average level change of the same period. This comes to $5481.4 mil. ($5107.6 + $373.8).

TABLE 2
SINGLE MOVING AVERAGE PERCENT CHANGE

Period	Sales of Jewel Co. (Mil. of $)	Level Change (Mil. of $)	% Change	3-Period Moving Total of % Changes	3-Period Moving Avg. of % Changes
(1)	(2)	(3)	(4)	(5)	(6)
1	2009.3	---	---	---	---
2	2219.6	210.3	10.47	---	---
3	2598.9	379.3	17.09	---	---
4	2817.8	218.9	8.42	35.98	11.99
5	2981.4	163.6	5.81	31.32	10.44
6	3277.7	296.3	9.94	24.17	8.06
7	3516.4	238.7	7.28	23.03	7.68
8	3764.3	247.9	7.05	24.27	8.09
9	4267.9	503.6	13.38	27.71	9.24
10	5107.6	839.7	19.67	40.10	13.37

$$\hat{Y}_{11} = \$5107.6 + (\$5107.6 \times .1337)$$
$$= \$5790.5 \text{ mil.}$$

How does this method perform? Since the actual of this period is $5650.0 mil., the error comes to $168.6 mil., or 3%.

Double Moving Average Percent Change Method

The double moving average percent change model works the same way as the double moving average change model. The only difference is that this model assumes that the next period value will increase or decrease by the double moving average percent change instead of by the double moving average level change. The process of computation is shown in Table 4. Steps, which are used for preparing a forecast with this model, are as follows:

Steps 1-5: The first 5 steps are the same as followed in the single moving average percent change model. Therefore, Col. 1-6 in Table 3 are the same as in Table 2.

Step 6: Compute 3-period double moving total of percent changes. This is done by adding first three single moving average percent changes given in Col. 6 (i.e. of periods 4, 5 and 6). Their total comes to 30.49% (11.99% + 10.44% + 8.06%). Enter the total next to the period 6 in Col. 7. Then, drop one change from the top (i.e. of period 4) and add one change from the bottom (i.e. of period 7). Their total comes to 26.18% (10.44% + 8.06% + 7.68%). Enter that total next to the period 7 in Col. 7. Similarly, compute 3-period double moving percent change total of other periods.

Period	Sales of Jewel Co.	Level Change	3-Period Mov. Total of Changes	3-Period Mov. Avg. of Changes	3- Period Double Mov. Total of Changes	3- Period Double Moving Avg. of Changes
	(Mil. of $)	(Mil. of $)	(Mil. of $)	(Mil. of $)	(Mil. of $)	(Mil. of $)
(1)	(2)	(3)	(4)	(5)	(6)	(7)
1	2009.3	---	---	---	---	---
2	2219.6	210.3	---	---	---	---
3	2598.9	379.3	---	---	---	---
4	2817.8	218.9	808.5	269.5	---	---
5	2981.4	163.6	761.8	253.9	---	---
6	3277.7	296.3	678.8	226.3	749.7	249.9
7	3516.4	238.7	698.6	232.9	713.1	237.7
8	3764.3	247.9	782.9	261.0	720.2	240.1
9	4267.9	503.6	990.2	330.1	824.0	274.7
10	5107.6	839.7	1591.2	530.4	1121.5	373.8

TABLE 3
DOUBLE MOVING AVERAGE LEVEL CHANGE

$$\hat{Y}_{11} = \$5107.6 + \$373.8$$
$$= \$5481.4$$

Step 7: Compute 3-period double moving average percent change. This is done dividing the moving total given in Col. 7 by 3. Since each total in this column is a sum-total of three changes, the average will be computed by dividing each by 3. The double moving average percent change of period 6 is 10.16% (30.49% ÷ 3). The value is entered next to the period 6 in Col. 8. The double moving percent change of period 7 is 8.73% (26.18% ÷ 3). Following this way compute double moving average percent change of other periods.

Step 8: Prepare a forecast. The forecast of period 11 will be the actual of period 10 plus 10.23 % of it. Here 10.23% is used because it is the double moving average percent change of that period. The forecast comes to $5630.1 mil. [($5107.6) + ($5107.6 × 0.1023)].

How does this model perform? This can be determined by comparing the forecast with the actual of this period. The error comes to $19.9 mil. ($5650 - $5630.1), or 0.4%.

DATA REQUIREMENT

The data requirement of moving average models depends on: (1) Periods of moving average, and (2) type of moving average — single or double. The larger the periods of moving average, the greater will be the data requirement. In a single moving average change model, for 2-period moving average, at least 3 periods of data will be needed to prepare a forecast; and for 3-period moving average, at least 4 periods of data will be needed. The use of single or double moving average also makes difference. The double moving average needs more data than the single moving average. In the single moving average level change model, for a 3-period moving average, at least 4 periods of data will be needed to prepare a forecast. Whereas, in the double moving average level change model, for the same moving average, at least 6 periods of data will be needed.

TABLE 4
DOUBLE MOVING AVERAGE PERCENT CHANGE

Period	Sales of Jewel Co. $Mil.	Level Change $Mil.	% Change (%)	3- Period Mov. Total of % Changes (%)	3- Period Mov. Avg. of % Changes (%)	3- Period Double Mov. Total of % Changes (%)	3- Period Double Mov. Avg. of % Changes (%)
(1)	(2)	(3)	(4)	(5)	(6)	(7)	(8)
1	2009.3	---	---	---	---	---	---
2	2219.6	210.3	10.47	---	---	---	---
3	2598.9	379.3	17.09	---	---	---	---
4	2817.8	218.9	8.42	35.98	11.99	---	---
5	2981.4	163.6	5.81	31.32	10.44	---	---
6	3277.7	296.3	9.94	24.17	8.06	30.49	10.16
7	3516.4	238.7	7.28	23.03	7.68	26.18	8.73
8	3764.3	247.9	7.05	24.27	8.09	23.83	7.94
9	4267.9	503.6	13.38	27.71	9.24	25.01	8.34
10	5107.6	839.7	19.67	40.10	13.37	30.70	10.23

$$\hat{Y}_{11} = \$5107.6 + (\$5107.6 \times .1023)$$
$$= \$5630.1 \, mil.$$

CHAPTER 42

EXPONENTIAL SMOOTHING

Chaman L. Jain
St. John's University

Exponential smoothing models are also members of the time series family. They differ from average change and moving average change models in one important way. In average change and moving average change models each observation gets the same amount of weight, which is one. But in exponential smoothing more weight is given to most recent observations and less to others, and the weight exponentially decreases as we go back. There are different types of exponential smoothing models — single, double, and triple. Within each one of them, there are some variations. For example, within single exponential smoothing, it can be single exponential smoothing (normally used) and single exponential smoothing with an adaptive approach. Within double exponential smoothing, it can be double exponential smoothing with Brown's one parameter and double exponential smoothing with Holt's two parameters. Because of the complexity in their computations, we will describe only two simple models — (1) single exponential smoothing and (2) double exponential smoothing with Brown's one parameter. Forecasting packages such as Smart Forecast and Forecast Pro are available which can be used to prepare forecasts with these and other models.

SINGLE EXPONENTIAL SMOOTHING

There are two basic properties of single exponential smoothing model. One, it gives more weight to the most recent data and less to others. In fact, this is true with all exponential smoothing models. Two, it automatically adjusts for the error experienced in the current period. We can demonstrate both these properties with the help of a formula of single exponential smoothing, which is:

$$F_{t+1} = \alpha X_t + (1-\alpha) F_t \qquad \qquad \dots (1)$$

where

F_{t+1}	=	Forecast of the next period
α	=	Smoothing constant
X_t	=	Actual value of the current period
F_t	=	Forecast value of the current period

Property 1: It gives more weight to the most recent value and less to others. The amount of weight decreases exponentially as we go backward. How much weight is given to each value depends on the size of the alpha (α) value used in the formula. The α value varies between 0 and 1. The larger the α value, the greater will be the weight.

Let us say that there are four observations. If $\alpha = .2$, then the weights assigned to past observations will be as follows:

$$
\begin{aligned}
X_t &= .2 &&= (.2)(1 - .2)^0 \\
X_{t-1} &= .16 &&= (.2)(1 - .2)^1 \\
X_{t-2} &= .128 &&= (.2)(1 - .2)^2 \\
X_{t-3} &= .1024 &&= (.2)(1 - .2)^3
\end{aligned}
$$

Property 2: It automatically adjusts for the error experienced in the current period. The size of adjustment depends on the size of α value. The larger the α value, the larger will be the adjustment for error. As mentioned earlier, the α value varies between 0 and 1. There will be no adjustment for the error if $\alpha = 0$, and maximum adjustment, if $\alpha = 1$. We can demonstrate this with the help of formula of a single exponential smoothing model, which is:

$$ F_{t+1} = \alpha\, X_t + (1 - \alpha)\, F_t \qquad \qquad \text{... (2)} $$

This can be re-written as:

$$
\begin{aligned}
\text{or} \quad & = \alpha\, X_t + F_t - \alpha\, F_t \\
\text{or} \quad & = F_t + \alpha\, X_t - \alpha\, F_t \\
\text{or} \quad & = F_t + \alpha\, (X_t - Ft) \qquad \qquad \text{... (3)}
\end{aligned}
$$

If we express $X_t - F_t$ (actual - forecast) as e_t (forecast error of the current period), then:

$$ X_t - F_t = e_t \qquad \qquad \text{... (4)} $$

The equation (3) becomes:

$$ F_{t+1} = F_t + \alpha\, (e_t) \qquad \qquad \text{... (5)} $$

This equation states that the forecast of the next period (F_{t+1}) is equal to the forecast of the current period (F_t) plus alpha (α) times forecast error (e_t) experienced in the current period. In other words, the forecast of the next period is equal to the forecast of the current period plus the value adjusted for the error in the current period. The adjusted value depends on the size of the α value. The larger the α value, the greater will be the adjustment for the error.

Here is a step-by-step procedure for preparing a forecast with single exponential smoothing model using sales data of Jewel Company (See Table 1):

Step 1: Determine the optimal α value. As mentioned earlier, the α value ranges between 0 and 1. To arrive at the optimal value, one has to prepare forecasts by using all the values between 0 and 1, i.e., .1, .2 and .3, to find out which value, on the average, yields the least amount of error. The value that yields the lowest error is the optimal value. It is difficult to go through this procedure manually. But every software package of single exponential smoothing goes through this iteration to arrive at this value. In case of Jewel Company, the computer came up with the optimal value of .99.

Step 2: Initialize the forecast. As can be seen from the formula given in Equation (1), if one wishes to make a forecast of period one, one needs a forecast of the previous period, which we don't have. Also, in order to make a forecast of period 11, which is the objective of this demonstration, one has to make forecasts of all the periods starting with period 1. So, we initialize the forecast by assuming that forecast of period 1 is the same as the actual, which is, \$2009.30. (See Table 1, Col. 3.)

Step 3: Prepare forecasts. First, we have to prepare a forecast of period 2. (This is the first period for which forecast can be prepared.) Keep in mind we are in period 1 and making a forecast of period 2. This can be done by plugging the values in Equation (1). Here:

$$\alpha = .99$$
$$X_t = 2009.30$$
$$F_t = 2009.30$$

The forecast of period 2 will be:

$$F_2 = [(.99)(2009.30)] + [(1-.99)(2009.30)]$$

$$= 2009.30$$

If we are in period 2 and wish to make a forecast of period 3, then:

$$X_t = 2219.60$$
$$F_t = 2009.30$$

The forecast of period 3 will be:

$$F_3 = [(.99)(2219.60)] + [(1 - .99)(2009.30)$$

$$= 2217.49$$

Similarly, if we are in period 10 and wish to make a forecast of period 11, then:

$$X_t = 5107.60$$
$$F_t = 4262.84$$

The forecast of period 11 will be:

$$F_{11} = [(.99)(5107.60)] + [(1 - .99)(4262.84)]$$

$$= \$5099.15 \text{ mil.}$$

TABLE 1
SINGLE EXPONENTIAL SMOOTHING

Period (1)	Sales of Jewel Co. (Mil. Of $) (X) (2)	Forecast (Mil. of $) (F) (3)
1	2009.30	2009.30
2	2219.60	2009.30
3	2598.90	2217.49
4	2817.80	2595.09
5	2981.40	2815.57
6	3277.70	2979.75
7	3516.40	3274.72
8	3764.30	3513.99
9	4267.90	3761.80
10	5107.60	4262.84
11		5099.15

DOUBLE EXPONENTIAL SMOOTHING WITH BROWN'S ONE PARAMETER

Since the single exponential smoothing model does not account for a trend in the data, the forecasted value computed by this model will lag behind the actual value particularly where there is a trend in the data. The double exponential smoothing with Brown's one parameter model overcomes this problem by adjusting the forecasted value for the trend.

Here is a step-by-step procedure for preparing forecasts with double exponential smoothing. We will again use sales data of Jewel company. (See Table 2)

Step 1: Determine the optimal α value. Here again one has to prepare forecasts of all the periods using all the α values between 0 and 1 and then determine which value on the average yields the lowest error. The optimal α value came to .70.

Step 2: The formula for computing forecast with double exponential smoothing is:

$$Y_{t+p} = a_t + b_t (P) \quad\quad ... (6)$$

where

$$Y_{t+p} = \text{Forecast value of the "P" period}$$

a_t	=	"a" value of the current period
b_t	=	"b" value of the current period
P	=	Number of periods ahead to be forecasted (If you wish to forecast one period ahead P = 1, if you wish to forecast two periods ahead, P = 2, and so on.)

TABLE 2
DOUBLE EXPONENTIAL SMOOTHING WITH
BROWN'S ONE PARAMETER

Period	Sales of Jewel Co. ($ Mil.)	S	D	a	b	Forecasts ($ Mil.)
(1)	(2)	(3)	(4)	(5)	(6)	(7)
1	2009.30	2009.30	2009.30	2009.30	000.00	---
2	2219.60	2156.51	2112.35	2200.67	103.03	2009.30
3	2598.90	2466.18	2360.04	2572.32	247.62	2303.70
4	2817.80	2712.31	2606.63	2817.99	246.55	2819.94
5	2981.40	2900.67	2812.46	2988.88	205.79	3064.54
6	3277.70	3164.59	3058.95	3270.23	246.46	3194.67
7	3516.40	3410.86	3305.29	3516.43	246.29	3516.69
8	3764.30	3658.27	3552.38	3764.16	247.04	3762.72
9	4267.90	4085.01	3925.22	4244.80	372.79	4011.20
10	5107.60	4800.82	4538.14	5063.50	612.83	4617.59
11						5676.33

Notes: S = Single exponential smoothing
D = Double exponential smoothing

To compute the value of "a" and "b," we need to compute single smoothed value (S) and double smoothed value (D). Next step is to compute S value for each period, the formula for which is:

$$S_t = \alpha X_t + (1 - \alpha)S_{t-1} \qquad \ldots (7)$$

where

S_t	=	Single smoothed value of the current period
α	=	Smoothing Constant
X_t	=	Actual value of the current period
S_{t-1}	=	Single smoothed value of one period before the current period

As can be seen from the above formula, to compute S value of period 1, we need S value of one period before (S_{t-1}) which we don't have. So, to initialize it, we assume S value of period 1 is the same as actual ($2009.30). The other S values we can compute by plugging the appropriate values in Equation (7). The S value of periods 2 comes to:

$$S_2 \quad = \quad (.70)(2219.60) + (1 - .70)(2009.30)$$

$$= \quad 2156.51$$

The S value of period 3 comes to:

$$S_3 \quad = \quad (.70)(2598.90) + (1 - .70)(2156.51)$$
$$= \quad 2466.18$$

Similarly, we can compute other S values which are given in Table 2, Col. 3.

Step 3: Compute double smoothed value (D) of each period. The formula for computing D is:

$$D_t \quad = \quad \alpha S_t + (1 - \alpha)D_{t-1} \qquad \qquad \text{... (8)}$$

where

D_t = Double smoothed value of the current period

α = Smoothing constant

D_{t-1} = Double smoothed value of one period before the current period

Here again to compute the D value, we need the D value of the previous period, which we don't have. Therefore, to initialize it, we assume the D value (double smoothed value) of the first period is the same as the S value of that period (which is $2009.30). Thereafter, we compute their values by plugging appropriate values in Equation (8). The D value of period 2 comes to:

$$D_2 \quad = \quad (.70)(2156.51) + (1 - .70)(2009.30)$$
$$= \quad 2112.35$$

The D value of period of 3 comes to;

$$D_3 \quad = \quad (.70)(2466.18) + (1 - .70)(2112.35)$$
$$= \quad 2360.04$$

Similarly, we can compute D values of other periods which are given in Table 2, Col. 4.

Step 4: Compute "a" value for all the periods. The formula for computing "a" value is:

$$a_t \quad = \quad 2(S_t) - (D_t) \qquad \qquad \text{... (9)}$$

We can compute "a" values of all the periods by plugging appropriate values in equation (9). The "a" value of period 1 comes to:

$$a_1 \quad = \quad 2(2009.30) - (2009.30)$$
$$\quad = \quad 2009.30$$

The "a" value of period 2 comes to:

$$a_2 \quad = \quad 2(2156.51) - (2112.35)$$
$$\quad = \quad 2200.67$$

Similarly, we can compute other "a" values which are given in Table 2, Col. 5.

Step 5: Compute "b" value of all the periods. Its formula is:

$$b_t \quad = \quad [(\alpha)/(1 - \alpha)] \times [(S_t - D_t)] \qquad \qquad \dots (10)$$

Here again we can compute "b" values of all the periods by plugging the appropriate values in Equation (10). The "b" value of period 1 comes to:

$$b_1 \quad = \quad [(.70)/(1 - .70)] \times [(2009.30 - 2009.30)]$$
$$\quad = \quad 0$$

The "b" value of period 2 comes to:

$$b_2 \quad = \quad [(.70)/(1 - .70)] \times [(2156.51 - 2112.35)]$$
$$\quad = \quad 103.03$$

Similarly, we can compute "b" values of other periods which are given in Table 2, Col. 6.

Step 6: Prepare forecasts. Forecasts can be prepared by plugging the "a" and "b" values in Equation (6). Let us say we are in period 1 and wish to make a forecast of period 2. Here P will be 1 because we are making one period ahead forecast. The forecast will come to:

$$F_2 \quad = \quad (2009.30) + (000.00)\,(1)$$
$$\quad = \quad \$2009.30$$

If we are in period 2 and wish to make a forecast of period 3, then:

$$F_3 \quad = \quad (2200.67) + (103.03)\,(1)$$
$$\quad = \quad \$2303.70$$

Similarly, if we are in period 10 and wish to make a forecast of period 11, it will be:

$$F_{11} \quad = \quad (5063.50) + (612.83)\,(1)$$
$$\quad = \quad \$5676.33$$

OTHER EXPONENTIAL SMOOTHING MODELS

The two models discussed above are not the be all and end all of exponential smoothing models. There are many other variations in exponential smoothing, though the ones discussed above are most often mentioned in the forecasting literature. Others include single exponential smoothing with an adaptive approach, double exponential smoothing with Holt's two parameters, triple exponential smoothing with Brown's one-parameter quadratic approach, and triple exponential smoothing with Winters' three-parameter trend and seasonality. The single exponential smoothing model with an adaptive approach allows the α value to change in a controlled manner to capture a change in the data pattern. Though both double exponential smoothing with Brown's one parameter and double exponential smoothing with Holt's two parameters adjust the forecast value for level and trend, the former uses the same smoothing weight for both and the latter uses one for level and another for trend.

Both single and double exponential smoothing models assume a linear data pattern. But the data pattern may very well be curvilinear. The triple exponential smoothing models account for the curvilinear pattern in the data. The difference between the triple exponential smoothing with Brown's one-parameter quadratic approach and triple exponential smoothing with Winters' three-parameter trend and seasonality is that the latter adjusts for, among other things, seasonality in the data whereas the former does not.

CHPATER 43

TREND LINE

Chaman L. Jain
St. John's University

A trend line model is often used to determine the long-term trend in a time series data. There are a number of models used to fit a line to a set of data. The objective here is to fit a line to a set of data so that deviations of observations from the line are very small. The model, which is often used, is the method of least squares – the one we will discuss in this chapter. How to prepare a forecast with a least squares trend line model depends on whether the number of observations are odd or even. We will show what to do in each case.

PREPARING A FORECAST WHERE NUMBER OF OBSERVATIONS IS ODD

Here is a step-by-step procedure for preparing a forecast with a trend line model where the number of observations is odd. We will use the data of K-Mart Stores as given in Table 1. We have sales data of nine periods and will make a forecast of the tenth period. The trend line equation is written as follows:

$$T = a + bX \qquad \qquad \dots (1)$$

where

T	=	Trend value (forecast)
a	=	Intercept
b	=	Slope of the line
X	=	Coded value which we assign

If we know the values of a, b and X, we can get the trend value, which is forecast. The steps are as follows:

Step 1: Assign code values, which are X values (Table 1, Col. 3). The assignment of code values depends on whether the number of observations is odd or even. In this example, the number of observations is nine, which is odd. In that case, take the mid period, which is, period 5, and assign it the value of zero. Then, decrement by one going backward, and increment by one going forward. In other words, the code value of period 4 will be –1, period 5, -2, and so on.

Similarly, code value of period 6 will be +1, period 7, +2, and so on. (See Table 1, Col. 3) There are a number of ways of assigning code values, but this is the one most often used.

Step 2: Compute "a" and "b" by plugging the values in their formulas:

$$a = \frac{\Sigma Y}{N} = \frac{77,758}{9} = 8,639.78$$

$$b = \frac{\Sigma XY}{\Sigma X^2} = \frac{81,225}{60} = 1,353.75$$

Step 3: Forecast value of period 10. Once values of "a" and "b" are computed, the trend line equation, as shown in Equation 1, becomes:

$$T = 8,639.78 + 1,353.75X$$

The "X" value of period 10 will be 5. By plugging its value in the above equation, we get forecast value of period 10, which comes to:

$$T_{10} = 8,639.78 + (1,353.75)(5) = \$15,408.53 \text{ mil.}$$

PREPARING FORECAST WHERE NUMBER OF OBSERVATIONS IS EVEN

The procedure of forecasting is the same except the way X values are assigned. Here is a step by step procedure:

Step 1: Assign code values, which are our X values (Table 2, Col. 3). Here we have even number of observations — 10 in total. Take two central periods, which in this case are periods 5 and 6. Assign a value of –1 to period 5 and +1 to period 6. Then, decrement by two going back, that is, assign a value of –3 to period 4, -5 to period 3, and so on. Increment by two going forward, that is, assign a value of +3 to period 7, +5 to period 8, and so on.

Step 2: Compute "a" and "b" by plugging values into the same formulas:

$$a = \frac{\Sigma Y}{N} = \frac{80,859}{10} = 8,085.9$$

$$b = \frac{\Sigma XY}{\Sigma X^2} = \frac{212,299}{330} = 643.33$$

TABLE 1
COMPUTATION OF TREND BASED FORECAST

(Where number of observations are odd)
K-Mart Stores

Period	Sales (Mil. of $) Y	X	XY	X^2
(1)	(2)	(3)	(4)	(5)
1	3,837	-4	-15,348	16
2	4,633	-3	-13,899	9
3	5,536	-2	-11,072	4
4	6,798	-1	-6,798	1
5	8,382	0	0	0
6	9,941	+1	9,941	1
7	11,696	+2	23,392	4
8	12,731	+3	38,193	9
9	14,204	+4	56,816	16
Total	77,758		81,225	60
	ΣY		ΣXY	ΣX^2

$$a = \frac{\Sigma Y}{N} = \frac{77,758}{9} = 8,639.78$$

$$b = \frac{\Sigma XY}{\Sigma X^2} = \frac{81,225}{60} = 1,353.75$$

$T = 8,639.78 + 1,353.75X$

$T_{10} = 8,639.78 + (1,353.75) \times 5 = \$15,408.53$ mil.

Step 3: Forecast the value of period 11 by plugging the values of "a," "b" and "X," in Equation (1). X value of period 11 will be 11. The forecast comes to:

$T_{11} = 8,085.9 + (643.33) \times (11) = \$15,162.53$ mil.

TABLE 2
COMPUTATION OF TREND VALUE

(Where number of observations are even)
K-Mart Stores

Period (1)	Sales (Mil. of $) Y (2)	X (3)	XY (4)	X^2 (5)
1	3,101	-9	-27,909	81
2	3,837	-7	-26,859	49
3	4,633	-5	-23,165	25
4	5,536	-3	-16,608	9
5	6,798	-1	-6,798	1
6	8,382	+1	8,382	1
7	9,941	+3	29,823	9
8	11,696	+5	58,480	25
9	12,731	+7	89,117	49
10	14,204	+9	127,836	81
Total	**80,859** ΣY		212,299 ΣXY	330 ΣX^2

$$a = \frac{\Sigma Y}{N} = \frac{80,859}{10} = 8,085.9$$

$$b = \frac{\Sigma XY}{\Sigma X2} = \frac{212,299}{330} = 643.33$$

$$T_{11} = 8,085.9 + (643.33) \times (11) = \$15,162.53 \, \text{mil.}$$

CHAPTER 44

CLASSICAL DECOMPOSITION

Chaman L. Jain
St. John's University

The classical decomposition is another method of times series. It assumes that each value has four components: (1) trend, (2) seasonal, (3) cyclical and (4) random/irregular. To make a forecast for the next period, one has to first estimate the values of these components. The decomposition method can be additive and multiplicative. In additive, we add these components to get a forecasted value, whereas in multiplicative, we multiply them. The approach which is most often used is multiplicative, and this is the one we will discuss in this chapter.

Before proceeding further one has to understand what these components are and what they imply. The trend component refers to a long-term trend in the data. The sales move up and down from one period to the next but the overall trend may be either upward or downward.

The seasonal component measures seasonal variations, which occur regularly and periodically, and the length of a cycle is always less than one year. The sales of a department store reach peak in the month of December because of Christmas. This occurs regularly (because it happens every year) and periodically (because it happens at the same time).

The seasonal variations are caused by customs and traditions (as in the case of Christmas), as well as by weather. The sales of certain sporting goods such as tennis racquets go up during summer and go down during winter. This happens regularly and periodically.

The length of a cycle can be measured either from trough to trough or from peak to peak, that is, how much time it takes for sales to go from one trough to the next or from one peak to the next. In the case of a seasonal cycle, the cycle is completed within a year. For a department store, sales reach peak in the month of December. Its seasonal cycle is completed within a year, that is, from December of one year to December of the next year. This means if you are preparing forecasts for a period less than one year, say, for weeks, months and quarters, you have to be concerned about seasonality. Otherwise, you don't have to be concerned about this component.

TABLE 1
SALES DATA OF FANTASTIC RUBBER COMPANY

Mos	1996			1997			1998			1999			2000		
	Sales $Mil	Seasonal Factor	Specific Seasonal Index	Sales $Mil	Seasonal Factor	Specific Seasonal Index	Sales $Mil	Seasonal Factor	Specific Seasonal Index	Sales $Mil	Seasonal Factor	Specific Seasonal Index	Sales $Mil	Seasonal Factor	Specific Seasonal Index
(1)	(2)	(3)	(4)	(5)	(6)	(7)	(8)	(9)	(10)	(11)	(12)	(13)	(14)	(15)	(16)
Jan	18	× 6.1224	= 110.2	25	× 4.4776	= 111.9	32	× 3.7736	= 120.8	38	× 3.0303	= 115.2	48	× 2.3211	= 111.4
Feb	16	× 6.1224	= 98.0	23	× 4.4776	= 103.0	29	× 3.7736	=109.4	32	× 3.0303	= 97.0	45	× 2.3211	= 104.4
Mar	15	× 6.1224	= 91.8	22	× 4.4776	= 98.5	27	× 3.7736	= 101.9	30	× 3.0303	= 90.9	41	× 2.3211	= 95.2
Apr	15	× 6.1224	= 91.8	23	× 4.4776	= 103.0	27	× 3.7736	= 101.9	31	× 3.0303	= 93.9	41	× 2.3211	= 95.2
May	16	× 6.1224	= 98.0	18	× 4.4776	= 80.6	23	× 3.7736	= 86.8	28	× 3.0303	= 84.9	39	× 2.3211	= 90.5
Jun	13	× 6.1224	= 79.6	16	× 4.4776	= 71.7	20	× 3.7736	= 75.5	27	× 3.0303	= 81.8	35	× 2.3211	= 81.2
Jul	12	× 6.1224	= 73.5	15	× 4.4776	= 67.2	20	× 3.7736	= 75.5	28	× 3.0303	= 84.8	38	× 2.3211	= 88.2
Aug	15	× 6.1224	= 91.8	21	× 4.4776	= 94.0	23	× 3.7736	= 86.8	31	× 3.0303	= 84.8	41	× 2.3211	= 95.2
Sept	17	× 6.1224	= 104.1	23	× 4.4776	= 103.0	25	× 3.7736	= 94.3	33	× 3.0303	= 100.0	43	× 2.3211	= 99.8
Oct	19	× 6.1224	= 116.3	26	× 4.4776	= 116.4	26	× 3.7736	= 98.1	37	× 3.0303	= 112.1	48	× 2.3211	= 111.4
Nov	22	× 6.1224	= 134.7	30	× 4.4776	= 134.3	35	× 3.7736	= 132.0	42	× 3.0303	= 127.3	52	× 2.3211	= 120.7
Dec	18	× 6.1224	= 110.2	26	× 4.4776	= 116.4	31	× 3.7736	= 117.0	39	× 3.0303	= 118.2	46	× 2.3211	= 106.8
	---	× 6.1224	---	---	× 4.4776	---	---	× 3.7736	---	---	× 3.0303	---	---	× 2.3211	---
	196		**1200.0**	**268**		**1200.0**	**318**		**1200.0**	**396**		**1200.0**	**517**		**1200.0**

Factor = 1200 ÷ 196 = 6.1224

Factor = 1200 ÷ 268 = 4.4776

Factor = 1200 ÷ 318 = 3.7736

Factor = 1200 ÷ 396 = 3.0303

Factor = 1200 ÷ 517 = 2.3211

TABLE 2
TYPICAL SEASONAL INDICES

	Line	Rank (1)	Jan (2)	Feb (3)	Mar (4)	Apr (5)	May (6)	Jun (7)	Jul (8)	Aug (9)	Sept (10)	Oct (11)	Nov (12)	Dec (13)	Sum (14)
Lowest	1	1	110.2	97.0	90.9	91.8	80.6	71.7	67.2	86.8	94.3	98.1	120.7	106.8	
	2	2	111.4	98.0	91.8	93.9	84.9	75.5	73.5	91.8	99.8	111.4	127.3	110.2	
	3	3	111.9	103.0	95.2	95.2	86.8	79.6	75.5	93.9	100.0	112.1	132.0	116.4	
	4	4	115.2	104.4	98.5	101.9	90.5	81.2	84.8	94.0	103.0	116.3	134.3	117.0	
Highest	5	5	120.8	109.4	101.9	103.0	98.0	81.8	88.2	95.2	104.1	116.5	134.7	118.2	
Total of 3 Central Values	6		338.5	305.4	285.5	291.0	262.2	236.3	233.8	279.7	302.8	339.8	393.6	343.6	
Modified Avg.	7		112.8	101.8	95.2	97.0	87.4	78.8	77.9	93.2	100.9	113.3	131.2	114.5	= 1204
Typical Seasonal Index	8		112.4	101.5	94.9	96.7	87.1	78.5	77.6	92.9	100.6	112.9	130.8	114.1	= 1200

241

242

TABLE 3
COMPUTATION OF TREND AND CYCLICAL VALUES

Period (1)	Year & Month (2)		Sales ($Mil.) (3)	Seasonal Values (4)	TCR (Col.3 ÷ Col.4) (Y) (5)	Code (X) (6)
1	1996	Jan	18	1.124	16.01	-59
2		Feb	16	1.015	15.76	-57
3		Mar	15	0.949	15.81	-55
4		Apr	15	0.967	15.51	-53
5		May	16	0.871	18.37	-51
6		June	13	0.785	16.56	-49
7		July	12	0.776	15.46	-47
8		Aug	15	0.929	16.15	-45
9		Sept	17	1.006	16.90	-43
10		Oct	19	1.129	16.83	-41
11		Nov	22	1.308	16.82	-39
12		Dec	18	1.141	15.78	-37
13	1997	Jan	25	1.124	22.24	-35
14		Feb	23	1.015	22.66	-33
15		Mar	22	0.949	23.18	-31
16		Apr	23	0.967	23.78	-29
17		May	18	0.871	20.67	-27
18		June	16	0.785	20.38	-25
19		July	15	0.776	19.33	-23
20		Aug	21	0.929	22.60	-21
21		Sept	23	1.006	22.86	-19
22		Oct	26	1.129	23.03	-17
23		Nov	30	1.308	22.94	-15
24		Dec	26	1.141	22.79	-13
25	1998	Jan	32	1.124	28.47	-11
26		Feb	29	1.015	28.57	-9
27		Mar	27	0.949	28.45	-7
28		Apr	27	0.967	27.92	-5
29		May	23	0.871	26.41	-3
30		June	20	0.785	25.48	-1
31		July	20	0.776	25.77	1
32		Aug	23	0.929	24.76	3
33		Sept	25	1.006	24.85	5
34		Oct	26	1.129	23.03	7
35		Nov	35	1.308	26.76	9
36		Dec	31	1.141	27.17	11
37	1999	Jan	38	1.124	33.81	13
38		Feb	32	1.015	31.53	15
39		Mar	30	0.949	31.61	17
40		Apr	31	0.967	32.06	19
41		May	28	0.871	32.15	21
42		June	27	0.785	34.39	23
43		July	28	0.776	36.08	25
44		Aug	31	0.929	33.37	27
45		Sept	33	1.006	32.80	29
46		Oct	37	1.129	32.77	31
47		Nov	42	1.308	32.11	33
48		Dec	39	1.141	34.18	35
49	2000	Jan	48	1.124	42.70	37
50		Feb	45	1.015	44.33	39
51		Mar	41	0.949	43.20	41
52		Apr	41	0.967	42.40	43
53		May	39	0.871	44.78	45
54		June	35	0.785	44.59	47
55		July	38	0.776	48.97	49
56		Aug	41	0.929	44.13	51
57		Sept	43	1.006	42.74	53
58		Oct	48	1.129	42.52	55
59		Nov	52	1.308	39.76	57
60		Dec	46	1.141	40.32	59
					ΣY 1697.36	

		TABLE 3			
		COMPUTATION OF TREND AND CYCLICAL VALUES			
XY	X²	Trend Value T	(CR) (Col. 5 ÷ Col 9)	3 Month Moving Total	3 Month Moving Average
(7)	(8)	(9)	(10)	(11)	(12)
-944.84	3481	12.95	1.24	-	-
-898.52	3249	13.47	1.17	-	-
-869.34	3025	13.99	1.13	-	-
-822.13	2809	14.51	1.07	3.54	1.18
-936.85	2601	15.03	1.22	3.37	1.12
-811.46	2401	15.55	1.06	3.42	1.14
-726.80	2209	16.07	0.96	3.36	1.12
-726.59	2025	16.59	0.97	3.25	1.08
-726.64	1849	17.11	0.99	3.00	1.00
-689.99	1681	17.63	0.95	2.92	0.97
-655.96	1521	18.15	0.93	2.92	0.97
-583.70	1369	18.67	0.84	2.87	0.96
-778.47	1225	19.19	1.16	2.73	0.91
-747.78	1089	19.71	1.15	2.93	0.98
-718.65	961	20.23	1.15	3.15	1.05
-689.76	841	20.75	1.15	3.45	1.15
-557.98	729	21.27	0.97	3.44	1.15
-509.55	625	21.79	0.94	3.26	1.09
-444.59	529	22.31	0.87	3.05	1.02
-474.70	441	22.83	0.99	2.77	0.92
-434.39	361	23.35	0.98	2.79	0.93
-391.50	289	23.87	0.96	2.84	0.95
-344.04	225	24.39	0.94	2.93	0.98
-296.23	169	24.91	0.91	2.88	0.96
-313.17	121	25.43	1.12	2.82	0.94
-257.14	81	25.95	1.10	2.97	0.99
-199.16	49	26.47	1.07	3.14	1.05
-139.61	25	26.99	1.03	3.30	1.10
-79.22	9	27.51	0.96	3.21	1.07
-25.48	1	28.03	0.91	3.07	1.02
25.77	1	28.55	0.90	2.90	0.97
74.27	9	29.07	0.85	2.77	0.92
124.25	25	29.59	0.84	2.66	0.89
161.20	49	30.11	0.76	2.59	0.86
240.83	81	30.63	0.87	2.46	0.82
298.86	121	31.15	0.87	2.48	0.83
439.50	169	31.67	1.07	2.51	0.84
472.91	225	32.19	0.98	2.81	0.94
537.41	289	32.71	0.97	2.92	0.97
609.10	361	33.23	0.96	3.01	1.00
675.09	441	33.75	0.95	2.91	0.97
791.08	529	34.27	1.00	2.88	0.96
902.06	625	34.79	1.04	2.92	0.97
900.97	729	35.31	0.95	2.99	1.00
951.29	841	35.83	0.92	2.99	1.00
1015.94	961	36.35	0.90	2.90	0.97
1059.63	1089	36.87	0.87	2.76	0.92
1196.32	1225	37.39	0.91	2.69	0.90
1580.07	1369	37.91	1.13	2.69	0.90
1729.06	1521	38.43	1.15	2.91	0.97
1771.34	1681	38.95	1.11	3.19	1.06
1823.16	1849	39.47	1.07	3.39	1.13
2014.93	2025	39.99	1.12	3.34	1.11
2095.54	2209	40.51	1.10	3.30	1.10
2399.48	2401	41.03	1.19	3.29	1.10
2250.81	2601	41.55	1.06	3.41	1.14
2265.41	2809	42.07	1.02	3.36	1.12
2338.35	3025	42.59	1.00	3.27	1.09
2266.06	3249	43.11	0.92	3.08	1.03
2378.62	3481	43.63	0.92	2.94	0.98
ΣXY 18,595.07	ΣX² 71,980				

The cyclical component measures cyclical variations, which occur regularly but not periodically. The length of a cycle is always more than one year. The sales, for example, go up for a certain period of time, hits the peak and then start falling. The cyclical variations do not occur periodically because it is not certain how much time it will take for sales to go from trough to peak or from peak to trough. One time it may take sales to go from trough to peak three years, and another time, five years. As such, the length of a complete cyclical cycle varies from one cycle to the next.

The random/irregular component measures variations, which occur randomly/irregularly. The sales of a company in one period may go down because of a labor strike, riot, snowstorm or hurricane. In another period, sales may go up because of a visit by Pope, Olympic game or World's Fair. Such events have a strong impact on certain businesses. On October 3, 1995, between 1 and 1:15 P.M., for example, the TV rating of all major channels shot up because at that time the verdict on the nationally publicized case, People vs. O. J. Simpson, was announced. At that time 49.4% of the nation's 95.9 million households tuned in to their TV set. This compares with 30%, normal level at that time of a day. Since such events occur randomly/irregularly, they are by definition unpredictable. We make adjustments in the historical data for such variations but we do not include them in the computation of forecasts. In other words, forecasts are prepared with an assumption that normal conditions will prevail, that is, no random event will occur during the forecast period. Next we will show how to compute each of these components.

SEASONAL COMPONENT

The seasonal component refers to a seasonal index. The seasonal indices are based on the average of 100. If the seasonal index of January is 120, it means that January performs 20% better than the average — average of 12 months. If it is 85, it means it performs 15% poorer than average. The average, which is 100, is the average of all the indices of 12 months. Any month having an index of more than 100 means that it performs better than the average. Any month having an index of less than 100 means that it performs poorer than the average.

Since there are 12 months in a year and the average of their indices is 100, the sum-total of all the indices will be 1200. Similarly, the sum-total of quarterly indices will be 400, since there are 4 quarters in a year.

There are two types of seasonal indices — specific and typical. The specific seasonal index is based on the data of just one year, whereas the typical seasonal index is based on the data of two or more years. The typical seasonal index is an average of specific seasonal indices.

Specific Seasonal Index

We will demonstrate the computation of specific seasonal index using the 1996 sales data of Fantastic Rubber Company as given in Table 1. There are several ways of doing it. The one we will show is the simplest one. Here is a step-by-step procedure:

Step 1:   Add up the sales of all the months of 1996, which comes to 196 (see Table 1, Col. 2).

Step 2:   Determine the factor, which is computed as follows:

$$\text{Factor} = \frac{1200}{\text{Total Sales}}$$

or

$$= \frac{1200}{196} = 6.1224$$

Since we are computing monthly seasonal indices, the numerator will be 1200 (100 × 12). This is because there are 12 months in a year, and the average value of a seasonal index is 100. Similarly, if we wish to compute quarterly seasonal indices, the numerator will be 400 (100 × 4).

Step 3: Multiply the sales of each month by the factor, which is 6.1224. This will give us seasonal index of each month. The sales index of January comes to 110.2 (18 × 6.1124), the sales index of February comes to 98.0 (16 × 6.1224), and so on. These are specific seasonal indices, which are given in Table 1, Col. 4.

Typical Seasonal Index

The typical seasonal index is the average of specific seasonal indices. There are several ways of computing it. Here is the simplest way. Its procedure is as follows:

Step 1: Compute specific seasonal indices of sales of all the five years (1996-2000) the same way as shown above. The specific seasonal indices are given in Table 1, Cols. 4, 7, 10, 13, and 16.

Step 2: Rank the index values of each month given in Cols. 4, 7, 10, 13, and 16, Table 1, from the lowest to the highest so that there are five values appearing under each month. The ranked index values are given in Table 2, Cols. 2 -13).

Step 3: Sum the three central values of each month. In other words, eliminate one value from the top and one value from the bottom. The sum of three central values of January is 338.5; of February, 305.4; and so on. (See Table 2, Line 6) The objective of this step is to remove from consideration extreme values (the lowest and the highest), which may represent periods of abnormal sales, periods of extremely high or low sales. The three central values are most likely the representative of the "norm."

Note: There is no hard and fast rule about eliminating the highest and lowest values. It would not be necessary to eliminate any value if the year-to-year variations in each month are very small. Also, since we have five values of each month, we could afford to eliminate one value from the top and one value from the bottom. If we had just three values we could not do that. On the other hand, if we had more than five values, we could afford to eliminate more than one value from the top and bottom.

246

Step 4: Compute the modified average of the three central values by dividing their sum by the number of central values, which is three in this case. The modified average of January comes to 112.8 (338.5 ÷ 3); of February, 101.8 (305.4 ÷ 3); and so on. (See Table 2, Line 7)

Step 5: Sum the modified averages of all the months. This comes to 1204 (See Table 2, Line 7). But this total should be 1200. To bring the total to 1200, we will re-compute seasonal indices the same way as we did before.

Step 6: Compute the factor. This is done by dividing 1200 by the sum-total, 1204. This comes to:

$$\text{Factor} = \frac{1200}{1204} = .99667$$

Step 7: Find the typical seasonal index for each month by multiplying the modified average of each month with the factor (.99667) computed above. The typical seasonal index of each month is given in Table 2, Line 8. (The sum of this line has to be 1200. If not, check the calculations for the error.)

Trend

Next step is to compute trend values, that is, T. To do this, we have to deseasonalize the sales data. We will compute trend values from the deseasonalized sales data. As mentioned earlier, in decomposition model, sales (Y) = T × S × C × R, or TSCR. If we divide this by S (seasonal index), it will leave with us TCR (TSCR ÷ S) — deseasonalized sales or sales without a seasonal component. Col. 4, Table 3 gives typical seasonal indices of all the months which we computed earlier — Line 8, Table 2. The only thing we did here is that we divided each index by 100. In other words, we listed the seasonal index of January as 1.124 (112.4 ÷ 100); of February, 1.015 (101.5 ÷ 100); and so on. Also, note that we listed the same seasonal index of each month of each year. In other words, the index of January 1996 is the same as of January 1997, January 1998, January 1999, and January 2000. The 112.4 index of January means that January on the average performs 12.4% better than the average. This is true with the January of 1996, January of 1997 and of any other year. This will remain so until we re-compute its index. For this reason, we list the same index of each month of each year of five years. We deseasonalize the sales data by dividing the sales of each month by its seasonal index. For example, deasonalized sales of January 1996 is 16.01 (18 ÷ 1.124); of February 1996, 15.76 (16 ÷ 1.015); and so on. The deseasonalized sales data of all the months of all the five years are given in Col. 5. Next step is to compute the trend value (T) from the deseasonalized data. The equation of trend line is:

T = a + bX

where

T = Trend
a = Constant

b = Slope of the line

X = Coded value which we assign

Since a date cannot be used in the equation, it is necessary to assign a numerical value to each period. There are different ways of assigning the value of X. The one, which is often used, is as follows:

Step 1: Determine whether the number of observations is odd or even. In our example, the number of observations is 60, which is even. In that case, find two central periods in the series. These are months 30 and 31 in the 60-month example shown in Table 3.

Step 2: Assign a negative 1 (-1) to the first central period (month 30 in the example) and positive 1 (+1) to the second central period (month 31) in the example).

Step 3: Go backward in time, decrementing by two, and go forward in time, incrementing by two. In other words, period 29 will get a value of –3; period 28, a value of –5; period 27, a value of –7; and so on. Similarly, period 32 will get a value of +3; period 33, a value of +5; period 34, a value of +7; and so on.

All the X values (coded values) are given in Col. 6, Table 3. The next step is to find the values of a and b in the trend line equation. Their formulas are:

$$a = \frac{\sum Y}{N} \qquad \qquad \text{... (1)}$$

$$b = \frac{\sum XY}{\sum X^2} \qquad \qquad \text{... (2)}$$

where

Y	= Deseasonalized sales
N	= Number of periods
X	= Coded values of periods
Σ	= Symbol for "sum of"

By plugging the values in Equations (1 and 2), we get:

$$a = \frac{1697.36}{60} = 28.29$$

$$b = \frac{18,595.07}{71,980} = 0.26$$

The trend line equation then becomes:

$$T = 28.29 + 0.26 X \qquad\qquad\qquad ... (3)$$

By using the Equation (3), we can compute trend value of each month of each year. The only thing we have to do is to plug in the value of X. For example, the X value of January 1996 is −59 (See Col. 6), its trend value comes to 12.95 (28.29 + 0.26 × -59). The X value of February 1996 is −57, its trend value comes to 13.47 (28.29 + 0.26 × -57). This way we can compute the trend values of all other months. All the trend values are given in Col. 9.

Since we now have numerical values of trend, we can determine the values of cycle and random factors (CR) of each month. Recall that TCR represents deseasonalized sales. Thus, by dividing deseasonalized sales in Col. 5 by the trend values in Col. 9, we will arrive at the combined values of cycle and random factors (CR) which appear in Col. 10 (TCR ÷ T = CR). For example, the CR value of Jan. 1996 comes to: 1.24 = 16.01 (Period 1, Col. 5) ÷ 12.95 (Period 1, Col. 9); and of February 1996, 1.17 = 15.76 (Period 2, Col. 5) ÷ 13.47 (Period 2, Col. 9).

Next step is to quantify the values of C and R. Since by definition a random occurrence cannot be predicted (e.g., a warehouse fire or a strike occurs without warning and with no regularity), it cannot be estimated directly. So, it has to be done indirectly. One way to get rid of random (irregular) variations is to smooth the CR data by computing moving average. When the data is smoothed, random (irregular) variations disappear.

Moving Average

What is a moving average, and how is it computed? A moving average is a technique that is used to smooth data (average the actual data of a number of periods). The exercise tends to reduce any skew in the data caused by random, or non-recurring events. Moving averages can be computed on the basis of any number of periods from 2 or up. Here is how to compute moving averages using three periods (a three-period moving average):

Step 1: Compute the moving total by summing the first three data points of a series for which moving averages are required. In this case, moving averages of the CR values of each month are required (The CR values appear in Col. 10, Table 3). The sum of the first three values of CR in the example is 3.54 (1.24 + 1.17 + 1.13).

Step 2: Enter the first moving total in the column adjacent to the CR value (Col. 11 in the example) and in the period immediately following the last data point included in the sum (Period 4). Then compute the second moving total by dropping one value from the top and adding one value from the bottom. This comes to 3.37 (1.17 + 1.13 + 1.07). All the moving totals are given in Col. 11.

Step 3: Compute moving averages that are computed by dividing each moving total by the number of data points included in the moving total, which is 3. The first moving average comes to 1.18 (3.54 ÷ 3). The second moving average comes to 1.12 (3.37 ÷ 3). This way we can compute moving averages of other months, which are given in Col. 12.

Here one has to decide how many periods one has to use in computing moving averages.

There is no set rule. One has to do trial and error to arrive at the optimum number. The best way is to prepare ex-post forecasts with different number of periods and use the one which on the average gives you the best forecast. As mentioned earlier, the moving average smoothes the data. When data is smoothed, it means that random (irregular) variations are eliminated.

FORECAST

Next step is to prepare a forecast of the next period, which in this case is period 61 or January 2001. As mentioned earlier, the classical decomposition model is:

Forecast $= T \times S \times C$

In the above equation R is missing. Remember, R (random or irregular variation) by definition is unpredictable. So we make a forecast with an assumption of normal conditions. So, to make a forecast we need the values of T, S and C of that period. Since we are making a forecast of January 2001, we need these values of that period. First we compute the T value of January 2001 by using the Equation (3), which is:

$T = 28.29 + 0.26\ X$

For this we need the value of X. January 2001 is period 61. The X value of period 61 also comes to 61 (59 + 2). Then:

$$T_{Jan\ 2001} = 28.29 + 0.26 \times 61$$
$$= 44.15$$

S value we already know it, which is, 1.124. C value, 3 month moving average of last 3 months (October, November and December 2000), is computed as follows:

$$C_{Jan2001} = \frac{1.00 + 0.92 + 0.92}{3}$$

$$= 0.95$$

Now we have all the values we need to prepare a forecast. The forecast becomes:

$$\text{Forecast}_{Jan\ 2001} = 44.15 \times 1.124 \times 0.95$$
$$= 47.14 \text{ or } \$47,140,000$$

Bear in mind with this model one can make a forecast of only one period ahead. In the above example, we cannot make a forecast beyond January 2001. Also, seasonal variations exist in the data of less than one year — in quarterly, monthly or weekly data. Where seasonal variations exist we have to include S in the computation of forecast. However, if we are making an annual forecast, we don't need S. In that case, the Decomposition model will look like this:

Forecast $= T \times C \times R$

CHAPTER 45

SALES RATIO

Chaman L. Jain
St. John's University

The sales ratio is another time series method of forecasting. Here we need one or more months of sales data to make a forecast of the whole year. For example, to make a forecast of the year 2001, we will need one or more months of actual sales of the same year. This method assumes that each month or quarter contributes a certain percentage to the total sales of a year, and that percentage remains fairly stable over time. If we know the sales of one month or one quarter, we can predict the sales of the whole year. This is a quick and easy way to determine how the sales are coming along and/or to verify the forecast number prepared by another method.

METHODOLOGY

Here is a step-by-step procedure for computing sales ratios and preparing forecasts. The sales data of Delphi Enterprise are used to illustrate the procedure.

Step 1: Table 1 gives two years of monthly sales data of 1999-2000. First step is to compute sales ratio of each month to the total of that year. For example, sales ratio of January 1999 is 0.074 [(194,529 / 2,637,598)] and sales ratio of February 1999 is 0.068 (180,053 / 2,637,598). This way we can compute the sales ratios of all the months of both years, that is, of 1999 and 2000. They are given in Cols. 3 and 5 in Table 1.

Step 2: Compute average sales ratios of both the years. The average of January is 0.075 [(0.074 + 0.077) / (2)]; of February, 0.071 [(0.068 + 0.074) / (2)]; and so on. All the average sales ratios are given in Col. 6, Table 1. The average sales ratio of 0.075 of January means that, on the average, 7.5% of the annual sales comes in the first month, that is, January; 0.071 of February means that 7.1% of the annual sales comes in the second month, that is, February; and so on. We compute average because monthly ratios do change somewhat from one year to the next. The average tends to give a better idea as to what percent each month contributes to the total of a year. At time, it may be advisable to eliminate a certain month of a year from the average because that month shows an unusual contribution, either too low or too high. In one month, sales might have gone down sharply because of a riot, snowstorm or strike at the factory. In another month, sales might have gone up sharply because of one big order from Saudi Arabia, Wal-Mart Opened a new store, or one of the competitors had a fire at its plant. Such elements distort the normal pattern. When you observe such values, the best thing to do is to eliminate those months from the average.

TABLE 1					
AVERAGE SALES RATIO					
DELPHI ENTERPRISE					
Month	**1999 Sales ($ Mil.)**	**Sales Ratio**	**2000 Sales ($Mil.)**	**Sales Ratio**	**Average Sales Ratio**
(1)	**(2)**	**(3)**	**(4)**	**(5)**	**(6)**
January	194,529	0.074	204,011	0.077	0.075
February	180,053	0.068	197,708	0.074	0.071
March	193,489	0.073	186,805	0.070	0.072
April	178,690	0.068	173,225	0.065	0.0.66
May	175,083	0.066	183,138	0.069	0.068
June	245,968	0.093	273,495	0.103	0.098
July	203,194	0.077	186,384	0.070	0.074
August	233,556	0.089	225,785	0.085	0.087
September	252,654	0.096	259,797	0.098	0.097
October	243,747	0.092	259,425	0.098	0.095
November	295,889	0.112	265,051	0.100	0.106
December	240,746	0.091	244,524	0.092	0.092
Total	**2,637,598**	**1.000**	**2,659,348**	1.000	1.000
Note: Because of rounding some totals may not add up.					

Step 3: Prepare forecasts. When the sales of January are in, we can project the sales of the whole year. Let us say we are in 2001. We have so far got only the sales of January of that year. We can then use the average sales ratio of January (based on the sales data of 1999 and 2000) to project the sales of the whole year of 2001. The sales of January 2001is $198,947mil. (See Table 2) According to our average sales ratio, this month sales represent only 7.5% of the whole year. This means then the sales of the whole year will be $2,652,627 mil. (198,947 / 0.075). This compares with the actual sales of $2,564,943 (an error of 3.42%). When the sales of February 2001are in, we can once again make a forecast for the whole year to see if the numbers are coming along the same way as we projected earlier. The average sales ratio of February is 0.071, meaning, on the average, 7.1% of the annual sales comes in that month. Then the forecast of the whole year of 2001 will be $2,613,479 mil ($185,557 / 0.071). This gives us an error of 1.89%. When the sales data of the third month are in, we can once again compute the forecast for the whole year of 2001. Table 2 gives annual forecasts of 2001 based on the sales data of all the months and their percent errors. As we can see from the table, error ranged anywhere from 1.22% to 22.14%. (See Col. 6, Table 2) The error went up in those months which

did not have a stable ratio. In other words, the annual forecasts of only those months would be reliable which have somewhat stable ratios.

	TABLE 2 2001 FORECASTS BASED ON AVERAGE SALES RATIO DELPHI ENTERPRISE			
Month (1)	2001 Sales ($Mil.) (2)	Avg. Ratio Based on 1999 & 2000 Sales Data (4)	Projected Sales of 2001 (5)	% Error (6)
January	198,947	0.075	2,652,627	-3.42
February	185,557	0.071	2,613,479	-1.89
March	177,166	0.072	2,460,639	4.07
April	179,221	0.066	2,715,470	-5.87
May	168,905	0.068	2,483,897	3.16
June	226,617	0.098	2,312,418	9.85
July	231,820	0.074	3,132,703	-22.14
August	241,445	0.087	2,775,230	-8.20
September	214,259	0.097	2,208,856	13.88
October	240,701	0.095	2,533,695	1.22
November	256,150	0.106	2,416,509	5.79
December	244,156	0.092	2,653,870	-3.47
Total	**2,564,944**	**1.000**		

Note: Because of rounding total may not add up.

CUMULATIVE SALES RATIO

Very often seasonality is driven by the promotional calendar. Seasonality refers to the performance of different months. If the promotional calendar changes, so will be the performance of different months.

TABLE 3
CUMULATIVE SALES RATIOS
DELPHI ENTERPRISE, INC.

| Month | 1999 | | 2000 | | Average |
| | Sales Ratio | Cum. Sales Ratio | Sales Ratio | Cum. Sales Ratio | Cum. Sales Ratio |
(1)	(2)	(3)	(4)	(5)	(6)
January	0.074	0.074	0.077	0.077	0.075
February	0.068	0.142	0.074	0.151	0.147
March	0.073	0.215	0.070	0.221	0.218
April	0.068	0.283	0.065	0.286	0.285
May	0.066	0.350	0.069	0.355	0.352
June	0.093	0.443	0.103	0.458	0.450
July	0.077	0.520	0.070	0.528	0.524
August	0.089	0.608	0.085	0.613	0.611
September	0.096	0.704	0.098	0.711	0.707
October	0.092	0.797	0.098	0.808	0.802
November	0.112	0.909	0.100	0.908	0.908
December	0.091	1.000	0.092	1.000	1.000
	1.000		1.000		

Let us say in one year the company decides to do its promotion in February rather than in January. In that case, the contribution of January to the total of that year will go down and of February, go up. In other words, the sales ratio of January will decrease and of February, increase. These things do happen which distort the sales ratio pattern. This causes changes in sales ratios and consequently our ability to forecast. However, this problem can be overcome somewhat by using cumulative sales ratios instead of sales ratios. Here is a step-by-step procedure for using cumulative sales ratios:

Step 1: Cumulate the sales ratios of each year. In our above example of Delphi Enterprise, the cumulative sales ratio of January 1999 will be the same as the sales ratio. The cumulative ratio of February will be 0.142 (0.074 + 0.068); of March 0.215 (0.142 + 0.073), and so on. (See Col. 3, Table 3) This way we can compute the cumulative ratios of all the months of both years. (See Cols. 3 and 5, Table 3)

TABLE 4					
2001 FORECASTS BASED ON CUMULATIVE SALES RATIOS					
Month	**2001 Sales ($Mil)**	**2001 Cumulative Monthly Sales ($Mil.)**	**Cumulative Sales Ratio**	**Projected Sales of 2001**	**% Error**
(1)	**(2)**	**(3)**	**(4)**	**(5)**	**(6)**
January	198,947	198,947	0.075	2,652,627	-3.42
February	185,557	384,504	0.147	2,615,673	-1.98
March	177,166	561,670	0.218	2,576,468	-0.45
April	179,221	740,891	0.285	2,599,618	-1.35
May	168,905	909,796	0.352	2,584,648	-0.77
June	226,617	1,136,413	0.450	2,525,362	1.54
July	231,820	1,368,233	0.524	2,611,132	-1.80
August	241,445	1,609,678	0.611	2,634,498	-2.71
September	214,259	1,823,937	0.707	2,579,826	-0.58
October	240,701	2,064,638	0.802	2,574,362	-0.37
November	256,150	2,320,788	0.908	2,555,934	0.35
December	244,156	2,564,944	1.000		
Total	**2,564,944**				

Step 2: Compute average cumulative sales ratios. The average cumulative sales ratio of January is 0.075 [(0.074 + 0.077) / (2)], of February, 0.147 [(0.142 + 0.151) / (2)], and so on. Average cumulative sales ratios of all the months are given in Col. 6, Table 3.

Step 3: Prepare a forecast. Here again when sales of January are in we can forecast the total sales of 2001, which will be the same as computed on the basis of sales ratio. The actual sales of January were $198,947. The projected sales of 2001came to $2,652,627 (198,947 / 0.075). When the sales of February came in we cumulated the sales of January and February because our average cumulative sales ratio is based on both months. This ratio is 0.147, meaning that, on the average, sales of January and February represent 14.7% of the annual sales. The projected sales of the whole year came to $2,615,673 ($384,504 / 0.147). Since our actual sales of 2001were $2,564,943, the percent error came to 1.98%. Similarly, we can prepare forecasts of 2001 based on the cumulative sales ratios of other months. Table 4 gives forecasts of 2001as well as their % error. The percent error here ranges between 0.35% and 3.42%, much lower than what we experienced when we used average sales ratios. (See Col.6, Table 4)

CHAPTER 46

ABC OF BOX-JENKINS MODELS

George Kress and John Snyder
Colorado State University

Box-Jenkins models are an anomaly among sales forecasters. Experts praise them for their accuracy in forecasting short-term sales. Professors allocate a great deal of instruction time to them in sales forecasting courses. In addition, formats for their usage are included in many of the time series forecasting packages presently available for use with personal computers. Yet, with all of these positive factors, they are among the models least used by sales forecasting practitioners. They seemingly are just tools for a certain "elite" cadre of sales forecasters. Why?

An opinion forwarded in the Summer 1987 issue of the Journal of Business Forecasting suggests that the complexity in the Box Jenkins model contributes to its lack of use. This chapter attempts to present a concise, understandable description of Box Jenkins models.

Some sales forecasters probably feel the words "concise" and "understandable" cannot even be used in the same sentence with Box Jenkins. Other skeptics view a "simple, concise explanation of Box Jenkins" as similar to a correspondence course entitled, "How to become a brain surgeon in three easy lessons." We feel that the model can be explained in an easy to understand language, and we decided to cover the topic by using a question/answer format.

BOX-JENKINS MODELS

Q. Just what are Box-Jenkins models?

A. They are a family or group of forecasting models that use an approach similar to that used when choosing explanatory variables for multiple regression models. Each model assigns different weights and uses different combinations of variables, depending on the nature of the data being forecasted. Box Jenkins models are best suited for short-term forecasts, and generally, the more data the better. Most experts recommend a minimum of 40 to 50 periods of data for accuracy. By the way, the name for these models comes from their developers—G.E. Box and G.M. Jenkins

Q. I see the acronym ARIMA used regularly with Box Jenkins, what does it mean?

A. Box Jenkins models combine autoregressive (AR) terms with moving average (MA) terms and differencing (the I or integrative term). That combination is depicted by the letters ARIMA.

Q. I'm familiar with moving average models and regression models, but not with autoregressive models. Could you explain autoregressive models and also let me know if my concept of moving averages is correct?

A. Sure, as you know, in normal regression you associate values of dependent variable with values of an independent variable(s). Well, in an autoregressive model you do the same thing except the independent variable used is merely a past value of the dependent variable. In other words, you determine the relationship between a variable and itself (auto) at earlier time periods. As you suspected, the term "moving average" has a different meaning in Box-Jenkins models than the one generally associated with it. Its use, by conventional terms, is not truly a moving average. It refers to a regression model in which past random shocks (a random variable) are used as independent variables. While it may appear strange using a random variable to make forecasts, it is this term that ARIMA uses to generate stochastic (probabilistic) forecasts.

Q. Can Box-Jenkins models be used with any type of time series data?

A. The data should either be stationary or convertible to stationary data. Stationary data fluctuate around a constant mean with no trend over time. If the data are not stationary, "differencing" can be used to create a stationary series with the same volatility as the original series. This is the "I" term in ARIMA.

Q. Why differencing? How do we do it?

A. Differencing enables data with a trend (non-stationary data) to be converted into stationary data. This is accomplished by subtracting successive values of a variable, and then using the differences as a new variable. (See Table 1) This original data series of five values has an upward trend. We can remove this trend by finding differences between each value and using the differences to create a new series of stationary data. Note that while the original series had an upward trend, the four new values are stationary. Sometimes it may be necessary to perform a second round of differencing before the new data become stationary.

TABLE 1 DIFFERENCING	
Original Series	**Differenced Series**
22	
>	1 (23 – 22)
23	
>	2 (25 – 23)
25	
>	2 (27 – 25)
27	
>	1 (28 – 27)
28	

Q. OK, we need stationary data, at least 50 data points, and we integrate autoregressive models with moving average models. Now explain how the whole process works!

A. As mentioned earlier Box-Jenkins forecasting is a marriage between time series and regression analysis. It takes past sales values, alters them, and then uses these altered values as the explanatory (independent) variables in a regression equation. The AR and MA terms are merely different forms of the past values in the time series. If a trend exists in the data, that trend is removed through differencing. Then the AR and MA terms are used in a regression equation to explain the fluctuations remaining in the data series.

Q. But if the trend is removed, how can realistic forecasts be made?

A. The trend is removed to allow a more accurate assessment of other fluctuations in the data. Once a forecast has been made of these fluctuations (the differenced series), they are simply added to the original data.

Q. But what if you can't tell from looking at the data whether it is stationary?

A. In those situations, just try identifying AR and MA terms from the original data. If a trend does exist, it will be uncovered in the ensuing analysis.

Q. What do you mean by "identifying AR and MA terms?"

A. Remember, we are trying to determine what patterns exist in the past data so that we can use that information to forecast future sales. We want to identify seasonal influences and any other patterns in the data that can improve our forecasts. Either autoregressive term(s) (AR), error terms (MA), or a combination of both will generally identify these patterns and influences. Thus, the first step is to identify the MA and AR terms that look like they will best fit our set of data. This is usually called the "identification phase" and it involves looking at plotted values of the AR and MA characteristics in the data. Then, based on these plotted values, you decide how many AR and MA terms are needed in your equation.

Q. You lost me here. What do you mean by plotted values?

A. Through computer analysis, sets of plotted data are developed from autocorrelation and partial autocorrelation values. The autocorrelation plots represent the correlation coefficients (r values) between the values in the time series in period 5 with those values in periods t-1, t-2, t-3, etc. Since they are correlated with their own past values, which we call them "auto" correlations. Most computer programs will show these results as a plot and also list the actual correlation coefficients. The printouts shown here come from Quantitative Micro Software's statistical software package called MicroTSP. For example, in Figure 1 plots of quarterly S & P 500 values are shown. Each time lag has an associated r value (AC). The values in this time series have a reasonably high association (r = .90) with values lagged one period (t-1), a lower association (r = .77) with values lagged two periods, etc. If there is seasonality in quarterly (or monthly) data, there will also be a high association between period t and period t-4 (t-12). There is no seasonality in this data series.

As with the autocorrelation coefficients, the partial autocorrelation (PAC) coefficients measure the observed values of the time series in period t and the values of the time series in periods t-1, t-2, t-3, etc. However, while the autocorrelation coefficient measures the relationship between two values (such as the one in time period t and one in period t-3), the partial autocorrelation measures the residual relationship between the values in period t-1, t-2 and t-n after the relationships between t and t-l, t-2, ..., t-n, have been accounted for. As you can see in Figure 1, the r value for PAC at period t-l is high (.90) but then drops off rapidly for ensuing time periods.

FIGURE 1
AC AND PAC FOR QUARTERLY S&P 500VALUES

(1975-1985)

```
==========================================================================
  Autocorrelations  Partial Autocorrelations         ac        pac
==========================================================================
I        |********* I        |********* I   1     0.9020     0.9020
I        |******** I         *** I            2     0.7661    -0.2541
I        |******* I           |*  I            3     0.6518     0.0825
I        |****** I            |   I            4     0.5665     0.0420
I        |***** I             |*  I            5     0.5074     0.0557
I        |***** I             |*  I            6     0.4751     0.0897
I        |**** I              |   I            7     0.4465    -0.0241
I        |**** I            * |    I           8     0.4042    -0.0550
I        |** I              * |    I           9     0.3399    -0.0983
I        |** I             ** |    I          10     0.2398    -0.2027
I        |* I               |   I             11     0.1426     0.0022
I        |* I              * |    I           12     0.0598    -0.0701
I        | I                |** I             13     0.0260     0.1592
I        | I                |   I             14     0.0265     0.0382
I        | I               * |    I           15     0.0118    -0.1461
I        | I                |* I              16    -0.0054     0.0857
I        | I                |   I             17    -0.0231    -0.0030
I      * | I               * | I              18    -0.0663    -0.1197
==========================================================================
 S.E. of Correlations  .1543034      Q-Stat. (18 lags)    134.2186
==========================================================================
```

Q. Let's stop a minute and see if I understand what is going on here. You are trying to build a regression equation using MA and/or AR terms as the independent variables. This means you have to determine how many total terms (independent variables) will be in the equation, and you also have to use a procedure to estimate their coefficients (bi values).

A. Right. You really are paying attention.

Q. Let's now get back to the plotted data and see how they are used to determine the types and number of terms in my model.

A. We simply look at the plots and apply some rules of thumb to identify the components of the initial model. The plots of the autocorrelation functions (AC) will determine whether AR terms are needed. If the AC plots have a gradual exponential decline, this suggests AR terms should probably be used in the model. Then the plots of the partial autocorrelation functions (PAC) are studied to see if MA terms are needed. If the PAC plots have a gradual exponential decline, then MA terms should probably be used. If either of those two functions declines gradually in a straight line, then a trend probably exists in the data and it should be removed by differencing. For example, in the S&P 500 data in Figure 1, the autocorrelation values have a gradual decline which may be a straight or exponential decline. This indicates that AR term(s) are appropriate, or the series should be differenced. Since we are not sure, we can continue without differencing. It will soon become evident if we are wrong and need to difference the data.

Q. You have talked about MA terms and AR terms. How do I know how many and which terms should be included in my model?

A. We must start by already knowing whether we want MA or AR terms, or both in the model. In the S&P 500 data we determined that AR terms are appropriate. Then we look at the opposite plot to determine the terms. For the number of AR terms we look at the PAC plots and for the number of MA terms we review the AC plots. A large coefficient indicates a strong association between the two sets of values, and that means that term should be used in the model. Let's look at the sample plots shown in Figure 1 again. This is a typical computer printout for a Box Jenkins model since it identifies the PAC and AC values in both numeric and graphic formats. For example, the autocorrelation between the original data (t) and data lagged by one period (t-1) is depicted by a value of .90 as well as the length of the adjacent line. The value for autocorrelations (AC) in (t-2) is .77, which is represented by a shorter line. The decline continues through the remaining periods. The value for PAC for period (t-1) is also .90, but it then drops off rapidly to zero where it fluctuates in a random manner.

Q. So the plotted lines in Figure 1 identify the amount of association between the original time series and itself at different time lags — the longer the plotted line, the greater the association.

A. That's right.

Q. In this case we first determine that AR terms are needed because the AC plot declined slowly, and then it is determined that only an AR (1) term is appropriate because the first PAC is much larger than the other PACs.

A. Yes, that is correct. Would you like some more examples?

Q. Sure

A. Figure 2 illustrates the case where the PAC plot declines exponentially indicating the need for MA term(s). The single spike (a significant "r" value) in the AC at one lag (t-l) indicates that only one MA term is needed. Thus, this model is a MA (1).

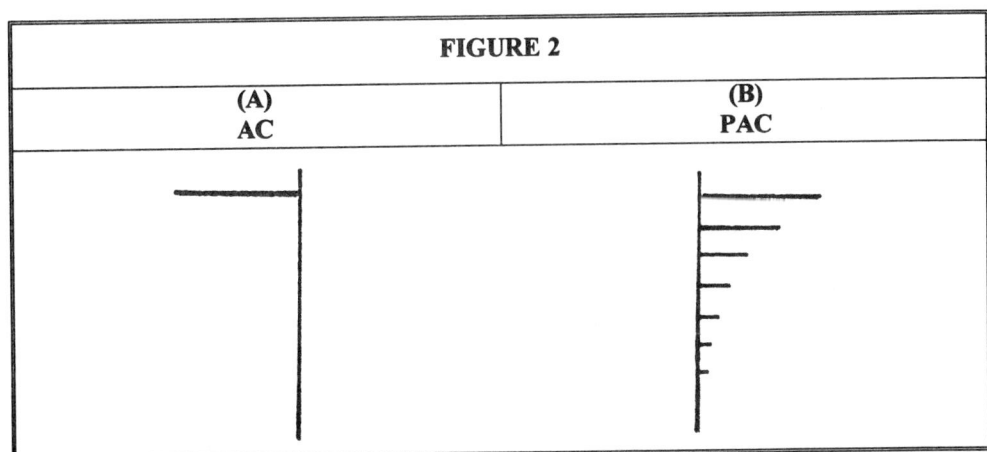

FIGURE 2	
(A) **AC**	**(B)** **PAC**

Figure 3 shows another example. In this case the AC plot declines exponentially indicating the need for AR term(s). The two spikes in the PAC indicate two AR terms are needed, i.e. AR (1) and AR (2). Now that you understand how to identify our initial model, let's advance to the evaluation phase.

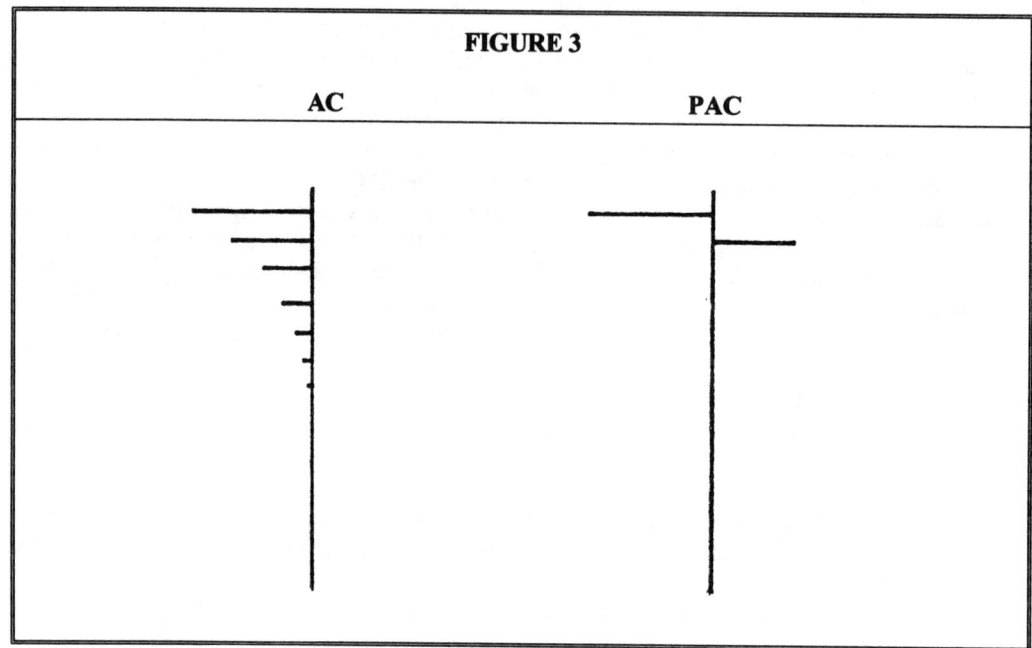

FIGURE 3

AC   PAC

Q. You seem to be suggesting that it is a common practice to use AC and PAC plots to help determine the ARIMA model. I have heard that some forecasters don't agree with this practice.

A. It is true that some forecasters believe matching AC and PAC plots is too subjective. They also may argue that economic business data do not behave in predictable patterns and therefore matching plots is a sub-optimal technique. However, I believe that the technique as explained here is an excellent way to acquaint yourself with ARIMA forecasting. As you continue to learn more about Box-Jenkins forecasting, other methods of choosing terms will evolve.

Q. That makes sense to me. Now what?

A. Once the initial model is identified, the model builder will run a regression using maximum likelihood estimation (MLE) procedures. (In some software packages, this change from ordinary least squares to MLE occurs automatically when you put an AR or MA term into the list of explanatory variables.) Then, the model builder evaluates the output of the regression to determine if the model is good or if another model should be tried. In this evaluation you look for statistical strength, stationarity, invertability and redundancy.

Q. Those sound like typical academic jargon, what do they mean?

A. Statistical strength is measured in a Box-Jenkins model the same way as in a multiple regression model. We first want the model to have a high R^2 value. (R^2 is the percent of variation in the original series explained by variation in the AR and MA terms.) The larger the R^2, the greater will the power of the model. An R^2 of over 90% is quite common. In addition to R^2, the model builder should look at the statistical strength of each term in the model. A 95% (or greater) confidence level is used to determine if each term's coefficient is significantly different from zero. The hypotheses are:

Ho: bi=0 (the coefficient is zero)
Ha: bi=0 (the coefficient is different from zero)

Those terms, for which the null hypothesis (Ho) is rejected (bi is significantly different from 0), are included in the model. These two statistics provide the basic information to build a model.

Q. How about "stationarity" and "invertability."
A. You show great insight in categorizing them together, because not only are they sets of conditions which a properly built model must meet, also they are very similar. As shown in Figure 4, these conditions are identical except that stationarity conditions apply to AR term(s) and invertability conditions apply to MA term(s). If they are met, then the model does not need an integrated (I) term. That means if the data series identified with the AR term(s) is stationary, then the model cannot be improved via differencing. To see if a model meets these conditions, the model builder simply checks its coefficients using the requirement(s) listed in Table 2. The final condition required for an acceptable model is called redundancy. Since the AR term(s) and the MA term(s) are mathematically related, there exists a danger that one can mistakenly offset (cancel) the other. When this happens the model has coefficients near (or at) redundancy, and they are generally of low quality. As a practical rule, if the coefficient of the AR term equals the coefficient of MA term, a better model will exist by using only one of the terms.

In conclusion, when the above conditions — statistical strength, stationarity, invertability, redundancy — are met, the model is complete. If not, the model builder must try a new form of the model. This entails a second look at the AC and PAC plots to identify ways of modifying the model. This process is repeated until either a satisfactory model is derived or the potential versions are exhausted with no satisfactory model. When two or more models both meet the requirements, the model with the least number of AR and MA terms and/or the one which does not mix MA and AR terms is preferred.

TABLE 2
CONDITIONS OF STATIONARITY AND INVERTABILITY

Stationarity	Invertability
1 AR term: $\|coef\| < 1$	1 MA term: $\|coef\| < 1$
2 AR terms: 2nd coef < 1	2 AR terms: 2nd coef < 1
$1^{st} + 2^{nd} < 1$	$1^{st} + 2^{nd} < 1$
$2^{nd} - 1^{st} < 1$	$2^{nd} - 1^{st} < 1$

AN EXAMPLE

Q. OK, I think I understand. How about an example to make sure?
A. Let's try forecasting the quarterly sales of Steam Mist Hot Tubs. As you remember, the first step requires identification and plotting of the AC and PAC functions. These appear in Figure 4. The slow decline in the autocorrelation plot indicates a need for AR term(s). The large spike in the

PAC plot at t-1 indicates that the AR large spike in the PAC plot at t-1 indicates that the AR terms should be an AR (1). In addition, a medium spike (PAC = -0.4131) exists in the PAC plot at t-2. This indicates that you might also try an AR (2) term.

From this information you initially run a regression using the sales of hot tubs as the dependent variable, AR (1) as the independent variable, and of course a constant term (C). The results of this regression equation are shown in Table 3. Notice that R^2 is about 91%, then by looking at the 2 tail significance column we see that the coefficient on the AR (1) term is statistically different from 0 at more than .999 level. Also, the stationarity and invertability conditions are met. This is determined by taking the coefficient of the AR (1) term (0.934) and seeing if it meets the stationarity conditions listed in Table 2 ([coef]<1). Since the coefficient is less than one, it meets the stationarity condition. Since there is no MA term, by definition, it meets the invertability condition. The requirement for redundancy is not applicable here since AR and MA terms are not used together. The model looks good, but remember, the AC and PAC plots indicated that an AR (2) term may provide additional explanatory power.

Q. So now we try a model with both an AR (1) term and an AR (2) term.

A. That's right. The results of that regression are shown in Table 4. As you can see, R^2 has increased to almost 93%, the AR (1) coefficient remains significantly different from 0 at a confidence level greater than .999, and the AR (2) coefficient is statistically different from zero at .998 confidence level. You now check the conditions of stationarity and invertability. As in all cases, since there is no MA term, the model, by definition, meets the invertability condition. As in the AR (1) model, checking for stationarity entails entering the values for the coefficients into the conditions listed in Table 2. Since the second coefficient is -.466, it is less than 1. Since the first coefficient plus the second coefficient [1.386+(-.466)] equals .92, it is less than 1. Since the second coefficient minus the first coefficient (-0.466 - 1.386) equals -1.852 it is less than 1. Therefore, all three conditions for stationarity in an AR (2) model are met. Since the second model has better statistics, and meets all the conditions, it is superior to the one using only a single independent variable.

TABLE 3 REGRESSION RESULTS				
Variable	**Coefficient**	**Std. Error**	**T-Stat**	**2-Tail Significance**
C	394.09452	122.00389	3.230180	0.003
AR (1)	0.9344924	0.0483970	19.308910	0.000
R-squared	0.907531	Mean of dependent variable		330.2750
Adj. R-squared	0.905098	S.D. of dependent variable		149.3689
S.E. of regression	46.01488	Sum of squared residuals		80460.03
Durbin-Watson stat.	1.103650	Log likelihood		208.8903

Q. Okay. So all I have to do with a typical software package containing the Box-Jenkins model is review the r values and plots the autocorrelation and partial autocorrelation and then determine whether AR, MA or some combination of these terms are needed. Then I plug that information into the computer, and evaluate the regression results to see if it is a good model. If it's a good model, we will use the information in the printout (Table 4 in the example) to make a forecast.

FIGURE 4
AC AND PAC PLOTS FOR STEAM MIST HOT TUBS
(1976-1988)

```
================================================================
    Autocorrelations  Partial Autocorrelations      ac      pac
================================================================
|           |********* |          |********* |  1   0.9406   0.9406
|           |******** |          |**** |         2   0.8370  -0.4131
|           |******* |           |* |            3   0.7180  -0.0626
|           |****** |            |* |            4   0.5899  -0.1138
|           |***** |             |* |            5   0.4541  -0.1202
|           |*** |               | |              6   0.3272   0.0376
|           |** |                |** |           7   0.2353   0.2088
|           |** |                | |              8   0.1743   0.0314
|           |* |                 |** |           9   0.1138  -0.2364
|           |* |                 |* |            10   0.0548  -0.0549
|           | |                  |* |            11   0.0004  -0.0723
|         * |                    |** |           12  -0.0599  -0.1527
|         * |                    | |             13  -0.1315  -0.0467
|        ** |                    |* |            14  -0.2029   0.0724
|       *** |                    |** |           15  -0.2746  -0.1655
|       *** |                    | |             16  -0.3364  -0.0220
|      **** |                    |* |            17  -0.3831   0.0537
|      **** |                    | |             18  -0.4092  -0.0102
================================================================
   S.E. of Correlations  .1543034      Q-Stat. (18 lags)  144.0011
================================================================
```

TABLE 4
REGRESSION RESULTS
AR (1) Model

Variable	Coefficient	STD. Error	T-Stat	2-Tail Sig.
C	359.40377	82.741713	4.3436830	0.000
AR (1)	1.3856519	0.1435446	9.6531079	0.000
AR (2)	-0.4663885	0.1415626	-3.2945736	0.002
R-Squared	0.928499	Mean of Depend. Var.		330.2750
Adj. R-Squared	0.924634	S. D. of Depend. Var.		149.3689
S.E. of	41.00600	Sum of Squared Resid.		62215.20
Regression	2.029230	Log Likelihood		-203.7470
Durbin-Watson Stat.				

A. That's correct. Let's start making our forecast by writing the equation estimated by the regression equation in Table 4. Hot Tub Sales = 359.40+ 1.386[AR (1) - 0.466 AR (2)]

Then plug in the values for AR (1) and AR (2) (which you remember are past values for hot tub sales) and make the forecast. Most computer software programs do this for you.

Q. Great, now it's time to sit back in my hot tub, and see how accurate this Box- Jenkins forecast is.

A. Just remember this is only an introduction to basic Box-Jenkins techniques. If you continue your study of them, you'll have more precise explanations and some of our terms will take on new meanings.

REFERENCES

1. Iceman, Joe D., Lover, Kenneth S., Abdulkader, AKiullah A. "Time Series Models: How Well Do They Forecast Sales?" **The Journal of Business Forecasting.** Spring 1985, pp. 18-22.

2. Kress, George, J. "Forecasting Courses Aimed At Managers, Not Technicians." **The Journal of Business Forecasting.** Spring 1985, pp. 10-11.

3. Mentzcr, J. T. and Cox, J.E. "Familiarity, Application and Performance of Sales Forecasting Techniques." **Journal of Forecasting.** Vol. 3. No. 1. 1984, pp. 27-36.

4. Pankratz, Alan. **Forecasting with Univariate Box-Jenkins Models.** New York: John Wiley and Sons, 1983.

5. Wheelwright, Steven C. et.al. "The Accuracy of Extrapolation (Time Series) Methods." **Journal of Forecasting.** Vol. 2. No. 3. 1982, pp. 259-312.

CHAPTER 47

FAMILY MEMBER FORECASTING

Chaman L. Jain
St. John's University

For production planning and scheduling purposes, forecasts have to be broken down to the lowest level, that is, the SKU (stock keeping unit, item) level. Generally speaking, forecasts can be categorized into three levels, aggregate, category, and SKU. The aggregate level forecast is referred to the forecast of the company as a whole. A given company manufactures or sells products of different categories. For example, a manufacturer of men's clothing manufactures gents suits (one category), casual wears (second category), dress shirts (third category), neckties (fourth category), and so on. Then, each category is broken down into SKUs. For example, forecasts of shirts can be broken down into different SKUs — 15 size, half sleeves and white color is one SKU; 16 size, half sleeves and white color is the second SKU; 17 size, half sleeves and white color is the third SKU; and so on. So there can be hundreds of SKUs within a category. Production people need a forecast of each SKU to set their production plans.

As mentioned earlier, forecasts can be initiated from the top (top-down), bottom (bottom-up), and somewhere in the middle. If the forecast is initiated from the top, then the forecast has to be broken down into categories and then each category into SKUs. Very often, forecasts in business are prepared somewhere in the middle, that is, they are prepared at the category level. When the category level forecasts are prepared, for production purposes, they have to be broken down into SKUs. Of course, if forecasts are initiated from the bottom (bottom-up), then we have the SKU level forecasts right from the beginning. But if a forecast is initiated at the aggregate level, it has to be broken down into categories and SKU. Similarly, if a forecast is initiated at a category level, it has to be broken down into SKUs. The family member forecasting is a way of breaking down the aggregate level forecast into category level forecasts, and category level forecasts into SKU level forecasts.

METHODOLOGY

There are a number of ways of disaggregating aggregate or category level forecasts. The method we will explain is the one which is commonly used and is easy to work with. Let us say we want to disaggregate a category level forecast into SKU level forecasts. Let us say we have prepared a forecast of a category (family) of shirts for the month of March 2001, using a certain time series model. The forecast comes to $25 mil. The family of shirts is keyed as 5200. (See Table 1) There are five SKUs within that family, which are 5200-1 (14 size), 5200-2 (14.5 size), 5200-3 (15 size), 5200-4 (15.5 size), and 5200-5 (16 size). We want to break up the family (category) level forecasts into five SKUs. Here is a step-by-step procedure:

Step 1: Col. 3, Table 1 gives actual monthly sales of the most recent 12 months of all the five SKUs, along with their sum-total. The first step is to compute the ratio of each SKU to the total sales of that family (category). For example, the ratio of SKUs, 5200-1, comes to 0.252 (35 ÷ 139), the ratio of SKUs, 5200-2, comes to 0.072 (10 ÷ 139), and so on. All these ratios are given in Col. 4. The ratio 0.252 of 5200-1 means that during last 12 months 25.2 % of the total sales of that family (category) came from that SKU.

Step 2: The projected sale of March 2001 is $25 mil. Then the next step is to breakdown the $25 million dollars into five SKUs using their ratios. The forecast of SKUs 5200-1 comes to $6.3 mil. (25 × 0.252), the forecast of SKU 5200-2 comes to $1.8 mil. ($25 × 0.072), and so on. The forecasts of all the SKUs are given in Col. 5. Here we assume that the ratios of the last 12 months will hold in the future. There is no hard and fast rule how many months should be used to develop these ratios. If the market dynamic of your product change very quickly, you may like to use fewer months, say, 9 months or 6 months in creating these ratios.

One should always use the rolling total of months, which is, 12 months in our example. If the next month you wish to update your forecasts, you should use total of rolling 12 months sales, that is, in computing these ratios, drop one month from the top and add one month from the bottom. In other words, in each case you should use the most recent 12-month sales in developing these ratios.

TABLE 1 FAMILY MEMBER FORECASTING				
Product Code (1)	Description (2)	Rolling 12 Month Total of Actual Sales (Mil. of $) (3)	Ratio of a Member to the Family (4)	Forecasts of March (Mil. of $) (5)
5200	Category/Family	139	....	25.0
5200-1	SKU	35	.252	6.3
5200-2	SKU	10	.072	1.8
5200-3	SKU	9	.065	1.6
5200-4	SKU	64	.460	11.5
5200-5	SKU	21	.151	3.8

PART IX

REGRESSION MODELS

INTRODUCTION

With an increase in the recognition of the role of forecasts in the decision making process, as well as in the level of sophistication of business forecasters, more and more forecasters are now moving in the direction of regression-based modeling. The advancement in computer technology and the development of various software which handle regression have also encouraged its use. At present, even the spreadsheet packages such as Microsoft Excel and Lotus have a feature to prepare forecasts with regression. Furthermore, the regression-based modeling is a must where a cause and effect relationship is strong, the forecaster wants to know not only the forecast but also what drives it and how much each one contributes. It also helps to develop a marketing strategy. If you want to hit a certain sales target, it can tell you what you have to do in terms of advertisement, price or any other driver you control to hit a set target.

CHAPTER 48

SIMPLE REGRESSION MODELS

Chaman L. Jain
St. John's University

The cause-and-effect models are one of the three types of forecasting models. The other two are time series and judgmental models. Within the cause-and-effect models, the regression models are the most popular ones. In this chapter, we deal with the cause and effect relationship. Suppose sales of a company are a function of price and advertising expenditures. Then sales are the effect, and price and advertising expenditures are the cause. We develop a relationship between the cause and effect, based on the historical data, and then use that relationship to prepare a forecast of a future period. The regression-based models are the most appropriate:

1. **Where there exists a strong cause-and-effect relationship and the relationship is somewhat stable.** Let us say that sales are a function of advertisement. Based on the past data we find that the relation between them is 1:8. It means then when the amount of money spent on advertisement increases by one unit (say, $1000), the sales will increase by 8 units (say, $8 million). (Here advertisement is expressed in thousands of dollars and sales in millions of dollars.) To make a forecast of a future period, we will use this relationship, that is, of 1:8. If this relationship does not remain stable, then our forecast will not be very accurate. It is recognized that such a relationship will change somewhat over time. But as long as it does not change dramatically from one period to the next, it will provide a good forecast.

2. **Where independent variables are either known or highly predictable.** Independent variables are the cause factors (drivers). In the above example, advertisement is the independent variable because it drives the sales. To predict the sales of 2002, we need to know how much money we will be spending on advertisement, which may very well be known. But, if we say that sales are a function of advertisement and GDP (Gross Domestic Products); then, in order to forecast sales of 2002, we need to know not only how much we will be spending on advertisement but also what would be GDP in that period. If we cannot forecast GDP fairly accurately, we will have a problem in forecasting sales.

3. **Where "what if game" has to be played to optimize the firm's position.** That is, what will happen if we raise the advertisement by 5%? What will happen if we raise the price by 2

cents. The regression-based model can provide answers to such questions. If we have such answers, we can determine our optimal strategy.

4. **Where sensitivity analysis is needed, that is, how sensitive the demand is with respect to price and advertisement.** The demand is highly price sensitive (elastic) if a small change in price is followed by a large change in demand. In that case, the company has to think twice before it raises its price because it will cause a sharp decline in demand. The regression-based model can provide such an answer based on the historical data.

INDEPENDENT AND DEPENDENT VARIABLES

The variables used in regression can be categorized into two types: (1) Independent variable and (2) Dependent variable. Independent variable(s) is the cause and dependent variable is the effect. Independent variables can be one or more. For example, sale of a product is a function of price and GDP. Here we have two independent variables, price and GDP. But the dependent variable is always one, which is sale in this case. Independent variables can be categorized into two: Internal (endogenous) and external (exogenous). Internal variables are those which are under our control, that is, we can change them in any way we want. In the above example, price is an internal variable. We can change it if it is so desired. But the other independent variable, GDP, is not under our control. We cannot change it. We have to accept as it is. Table 1 gives a list of various internal and external independent variables.

TABLE 1 INDEPENDENT VARIABLES	
Internal/Endogenous	**External/Exogenous**
Price of a product Advertising Expenditure Number of products to be introduced Number of products to be discontinued Number of Stores Etc.	Competitive price Gross National Product Consumer price index Housing starts Auto Sales Etc.

TYPES OF REGRESSION MODELS

Regression models come in all shapes and colors. The ones that are often mentioned in the literature are:

1. Simple vs. multiple regression models
2. Linear vs. curvilinear regression models
3. Time series vs. cross-sectional regression models
4. Step-wise regression model
5. Probit and logit regression models

Simple vs. Multiple Regression Models

Regression is called simple regression model if it has only one independent variable. If there is more than one independent variable, it is called multiple regression model. In other words, if the model assumes that sale is only a function of price, then it is a simple regression model. Here there is only one independent variable. If we say that sales is a function of price and GDP, then we have two independent variables. The model will be a multiple regression model.

Linear vs. Curvilinear Regression Models

Linear regression models assume that the relationship between the independent and dependent variables is linear. Let us say, based on the historical data, our regression model comes with a relation of 1:2 between price and sales, and the relationship is negative. This means, other things remaining constant, if price goes down by one cent, sales will increase by $2 million; if it goes down by 2 cents, sales will increase by $4 million; if it goes down by three cents, sales will increase by $6 million; and so on. This is a case of a linear regression model. The relationship between sales and price is fixed. If the model states, with a one cent decrease in price, sales will increase by one million dollars; with 2 cents decrease in price, sales will increase by 1.5 million dollars; and with 3 cents decrease in price, sales will increase by 1.75 million dollars; then it is a case of a curvilinear regression model. The relationship between price and sales is not fixed. It changes with a change in price.

Time Series Vs. Cross-section Regression Model

A time series regression model is based on consecutive time periods. For example, a sales model of Eastman Kodak Company based on its sales data of the last 15 years. In a cross-section regression, the model is based on only one time period. If we wish to predict the height of a son based on the height of a father, we may use the data of heights of fathers and sons of one given period.

Probit and Logit Regression Models

These types of models are used where the objective is to estimate the probability of occurrence of an event (dependent variable) which takes the value of 1 and 0 — 1 for "yes" and 0 for "no." Such models are used for developing a bankruptcy model — to determine the probability of a certain company to succeed or fail. In credit card business, such models are used to predict the probability of default on payment.

FOUR STEPS TO BUILD A MODEL

There are four steps to build a regression model, which are:

1. Specification
2. Estimation
3. Validation
4. Forecast

The first step to build a regression model is to specify the model. Let us say we want to build a sales model of Walgreens. The first step is to think of all the possible factors that drive Walgreens' sales. Let's say we come up with following factors: price (P), media spending (M), GDP and personal consumption expenditures (PCE). Then the model becomes:

Sales = f (P, M, GDP, PCE)   ... (1)

Here f stands for function, that is, sales are a function of P, M, GDP and PCE. To see how good each of these variables are, we run a partial coefficient of correlation, that is, between sales and price, sales and media spending, and so on. The coefficient of correlation gives the degree of association between variables, that is, how sales are associated with price, how sales are associated with media spending, and so on. The higher the association is, the better. The coefficient of correlation runs between zero and one. Zero means that there is no association between them whatsoever. One means that there is a perfect association between them.

The coefficient of correlation can be negative or positive, which describes the direction of causality. Price usually has a negative coefficient of correlation, meaning when price increases, sales drop, and vice versa.

Let us say among these four variables, GDP has the highest coefficient of correlation, so we select the GDP as an independent variable. (Since this is a chapter on simple regression, we have to select only one independent variable.) Then, the model becomes:

Sales = f (GDP)   ... (2)

Now our model is specified, that is, sales are a function of GDP. Once the model is specified, the next step is to estimate the model, that is, to compute the regression. Simple regression can be computed manually as well as with the help of a software. We will show both ways. Let's first compute it manually.

Estimation

The regression model in this case will be expressed as follows:

Y = a + bX   (standard linear form)   ... (3)

where

    Y = Sales (variable we wish to forecast)
    a = Constant (intercept)
    b = Slope of the line (regression coefficient)
    X = GDP (independent variable)

This means that we have to compute the values of a and b. Their formulas are as follows:

$$b = \frac{n \sum XY - \sum X \sum Y}{n \sum X^2 - (\sum X)^2}$$ ... (4)

$$a = \frac{\sum Y}{n} - b \, (\frac{\sum X}{n}) \qquad \qquad \qquad \dots (5)$$

The values of $\sum Y$, $\sum X$, $\sum XY$ and $\sum X^2$ are given in Table 2. By substituting the values in the above equations, we get:

$$b = \frac{(12)(337,828,045) - (99,685)(40,446)}{(12)(830,196,863) - (99,685)^2} = 0.8739$$

$$a = \frac{40,446}{12} - 0.8739 \left(\frac{99,685}{12} \right) = -3888.92$$

By plugging the values of a and b in Equation 3, we get the regression (predictive) model, which is:

$$\hat{Y} = -3888.92 + 0.8739X \qquad \qquad \qquad \dots (6)$$

Here Y hat ($\hat{Y}$) represents forecast.

ESTIMATING REGRESSION MODELWITH EXCEL

Instead of doing it manually, we can easily estimate the regression model with Microsoft Excel. The step-by-step instructions for doing it with Excel are given in Appendix I. The Excel based regression output, using the same data, that is, of Walgreens (1996-Q1 thru 1998-Q4), is given in Table 3.

We came up this model:

$$\hat{Y} = -3888.922 \text{ (intercept)} + 0.8739 \text{ (coefficient of X variable 1) X} \qquad \dots (7)$$

This estimated regression model is the same as what we manually computed, which is given in Equation (6). Now the model has been estimated. Before we use it for making a forecast, we want to know how good this model is. In other words, whether or not this model is valid, which is the objective of the next section.

VALIDATION

We can evaluate a model with five commonly used diagnostic tests, which are:

1. Adjusted R^2
2. t test
3. F test
4. Durbin Watson (DW) Test

5. Ex-post forecasts

TABLE 2 SALES OF WALGREENS					
Period	**Y** **Sales** **(Mil. Of \$)**	**X** **GDP** **(Bil. of \$)**	**XY**	X^2	Y^2
1996-Q1	2,693	7,630	20,547,590	58,216,900	7,252,249
1996-Q2	3,179	7,783	24,742,157	60,575,089	10,106,041
1996-Q3	2,989	7,859	23,490,551	61,763,881	8,934,121
1996-Q4	2,917	7,981	23,280,577	63,696,361	8,508,889
1997-Q1	3,054	8,124	24,810,696	65,999,376	9,326,916
1997-Q2	3,603	8,280	29,832,840	68,558,400	12,981,609
1997-Q3	3,403	8,391	28,554,573	70,408,881	11,580,409
1997-Q4	3,303	8,479	28,006,137	71,893,441	10,909,809
1998-Q1	3,485	8,635	30,092,975	74,563,225	12,145,225
1998-Q2	4,093	8,722	35,699,146	76,073,284	16,752,649
1998-Q3	3,887	8,829	34,318,323	77,951,241	15,108,769
1998-Q4	3,840	8,972	34,452,480	80,496,784	14,745,600
	40,446	**99,685**	**337,828,045**	**830,196,863**	**138,352,286**
	ΣY	ΣX	ΣXY	ΣX^2	ΣY^2

$$R^2$$

R^2 (also called the coefficient of determination) shows what percent of variations in the dependent variable (sales in our example) can be explained by the independent variables (GDP in our example). The more the independent variables explain the variations in the dependent variable, the better it is. Table 3 shows that, in our example, R^2 came to 0.79. This means that 79% of the variations in the sales of Walgreens can be explained by GDP, and the other 21% are due to something else. The closet R^2 comes to one, the better.

The R^2 increases when we add more independent variables, this is because the way it is computed. Thus, the increase in R^2 resulting from more variables does not necessarily mean that the improvement is real. For that, we adjust the R^2 for the number of independent variables to arrive at the real R^2, which we call adjusted R^2. Of course, the interpretation is the same. The closet the adjusted R^2 is to one, the better.

TABLE 3 WALGREENS SALES MODEL SUMMARY OUTPUT (1996-Q1 - 1998-Q4)					
Regression Statistics					
Multiple R	0.8901				
R Square	0.7924				
Adjusted R Square	0.7716				
Standard Error	205.2593				
Observations	12				
ANOVA					
	Df	**SS**	**MS**	**F**	**Significance F**
Regression	1	1607729.1	1607729	38.159889	0.0001045
Residual	10	421313.89	2131.39		
Total	11	2029043.0			
	Coefficient	Stand. Err	t Stat	P-Value	Lower 95%	Upper 95%
Intercept	-3888.922	1176.6569	-3.3051	0.0079	-6510.6774	-1267.167
X Variable 1	0.8739	0.1415	6.1774	0.0001	0.5587	1.1891

t Test

The t test is used to determine the significance of coefficient of an independent variable. If it is not significant, we should eliminate that variable from the model. For a variable to be significant, its coefficient should be significantly different from zero. If not, we should exclude it from the model. We start out with a null hypothesis that it is not significantly different from zero, that is, there is no slope. Then we look at the table of t distribution at a set critical value, say, 5% (i.e., chances of being wrong is 5% or 95% level of confidence) at a given df (degree of freedom). The formula for computing df is: df = n – k - 1. Here n is the number of observations and k is number of independent variables.

In our example df comes to 10 (12 - 1 - 1). The table value at 5% critical value and 10 degree of freedom is 1.812. Our calculated t value for GDP, which is given in Table 3, is 6.18. Since the calculated value is greater than the table value (value given in the table of t distribution), we reject the null hypothesis, meaning that the coefficient of GDP is significant. We should keep that variable.

Rule of Thumb: If the calculated t value is greater than or equal to 2 for 20 or more observations, the coefficient is significant. We should keep that variable in. The higher the t value, the better it is.

F Test

Like R^2, F measures the significance of the overall relationship between Y (dependent variable) and Xs (independent variables). Another way of saying is that it measures the goodness of fit. Generally speaking, the larger the F is, the better. To conduct this test, we need two different degree of freedoms, one associated with the numerator of F statistic (NDF), the formula for which is: NDF = k, and another associated with the denominator of F statistic (DDF), the formula for which is: DDF = n - k - 1. (Again n is the number of observations and k is the number of independent variables.) We also have to decide about the critical value. In our example, NDF is 1; DDF is 10 (12 - 1 - 1), and we decide to use critical of value of .05 (95% level of confidence). With these, the F table gives a value of 4.96. However, our computed value of F, as given in Table 2, is 38.16. Since the computed value is significantly greater than the table value, it means that we have a good regression model.

Rule of Thumb: If the calculated value of F is 5 or above, it means that we have a significant regression model. In a business model, normally three years of data (36 months) and 2-5 independent variables are used. For these, F = 5 is sufficient. Of course, the greater the F value is, the better.

Durbin Watson Test

The Durbin-Watson test (DW) measures the autocorrelation in the residuals. The residual is the difference between the actual value and the predictive (fitted) value — value computed by the regression model. The residuals should be random. If they are random, they won't form any pattern. On the other hand, if there is autocorrelation in the residuals, it means that they form some kind of pattern, implying that independent variable(s) does not effectively explain the variations in the dependent variable. Excel does not give DW value but it gives residuals (actual – predictive value) which can be used to compute it. To get these values from Excel, one has to check residuals in the menu. The residuals obtained from Excel output, the formula and computation of DW are given in Table 4. The DW came to 2.17.

Rule of Thumb: The value of DW varies between 0 and 4. But it is safe to say that there is no autocorrelation among the residuals if the DW value falls between 1.5 and 2.5. Of course, the value close to 2 is the best.

Standard Error of Regression

The standard error measures deviations around the regression line. It is used to prepare range forecasts (low and high forecasts) at different levels of confidence. The smaller the standard error of regression is, the better. Because, with the lower standard of error of regression, the gap between the low and the high forecasts will be small. In our example, the forecast of 1999-Q1 comes to $4067.06 and standard error of regression is $205.26. (See Table 3)

Using the assumptions and characteristics of normal distribution, we can say if we want to be right 68 times out of hundred (68% level of confidence), the forecast range will be: $4067.06 ± (1) (205.26), that is, it can be as low as $3861.80 mil. and as high as $4272.32 mil. If you want to be right 95 times out of hundred (95% level of confidence), the forecast range comes to: $4067.06 ± (2) (205.26), that is, it can be as low as $3656.54 mil. and as high as $4477.58 mil. Again, if you want to be right 99 times out of hundred (99% level of confidence), the forecast will range between $4067.06 ± (3) (205.26), that is, as low as $3451.28 mil. and as high as $4682.84 mil. The range is based on the set characteristics of a normal distribution, that is, for 68% level of confidence, ± 1 standard error of regression; for 95% level of confidence, ± 2 standard errors of regression; and for 99% level of confidence, ± 3 standard errors of regression.

TABLE 4
COMPUTATION OF DURBIN WATSON (DW) STATISTIC BASED ON WALGREENS SALES DATA
Model: Y = f (GDP)

Period	Predicted Value	Residuals E_t	$E_t - E_{t-1}$	$(E_t)^2$	$(E_t - E_{t-1})^2$
1996-Q1	2778.81	-85.81		7,363.04	
1996-Q2	2912.51	266.49	352.30	71,015.70	124,112.36
1996-Q3	2978.93	10.07	-256.42	101.46	65,748.72
1996-Q4	3085.54	-168.54	-178.61	28,406.14	31,902.88
1997-Q1	3210.51	-156.51	12.03	24,494.29	144.83
1997-Q2	3346.83	256.17	412.67	65,621.88	170,299.99
1997-Q3	3443.83	-40.83	-297.00	1,667.36	88,209.63
1997-Q4	3520.74	-217.71	-176.90	47,408.58	31,294.22
1998-Q1	3657.06	-172.06	45.67	29,604.96	2086.13
1998-Q2	3733.09	359.91	531.97	129,536.09	282,994.37
1998-Q3	3826.59	60.41	-299.51	3,648.85	89,703.56
1998-Q4	3951.56	-111.56	-171.97	12,445.55	29,572.07
SUM				421,313.89	
					916,068.76

$$DW = \frac{\sum_{t=2}^{n}(E_t - E_{t-1})^2}{\sum_{t=1}^{n}E_t^2}$$

$$DW = \frac{916,068.76}{421,313.89} = 2.17$$

Ex-post Forecasts

The final test is how would this model have forecasted if we selected it? One way to do is to have hold-out periods, the periods which were not used in developing the model. Then prepare their forecasts using the model. Since we know the actuals of these periods, we can determine their errors. This will give us some idea what kind of error we can expect in the future with this model.

No matter what the other tests say, if the errors are acceptable, we should go ahead and use that model.

TABLE 5
SALES DATA OF WALGREEN AND GDP

Period	Sales (Mil. Of $)	GDP (Bil. Of $)
1999-Q1	4016	9104
1999-Q2	4691	9191
1999-Q3	4571	9341
1999-Q4	4560	9560

Let us first build a model based on the data of 1996-Q1 thru 1998-Q4, and then prepare the forecast of 1999-Q1. The model came to (Equation 6):

$$\hat{Y} = -3888.922 + 0.8739\,X \qquad\qquad \dots (8)$$

Here Y hat ($\hat{Y}$) stands for the forecast. In order to make a forecast of Q1-1999, we need the GDP of that period which is $9104 bil. The sales of Walgreens and GDP from 1999-Q1 to 1999 Q4 are given in Table 5. The forecast comes to:

Forecast 1999-Q1   = -3888.922 + 0.8739 (9104)
                    = $4067.06 mil.

Since the actual of this period is $4016 mil., the % forecast error comes to:

% Error   = -1.27 [(4016 – 4067.06) ÷ (4016)] × [100]

Now we are in 1999-Q1. We re-compute the model by using the data from 1996-Q1 thru 1999-Q1. The model comes to:

Y   = -3776.393 + 0.8600X

Then the forecast of 1999-Q1 comes to:

Forecast 1999-Q2   = -3776.393 + 0.8600 × 9191
                    = $4127.87 mil.

Since the actual of this period is $4691 mil., the % error comes to:

% Error   = 12.00% [(4691 – 4127.87) ÷ (4691)] × [100]

Now we are in 1999-Q2 and want to make a forecast of 1999-Q3. This means we will again compute the predictive model by using the data of 1996-Q1 thru 1999-Q2, and then make a forecast of 1999-Q3. We will do the same to prepare the forecast of 1999-Q4. In this case, we will use the data of 1996-Q1 thru 1999-Q3. The predictive models of all the four quarters, their forecasts and errors are given in Table 6. Their MAPE (mean absolute % error) comes to 4.81%. If this error is acceptable and you can live with it, it is a good model. Otherwise, you have to go back to the first step and re-specify the model, and then follow all these steps again.

In preparing ex-post forecasts, don't depend on just one or two forecasts because they can be misleading. Prepare ex-post forecasts of a number of periods. Because one or two forecasts may not be representative of what that model can do. Let us say that you have a bag full of marbles, which contains 80 black marbles and 20 red marbles. If you mix them thoroughly and then pick randomly one marble, you have an 80% probability that you will pick the black marble but in any given time you may wind up with a red one. But if you continue picking them, 80% of the time you are likely to pick a black marble. Similarly, in a particular period, you may experience an error, which is way above 4.81% or way below 4.81%. But if you prepare a number of forecasts with that model, there are good chances that the average % error will come close to that number.

TABLE 6 PREDICTIVE MODELS, ACTUALS, FORECASTS AND ABSOLUTE % ERRORS				
Period	Model	Actual	Forecast	Abs. % Error
1999-Q1	Y = -3888.92 + 0.8739 X	4016	4067.06	1.27
1999-Q2	Y = -3776.39 + 0.8600 X	4691	4127.87	12.00
1999-Q3	Y = -4828.62 + 0.9896 X	4571	4415.29	3.41
1999-Q4	Y = -5093.24 + 1.0220 X	4560	4677.12	2.57
	MAPE			4.81

ASSUMPTIONS OF AN ORDINARY LEAST SQUARE MODEL

The predictive model described above was computed with the Ordinary Least Squares model (OLS), the one commonly used. The model assumes:

1. The relation between Y and Xs is linear.
2. The residuals are normally distributed with a zero mean.
3. The successive residuals are not correlated. That is, there is no autocorrelation.
4. The residuals have a constant variance. That is, there is no heteroscedasticity.
5. The X variables are not linearly correlated. That is, there is no multicollinearity.

For the least squares procedure to work efficiently, all the five assumptions should hold. But it is rare in business modeling. A violation of any of the assumptions can affect the model performance, thereby requiring either a special treatment of data and/or special procedure for estimating the procedure.

The first assumption states that Y and Xs are linearly related. There is rarely a business data series where Y has a perfect linear relation with each of Xs, yet OLS type models are used, and used successfully. However, where data reveal a distinct curvilinear relationship, one has to look into a curvilinear regression model.

The second assumption of zero mean is always fulfilled, the way the least squares estimations are made.

The third assumption refers to autocorrelation, which means that the successive residuals are not correlated. Residual is actual value minus fitted value (value derived by using the regression model). The Durbin Watson Statistic measures the presence of autocorrelation. Its presence does not cause a bias in the estimation of model coefficients but it reduces the efficiency of a model to forecast. There are number of procedures available to correct it including the Cochran-Orcutt Iterative Procedure.

The fourth assumption refers to heteroscedasticity where residuals do not have a constant variance. It is usually found more in cross-sectional data than in time series data. It occurs where data values have a large range between the smallest and the largest value; where the growth rates between the dependent and independent variables vary significantly during the modeling period, and where data are highly heterogeneous. The problem of heteroscedasticity is often handled by transforming the data (inverse transformation, logarithmic transformation, etc.).

The fifth assumption refers to multicollinearity where X variables are correlated with each other. Although it is found in most of the data series, perfect multicollinearity is rare. It is acceptable as long as the estimated coefficients are statistically significant and have correct signs. Also, muticollinearity does not present a serious problem as far as forecasting is concerned, though with its presence we cannot estimate the precise contribution of each independent variable to the dependent variable. There are a number of procedures available to correct it, One way to handle this is to eliminate one of the two variables which create multicollinearity. The issue of multicollinearity does not arise when there is only one independent variable, which is the case with simple regression, the subject of this chapter. However, in the next chapter, where we will deal with more than one independent variables (multiple regression), this issue will arise.

APPENDIX 1

HOW TO COMPUTE A REGRESSION MODEL WITH MICROSOFT EXCEL

To compute any statistical function, one needs "Data Analysis" as a selection in the Tool Menu. If it is not there, follow these steps:

1. Click Tool on menu bar.
2. From Tool menu, click Add-Ins.
3. Select the "Analysis ToolPak," that is, check that box.
4. Click "OK."

This will place "Data Analysis" as a selection in the Tool menu.

Regression

Once the "Data Analysis" is incorporated, follow these steps:

1. Click "Tool" on menu bar.
2. Click "Data Analysis."
3. Click Regression
4. In this menu you have to indicate the data you wish to use.

    i. In "Input Y Range" indicate from where the Y value starts and where it ends.
    ii. In "Input X Range" indicate from where X value starts and where it ends.
    iii. In "Output Range" indicate where you want the output to be written.
    iv. If you need any of the following information, click its box:

        a. Residual
        b. Standardized Residuals
        c. Residual Plot
        d. Line Fit Plot

CHAPTER 49

MULTIPLE REGRESSION MODELS

Chaman L. Jain
St. John's University

Very often there are multiple drivers (independent variables) which drive sales. Sales may be driven by various internal factors such as advertisement, price and number of new products to be introduced, and external factors such as GDP, interest rates and competitive prices. The multiple regression is referred to a model where two or more independent variables are used. In contrast, simple regression is referred to a model where there is only one independent variable. Though there are a number of different approaches to build a multiple regression model, the one which is often used is the Ordinary Least Squares (OLS). This is the one we will describe in this chapter.

The assumptions of an OLS model are the same as what we described in the previous chapter, which are: (1) The relation between Y and Xs is linear. (2) The residuals are normally distributed with a zero mean. (3) The successive residuals are not correlated (i.e., no autocorrelation). (4) The residuals have a constant variance (i.e., no heteroscedasticity). (5) The X variables are not linearly correlated (i.e., no multicollinearity). Also, the steps to build such a model are the same, that is, specification, estimation, validation and forecast.

MULTIPLE REGRESSION MODEL

Let us build a multiple regression model for Walgreens using two independent variables, GDP and Personal Consumption Expenditures (PCE). Then, the model is specified as follows:

$$Y = f(GDP, PCE)$$

The next step is to estimate the model, which we will do by using the data from 1996-Q1 to 1998-Q4. When there are two or more independent variables, it is very difficult to estimate the model manually. We will use Microsoft Excel to perform the calculation. Table 1 gives the data, and Table 2 gives the output of regression as computed by Excel. The model becomes:

$$\hat{Y} = -3708.4867 + 1.2559 X_1 - 0.6054 X_2 \qquad \ldots (1)$$

Here Y hat $(\hat{Y})$ stands for a predictive value. The next step is validation. The objective here is to see if the model we have constructed is valid. We will look at three key diagnostic statistics, which Excel produces, as well as ex-post forecasts. As mentioned in the previous chapter, in order to evaluate a model, we should look at a number of ex-post forecasts instead of just one. For that reason, we kept four holdout periods — 1999-Q1, 1999-Q2, 1999-Q3, and 1999-Q4. We first developed a model based on the data of 1996-Q1-1998-Q4, which is given in Equation (1). In order to prepare a forecast of 1999-Q1, we need the values of GDP (X_1) and PCE (X_2) for the same period, which are $9104 bil. and $6095.3 bil., respectively. By plugging these values in Equation (1), we get a forecast of 1999-Q1, which is:

$$\hat{Y}_{99\text{-}Q1} = -3708.4867 + (1.2559 \times 9{,}104) - (0.6054 \times 6095.30)$$

$$= \$4035.13 \text{ mil.}$$

TABLE 1
SALES OF WALGREENS, GDP AND PERSONAL CONSUMPTION EXPENDITURES

Period	Sales (Mil. of $)	GDP (Bil. of $)	PCE (Bil. Of $)
1996 Q1	2,693	7,630	5,130.5
1996 Q2	3,179	7,783	5,218.0
1996 Q3	2,989	7,859	5,263.7
1996 Q4	2,917	7,981	5,337.9
1997 Q1	3,054	8,124	5,429.9
1997 Q2	3,603	8,280	5,470.8
1997 Q3	3,403	8,391	5,575.9
1997 Q4	3,303	8,479	5,640.6
1998 Q1	3,485	8,635	5,712.6
1998 Q2	4,093	8,722	5,811.4
1998 Q3	3,887	8,829	5,893.4
1998 Q4	3,840	8,972	5,986.0
1999 Q1	4,016	9,104	6,095.3
1999 Q2	4,691	9,191	6,213.2
1999 Q3	4,571	9,341	6,319.9
1999 Q4	4,560	9,560	6,446.2

Note: PCE= Personal consumption expenditures

Since the actual of that period is $4016 bil., the % error comes to -.48% [(4016 – 4035.13)/ (4016)] × [100]. Then, we prepare another model based on the data of 1996-Q1 – 1999-Q1, and use it to prepare the forecast of 1999-Q2, and the resulting error. At this point in time, we are in 1999-Q1. We use all the information available at that time to prepare the forecast of the next period. Similarly, we use the data of 1996-Q1 - 1999-Q2 to prepare the forecast of 1999-Q3, and of 1996-Q1 - 1999-Q3 to prepare the forecast of 1999-Q4.

TABLE 2 WALGREENS SALES MODEL SUMMARY OUTPUT (1996-Q1 – 1998-Q4)					
Regression Statistics					
Multiple R		0.8908			
R Square		0.7935			
Adjusted R Square		0.7476			
Standard Error		215.7890			
Observations		12			
ANOVA					
	Df	**SS**	**MS**	**F**	**Significance F**
Regression	2	1609958.826	804979.4	17.28725	0.00082707
Residual	9	419084.174	46564.91		
Total	11	2029043.000			
	Coefficient	Stand. Err	T Stat	P-Value	Lower 95%	Upper 95%
Intercept	-3708.4867	1486.6496	-2.4945	0.0342	-7071.5242	-345.499
X Variable 1	1.2559	1.7519	0.7169	0.4916	-2.7072	5.2189
X Variable 2	-0.6054	2.7666	-0.2188	0.8317	-6.8640	5.6531

All the four models, and their corresponding diagnostics statistics and absolute % errors are given in Table 3. It shows that the adjusted R^2 run between 0.75 and 0.86, which are not the greatest. T vales of both X_1 and X_2 are very poor in all the four models. In each case, it is less than 2. F values, of course, are acceptable. There is a problem of multicollinearity between GDP and PCE because the coefficient correlation between them is close to 1. The forecasting error runs between 0.48% to 13.49%, with a MAPE (mean absolute percent error) of 4.80%. The next question is what we can do to improve the model and, consequently, the forecasts, which we will discuss later.

DUMMY VARIABLES

At times, dummy variables can be helpful in improving the quality of a model. Before we go into that, we will explain what they are, and when, where and why they are used. Dummy variables assume the value of "zero" and "one." They are used:

1. Where the variable cannot be quantified as needed in regression. For example, a strike or a fire at the plant has an impact on sales but it cannot be quantified.

2. To capture seasonality. A company in certain months or quarters does very well, while in other months or quarters, very poorly. This happens every year because of weather, custom and tradition, or for any other reason. Department stores, for example, do very well during Christmas. This happens every year and at the same time.

TABLE 3
WALLGREENS' MODELS AND DIAGNOSTIC STATISTICS

Data Used	Forecast Period	Model	T Value	Adj. R^2	F Value	Absolute % Error
96-Q1 – 98-Q4	99-Q1	Y= -3708.49 + 1.2559X_1 – 0.6054X_2	X_1 = 0.72 X_2 = -0.22	0.75	17.29	0.48
96-Q1 – 99-Q1	99-Q2	Y= -3651.34 + 1.3077X_1– 0.6937X_2	X_1 = 0.89 X_2 = -0.31	0.79	23.78	13.49
96-Q1 – 99-Q2	99-Q3	Y= -4812.50 – 0.5808X_1 + 2.3490X_2	X_1 = -0.47 X_2 = 1.29	0.83	31.89	0.80
96-Q1 – 99-Q3	99-Q4	Y= -4766.26 – 0.5137X_1 + 2.2400X_2	X_1 = -0.49 X_2 = 1.47	0.86	45.66	4.44
					MAPE	4.80

3.   To account for an outlier (unusual value). Sales in one given year went up sharply because the company received a special order from the government or went down sharply because of a riot or heavy snowstorm. Among other things, the outlier(s) has to be accounted for to have a good forecasting model.

Table 4 gives sales and advertising expenditures of a company, TVI.com. The company has a strike in periods 4 and 8. We create another independent variable for strike. This means that we now have two independent variables, X_1 for advertising expenditure, and X_2 for strike. In the case of strike, we assign a value of "zero" to those periods when we did not have a strike, and assign a value of "one" to periods when we had a strike. As shown in Table 4, Col. 4, we had a strike in the 4th and 8th periods, as such they get a value of "one," and all other periods get a value of "zero." Then, we compute the regression model, the same way as we did before. The regression model comes to:

$$\hat{Y} = 3.8610 + 4.3868 X_1 - 7.875X_2$$

Here Y hat ($\hat{Y}$) stands for a predictive value. If we want to make a forecast of period 11, we need to know how much money we will spend on advertisement in that period. Let us say it is $20 thousand (i.e., X_1 = $20 thousand). We expect no strike in that period (i.e., X_2 = 0). Then the forecast for that period will be:

$$\hat{Y}_{11} = 3.8610 + (4.3868) (20) - (7.875)(0)$$
$$= \$91.597 \text{ mil.}$$

If we had a strike as well as fire during those 10 periods, then we will add one more independent variable, that is, X_3 as shown in Table 5, and then compute the regression model the same way as we did before. The only difference is that we have now three independent variables instead of two. Similarly, if we have an outlier in the data, we will add one more independent variable for the outlier. Here too, we will assign a value of "one" to the period which has an outlier, and assign a value of "zero" to other periods. When we use that model for preparing a forecast, we will plug a value of "zero" for that independent variable because we don't expect any unusual thing to happen in that period.

TABLE 4 TVI. COM USING DUMMY VARIABLES FOR STRIKE			
Period	**Sales (Mil. of $)**	**Advertising Expenditures (Thousands of $)**	**Strike**
	Y	X_1	X_2
(1)	**(2)**	**(3)**	**(4)**
1	10	2	0
2	15	2	0
3	14	2	0
4	12	3	1
5	20	4	0
6	30	7	0
7	40	8	0
8	37	10	1
9	60	12	0
10	70	15	0

Predictive Model:

$$\hat{Y} = 3.8610 + 4.3868\, X_1 - 7.875\, X_2$$
If

$X_1 = \$20$ Thousand
$X_2 = 0$

Then

$\hat{Y}_{11} = 3.8610 + (4.3868)(20) - (7.875)(0)$
$= \$91.597$ mil.

In a regression model, seasonality is also captured with dummy variables. In the case of quarterly data, we add three dummy variables, one less than the total number of quarters in a year. In the case of monthly data, we add eleven dummy variables, again, one less than the total number of months in a year. Table 6 shows how the dummy variables are assigned to capture seasonality. We have a total of five independent variables (X_1 thru X_5) where X_3 is for Q1, X_4 for Q2, and X_5 for Q3. For the sales of 1996-Q1, we put "one" under Q1 (X_3) and "zero" under Q2 (X_4) and Q3 (X_5). For the sales of 1996-Q2, we put "zero" under Q1 (X_3), "one" under Q2 (X_4) and "zero" under Q3 (X_5). Similarly, for the sales of 1996-Q3, we put "zero" under Q1 (X_3) and Q2 (X_4), and 'one" under Q3 (X_5). For 1996-Q4, we put "Zero" under each of Q1 (X_3), Q2 (X_4) and Q3 (X_5).

We do the same for all other periods. (See Table 6) How we build a model and then use it for forecasting will be shown in the next section.

Period	Sales (Mil. of $) Y	Advertising Expenditures (Thousands of $) X_1	Strike X_2	Fire X_3
1	10	2	0	0
2	15	2	0	0
3	14	2	0	0
4	12	3	1	0
5	20	4	0	0
6	30	7	0	0
7	40	8	0	1
8	37	10	1	0
9	60	12	0	0
10	70	15	0	0

TABLE 5
USING DUMMY VARIABLES FOR STRIKE AND FIRE

IMPROVING A MODEL

To improve a regression-based model, one has to understand the main principle on which it is built. The principle is to find the true drivers (independent variables), which are highly related to the variable we wish to forecast, both statistically and theoretically. The statistical relation can be looked at in terms of coefficient of correlation. The higher the coefficient of correlation, the better will be the model. The theoretical relation means that we can intuitively explain the cause and effect relationship between each driver and the variable we wish to forecast. Sometime ago, someone found a high degree of correlation between the number of divorces in England and the import of potatoes. This does not mean that we can forecast the number of divorces on the basis of bushels of potatoes imported. This has a statistical relationship, but not a theoretical one. The import of potatoes has nothing to do with the number of divorces in England. As such, the model built on this premise can fail you any time. Let us take the example of Click.com Company. Its sales data and the amount of money spent on advertisement over the last nine years are given in Table 7. In 1992, the company spent $2 thousand on advertisement and the sales were $10 mil. The ratio of sales to advertisement was 1:5. In 1993, the company spent $3 thousand on advertisement, and sales were $15 mil. The ratio again came to 1:5. The same ratio holds for all other years. This shows that advertisement is not only a true driver of sales, but also the relationship between sales and advertisement is stable, which is 1:5. With this information, we can easily and correctly forecast the sales of the company at any level of advertisement. If the company wishes to spend $20 thousand on advertisement in 2001, then its sales will be $100 mil. The coefficient of correlation between sales and advertisement is 1, which is a perfect relationship.

Period	Sales (Mil. of $) Y	GDP (Bil. of $) X_1	PCE (Bil. of $) X_2	Q1 X_3	Q2 X_4	Q3 X_5
TABLE 6 — USING DUMMY VARIABLES TO CAPTURE SEASONALITY (Sales of Walgreens)						
1996 Q1	2,693	7,630	5,130.5	1	0	0
1996 Q2	3,179	7,783	5,218.0	0	1	0
1996 Q3	2,989	7,859	5,263.7	0	0	1
1996 Q4	2,917	7,981	5,337.9	0	0	0
1997 Q1	3,054	8,124	5,429.9	1	0	0
1997 Q2	3,603	8,280	5,470.8	0	1	0
1997 Q3	3,403	8,391	5,575.9	0	0	1
1997 Q4	3,303	8,479	5,640.6	0	0	0
1998 Q1	3,485	8,635	5,712.6	1	0	0
1998 Q2	4,093	8,722	5,811.4	0	1	0
1998 Q3	3,887	8,829	5,893.4	0	0	1
1998 Q4	3,840	8,972	5,986.0	0	0	0
1999 Q1	4,016	9,104	6,095.3	1	0	0
1999 Q2	4,691	9,191	6,213.2	0	1	0
1999 Q3	4,571	9,341	6,319.9	0	0	1
1999 Q4	4,560	9,560	6,446.2	0	0	0

Now let us take another example of Fantastic.com Company. Its sales and advertising data of last nine years are given in Table 8. In 1992, the ratio of advertisement to sales was 1:10; in 1993, 1:11; in 1994, 1:1.1, and so on. The coefficient of correlation between sales and advertisement is 0.63. This means that their relationship is neither good nor stable. In that case, it would be very difficult to make a good forecast. So, what we have to do is to either find another variable(s), which is highly related to the sales and/or make a systematic modification in the data of advertisement so that it becomes more correlated with the sales. The systematic modification of data is called transformation. Therefore, to improve a model, we have to find one or more variables, which are highly related to the variable we wish to forecast. If not, transform them in such a way so that they become more correlated. There are a number of ways of transforming a data set, which we will describe later.

Here are the steps one can take to improve a model:

1. Check for seasonality.
2. Check for outliers

3. Add or delete variables.
4. Try all possible regression models.
5. Transform data.

TABLE 7 CLICK.COM		
Year	Sales (Mil. of $)	Advertising Expenditures (Thousands of $)
1992	10	2
1993	15	3
1994	15	3
1995	25	5
1996	40	8
1997	45	9
1998	60	12
1999	75	15
2000	85	17

Note: Coefficient of correlation (R) = 1

Check for Seasonality

The first step is to see if the data have seasonality, that is, certain months or quarters consistently (year in and year out) perform in a certain way. That is, a company, for one reason or another, does well in certain months or quarters, and does poorly in other months or quarters. If the data contain seasonality, the model will improve when we account for it.

To determine whether the sales data of Walgreens have seasonality, we computed the sales ratios of all the four quarters of all the four years. The sales ratios are what the sales of Q1, Q2, Q3 and Q4 are of the whole year. The sales ratio of Q1 of 1996 is 0.23, meaning 23% of the total sales of the year came in that quarter. The sales ratio Q2 of 1996 is 0.27, meaning 27% of the sales of the year came in Q2, and so on. The sales ratios of all the four quarters of all the four years are given in Table 9. It shows that there is a fair amount of consistency in the performance of all the four quarters. By and large, Q2 is the best, and Q1 is the worst. In all the four years, the sales in the Q1 were 23% of the total annual sales. The sales of Q2 is 27% of the total annual sales in all the years except 1999 in which year it was 26%, one percentage point below the other years. Also, the performance of Q3 and Q4 is pretty much consistent. This means that the data contains seasonality and the performance of the model will improve if we incorporate seasonality into the model.

Let us now build a model using five independent variables, GDP (X_1), PCE (X_2), and three dummy variables for quarters, that is, Q1 (X_3), Q2 (X_4) and Q3 (X_5). This way the model will capture seasonality in the data. Here again we build four models: One is based on the data of 1996-Q1 – 1998-Q4 to forecast the sales of 1999-Q1. The second one is based on the data of

1996-Q1 – 1999-Q1 to forecast the sales of 1999-Q2. The third one is based on the data of 1996-Q1 – 1999-Q2 to forecast the sales of 1999-Q3. The fourth one is based on the data of 1996-Q1 – 1999-Q3 to forecast the sales of 1999-Q4. The data are given in Table 6 and the results are given in Table 10.

TABLE 8 FANTASTIC.COM		
Year	Sales (Mil. of $)	Advertising Expenditures (Thousands of $)
1992	10	1
1993	11	1
1994	11	10
1995	12	2
1996	13	5
1997	13	3
1998	14	1
1999	13	2
2000	16	25
Note: Coefficient of correlation (R) = 0.63		

TABLE 9 SALES RATIOS OF WALGREENS				
Period	1996	1997	1998	1999
Q1	0.23	0.23	0.23	0.23
Q2	0.27	0.27	0.27	0.26
Q3	0.25	0.25	0.25	0.26
Q4	0.25	0.25	0.25	0.26
Total	1.00	1.00	1.00	1.00

The results show that we improved the model practically in every respect. In Table 10, under the heading of X_1 and X_2 are the results of a model where only these two independent variables were used, and seasonality was not accounted for. Under the heading, X_1, X_2, DV, on the other hand, are the results of a model, which uses these two variables plus dummy variables to account for seasonality. DV here stands for dummy variables. The adjusted R^2 went up — it varies between 0.994 and 0.997. In the previous model, where seasonality was not accounted for, the adjusted R^2 varied between 0.748 and 0.864. As we know, the higher the adjusted R^2, the better it is. The F value also went up. The model, which accounts for seasonality, the F value varied between 352.10 and 930.11, whereas in the other model where seasonality was not accounted for, it varied between 17.29 and 45.66. Here too, the higher the F value, the better it is. However, on the t statistics, we did not make much progress. But we have substantially improved the mean absolute % error (MAPE), from 4.80% to 0.96%. (See Table 10)

Check for Outliers

Before a building a model one should look very closely at the data for extreme values (too high or too low values), which don't fit into the data pattern but they are there. Outliers have to be accounted for in order to have a good model. When you find an outlier, first thing to do is to account for, that is, what caused it. The sales of one manufacturer in one given period rose sharply because Walmart opened a new store or government of Saudi Arabia placed one large order. In another period, the sales dropped sharply because of a snowstorm, riot, or strike at the plant. In a regression-based model, one can account for outliers by using dummy variables. There are two reasons why outliers should be accounted for. One, if you know the cause of each outlier, one can create a separate X variable for each circumstance. Two, if you know why it happened, you may have some idea whether or not that circumstance will recur in the period you are forecasting. As you know in a regression-based model, we need to plug a value for each X variable for the forecasting period. If we have an idea whether or not that circumstance will recur, we know what value we should plug in, that is, whether we should plug in "zero" or "one' for that circumstance.

Add or Delete a Variable

If a given variable is not giving you a good partial coefficient of correlation, R value, you may like to delete that variable. At the same time, you may like to add one or more other variables. Although we look at various statistics such as partial coefficient of correlation, t value, adjusted R^2 and F value, the final test is which variables either individually or in combination with others give the best forecasts. These are the variables you want to keep in a model.

Try All Possible Regression Models

To arrive at the best model, one has to try different regression models based on different independent variables. Step-wise regression is designed to go through various combinations and then come up with the one which gives the best results. In other words, if we have three independent variables (X_1, X_2, X_3), the step-wise procedure will test all the various combinations of these variables and then come up with the one which gives the best result. It may first build a model by using just X_1, X_2 or X_3, then in combination such as: X_1 and X_2; X_1 and X_3; and X_2 and X_3. To do that one has to decide about the criteria for the best. It may be the highest adjusted R^2, the highest F value or any other indicator. For Walgreens data, we tried some different combinations, and their results are given in Table 10.

Transform Data

As described earlier, the best way to improve a model is to find either a single variable or a combination of different variables, which are highly associated with the variable we wish to forecast. If not, modify them in a systematic way so that they become highly associated. The process of systematically modifying a data series is called transformation. Although there are number of ways of transforming the data, here are the ones commonly used:

1. *Disaggregating some of the independent variables.* For example, disaggregate the total advertising spending into direct mail, space, TV and radio, then use each one as a separate independent variable.

2. *Adding a constant number to a given independent variable.* For example, add 10 or any other number to a given independent variable.

TABLE 10
RESULTS OF DIFFERENT MODELS
WALGREENS

1999	X_1, X_2	$X_1, X_2,$ DV	$X_1,$ DV	$X_2,$ DV	$X_1 \times X_2,$ DV	$1/X_1,$ $1/X_2,$ DV	$(X_1)^2,$ $(X_2)^2,$ DV	$X_{1(t-1)},$ $X_{2(t-1)},$ DV	$(X_1/X_2),$ $(X_1 \times X_2),$ DV
	1	2	3	4	5	6	7	8	9
					Adjusted R^2				
Q1	0.748	0.994	0.984	0.995	0.994	0.990	0.995	0.992	0.995
Q2	0.792	0.995	0.986	0.995	0.995	0.992	0.995	0.994	0.996
Q3	0.826	0.997	0.981	0.997	0.995	0.995	0.997	0.995	0.997
Q4	0.864	0.997	0.979	0.997	0.995	0.995	0.998	0.996	0.997
Avg.	0.808	0.996	0.983	0.996	0.995	0.993	0.996	0.994	0.996
					F Statistic				
Q1	17.29	352.10	173.74	506.30	472.66	214.14	429.42	235.23	431.28
Q2	23.78	459.93	214.27	657.04	638.91	296.87	524.20	338.68	532.61
Q3	31.89	776.92	174.67	1010.36	677.81	505.29	875.29	530.15	859.25
Q4	45.66	930.11	164.42	1043.65	697.49	510.04	1149.30	726.36	1088.94
Avg.	29.65	629.76	181.77	804.34	621.72	381.59	744.55	457.60	728.02
					t Value				
Q1	$X_1=.7$ $X_2=-.2$	$X_1=-0.1$ $X_2=1.6$	$X_1=23.1$	$X_1=39.5$	$X_1=38.2$	$X_1=1.2$ $X_2=-3.6$	$X_1=0.4$ $X_2=-3.1$	$X_1=0.5$ $X_2=2.3$	$X_1=-1.4$ $X_2=34.5$
Q2	$X_1=.9$ $X_2=-.3$	$X_1=00$ $X_2=3.8$	$X_1=28.1$	$X_1=49.2$	$X_1=48.6$	$X_1=1.4$ $X_2=-4.5$	$X_1=1.0$ $X_2=3.1$	$X_1=0.5$ $X_2=2.9$	$X_1=-1.2$ $X_2=46.3$
Q3	$X_1=-.5$ $X_2=1.3$	$X_1=0.2$ $X_2=0.3$	$X_1=23.4$	$X_1=56.4$	$X_1=46.2$	$X_1=2.7$ $X_2=-7.1$	$X_1=0.5$ $X_2=5.6$	$X_1=-0.1$ $X_2=3.9$	$X_1=-2.5$ $X_2=58.0$
Q4	$X_1=-.5$ $X_2=1.5$	$X_1=-1.5$ $X_2=7.8$	$X_1=23.2$	$X_1=58.4$	$X_1=47.8$	$X_1=-3.4$ $X_2=-7.9$	$X_1=0.1$ $X_2=7.0$	$X_1=-.9$ $X_2=6.6$	$X_1=-3.2$ $X_2=63.7$
					Absolute % Error				
Q1	0.48	0.82	1.54	0.63	0.24	0.18	1.12	0.20	1.03
Q2	13.49	1.06	4.55	1.06	2.08	1.20	1.09	1.47	1.18
Q3	0.80	1.25	4.37	1.61	1.97	2.21	0.80	1.03	0.95
Q4	4.44	0.72	2.73	1.04	0.47	2.57	0.25	0.80	0.16
Avg.	4.80	0.96	3.30	1.09	1.19	1.54	0.82	0.88	0.83

Note: DV= Dummy variables

3. *Convert current dollars into constant dollars.* For example, use GDP in current dollars instead of constant dollars.

4. *Using an interaction variable.* That is, use the product of two variables. (See Table 11 where we use a product of GDP and PCE, making two variables into one.) In this case, we have four independent variables, interaction variables plus three dummy variables for seasonality.

5. *Using inverse transformation*. This is one divided by an independent variable (1/X), or one independent variable divided by another (X_1 / X_2). (See Table 12, where we use inverse transformation of two variables, that is, of GDP and PCE.) Now we have five independent variables in total.

6. *Using the second order polynomial*. Here we square each value of an independent variable, that is, X^2. (See Table 13, where we square each value of GDP and PCE.). Here we have a total of five independent variables.

7. *Using two different transformations in two different variables*. We can use X_1/X_2 as one transformation and $X_1 \times X_2$ (interaction) another. (See Table 14)

8. *Converting a variable into a natural log*. All the variables don't have to be converted. Convert one or more variables depending on what works.

This is, by no means, a complete list of ways the data can be transformed. In fact, every time you modify the data one way or the other, you land on a different transformation. To determine the best model for Walgreens, we tested nine different models, which are:

1. X_1, X_2
2. X_1, X_2, DV
3. X_1, DV
4. X_2, DV
5. $X_1 \times X_2$, DV
6. $1/X_1$, $1/X_2$, DV
7. $(X_1)^2$, $(X_2)^2$, DV
8. $X_{1(t-1)}$, $X_{2(t-1)}$, DV
9. (X_1/X_2), $(X_1 \times X_2)$, DV

The results of all these models are given in Table 10. Note that in model 8, we lagged the both variables (X_1 and X_2) by one period, i.e., we put the GDP of 1996-Q1 next to 1996-Q2, of 1996-Q2 next to 1996-Q3, and so on. We did the same thing with the PCE data. Within each model, we prepared four different models for four different quarters of 1999. For example, the first model used the data of 1996-Q1 – 1998-Q4; the second one, of 1996-Q1 – 1999-Q1; the third one, of 1996-Q1 – 1999-Q2; and fourth one, of 1996 Q1 – 1999-Q3. The results show that an increase in adjusted R^2, and F statistic and t value tend to improve the forecast accuracy, but not all the time. The average highest adjusted R^2 is .996. The four different models (Models 2, 4, 7 & 9) have such a value but the highest average F value is of Model 4, which is, 804.34. Its t values are also fairly high. But the lowest mean absolute % error (MAPE) is of Model 7, which is, 0.82%. The next lowest MAPE is of Model 9, which is, 0.83. (See Table 10)

WHAT IF GAME

The regression model is used not only to prepare a forecast but also to play 'what if game,' that is, what will happen if I lower or raise the price by "X" amount and/or lower or raise the media spending by "Y" amount. Also, if the forecast number is not meeting the target the management has set for, what we can do in way of increasing the media spending or anything else to hit it. The regression model can provide all these answers. Let us say a company comes up with this model:

$$\hat{Y} = 120 - .4\,X_1 + 2\,X_2$$

Here

X_1 = Price
X_2 = Media spending

If

X_1 = \$10 per unit
X_2 = \$ 2 mil.

Then

$$\hat{Y} = 120 - (.4)(10) + (2)(2)$$
$$= 120 - 4 + 4$$
$$= \$120 \text{ mil.}$$

If the company decides to raise media spending from \$2 mil. to \$3 mil., and keeps the price unchanged, then its forecast will be:

$$\hat{Y} = 120 - (.4)(10) + (2)\,(3)$$
$$= \$122 \text{ mi.}$$

Let us say now that management of the company wants the total sales to reach \$130 mil. Keep in mind that the forecast is based on a set plan — plan about how much money will be spent on media, what price will be charged, and so on. To change the forecast, we have to change the plan. Let us say in order to hit the target of \$130 mil. the company is willing to increase the media spending, but everything else will remain the same. In that case, we can solve for X_2 to find out how much media spending we need to hit the target.

$$130 = 120 - (.4)(10) + 2\,X_2$$
$$X_2 = \$7 \text{ mil.}$$

THINGS TO REMEMBER

In preparing a regression model, one should remember:

1. The independent variables you use are not only statistically valid but also theoretically sound. In other words, the independent variables logically explain the behavior of the dependent variable over time.
2. The independent variables have the correct signs. For example, the relationship between price and sales should be negative. If you come up with a positive sign, make sure that you can explain why. Maybe the higher price gives an image of better quality. As such, sales go up with an increase in price.

TABLE 11
WALGREENS: AN EXAMPLE OF INTERACTION VARIABLE

Period	Sales (Mil. of $)	GDP × PCE	Q1	Q2	Q3
	Y	X_1	X_2	X_3	X_4
1996 Q1	2,693	39,145,715.0	1	0	0
1996 Q2	3,179	40,611,694.0	0	1	0
1996 Q3	2,989	41,367,418.3	0	0	1
1996 Q4	2,917	42,601,779.9	0	0	0
1997 Q1	3,054	44,112,507.6	1	0	0
1997 Q2	3,603	45,298,224.0	0	1	0
1997 Q3	3,403	46,787,376.0	0	0	1
1997 Q4	3,303	47,826,647.4	0	0	0
1998 Q1	3,485	49,328.301.0	1	0	0
1998 Q2	4,093	50,687,030.8	0	1	0
1998 Q3	3,887	52,032,828.6	0	0	1
1998 Q4	3,840	53,706,392.0	0	0	0
1999 Q1	4,016	55,491,611.2	1	0	0
1999 Q2	4,691	57,105,521.2	0	1	0
1999 Q3	4,571	59,034,185.9	0	0	1
1999 Q4	4,560	61,625,672.0	0	0	0

3. Models do age with time. Because of the changing market dynamic it is not unusual to find a model that worked well in the past but is not working now. So, it is important to monitor regularly the performance of a model. If a model discontinues to work as efficiently as it used to, it is the time to re-specify it.

4. Statistics such as partial R, multiple R^2, adjusted R^2, F and t should be used as a guide and not as a Bible to arrive at an optimum model. Because they do not guarantee an optimum model. Furthermore, in business, one or more statistics (adjusted R^2, F value, etc.) may not be satisfied. This does not necessarily invalidate the model and its forecasts.

5. The ultimate goal of a forecaster is to come up with a model that gives the least amount of error (the error you can live with). Then, why not concentrate more on the error than anything else. For example, if a model has an adjusted R^2 of .75, but gives an error of 5% with which you can live with, then the model should be acceptable.

6. Because of interaction among variables, a certain independent variable may not work well when used alone, but works well when used with another variable(s).

7. A partial coefficient of correlation explains the degree of association between two variables, but not the cause and effect relationship. You have to make your own judgment whether the relationship runs from "A" to "B" or from "B" to "A."

TABLE 12
WALGREENS: AN EXAMPLE OF INVERSE TRANSFORMATION

Period	Sales (Mil. of $) Y	1/GDP X_1	1/PCE X_2	Q1 X_3	Q2 X_4	Q3 X_5
1996 Q1	2,693	0.00013106	0.00019491	1	0	0
1996 Q2	3,179	0.00012849	0.00019164	0	1	0
1996 Q3	2,989	0.00012724	0.00018998	0	0	1
1996 Q4	2,917	0.00012530	0.00018734	0	0	0
1997 Q1	3,054	0.00012309	0.00018417	1	0	0
1997 Q2	3,603	0.00012077	0.00018279	0	1	0
1997 Q3	3,403	0.00011918	0.00017934	0	0	1
1997 Q4	3,303	0.00011794	0.00017729	0	0	0
1998 Q1	3,485	0.00011581	0.00017505	1	0	0
1998 Q2	4,093	0.00011465	0.00017208	0	1	0
1998 Q3	3,887	0.00011326	0.00016968	0	0	1
1998 Q4	3,840	0.00011146	0.00016706	0	0	0
1999 Q1	4,016	0.00010984	0.00016406	1	0	0
1999 Q2	4,691	0.00010880	0.00016095	0	1	0
1999 Q3	4,571	0.00010705	0.00015823	0	0	1
1999 Q4	4,560	0.00010460	0.00015513	0	0	0

TABLE 13
WALGREENS: SECOND ORDER POLYNOMIAL TRANSFORMATION

Period	Sales (Mil. of $) Y	$(GDP)^2$ X_1	$PCE)^2$ X_2	Q1 X_3	Q2 X_4	Q3 X_5
1996 Q1	2,693	58,216,900	26,322,030.3	1	0	0
1996 Q2	3,179	60,575,089	27,227,524.0	0	1	0
1996 Q3	2,989	61,763,881	27,706,537.7	0	0	1
1996 Q4	2,917	63,696,361	28,493,176.4	0	0	0
1997 Q1	3,054	65,999,376	29,483,814.0	1	0	0
1997 Q2	3,603	68,558,400	29,929,652.6	0	1	0
1997 Q3	3,403	70,408,881	31,090,660.8	0	0	1
1997 Q4	3,303	71,893,441	31,816,368.4	0	0	0
1998 Q1	3,485	74,563,225	32,633,798.8	1	0	0
1998 Q2	4,093	76,073,284	33,772,370.0	0	1	0
1998 Q3	3,887	77,951,241	34,732,163.0	0	0	1
1998 Q4	3,840	80,496,784	35,832,196.0	0	0	0
1999 Q1	4,016	82,882,816	37,152,682.1	1	0	0
1999 Q2	4,691	84,474,481	38,603,854.2	0	1	0
1999 Q3	4,571	87,254,281	39,941,136.0	0	0	1
1999 Q4	4,560	91,393,600	41,553,494.4	0	0	0

TABLE 14
WALGREENS: AN EXAMPLE OF TWO DIFFERENT TRANSFORMATIONS

Period	Sales (Mil. of $) Y	GDP/PCE X_1	GDP × PCE X_2	Q1 X_3	Q2 X_4	Q3 X_5
1996 Q1	2,693	1.4872	39,145,715.0	1	0	0
1996 Q2	3,179	1.4916	40,611,694.0	0	1	0
1996 Q3	2,989	1.4931	41,367,418.3	0	0	1
1996 Q4	2,917	1.4952	42,601,779.9	0	0	0
1997 Q1	3,054	1.4962	44,112,507.6	1	0	0
1997 Q2	3,603	1.5135	45,298,224.0	0	1	0
1997 Q3	3,403	1.5049	46,787,376.9	0	0	1
1997 Q4	3,303	1.5032	47,826,647.4	0	0	0
1998 Q1	3,485	1.5116	49,328,301.0	1	0	0
1998 Q2	4,093	1.5008	50,687,030.8	0	1	0
1998 Q3	3,887	1.4981	52,032,828.6	0	0	1
1998 Q4	3,840	1.4988	53,706,392.0	0	0	0
1999 Q1	4,016	1.4936	55,491,611.2	1	0	0
1999 Q2	4,691	1.4793	57,105,521.2	0	1	0
1999 Q3	4,571	1.4780	59,034,185.9	0	0	1
1999 Q4	4,560	1.4830	61,625,672.0	0	0	0

8. It is not uncommon to find multicollinearity in a business model. (Multicollinearity is referred to a situation where X variables are correlated.) There are a number of procedures available to correct it. But don't panic if it still persists. With multicollinearity you may not be able to determine precisely the contribution of each X variable, but often it does not affect its ability to forecast.

9. Monitor not only the forecasts but also how regression coefficients of independent variables are changing over time.

10. A good forecasting model does not have to include all the relevant variables. All it needs is a few important variables. If two models yield more or less the same amount of accuracy, one with few variables should be preferred over the other (Principle of Parsimony).

11. When testing a model with ex-post forecasts, prepare a number of forecasts. The results of just one ex-post forecast may be misleading.

PART X

FORECAST ERROR

INTRODUCTION

There is no single measure of measuring forecast error. Each measure looks at different aspects of an error. This part discusses various methods of measuring forecast error and what each measure reveals. This, of course, does not include every measure discussed in the forecasting literature but it covers the ones that are applicable to business. Forecast error helps in three important ways: (1) It helps to set up a goal, that is, what forecast error a company has and what it should aim at. (2) It helps to improve accuracy. The purpose of a forecast error is not only to determine what the error is but also where it came from. If we can determine the source of an error, we can find a way to improve it. (3) It helps to manage the risk. If, for example, production people know what kind of error they can expect, then they know what they have do in way of safety stock to meet their customers' needs. No matter what we do, we will have a certain amount of error. Therefore, our resources should be directed in reducing the error rather than eliminating it. Also, we have to learn how to cope with an error. Remember, error is not a terrible thing as long as we don't repeat the same error, as long as it is within acceptable limits, as long as we learn from it, and as long as we can put it to our own advantage.

CHAPTER 50

DIFFERENT FORECASTING ERROR MEASURES

Chaman L. Jain
St. John's University

All forecasts are wrong regardless of the method used in their preparation. Since that is an uncontroversial fact, managers should devote their resources to cope with errors rather than to attempt to eliminate them. Two things are implicit in coping with error: (1) The size of an error can be measured. (2) The measure can be interpreted in such a manner as to improve significantly a manager's chances of making reasonable decisions.

Forecasters are often advised to prepare forecasts with different methods and choose the one that gives the smallest error. This is accomplished by preparing an "ex-post" forecast, a procedure under which a forecast is made for the most recent historical period for which actual data are available; the forecast is then compared with the actual outcome, and the error is calculated.

Which of a number of methods produces the "smallest" error depends on how the error is measured and interpreted. There is some good news and some bad news on this point. The good news is that there are many ways to measure error. The bad news is that there are so many ways to measure error that it can be confusing. To overcome the confusion we confine our discussion to five. These five methods share the attributes that are important to managers: they are easy to understand, easy to apply, and are practical. Moreover, they complement each other. All of them can be applied to any type of forecast — sales, cash flow, shipments, etc. — regardless of the forecasting method used. Each of the five error measurement methods requires only two sets of data: (1) Forecast of each of a number of periods. (2) Actual outcomes of each of the same periods.

TWO POINTS

Two important points need to be made if the forecast errors of different methods have to be compared to determine the best one: (1) The time lag between forecast preparation and the period for which forecast is to be prepared (forecast horizon) must be the same for all the methods. Example: In quarter 4 of 2000 you wish to prepare a forecast of the fourth quarter of 2001— a three quarter lag between the preparation of forecast and beginning of quarter 4 of 2001. In each case, we should be comparing forecast of each method of the same forecast horizon. Otherwise, we will be comparing apples with peaches. (2) Use the same set of data for each method. If we use monthly data, we should be using monthly data for preparing forecasts with each method. If we use quarterly data, we should be using quarterly data with all the methods. Following the above rules, we use the data of 10 periods, as shown in Table 1. Col. 2 gives sales of each period, and Col. 3, the forecasts of each of the periods.

ERROR MEASURES

The five error measures are:

1. Mean absolute percent error (MAPE)
2. Consistency of performance
3. Tendency to over or underestimate
4. Range of error (standard deviation)
5. Error behavior

Although there are many other ways of measuring error, these are the ones that can be used effectively in a business environment.

MEAN ABSOLUTE PERCENT ERROR (MAPE)

This is the error measure most often used in business. In business it is often referred to as average percent error — the average of percent errors with signs ignored. It is computed as follows:

Step 1: Compute forecast error, which is calculated by subtracting forecast value from the actual (i.e., Col. 2 – Col 3 in Table 1). For example, the forecast error of the first period is 1, of the second period, 3, and so on. All the forecast errors are given in Col. 4, Table 1.

Step 2: Error is an error whether it is positive or negative. When it is positive, actual value is greater than the forecasted value (a case of under-forecasting). When it is negative, actual value is less than the forecasted value (a case of over-forecasting). Whether we over-forecasted by 1 million units or under-forecasted by 1 million units in either case we made an error of 1 million units. So, the next step is to ignore the signs, otherwise in computing the average of error, the minus errors will cancel out the positive errors. Col. 5 gives errors in absolute values, that is, we remove the minus signs.

Step 3: Divide the absolute error of each period by the actual of the same period and then multiply the quotient by 100 to obtain percent difference (error) of each period. The percent error of the first period comes to 3.1% [(1 ÷ 32) × 100], the second period, 8.1% [(3 ÷ 37) × 100], and so on. All the percent errors are given in Col. 6.

Step 4: Sum the percent errors given in Col. 6 and then divide it by the number of observations, which is 10, to obtain average percent error. This comes to 3.3% (32.9 ÷ 10). This is called the Mean Absolute Percent Error (MAPE).

			TABLE 1		
		MEAN ABSOLUTE PERCENT ERROR (MAPE)			
		BASED ON THE FORECASTS PRODUCED BY METHOD A			
Period	Actual Sales ($Mil.)	Forecast ($Mil.)	Error	Absolute Error	% Error
(1)	(2)	(3)	(4)	(5)	(6)
1	32	31	1	1	3.1
2	37	34	3	3	8.1
3	42	40	2	2	4.8
4	47	46	1	1	2.1
5	52	55	-3	3	5.8
6	55	56	-1	1	1.8
7	61	60	1	1	1.6
8	67	66	1	1	1.5
9	72	73	-1	1	1.4
10	74	76	-2	2	2.7
Sum					32.9
MAPE =	3.3% (32.9 ÷ 10)				

Interpretation: This means that, on the average, forecasts prepared with this method, say, Method A, will be wrong by a factor of plus or minus 3.3%.

Assume at this point we have applied the MAPE to forecasts produced by say seven other forecasting methods besides the Method A. Assume further that we found that, on the average, Method A produces the forecast with the smallest error. Would be we justified in using this method for preparing forecasts? Before we decide we have to see whether or not this method consistently outperforms other methods; whether or not this method has a tendency to over- or under-estimate; what kind of range error it gives; and whether or not there is any change in the error behavior in recent periods. These are questions we will answer with the help of other error measures.

CONSISTENCY OF PERFORMANCE

This refers to the frequency with which a forecasting method produces an error that is equal to or smaller than a limit mandated by management. This limit is based on the lead-time required by managers to adjust their activities with respect to financing, shipping, manufacturing, purchasing, etc. Each manager determines the maximum size of forecast error with which he/she can cope with without adversely affecting company objectives. An error limit is set based on the different inputs from each department. Using the limit as a guide, count the number of periods in which the percent error stays within that limit, and what that is as a percentage of total number of periods.

304

Example: Assume that a company mandated a limit of 3.5% error in either direction (plus or minus). Data in Col. 6, Table 1 shows Method A produces an error equal to or less than 3.5% seven times out of ten, which is, 70%.

Interpretation: This means that there is a 70% chance that future forecasts produced by Method A will be within the company-mandated error limit. Good odds in our favor. But will the error be on the high side or low side? That question leads to the next method of error measurement — tendency to over or under estimate.

Thus far our analysis shows that, on the average, the error of Method A is ± 3.3%, and most of the time the error is within the company's ability to adjust its activities.

At times the average (MAPE in this case) can be misleading. Table 2 gives % errors of two methods, A and B, experienced over ten periods. If we look at just MAPE, Method A is superior to Method B because its average error is lower than the other (3.4% against 3.7%). However, if we look at the consistency, Method B is better than Method A because in 90% of the cases, the error was 3.5% or less (error mandated by the management), whereas in the case of Method A it was only in 40% of the cases.

TABLE 2
FORECAST ERROR

Period	Method A Forecast Error (%)	Method B Forecast Error (%)
1	2.5	2.5
2	3.6	2.2
3	3.7	12.5
4	3.6	2.3
5	2.9	3.1
6	3.6	2.2
7	3.8	2.8
8	3.2	2.9
9	3.4	3.2
10	3.6	3.2
MAPE	**3.4**	**3.7**

TENEDENCY TO OVER- OR UNDER-ESTIMATE

To some functions, it is important not only that the MAPE is the lowest but also whether the method has a tendency to over- or under-estimate. For example, production people are more comfortable with an over-estimate than with an under-estimate. In other words, they are more comfortable with over-stock than with under-stock. Finance people, on the other hand, are more comfortable with an under-estimate than with an over-estimate.

A forecasting method has a tendency to over-estimate if the forecast values over time are greater than actual values in more than 50 percent of the cases (periods), and a tendency to under-estimate if the forecast values over time are smaller than actual values in more than 50 percent of the cases.

Example: An examination of data in Col. 4, Table 1, shows that Method A over-estimated actual sales in 4 periods and under-estimated in 6 periods, implying that it over-estimated in 40% of the cases, and under-estimated in 60% of the cases.

Interpretation: Method A has a slight tendency to under under-estimate. The chances are that forecasts prepared by Method A will err on the low side.

Thus far our analysis of Method A shows that it errs at an average rate of ± 3.3%, that most of the time the error is within the company's ability to adjust its activities, and that the method will probably err on the low side.

What are the chances, though, that the error will exceed certain limits that may be beyond the company's ability to adjust? The range of error (standard deviation) has some answers for us.

RANGE OF ERROR

The range of error is the spread between the smallest and largest error a forecasting method is likely to produce. Technically, it is referred to as "standard deviation." It is computed as follows:

Step 1: Col. 2, Table 3, gives % error (with signs ignored). First step is to compute the average % error (mean), which is sum of % errors (32.9) divided by the number of observations, which is 10. It comes to 3.3% (32.9 ÷ 10).

Step 2: Compute deviation from the mean. This is obtained by subtracting each % error from the mean (3.3%). For the first period, it comes to –0.2 (3.1 – 3.3); for the second period, 4.8 (8.1 – 3.3); and so on. All these values are given in Col. 3, Table 3.

Step 3: Square the deviation of each period. For the first period, square of deviation comes to 0.04 (0.2 × 0.2); for the second period, 23.04 (-4.8 × -4.8); and so on. All these values are given in Col. 4.

Step 4: Sum the square of deviations, which comes to 45.37. (See Col. 4, Table 3)

Step 5: Divide the sum of square of deviations by the number of observations, which is 10. It comes to 4.537 (45.37 ÷ 10).

Step 6: Find out the square root of the quotation from Step 5 to obtain standard deviation. This comes to 2.13% ($\sqrt{4.537}$%).

Interpretation: The standard deviation measures the likely range of error between the forecast and the actual. There are three ranges most commonly used, each with a different probability of occurrence — 68%, 95%, and 99%. You select the probability with which you are most comfortable. If, for example, you need to be virtually certain that your forecast should fall within the high and low points of the range, you should select 99 % probability (level of confidence). As we shall see in a moment, however, the spread between the high and low points of the range increases as you increase the probability in your favor.

TABLE 3 RANGE OF ERROR			
Period (1)	% Error (Signs ignored) X (2)	$(X - \mu)$ (3)	$(X - \mu)^2$ (4)
1	3.1	-0.2	0.04
2	8.1	4.8	23.04
3	4.8	1.5	2.25
4	2.1	-1.2	1.44
5	5.8	2.5	6.25
6	1.8	-1.5	2.25
7	1.6	-1.7	2.89
8	1.5	-1.8	3.24
9	1.4	-1.9	3.61
10	2.7	-0.6	0.36
Sum	32.9		45.37

μ (Average % Error) $= 3.3\% \ (32.9 \div 10)$

$$SD \ (Standard \ Deviation) = \sqrt{\frac{(X-\mu)^2}{N}} = \sqrt{\frac{45.37}{10}} = 2.13\%$$

In using this procedure, it is important to distinguish between the standard deviation and the number of standard deviations. The procedure outlined above obtains the value of the standard deviation, whereas the number of standard deviations (SD) refers to the probabilities as follows: One SD = 68%, two SD = 95%, and three SD = 99 %.

Following is the procedure to obtain the error range for each probability:

68 % Probability

Step 1:   Multiply the value of the SD (2.13% in our example) by 1. (2.13% × 1= 2.13%)

Step 2: Subtract the product of Step 1 from the average percent error (3.3%) to obtain the lower end of the range, which comes to 1.17% (3.3% - 2.13%), and add the same value to the average percent error to obtain the higher end which comes to 5.43% (3.3% + 2.13%).

Interpretation: There is a 68 % chance that the forecast error produced by Method A will fall somewhere between 1.17% and 5.43%.

95 % Probability

Step 1: Multiply the value of the SD (2.13%) by 2 (2.13% × 2 = 4.26%).

Step 2: Subtract the product of Step 1 from the average percent error (3.3%) to obtain the lower limit of the range, which comes to –0.96% (3.3% - 4.26%), and add the same product to the average percent error to obtain the upper end of the range, which comes to 7.56% (3.3% + 4.26%).

Interpretation: Since the error cannot go below zero, a minus value is given a value of zero. This then means that there is a 95% chance that the forecast error produced by Method A will fall somewhere between zero and 7.56%.

99 % Probability

Follow the same two steps as above except multiply the value of the SD by 3 (2.13% × 3 = 6.39%) and subtract and add the product to the average percent error to obtain and high and low points of the range. This then means that at 99% probability the error can be as low as zero (3.3% - 6.39% = -3.09%) or as high as 9.69% (3.3% + 6.39%). Here again the value of –3.09% is interpreted as zero.

ERROR BEHAVIOR

The error behavior changes over time. If we look at the errors given in Col. 2, Table 3, we will notice that the errors in the first five periods are much higher than in the last five periods. This means that the performance of the forecasting method has improved over time. They are much more indicative of what we can expect in the future than all of the 10 historical periods combined. Therefore, to get a better picture of what kind of error we can expect in the future, we should refigure the average percent error, the consistency of performance, the over-and under-estimating tendency, and the SD on the basis of data of the most recent five periods.

The average percent error of the last five periods comes to 1.8% as opposed to 3.3%. This will have quite an impact on the other four measures. On the other hand, if the errors in the last five periods were higher than before, it may mean that our method of forecasting is no longer working. In that case, we may decide to discard this forecasting method and look for another one.

CHPATER 51

MEASURING FORECAST ACCURACY

Charles W. Chase Jr.
Wyeth-Ayerst Pharmaceuticals

The question regarding what calculation is best to measure forecast accuracy has been debated by both practitioners and academics for many years. In fact, you will find at least one chapter in every business forecasting textbook dedicated to this topic, measuring forecast accuracy. Nevertheless, the most frequently used measure in the corporate world is percent attainment of forecast rather than forecast error, which can lead to some biased interpretations of the results. Percent attainment is simply the actual occurrence divided by the forecast then multiplied by one hundred. It is written as, Attainment = (Actual ÷ Forecast) × (100). Its primary purpose is to measure actual performance as a percentage attainment of the forecast. When asked why attainment is the most preferred measure practitioners reply, "it is easier for Executive Management to understand." For the most part, it is used as a financial target or goal rather than an accuracy measurement. It's fine for financial purposes, but not for improving forecast accuracy. The intent of this editorial is to clarify any questions surrounding the theoretical formulation of forecast error and its implications on how it is utilized to measure forecast accuracy.

WHY MEASURE FORECAST ACCURACY?

Before describing the method by which error is calculated and its implications, it is important to be clear as to what we are trying to measure, "forecast accuracy," and why. In this case, the word accuracy refers to the accuracy of the future forecast or ex-ante forecast as compared to the actual outcome. Its primary purpose is not to measure how well we predicted the actual occurrence, but rather why the outcome occurred. By documenting the design, specifications, and assumptions that went into the forecast only then we can begin to learn the dynamics associated with the item(s) we are trying to predict. Forecast measurement should be a learning process, not a tool to evaluate performance. The best way to improve forecast accuracy is by measuring the outcome. However, tracking forecast error alone is not the solution. Instead of asking the question, "what is this month's forecast error?" we need to ask, "why was this month's error so high (or low), and has it improved since last month?" Ongoing documentation of the specifics that went into each forecast is actually more important if you are truly dedicated to improving your performance. Unfortunately, we will always be judged based on forecast error alone.

DEFINITION OF FORECAST ERROR

The basic assumption underlying the application of any forecasting technique (statistical or judgmental) is that the actual outcome observed will follow some pattern associated with seasonality, trend, and/or causal relationships plus some random influences. This is algebraically written as: Actual Outcome = Pattern + Randomness. This simple equation is really saying that even when the average pattern of the underlying data has been identified, some deviation will exist between the forecasting method applied and the actual occurrence. Our purpose as practitioners is to minimize these deviations or errors in the forecast. Those errors are defined as the difference between the actual value and what was forecasted. They can be written as:

$$e_i = X_i - F_i \qquad \qquad ... (1)$$

An error value is always associated with each observation for which there is both an actual and a predicted value. To simplify the manipulation of expressions involving the adding of many numbers, it's convenient to use a summation sign known as sigma, Σ.

The use of this sign and the elements of the notation mentioned previously can be demonstrated by using X_i as the actual sales value, F_i as the forecast value for sales, and e_i as the error, or difference between actual (Xi) and forecast (Fi) values of sales in time period i. The subscript i indicates that it is the error of the time period i being examined.

CALCULATING FORECAST ERROR

A number of specific measures of accuracy have been defined which are useful in determining forecast accuracy. Table 1 presents a set of data that can be used to illustrate these measures of accuracy. The data in this example represent monthly sales (in thousands of units) for a mass merchandiser over a 10-month period.

MEAN ERROR

One measure of accuracy that can be calculated is average error. The actual formulation can be written as:

$$AE = \frac{1}{n} \left[\sum_{i=1}^{n} (Xi - Fi) \right] \qquad \qquad ... (2)$$

Using the data in Table 1, if we simply add up the values of the errors and compute the average, we find that it is close to zero (.8), since many of the positive errors have canceled out the negative errors (see Col. 4). To avoid such problems we can compute the absolute errors (disregarding the plus or minus signs) and looking at what is commonly referred to as the mean absolute deviation (MAD).

					TABLE 1

MONTHLY MASS MERCHANDISER SALES

Month	Sales ($1000) X_i	Forecast F_i	Error $X_i - F_i$	Absolute Error $\|X_i - F_i\|$	Absolute Percentage Error $\frac{\|X_i - F_i\|}{X_i} \times 100$
(1)	(2)	(3)	(4)	(5)	(6)
1	100	100	0	0	0.0%
2	90	100	-10	10	11.1
3	120	110	10	10	8.3
4	140	110	30	30	21.4
5	110	140	-30	30	27.3
6	120	90	30	30	25.0
7	110	120	-10	10	9.1
8	70	110	-40	40	57.1
9	130	70	60	60	46.32
10	152	120	32	32	21.1
Sum			8	252	226.6
Mean			0.8*	25.2**	22.7***

* Mean Error
** Mean Absolute Deviation
*** Mean Absolute Percentage Error (MAPE)

MEAN ABSOLUTE DEVIATION

The mean absolute deviation (MAD) is calculated as follows:

$$MAD = \frac{1}{n}[\sum_{i=1}^{n} |Xi - Fi|] \qquad ...(3)$$

This is simply the mean absolute error over several periods. From Col. 5 in Table 1 we see that the value of the mean absolute deviation is 25.2. This second measure is often preferred to that of the mean error.

MEAN ABSOLUTE PERCENT ERROR

Another accuracy measure is the mean absolute percentage error (MAPE). It is the most widely used measure for calculating forecast error. MAPE is obtained by computing the average absolute percent error for each time period. The actual formulation is written as:

$$MAPE = \frac{1}{n}[\sum_{i=1}^{n} \left|\frac{Xi - Fi}{Xi}\right| \times 100] \qquad ...(4)$$

As a percentage, this measure is a relative one, and thus it is preferred to the mean error or the MAD as an accuracy measure. In other words, the MAPE is similar to MAD except that it is dimensionless. This makes it nice for communication purposes and helpful in making comparisons among forecasts from different scenarios. However, the MAPE has a bias favoring estimates or forecasts that are below the actual values. Therefore, you are penalized less if you over achieve your forecast than if you under achieve your forecast. This becomes obvious when we look at the extremes. For example, a forecast of 0 can never be off by more than 100%, but there is no limit to errors on the high side. When working with judgmental forecasters, it could become a problem in the event of an intentional biasing of their forecasts. Nevertheless, if this is not critical, then you should use the MAPE.

TABLE 2
SKU MASS MERCHANDISER STORE SALES
(March 2000)

SKU I	Sales ($000) X_I	Forecast F_I	% Attainment $(X_I \div F_I) \times 100$	Error $X_I - F_I$	Absolute Error $\|X_I - F_I\|$	Absolute Percentage Error $\dfrac{\|X_I - F_I\|}{X_I} \times 100$	Weighted Absolute % Error $\dfrac{\|X_I - F_I\| \times 100 \times X_I}{X_I}$
(1)	(2)	(3)	(4)	(5)	(6)	(7)	(8)
1	10	10	100	0	0	00.0%	00.0
2	9	10	90	-1	1	11.1	99.9
3	20	18	111	2	2	10.0	200.0
4	40	35	114	5	5	12.5	500.0
5	30	40	75	-10	10	33.3	999.0
6	100	90	111	10	10	10.0	1000.0
7	10	20	50	-10	10	100.0	1000.0
8	7	11	64	-4	4	57.1	399.7
9	13	7	186	6	6	46.2	600.6
10	20	32	63	-12	12	60.0	1200.0
Sum	259	273	964	-14	60	340.2	4999.2
Mean			96.4****	-1.4	6.0*	34.0	19.3***

*	Mean Absolute Deviation (MAD)
**	Mean Absolute Percentage Error (MAPE)
***	Weighted Mean Absolute Percentage Error (WMAPE)
****	Forecast Attainment

WEIGHTED MEAN ABSOLUTE PERCENT ERROR

Another problem to consider with MAPE is that it allocates equal weight to each period. In other words, it is scale dependent. This is fine when measuring error across periods of time but not for measuring error across SKUs (Stock Keeping Units) for one period of time. For example, when measuring mean forecast error across a group of items for a given period of time, say, March 2000, you need to consider using a method that accounts for each item's proportional weight to the total. A method that we have developed to address the issue of scale dependence is called weighted mean absolute percentage error (WMAPE).

Table 2 illustrates this method for measuring SKU level accuracy across product groups. It's preferred to MAPE because it accounts for each product's contribution to the total error by weighting the impact of the individual item value of each product within the group as it is related to the total. For example, if we were measuring SKU accuracy for a given point in time each corresponding SKU would only affect the outcome based on its contribution or unit volume proportion within the group. The actual formulation can be written as:

$$\text{WMAPE} = [\sum_{i=1}^{n} \left| \frac{Xi - Fi}{Xi} \right| \times 100 \times Xi] \div [\sum_{i=1}^{n} Xi] \qquad \dots (5)$$

The commonality of these algebraic measures is that they all relate to the difference between the actual value and the forecasted value. As such, these measures have an intuitive appeal. Subsequently, if we are serious about increasing forecast accuracy, it is desirable for each of these measures to be close to zero.

REFERENCES

1. J. Scott Armstrong, **Long-Range Forecasting: From Crystal Ball to Computer**. New York: Wiley-Inter-science, Second Edition, 1985, pp. 346-348.
2. Spyros Makridakis and Steven C. Wheelright. **Forecasting Methods for Management.** 5th Edition. New York: John Wiley & Sons, 1989, pp. 54-59.

CHAPTER 52

LIVING WITH FORECAST ERROR

William J. Drumm
U.S. Consumer Products, S.C. Johnson Wax

Perhaps the most underutilized aspect of the sales forecast function is learning to live with forecast error. While the priority should be the never ending process of improvement of the sales forecast, other functional areas of the organization will also benefit from the process if they share in the management of the risk attached with the forecast. Basic to this caveat is the need for the forecast function to play a "point role" in communicating the risks and assumptions attached with the forecast and key milestone dates when more/better data might be available to aid in managing the forecast. The key word is one that is not new to us; it's communication.

As the forecast function deals with improvement in the reliability of the forecast, one must also learn to manage around the fact that lead-times for other functional areas may not coincide with when the best estimate might be available from the forecast function. It is a pretty obvious phenomenon in most organizations that functional areas that feed on the sales forecast will "second guess" its output based on past experience with forecast error and the bias in the forecast. This is fine and healthy when trying to manage increased inventory turns and improved customer service as long as the forecasting function has made sure that they are "in the loop" during the process (vs. just issuing a forecast and then turning to the next batch of data/assumptions for the next forecast update). The longer the time span between forecast updates, the more important it is for the forecast function to communicate pending revisions so that other functional areas benefit from an environment that is more communicative, thus giving them a better chance to manage risk and help the organization run more efficiently.

It's up to the forecast function to create the environment in which forecast error is an "open book" where forecasters share with other functional areas the realism that the forecast "might be" wrong. Investing all of your time trying to perfect a given forecast(s) and/or system(s) does not allow this type of environment. The forecaster must take the time to be sure that either a written or person-to-person risk assessment of his/her latest estimate is shared with other functional groups. Forecasters can best serve themselves by accepting the challenge to both improve the forecast (look for more sources of "timely" information as opposed to a better Black Box) and by partnering with other functional areas in risk management via better communication of the pitfalls of a given estimate for a product line and/or singular SKU's.

By all means, try to measure forecast error at the item level and, hopefully, as an absolute measure so that the +/- variances do not offset each other at higher levels of aggregation. Also, always pick a frozen period of time to measure forecast error that is just outside your organization's average procurement/production lead-time. If this is a lead-time of a month, then you would take a "snapshot" of the forecast for February at the beginning of January and save it for a measure/comparison against actual results at the completion of activity for the month of February. Category or brand forecast error means nothing from an operational perspective when in fact you are manufacturing and carrying inventories at the SKU level. It's rather misleading to upper management and other functional areas when the balancing of +/-'s within a brand/category hide the real impact of forecast error on inventory turns and customer service levels. The reality of all is that performance attainment by other functional areas will not always credit a good forecast, but with poor performance you can bet that the forecast will be one of the major reasons they've missed a target. So be it ... learn to live with forecast error and make sure that other functional areas learn to live with it as well.

PART XI

PRESENTING AND SELLING FORECASTS

INTRODUCTION

No matter how good the forecasts are, if they are not accepted and used they are useless. The job of a forecaster is not only to prepare forecasts but also to sell them. This requires a special skill for presenting forecasts and building trust with your customers. One Director of Forecasting of a large corporation once remarked, "I would rather spend my time in preparing and improving forecasts than selling to the forecast users. But that is part of the job." This section explains what kinds of problems, political or otherwise, the forecaster often encounters and how to deal with them. The road to success in the forecasting function is long and arduous. But with determination, hard work and perseverance, the forecaster can win the trust of his or her customers.

CHAPTER 53

STRATEGY FOR PRESENTING A FORECAST

Robin Peterson
New Mexico State University

Technical competence is not the sole key to the success of a forecaster. Selecting an adequate prediction model, acquiring reliable data and making meaningful forecast subdivisions are important. But they are not enough for the success of a forecaster. Forecasts are made to be used. They will serve no purpose if managers (users of forecasts) neither recognize them as good forecasts nor use them. Therefore, it is equally important how forecasts are presented. This chapter outlines a strategy for presenting a forecast.

The presentation of a forecast is more an art than a science. It may differ from one company to another, from one forecaster to another. The best strategy for presenting a forecast is the one that works for an individual. Nevertheless, enough similarity exists among different forecasters to chart a definitive strategy.

The strategy for presenting a forecast involves two basic things: (1) Acquisition of information about the users of forecasts, and (2) strategy used in making the presentation. Since personal selling is more an art than a science, the implications of the suggestions differ from one company, and even one sales forecaster, to another. Nevertheless, enough similarity exists among the communication needs of diverse forecasters to permit the drawing of some relatively definitive conclusions.

Those sales representatives, who are most successful, gather considerable information about their prospects and their needs prior to calling upon them. Similarly, forecasters are well advised to seek out background material on the executives to whom they will provide data. Indeed, forecasters should keep in mind that their reason for being is to serve line executives—a very useful overall guiding philosophy.

Forecasters should attempt to determine the problems that executives are experiencing which forecasts can be of value in overcoming. This requires a working knowledge of the managers' jobs, including their objectives, personnel, policies constraints, and resources. It also requires estimates of how well the executives are performing and major obstacles, which may be preventing goal achievement.

In addition, forecasters are well advised to accumulate personal information about the forecast users. Examples are inputs regarding their personalities, backgrounds, hobbies, interests, education status, and family background. This information is useful in developing tailored messages that "fit" the forecast user's unique characteristics. Some executives, for instance, are very business-like and prefer a very formalized presentation of forecast methods and approach. Others like a relatively unstructured people-oriented start. This kind of background information can be acquired through observation, relatives and colleagues of executive, and discussions with other company personnel.

STRATEGY FOR PRESENTATION

A well-planned personal presentation is made up of five major activities: These are (1) the contact, (2) the presentation, (3) handling objections, (4) the close, and (5) post-presentation functions. In practice, these are not necessarily sequential and may overlap considerably. However, they should be planned in the order indicated above for maximum impact.

The contact takes place when the forecaster first approaches the line executive. If well-handled, it sets the stage for the remainder of the presentation. Besides including some small talk to establish friendly relations, the forecaster should attempt to stimulate attention and interest. This can be accomplished by promising reward —"I have some figures that will be very useful to you" or stimulating curiosity "what do you think next month's sales forecast will be?" If the forecaster makes a good impression at the contact stage the remainder of the presentation is likely to flow easily.

At the contact stage, the forecaster should attempt to establish similarities with the manager. This means bringing out various facets — such as common interests, hobbies, or philosophies that the two have in common. When forecasters are acquiring information about managers they should seek points of similarity. They can bring these out in the contact and the presentation.

At the presentation stage, the forecaster gives the forecasts along with some background on how they are derived, and makes an attempt to convince the manager of their value. For a presentation to numerous low-level executives, the forecaster may choose to use a "canned" approach that is planned in some detail and even memorized. In most cases, an extemporaneous approach is preferred, however. It is a necessity, of course, when dealing with higher level managers.

The presentation is most likely to be effective if the forecaster acts as a creative problem-solver, one who attempts to aid managers in resolving their difficulties. This requires a commitment to the satisfaction of the executives' (rather than the forecaster's) needs. It also requires empathy — the ability to mentally put oneself in the shoes of others — as a means of truly understanding managerial problems. In well-conducted presentations, forecasters are engaged in considerable listening to and observing of the executive's behavior in order to ascertain if the messages are getting across and what the managers' reactions are. Two-way communication is essential. The forecaster who monopolizes the conversation may quickly bore and alienate executives, and fail to react to their impressions. If possible, it is useful to allow the managers to participate in the presentation, as this promotes understanding and learning on their part. These individuals participate when they are allowed to talk; handle written reports, charts and graphs; make computations; and engage in other behaviors. Ideally, both the forecaster and the executives work together as joint problem solvers who are attempting to enhance the executives' effectiveness.

Those forecasters who make an impression of being both competent and trustworthy are most likely to obtain the cooperation of line managers. This impression is most likely to emerge if the forecasters are, in fact, knowledgeable, capable, and devoted to solving the problems of executives.

HANDLING OBJECTIONS

From time to time executives will raise objections. They may state that forecast levels are not realistic or that the methodology is unsound. Forecasters should be in a position to answer such objections. Generally, they should avoid arguments when objections are raised. Instead, they should point out how the forecasts can be of value to the line managers. Sometimes forecasters can benefit by asking a series of open-end questions designed to reveal the true underlying objections. They may ask, for instance, "Why do you feel that this forecast is too high?" "Why do you feel that the methodology is weak?" or, "What are your major objections to this technique?" Overall, the best means of responding to objections is to accent the positive — point out the strengths such as superior forecasting technology and successful past track records. These are indispensable rejoinders.

In the close, the forecaster attempts to complete the job of convincing line executives to accept and take action on the forecast. It may be undertaken directly, as when a manager is asked, "Will you use these forecast figures?" or a summary of the strong points of the forecast methodology may be presented. If forecasters simply conduct themselves in a manner that the forecast will be accepted and voted upon, managers are likely to react positively to the forecast. If the previous steps in the presentation have been undertaken in a well-conceived manner, the close will often flow smoothly.

POST-PRESENTATION FUNCTION

Forecasters should contact line executives from time to time after the presentation to ensure that the forecasts have been properly understood and are being used in an appropriate manner. Effective post presentation service promotes management satisfaction and makes future acceptance of forecasts more likely.

CHAPTER 54

TEN COMMANDMENTS OF SELLING FORECASTS TO FORECAST USERS

Chaman L. Jain
St. John's University

Preparing good forecasts is half of the job of a forecaster. The other half is to sell them. The more accurate the forecasts are, the better. But how good are the forecasts if they are neither accepted nor used. One forecasting director once remarked, "I would rather spend my time in refining and improving forecasts than selling them. But business realities don't permit." Therefore, it is important for a forecaster to learn not only how to prepare forecasts but also how to sell them. Here are the ten commandments of selling forecasts.

1. Know your customers.
2. Involve the users in the forecasting process.
3. Educate the users of forecasts.
4. Provide detailed report on forecasts.
5. Present forecasts in a professional manner.
6. Forecasts are just forecasts.
7. Sell to the boss.
8. Look for new uses of forecasts.
9. Appreciate management perspective.
10. Have patience.

KNOW YOUR CUSTOMERS

One of the keys to successful selling is to know your customers — who they are and what they want. Here customers are the forecast users. They are often production, logistics, sales, marketing, planning, and finance people. It would be easier to sell, if the forecasts are what the users are looking for. Therefore, before preparing forecasts, forecaster should assess the requirements of each customer. The requirements can be established in terms of: (1) What variables should be forecasted — shipments, orders, cash flow, etc.? (2) In what form forecasts should be prepared — dollars, units, percentage, etc.? (3) What levels of details are required? On a product level, forecasts may be required at category and SKU levels. On a geographical level, they may be required by sales division, distribution center, manufacturing location, broker and account. On a trade channel level, they may be required by food stores such as Pathmark, Shoprite and Public; by mass merchandisers such as Walmart, K-mart and Target; by drug stores such as Drug Emporium, Walgreens and CVS; by warehouse clubs such as Price Club and Sam; and by government unit. Of what time period forecasts are required? They may need forecasts by day, week, quarter and/or year. (4) How far ahead forecasts are required — one month ahead, one quarter ahead or one year ahead? (5) When are forecasts required? This depends on the lead-time required to make or change a plan. (6) What is the acceptable forecasting error?

The most important thing to senior management is not the forecast error but what drives the business, says Charles Chase, Assistant Vice President, Global Forecasting & Analysis, at Wyeth-Ayerst Pharmaceuticals. They want to know how promotional activities, competitive actions and price changes affect the business. They want to know what factors are controllable and what are not. They want the forecaster to tell them not what will happen, but what can happen and what they can do to change it.

INVOLVE YOUR CUSTOMERS IN THE FORECASTING PROCESS

The involvement of customers into the forecasting process can help not only in selling forecasts but also in improving them. Forecasting is not done in isolation but in an environment of interchange between forecaster and forecast users. Involvement can be in the form of obtaining input, establishing assumptions, determining most probable scenarios, going over preliminary forecasts, and following up how forecasts are used and difficulties encountered.

To prepare forecasts, forecaster needs not only sales history but also input about the market (what consumers are buying or not buying and why), competition, promotional strategy, products to be introduced or abandoned, and production and logistics issues. Salespeople are the eyes and ears of the market. They know more about what is happening in the marketplace than any one else. They know what consumers are buying and what competitors are doing. Such information can be useful to the forecaster.

Each forecast is based on a set of assumptions, assumptions about promotional strategy, which products will be introduced and which ones will be abandoned, and so on. Marketing can provide such information. In some cases, forecasts may be required under different scenarios, that is, what will happen if we raise the price by this much, reduce the advertising budget by this much, or go to a new market? Again, marketing can help you to determine the most likely scenarios.

Forecasts will be meaningless if the production people cannot produce and deliver on time. I remember one monthly forecast meeting I attended. In that meeting, the production person said that now we could manufacture and deliver customized steel doors in three weeks instead of four weeks. Salesperson immediately responded that in that case we would get more orders. Because he was not accepting orders where delivery was required in three weeks. By circulating preliminary forecasts, the forecaster can obtain the reaction of the forecast users. If the forecaster does not agree with them, he or she will know how to defend at the time of final presentation. The forecasting manager of Fujitsu America finds this procedure very helpful. Most of the differences are resolved before the final presentation.

The forecaster can further improve the involvement of the forecast users if he or she periodically follows up how forecasts are used, and if not, why? This will help not only to bring the forecaster and customers closer but also enable the forecaster to determine exactly the kinds of forecasts they need.

EDUCATE THE FORECAST USERS

It is important that the forecast users understand the basics of business forecasting. The more they know, the more they will appreciate. What they need to know is the basic concepts, not algorithm, how forecasts are prepared. What assumption is made when a time series model is used, that is, the past pattern will continue? What assumptions are made when a cause and effect model is used? Assumptions might have been made about the advertising budget, price, competitive action, and state of the economy. The forecast users have to understand that forecasts are a must for making a business plan. The option is either to use your own forecasts, which may be highly crude, or use the ones prepared by the professional. They have to understand that forecasts are neither a goal nor a plan, but based on a plan. They can to some extent influence the future by changing the plan. They have to understand that forecasts are not entirely mechanical, a certain amount of judgment goes into them. The more the forecast users understand the forecasting, the more they will appreciate and use them. The forecaster can play an important part in educating them. The education of the forecast users can be achieved by offering a seminar on forecasting and/or explaining something about it at the organization's regularly scheduled meeting. Carroll Mohan of Coca-Cola says that one way to accomplish this is to find a "rock" in an organization, a person who is likely to be around for a while, with and through whom professional understanding can be developed. No matter which approach you use, bear in mind, managers want to learn but they don't want to be taught.

PROVIDE DETAILED REPORT ON FORECASTS

The buy-in of forecasts depends very much on, among other things, how forecasts are reported and presented. Here are some cardinal rules of reporting forecasts.

i. Give forecasts in as much detail as needed.
ii. Indicate the assumptions used in preparing forecasts.
iii. If forecasts deviate substantially from the norm, give reasons.
iv. In some situations, forecasts under different scenarios may be needed.
v. Make sure forecasts are internally consistent, that is, each column adds up correctly. Forecast users often have a built in suspicion about forecasts. If one thing is wrong, then the whole thing will be considered wrong.
vi. Give forecasts along with actuals. This way they can see where we are and where we are going.
vii. Standardized the format of forecasting report. This way they will know right away where they can find what they are looking for.

PRESENT FORECASTS IN A PROFESSIONAL MANNER

How forecasts are presented can make the difference. Good presentation can turn the skeptics into believer. Here are some cardinal rules of presenting forecasts:

i.   Describe forecasts in simple, jargon-free language. Each business has its own culture, terminology and language. Use their terms and language in making presentation.

ii. Don't prove, demonstrate. A rigorous, deductive proof carries immense persuasion to another yogi but not to a kommissar. Show how good your forecasts were in the past by displaying graphically both actual and projected numbers. Turn your work into graphic presentation, particularly where cause and effect relationships (e.g., advertisement and sales) have to be demonstrated, says Bob Altabet, Vice President of Business Management in the Duracell North America Group of The Gillette Company.

iii. Indicate whether your model has a tendency to over- or underestimate. Also, indicate what you can forecast well and what you cannot. This will help to give credibility to your forecasts.

iv. Tell them not only what problems are but also how to deal with them.

v.   Keep your presentation as broad as possible. Top management is often not interested in the gory details or even the creative use of some statistical techniques you are proud of. Also, keep in mind you have a limited time for your presentation.

vi. Be diplomatic. Learn how to handle questions and non-believers. Be prepared for all circumstances. A good forecaster is never surprised. As far as possible, keep a neutral stance.

FORECASTS ARE JUST FORECASTS

Bear in mind that forecasts are just forecasts. The actuals may turn out to be somewhat higher or lower than the projected numbers. So, be ready to compromise. The users may, for one reason or another, wish to slightly raise or lower the numbers. In a monthly consensus meeting (often attended by people from various functions such as marketing, sales, planning, production and finance), statistical forecasts (forecasts provided by the professional) are often regarded as base-line forecasts. They become the final forecasts after the participants collectively overlay their judgment on them. But the overlay of judgment by various functions often improves the quality of forecasts. Telephone survey of forecasters of 10 large corporations, including Coca-Cola, S.C. Johnson, McCormick and AT&T, by the author shows that companies do overlay judgment over the forecasts prepared by the professional, and judgment does tend to improve the quality of forecasts. All the forecasters said that their forecasts had a layer of judgment in them. Furthermore, all the forecasters except one said that judgment improved their forecasts. The person who did not respond to this question was not sure because he never checked it.

SELL TO THE BOSS

Carroll Mohn of Coca-Cola says that one way to sell forecasts is to start a series of presentations, first one with the boss, then with the first line subordinates (in a meeting with the boss), and then with their line subordinates (in a meeting with their bosses), and so on. If you have a buy-in from the big boss, the others will follow.

LOOK FOR NEW USES OF FORECASTS

The discovery of new and better ways of using forecasts can increase the buy-in of forecasts. When Adam Pilarksi, Chief economist of Douglas Aircraft Company, McDonnell Douglas

Corporation, told his purchasing department how they could use forecasts of foreign exchange and inflation rates of different countries in negotiating contracts for purchasing parts from abroad, they were mighty pleased. These forecasts helped them to negotiate better deals with foreign sub-contractors, thereby, savings millions of dollars.

APPRECIATE MANAGEMENT'S PERSPECTIVE

To be considered a part of their own, not an outsider, the forecaster must appreciate the management's perspective. He or she must be sensitive to the organization's structure, limitations and priorities. At times, the forecaster may find that a given project is not viable yet management decides to hang on to it because it cannot afford to lay off so many people at one time, people from the top echelon have a special interest in the project or it is afraid of adverse publicity which may come with the termination of the project. Terminating a project is not like deleting a line on a computer.

The forecaster should never forget that he or she is not a boss. He or she does not make decisions. He or she simply provides input used for making decisions. Furthermore, the forecaster should not brag about good forecasts. At any one time, forecasts can go sour. People tend to remember bad forecasts far longer than good forecasts.

HAVE PATIENCE

To win the confidence of forecast users can be long and frustrating, but it is attainable with determination, patience, and perseverance. The forecast users often question why the crystal ball of the forecaster is better than their own. At Parke-Davis, it was an uphill task to sell forecasts to the marketing management, but with patience, determination and proper strategy they succeeded, says Debra M. Schramm, Manager of Sales Forecasting. They followed their strategy in two steps: First, they took a hard look at the information they were generating and asked themselves whether it would stand up to the scrutiny from both within the department and outside the department. They tracked system-generated forecasts in relation to the management-generated numbers. They identified their confidence level for each forecast and were prepared to defend their position. After that, they started introducing their forecasts into the management process. In the beginning, the management showed no interest whatsoever in their forecasts. Tactful persistence became a must. Each month, the forecast staff stressed those forecasts in which they had high confidence and documented how and why they were better than those generated by management. They issued a report that they thought would be useful, and with that included their own forecasts. Eventually, those attending the meeting became accustomed to seeing the forecasts, and began to question why their numbers were different from their own. That was a turning point. Today, forecasts prepared by the forecasting staff are an integral part of the management process.

CHAPTER 55

ANALYZING AND REPORTING FORECAST PERFORMANCE IN THE CONSUMER PRODUCTS INDUSTRY

James C. Felmley
Reckitt Benckiser

Most individuals who are, or have been, responsible for generating sales forecasts have been hard pressed to prepare the most realistic and accurate projections utilizing a variety of quantitative and subjective methodologies. Much time and effort is spent in gathering data, building models and discussing forecasts. The resulting forecasts of this dynamic process are the basis of many business planning and control activities. Forecast accuracy has become a crucial topic. It is discussed in boardrooms throughout America and abroad in an effort to reduce overhead costs and improve profit margins.

Unfortunately, forecasting is not an exact science. Many sleepless nights are spent, wondering if the forecasts generated today will be accurate tomorrow. With today's fluctuating economic environment along with numerous competitive pressures, one can no longer forecast in a vacuum. It has become considerably harder to forecast accurately due to the ever changing economic and business environments. The old adage of "living and dying" by the numbers can bring back unpleasant memories where undersells/oversells to the forecast have resulted in considerable turmoil within an organization. This turmoil results in a domino effect of anxiety and second-guessing, making its way back, and I may add rather quickly, to the source of the errant forecasts.

Many books, papers and articles have been written that have tried to assist those responsible for the generation of forecasts in improving forecast accuracy through a variety of qualitative and quantitative techniques. The fact of the matter is that there comes a point in every forecaster's life where they must accept the fact that, at least at the writing of this paper, there is no forecast model in existence that can predict the future with 100% accuracy on a regular basis. Although, it is extremely important to do one's best to improve forecast accuracy, we must learn to accept forecast error as an unavoidable occurrence. Once we have accepted the fact that forecast error is here to stay, we must learn to utilize it to our advantage. Faced with this reality, I have chosen to digress from the mainstream of published materials that tutor on the ways of improving forecast accuracy, and have chosen to focus on the progressive steps that an organization needs to take to effectively capture, measure, report and utilize forecast error to its benefit.

FITTING DATA TO THE BUSINESS PROCESS

The first step that an organization must undertake is the establishment of data requirements. Before a forecaster can begin to analyze forecast error of an individual product or group of products, he or she must initially define what type of "transaction" is to be measured. A transaction may be defined as: customer orders, factory shipments, sales bookings, inventory releases, etc. It is crucial that the transaction chosen for analysis be consistent and accurate so that data integrity can be maintained.

A consensus decision must be made to determine the frequency of forecast performance measurement and the span of data to be measured. For example, at Reckitt Benckiser, we have chosen to measure our forecast performance on a monthly basis and we utilize our Finance department's fiscal calendar to determine our monthly time span. In addition, many organizations will "lag" the forecast being measured. For example, in January, forecast projections will be generated for consecutive future months. Based on average manufacturing lead-times of two months, the projection for March is the forecast that our manufacturing facilities will produce to during January and February. To measure our forecast accuracy for March, we will measure March's actuals against the March forecast call previously generated in January.

MEASURING PERFORMANCE

Within an organization's infrastructure, there can exist a variety of forecast versions. For example, at Reckitt Benckiser, versions of the sales forecast mirror the monthly forecasting process. Initially a statistical forecast is generated by the Sales Forecasting Group and then circulated to Brand Marketing for review. Brand Marketing makes minor revisions to the statistical forecasts based on additional information that was not incorporated in the statistical forecast because it could not be quantified. The revised forecast version is saved as the Marketing forecast. Monthly meetings are then held to review the Marketing forecast. In attendance are representatives from the various functional business units: Sales, Finance, Brand Marketing, Sales Forecasting, Production Planning and Distribution Planning. Any revisions made to the Marketing forecast from discussions held in the forecast meetings are then saved as the Consensus forecasts. The Consensus forecasts are then transmitted to the various business units to drive the business planning and control activities.

One may ask why do we need so many versions of sales forecasts? The answer is quite simple. Through the combination of quantitative and qualitative input into sales forecasts, along with "buy-in" from representatives of the various functional groups, forecast accuracy is destined to improve. In addition, by consistently measuring forecast accuracy at different stages of forecast generation, performance records can be established. This "audit trail" can provide clues as to at which stage additional focus is needed. Also, it can serve as a means to open up communication channels among different functional groups. The most important aspect of the whole process is that the end result, the Consensus forecast, should be a group effort. No single person should be held solely responsible for poor forecast performance.

By speaking with many forecast practitioners, I have found that there are diverse ways of calculating and reporting forecast performance. I always wondered why there are so many means of reporting performance until I realized that the more techniques available to report forecast accuracy the better chance one has of hiding behind the numbers. Unfortunately, this tactic of providing management with "smoke screen numbers" is destined to result in distrust from peers and superiors, once the facade is exposed. One cannot underestimate the importance of trust when presenting results to others. I am a firm believer that forecast practitioners must learn to be consistent with the way they formulate forecast error statistics. It is also important to standardize the way findings are presented. I strongly believe that initial harsh measurements lend towards easier and more noticeable improvements.

One may ask how can I accurately report forecast error without jeopardizing my reputation? I personally have faced the same dilemma at Reckitt Benckiser. As a large manufacturer of consumer household and food products, our diverse portfolio of merchandise made it difficult to report forecast performance in a positive light when reporting at the detailed item level. Realizing this, we advised the upper management that before we can hope to improve our forecast accuracy at the item level, we need first to improve the error at aggregated levels. We chose to begin at the brand level, which consisted of 550+ products broken down into 47 product groups. A variety of simple and complex forecast models were built around these 47 product groupings. The resulting forecasts were then exploded down to the item level using simple historical ratios. Initially we focused on reporting forecast accuracy at the product group level. We consciously made this decision due to the fact that forecast error tends to decrease as one measures performance at higher levels of aggregation. This choice made it easier to report more desirable forecast results.

As expected, certain product groups performed well while others performed poorly. Those groups, which performed poorly, received additional focus. Sub-product groups were established for groups of items within brands that were performing poorly due to their unstable product profiles. The sub-forecast groups were forecasted using techniques similar to those used for their parent product groups.

In less than a year time this methodology resulted in average forecast improvement of 50% at the product group level. Only then we were prepared to concentrate additional effort on reducing error at the item level. The next step was to isolate items that continued to perform poorly when forecasted at an aggregated level. Individual forecast models were built around each of these items, providing more detailed and focused attention. This multi-tiered approach to forecasting at Reckitt Benckiser has provided us the flexibility to forecast at various levels of aggregation, isolate problematic items and give additional attention where needed most.

UTILIZING FORECAST ERROR

Forecast error is a useful measurement, which is frequently utilized by a variety of functional groups. To name a few of its uses: it can be utilized by Production Planning to establish safety stocks (a quantity of stock set aside in inventory to protect against fluctuations in demand); reduce transportation costs by calculating the minimum amount of inventory that should be stored at various warehouse sites based on demand fluctuations, thus reducing intra-warehouse transfers; track sales performance to determine if strategic objectives are being achieved by the Sales organization; or to isolate and identify items that are performing poorly. In addition to some of the standard uses of forecast error, there are subtle ways to utilize forecast error to your benefit. I've found that graphing forecast error that has shown improvement over a span of time (try using a moving average), can help build confidence in your forecasts. The increased forecast credibility will result in stronger alliances with other functional groups. It is also very important to quantify what impact forecast error has on your organization. Try to measure the impact of forecast error on inventory, customer service or lost revenues. You may be surprised to find the impact of forecast error may not always be as extreme as one might think. This exercise can also be useful in setting or re-establishing forecast accuracy objectives. On the same note, it is crucial to determine when the cost of improving forecast accuracy outweighs the benefits.

One must also be prudent when communicating forecast performance to the organization. Structure your presentation based on the technical competence of your audience. This helps in disseminating the "Black Box" syndrome. It is important to determine how detailed your performance measurements should be and remember that consistency is extremely important. Ascertain what level of hierarchy should you report findings. Don't forget that error tends to be more accurate and "digestible" by management at an aggregated level.

In closing, I would like to emphasize once again that forecast error is an unavoidable circumstance. Forecast practitioners must continue to strive for improvement, but must also come to grips with the fact that forecast error can be utilized to one's benefit.

CHAPTER 56

GETTING PEOPLE TO USE YOUR FORECASTS

Charles W. Chase Jr.
Wyeth-Ayerst Pharmaceuticals

All companies, regardless of size, develop sales forecasts and use those forecasts as the bases for their decision making and planning activities. Thus, the sales forecast is probably the one most critical piece of information for any company because it has major short- and long-term implications that impact both operational efficiencies and the use of marketing investments.

Unfortunately, in most mid-sized and small-sized companies, as well as in some larger companies, forecasting departments are non-existent mainly due to budget constraints and/or their view is it does not add any value. As a result, the forecasting task is usually assigned to associate product managers, field sales managers, and in many cases production planners. In these situations, the person developing the sales forecast is also the person who uses those same forecasts to guide their daily business decisions. In situations where there are staff people whose primary responsibility is to develop sales forecasts, the forecaster and the decision-makers (users) are not the same person. This can create some problems in the acceptance and use of the sales forecasts, particularly, if the forecasts in question don't meet the needs of the decision-maker (user).

Companies that devote entire departments to develop formal sales forecasts must establish an environment that entices decision-makers to use those forecasts. As a result, the success of the sales forecast is measured not only by its accuracy but to what extent it is used by key decision makers in the various functional groups (i.e., Sales, Marketing, Finance, and Operations). While efficient forecasts require strong technical and quantitative skills, effective sales forecasters also require excellent written and oral communication skills and a good understanding of the business (or industry). Subsequently, if decision-makers don't have confidence in the formal sales forecast, they will eventually develop their own informal forecasts to guide their decisions. When this happens, the company suffers because it can't operate in a coordinated manner due to multiple forecasts that are not driven by a common goal.

RATIONALE FOR DISSATISFACTION WITH SALES FORECASTS

A sales forecast is only useful if it is accepted by decision-makers, and in many cases obtaining such usage can be difficult. There are several issues that contribute to this situation that can include, distrust of sales forecasts because of a bad experience a decision maker has had with a previous forecast, because he/she does not feel the forecaster is really tuned into the marketplace, or because the decision maker does not understand how the forecast was developed. Most of these problems can be resolved if proper communication channels are established between forecasters and the users of the forecasts.

Technical Issues

In many cases, the sales forecast is not accepted because the users really don't understand how it was derived. This is called the "Black Box Syndrome." Most users, who need to base their decisions on a sales forecast number, will always want to understand how it was developed. They're not interested in the algorithm itself, but rather in assumptions made in preparing the forecast. For example, does the sales forecast reflect current seasonality, sales promotions, competitive activities, and trends? In many cases, techniques that have outstanding accuracy, like Box-Jenkins models, are not appreciated by the fact that many decision-makers do not understand how these models actually work.

Thus, in spite of their proven accuracy as forecasting tools, Box-Jenkins models are among the least used techniques in business today. On the other hand, Multiple Regression technique's lack of use is more of a database and information integrity issues, which have a high cost and resource support requirement. Most practitioners use these two issues as a scapegoat for their lack of knowledge regarding the application of the technique. This is unfortunate because more and more decision makers are becoming familiar with causal techniques and find them very useful in a highly competitive environment for strategic planning purposes.

Credibility Issues

Another set of reasons forecasts are not accepted by many decision-makers relates to the credibility of both the sales forecast and the forecaster. If too many previous sales forecasts have been extremely inaccurate, decision makers become reluctant to use or accept current versions. The most common reason for not accepting a potential forecast by users is disagreement with some of the forecast's premises. For example, a key assumption by the forecaster may have been that a price increase will cause significant forward purchases by channel distributors who are trying to avoid the price increase by stockpiling the product at the lower price. The user may disagree on the ground that the cost of financing such a large chunk of inventory would reduce their margin over time because of the increase in inventory carrying costs.

The lack of creditability as a result of the user's skepticism in general developed over the years is another aspect of dissatisfaction. In many companies, particularly the larger ones, forecasters are usually staff personnel, and many decision-makers feel those forecasters really don't understand the marketplace. Their vision of staff people is that they are centered around statistical models driven by numbers derived from "black box" calculations that are completely devoid of the human element. Another more common credibility issue evolves around senior management support or non-support of the formal sales forecast. For example, if personnel from all the various levels of management sense that senior management agrees with the formal sales forecast, they all rally behind it as the focal point of all decisions. On the other hand, if they sense that senior management is not in agreement with the formal sales forecast, different functional units of the company develop their own independent forecasts to guide their decisions. This will result in multiple forecasts, thereby causing a chaotic environment within a company.

POSSIBLE SOLUTIONS TO THESE ISSUES

Companies who develop formal sales forecasts need to establish an environment that fosters the use of those forecasts by decision-makers. First and foremost, forecasters need to be aware of the dates when key decisions are made and be prepared to have their sales forecasts available early enough to be utilized to make those decisions. For example, a sales forecast that is provided in the second week of the month is too late to help production planners schedule production for that month, resulting in either too much inventory or not enough. Both situations will have a financial impact on the business either in higher inventory carrying costs, or lost sales due to inventory shortages. On the other hand, if sales forecasts are not available during key decision times in the strategic marketing and planning cycles, decision makers may make sub-optimal marketing investment decisions resulting in lost sales volume and profit. In other words, you should always have your sales forecast available when it is needed.

It is important that your sales forecasts be in the appropriate format (i.e., in dollars, units, and physical cases). The forecast must also be broken down to the lowest level based on the decision-makers' needs (i.e., by product, channel, geographic location, and customer). In other words, understanding that a wide range of decision-makers will be using your sales forecast, a variety of formats will be required if the forecast is to effectively serve their diverse requirements. As a result, it will require forecasters to contact the user community on a regular basis to determine their required needs and desires. It's good to contact your users occasionally (at least once a year) not only to determine their informational needs, but also whether the current formats are meeting their immediate needs. It's not unusual for a report format to change over time as the organization evolves due to various reasons.

Always make sure your users understand the forecasting method you are employing. It is your responsibility, as a forecaster, to make sure that decision-makers are comfortable with the technique used to develop the sales forecast. Remember, it is more important to explain the assumptions used to generate the forecast, rather than explaining the techniques themselves. This is a fundamental problem that most forecasters get themselves into when explaining their forecasts. They tend to explain the algebraic content in detail rather than the assumptions that drive the forecast method. For example, explaining the reverse matrix of a multiple regression model is not as effective as explaining what marketing drivers have a causal relationship and why, based on their statistical significance. Furthermore, it is even more important to explain the assumptions made about those causal relationships to predict the future, and what are the likelihood of those predictions to occur. Finally, remember to explain the limitations of your forecast to alert users to the possible conditions that could occur either in a negative or positive way. Examples of such limitation statements can include "the model utilized is a time series model that only measures the effects of trend, seasonality and randomness based on past sales history and replicates it into the future" or "the forecast doesn't take into consideration the effects of a price decrease by one of our major competitors."

It is very important to provide different sales forecast scenarios. Most forecasts are usually based on the scenario most likely to occur at that point in time. The value of your forecasts can be increased if you provide decision-makers with both the "worst case" and "best case" situations. Such inclusion of extreme scenarios not only provide forecast ranges for users, but also alert them to the fact that such possibilities may occur. Most of all get management involved. Your sales forecasts will receive more credibility if there is strong evidence that senior management accepts the formal forecast figures and requires each functional area to use those figures in their decision-making activities.

Each company has its own corporate culture, and forecasters should strive to understand that culture, and ideally, be accepted as part of that culture. At many companies, forecasters are viewed as "quantitative techies" who really do not understand what is really going on in the marketplace. If forecasters want to shed that image, they need to be accepted as people who understand and accept the values and nomenclature of the company. This means communicating with decision-makers on a regular basis, obtaining their outlook of future changes in the marketplace and getting their initial reactions to the forecaster's assumptions and predictions of the market. Such communication will ensure your sales forecasts more palatability with decision-makers because they feel they participated in the process. This emphasis on strong communication skills also applies to the actual presentation of your sales forecasts to decision-makers. In many cases, forecasters are evaluated more on their ability to present or "sell" the forecast than they are for their technical expertise. Thus, it is critical that you spend time to prepare your forecast presentation and present it in a professional manner that will be eventually accepted by decision makers.

Finally, make sure your sales forecasts are available to all users. A forecast can only be used by decision-makers if they have easy access to it. The one mistake most forecasters make is assuming that if one person has access to the forecast in the management hierarchy that its distribution will be disseminated throughout the organization. A copy of the sales forecasting report should be made available to every individual who is likely to need the information.

Most of all remember the only critical factor determining whether a forecast is used in the decision-making process is the commitment that users have in its accuracy. All the actions prescribed above are for naught and will have little impact if decision-makers do not have confidence in the forecast. Such confidence hangs on the forecaster's past performance.

CHAPTER 57

HOW TO SELL FORECASTS TO MANAGEMENT

Debra M. Schramm
Parke-Davis

One of the universal problems forecasters have is 'selling' their forecasts to others, especially Marketing Management. Management is reluctant, at best, to use numbers from a group or individual who is viewed as only able to analyze numbers. They question why our crystal ball should be any better than theirs. Our company was no exception. Five years ago the forecast area was viewed as a department that did something with the sales numbers. No one seemed to know what our role was in the organization or how we meshed with the big picture. Although our forecasts were used to feed manufacturing and distribution, they were not considered in the management review process, which took place each month, to determine the division's sales numbers. It became our goal to change our image or the lack of it.

The process, though arduous and frustrating, was well worth it. First, we had to be sure we had confidence in our forecasts before we could instill the confidence in others. We had to take a hard look at the information we were generating and asked ourselves whether it would stand up to scrutiny from both within the department and outside the department. We tracked our system-generated forecasts in relation to the purely management-generated numbers, experimented with ways of estimating and incorporating changes to the system forecasts, made adjustments in procedure and continued tracking. The process lasted a considerable length of time but we were able to discover which product forecasts required special treatment and why. We also identified our confidence level for each forecast and were prepared to defend our position.

When we felt we were ready for step two, we introduced our forecasts into the management process. What transpired the first time we interjected our forecasts was a complete lack of interest in the fact that we even had one. Tactful persistence became a must. Slowly, each month we would stress those forecasts in which we had high confidence and documented how they were better than the ones generated by management. We issued a report that contained useful information, and just happened to include our forecasts. Those attending the meeting became accustomed to seeing the forecasts, and began to question why they were different from their numbers. This was truly a turning point in the process. It was up to us to continue to strengthen our position even if it meant admitting that we did not have confidence in some of our numbers and suggesting they not to be used. We began to include the forecasts directly on the report used during the meetings. We also became a supplier of other information: prescription data, pipeline data, data on inventory held by our large customers, and trade class buying patterns, to name a few.

Today the forecasting department and its forecasts are an integral part of the management process. Our system forecasts are used as a basis for the monthly review, the annual and longer term plans. We continue to support Marketing with reliable information, anticipating their future needs, and experimenting with external data in order to improve the forecasts. There is no point lower than to work at something, then find you are the only one who believes in what you do. If we as forecasters are to raise our image in business we must be able to prove ourselves and prove the integrity of the data we supply. The process can be long and frustrating, but it is attainable with determination, patience, and perseverance. Once achieved, it is immensely rewarding.

CHAPTER 58

MACHIAVELLIAN PRINCIPLES AS APPLIED TO BUSINESS FORECASTING

Robert A. Forrest
AT&T

Machiavelli's principles are applicable to forecasters as well as to a government. Here are some of the lessons that can be learned from him by a forecaster: (1) Know the people for whom you forecast and what their business needs and concerns are. (2) Be good to your staff members and other people on whom you rely. (3) Communicate with your clients and/or managers. (4) Be good at what you do. (5) Anticipate problems ahead of time and solve them before they become snarling arguments. (6) Avoid letting your work be misused or misrepresented. (7) Defend the validity of your work. (8) Be confrontational if that is what is required in the best interest of your company's business. (9) Avoid burning bridges and making enemies needlessly. (10) Be of service to forecast users on an on-going basis.

Forecasts in business are inherently political. In the forecasting process, there are people, an organization, potential conflicts, and therefore there are politics. We can turn for guidance to perhaps the most famous political thinker, Niccolo Machiavelli. Machiavelli lived from 1469 to 1527 in the city-state of Florence during an era of political instability and armed conflict. His book, *The Prince,* was written for the new ruler of Florence, Lorenzo de Medici, advising him on how to consolidate and retain his power. Machiavelli and his book have gotten a great deal of bad press over the centuries, probably because many people never bothered to read it. What Machiavelli attempted to promote was government that would last. He has given lessons about power and people. Forecasters have a very logical link with Machiavelli. Forecasters deal with data. Data processed are information. Information, when understood, becomes knowledge. Knowledge is power. Now, if, for a moment, you as a forecaster, see yourself as a prince, you will see what lessons Machiavelli has for you. Perhaps the first lessons to consider are those having to do with your knowledge of people and getting along with them.

UNDERSTAND COLLEAGUES

Many of you provide forecasts to planning, product management or sales people who are in many ways different from you. These people, every day, deal with issues such as product engineering, inventory levels, customer complaints, product liability, competition and a host of other matters. They also consider long-term issues such as product and brand loyalty, new technology, and profitability. You need to know what their jobs require and what goals they hope to achieve. Much of what they do is manage crises, leaving little or no time for long-term planning. To understand users of forecasts, attend product team meetings. Take a client to lunch. Machiavelli counseled princes, "...when states are acquired in a province differing in language, in customs and in institutions, then difficulties arise; and to hold them one must be very fortunate and very assiduous. One of the best, most effective expedients would be for the conqueror to go live there in person." Some of you may have gone into supervisory positions. You may have a staff of forecasters, market researchers, programmers, or other types, and they also need to understand the process and purposes they are supporting. Take your people to meet the clients. But be very selective when you hire your staff. Try to get people who are not only technically competent and bright but also affable and communicative. Machiavelli says, "The first opinion that is formed of a ruler's intelligence is based on the quality of the men he has around him."

In addition to people working directly for you and the people to whom you provide forecasts, there are a number of other people you have to deal with every day in order to get your work done. Clerks who must input raw data accurately, researchers who tabulate and summarize the data on which you rely, and programmers who work long hours at the CRT debugging programs that you, the forecaster, flow charted on the back of an envelope.

APPRECIATE GOOD WORK

When they do a good job, tell them so. Thank them. Send a note to their supervisors, detailing their contribution. Give them zucchini from your garden. Bring in cupcakes for them. Machiavelli says, "A prince should show his esteem for talent, actively encouraging able men, and paying honor to eminent craftsmen."

TALK THEIR LANGUAGE

Forecasters are in many ways different from other people. When two or more forecasters get together they talk about heteroscedasticity, Box Jenkins, etc., while product managers worry about the fading of ink on the packages which will make them less attractive to customers. In organizations, forecasters sometimes are social outcasts because they are kept away from the day-to-day operations. As a result, forecasters are often paranoid about their political position. Machiavelli says, "Men do harm either because they fear you or because they hate you." Forecasters should learn about the problems and goals of forecast users. Make them aware of your problems and goals. Let them know that you are committed to the business. Your role in the business is not unlike theirs, it just requires a level of quantitative sophistication. Communicate with them. They aren't bad people. They understand. You may have to meet them more than half way for they are often swamped with their own work.

DAZZLE THEM WITH YOUR BRILLIANCE

It is perfectly all right to dazzle forecast users with your brilliance and skill. Machiavelli recognized it when he said, "Nothing brings a prince more prestige than great campaigns and striking demonstrations of his personal abilities." Apply your full measure of creativity to their business problems. Make sure your product forecasts take into consideration the effects of different levels of marketing effort or sales force compensation. Where new products and services are concerned, you should be prepared to account for customer's resistance or desire to change. Understand thoroughly the positive responses (intention to buy) received from a market survey. Generally speaking, fewer people exhibit the positive purchase behavior than indicated in any survey.

TRUTH IN ADVERTISING

Sometimes there is a divergence of belief between what forecasters think they have been asked to provide and what managers or clients think they have asked for. Up-front communication is the answer. Ideally, in any dialogue between forecasters and managers, ego should be put aside. Machiavelli advises us: "When trouble is sensed well in advance, it can easily be remedied; if you wait for it to show itself off, any medicine will be too late because the disease will be incurable." Even though many forecasts are delivered on green and white paper with sprocket-holes on the sides, forecasting is not an exact science. Make your clients understand the uncertainties and even frailties associated with your forecasts. Educate your clients about the concept of "statistical error." Those of us who rely on your forecasts ask you to provide us with a single number, and you do, knowing that there is a range associated with that number. You could give us the range, in addition to a single number, but since we manager-types are congenitally optimistic, we will choose the upper limit of the range as our number. Let us know why we shouldn't do that.

Another area of misunderstanding is often what your clients call over-billing of a forecast and what forecasters consider the client's unrealistic expectations for granularity. Decide up-front whether a forecast needs to be applicable down to two-digit SIC codes. When you cut your data into 60 vertical markets, 7 regions, 5 establishment size classifications, and whether a location is a headquarter, branch, or single premise customer, you're probably out of sample points, and the reliability of your estimates may only be coincidental.

Forecasts are like weapons; teach people to use them cautiously. Strive for clarity in your forecasts, comparability between forecasts, adequate definitions, and caveats. Yes, write down warnings. On packages, a manufacturer sometimes claims no responsibility if the product is used in a manner inconsistent with its intended use. A misused forecast is a bastardization of your work, and you can't stand behind work that has been corrupted. After all, Machiavelli said: "...a prudent ruler cannot, and should not, honor his word when it places him at a disadvantage and when the reasons for which he made his promise no longer exist."

POLITICAL CONFRONTATIONS

The politics of forecasting have less to do with the actual methodologies employed than with the numbers themselves. Politically speaking, the main reason forecasts are wrong is because they don't always coincide with the recipient's presupposition of what the numbers should be. Let's take a typical scenario: a product manager thinks his or her new product is going to take the market by storm. This person is working 18 hours a day, six days a week to get the product developed, to design a marketing plan, and so on. The product manager is totally committed. The processes in your company dictate that all products pass a financial test, sometimes called a business case, before they can be introduced. Your research shows that the product is a dog. By definition, your forecast is wrong, and you will be pressured to raise it.

You, and even the executives above you, may be called on the carpet by your clients and their executives. You are charged with failure to support the product managers. You have a couple of choices: you can knuckle under and raise the forecast, or you can justify and defend your position. If you think you are right and have done your homework, fight for your viewpoint. Be prepared to talk about how you reached your conclusions, the reasonableness of your assumptions, and the underlying data. Always be prepared, for Machiavelli told you: "You are bound to meet misfortune if you are unarmed because, among other reasons, people despise you, and this. . . is one of the infamies a prince should be on his guard against."

When you think you are right you should take a position on it. Otherwise, you will allow the company's resources to be misallocated. When a project that should be terminated is allowed to continue, other opportunities may go un-pursued while the company continues to squander funds and effort on something that is doomed to fail in the market. Thus, if it is necessary, escalate your concerns, and let the executives decide. They may decide in favor of what you feel is the incorrect alternative, but you have done your job, that of seeking truth.

Throughout such a dispute, be up front with the clients, apprising them early that your differences must be adjudicated by a higher authority. If you have developed a good working relationship with them, if you have made the effort of going to their meetings, if you have in the past been a reliable part of their team, your relationship might not suffer as a result. You are walking on a tightrope. Be communicative, be professional, and be civil. It is best for your future relationship to have a good track record. Machiavelli counsels: "Whoever believes that with great men new services wipe out old injuries deceives himself."

You are professional forecasters, but I don't feel you owe your principal loyalty to your profession. Your first loyalty is to your employer, the person who signs your check. You must be concerned with the fortunes of your company. Forecasting is a quest for truth, and a forecast should not arbitrarily be jacked up in order for a product to pass a business case milestone that will result in the aggrandizement of a product manager's career, since he or she may have moved on to greater assignments by the time it becomes evident that the product didn't live up to its unrealistically high expectations.

A much more rare problem occurs when the client presupposes a smaller market than you project. In this instance, your company might miss out on a significant opportunity or be forced to incur exorbitant ramp-up costs in order to meet the unanticipated demand. Politically, this is usually easier to resolve without escalation. Talk over your differences. Perhaps you see a different or additional target market, and perhaps this point can be proven by existing research or by additional concept tests or in test marketing. Prove your point, for Machiavelli noted: " ... Men are generally incredulous, never really trusting new things unless they have tested them by experience."

Always stay in tune and in touch with your client base. Be available to run what-if simulations or to express your ideas about where the market is going based on the latest developments. Don't just come around when it is time for the annual or semi-annual review. Look for ways to add value on a consistent basis. Machiavelli counsels: "...men are won over by the present far more than by the past; and when they decide that what is being done here and now is good, they content themselves with that and do not go looking for anything else."

Finally, forecasters, in dealing with management, should always remember Machiavelli's words: "It cannot be called prowess to kill fellow citizens, to betray friends, to be treacherous, pitiless, irreligious. These ways can win a prince power but not glory."

(The Machiavellian quotes used in this article were taken from the 1961 Penguin Books Ltd edition of The Prince)"

CHAPTER 59

THE EFFECTS OF CORPORATE POLITICS ON BUSINESS FORECASTING

Charles W. Chase, Jr.
Wyeth-Ayerst Pharmaceuticals

Forecasting is a difficult task because it often requires a significant amount of high-quality data, insight, common sense, imagination and the preparer's willingness to stick his/her neck on the line. Before becoming serious about forecasting, one must understand the political realities. My initial encounter with corporate politics started seven years ago when I presented my first professional sales forecast. Management wanted accurate sales projections to reduce inventory while maintaining a 97% customer service line item fill rate. The plan was to implement a new program called "Just In Time." It seemed logical from an operational perspective. Heck, the Japanese and automobile industry have been doing it for years. For this reason, I used a somewhat sophisticated time series technique called, "Multiplicative Decomposition," to extrapolate sales by brand based on trend, seasonality, cyclical influences, and randomness. Apparently, management was not ready for such an obscure method. When I presented my findings to the Vice-President of Marketing at the monthly sales forecasting meeting, he basically fell on the floor. "Multi What?," he calmly repeated. He complained that my forecasts were ludicrous and too low. Fortunately, those numbers were very accurate, and over time my corporate reputation preceded me. It took many years and much criticism from users before I understood the politics that influenced their perceptions of the marketplace.

As Director of Forecasting at Johnson & Johnson Consumer Products, Inc., we used Multiple Regression methods (methods which many really did not understand, but were afraid to admit). One lesson that I've learned from my experience over the last several years is that users (management) often know many things that preparers do not. Also, the users are afraid to admit that their focus is not always on reality. Perhaps, initially, users have been over promised what forecasting could deliver. In many cases, by the lack of application. The users are often oblivious to the various dimensions of forecast applications.

UNREALISTIC EXPECTATIONS

A consistent problem concerning the Business Forecasting industry involves unrealistic goals and expectations. The market realities associated with diminishing returns, points of saturation, and competitive characteristics are often not recognized or considered in our forecasting efforts. This is even more evident when users develop their own forecasts based on enterprise or corporate needs rather than actual market conditions.

Most managers do not know enough about forecasting models themselves. One of the major problems is misapplication of a model. Once a manager of a large consumer brand explained to me that he used times series methods to forecast shipments and failed. He did not understand that the assumption of time series techniques did not match the conditions in his data set. I explained to him that the seasonality might have been disrupted with the use of annual trade promotions, and there might have been several variables other than the past historical trend which influenced his business. But his response was, "We tried mathematical forecasting methods and they didn't work." Since one method did not work, he abandoned the entire discipline.

This brings up another problem based on user's competitive desires to test preparer's abilities to forecast. Often preparers deliver lengthy orientations to users about why there is a need for a reasonable amount of data and that a forecasting method is going to be extremely accurate for some brands and miss others, but on average, will do a better job than what is currently being done. Furthermore, that the models need to be tested after each update so as to give them an accurate trial. In turn, users proceed to supply a history of 12 to 24 of the toughest, most unusual data sets that man has ever discovered. The test data contains erroneous sales entries, negative sales periods due to backorders, huge one-time order periods from some gulf war called "Desert Storm," that never occurred before and probably will never occur again. Then, with a straight face, the user says, "I got you this test data and we're anxious to see how well your model works." They continue, by saying, "We were only able to get 24 months of data because our records only go back that far." By the way, we didn't have time to get you the Nielsen data for price, inventory, consumption, distribution, and category that you requested. But you should be able to do something with the data you have.

WHAT INFORMATION TO PROVIDE?

Another problem associated with users, not knowing about various methods, is that they do not understand what information to provide preparers to enable them to build appropriate models. Business forecasting is tough enough when critical information is provided, when it is not, the work becomes virtually impossible. For example, when we began to develop the first series of multiple regression models at Johnson & Johnson Consumer Products, Inc., several of our brand shipments were tracking flat or slightly negative, while retail consumption for those same brands were increasing at an accelerated rate. During the same time frame, inventories (a key variable in the model) at the retail outlets were showing below normal levels. After several uneventful forecasts of shipments, we were told that the inventory data only reflected on-site store inventory. Off-site inventories were not included in the past historical data.

Eventually, after evaluating the past trade promotion calendar and speaking with brand management, we realized that our customers built up large inventories in their off-site warehouses as a result of our past trade promotions which they unloaded during several of their own lucrative consumer promotions. Fortunately, we were able to pick-up on this unusual occurrence within a relatively short time frame. We learned our lesson. Now we always account for off-site retail inventories in our models.

FORCING THE NUMBERS

Finally, the biggest problem that seems to be the most political in nature is that users believe they can force the numbers. In other words, plans are often developed in a vacuum. The forecasts represent what management would like to see from a corporate financial perspective. When forecasts do not reflect upper management's planned volumes, the plans are not changed based on the statistical results. Instead, the marching orders are to generate new forecasts based on their expectations. Many times they back into those higher/lower numbers, dismissing any prior recommendations from the forecasting group. What they are really looking for are forecasts that match what they would like to believe will happen, and then some how through an act of God will happen. It's that old familiar saying, "Well now we have the forecast, let's go get the statistics."

HIGH HOPES OF A NEW PRODUCT MANAGER

Another typical scenario is a product manager who thinks his/her product is going to take the market by storm. This person is working 16 hours a day, six days a week to get the product developed (redeveloped) and market plan made. The product manager is totally committed. The forecast model you have built, based on the product managers' suggestions, indicates the product is a dog. By definition, according to the product manager, your forecast is wrong and you will be pressured to raise it. You might even be charged with failure to support the product manager. At this point, you can either knuckle under and raise the forecast, or you can justify and defend your position. If you think you are right and have done your homework, fight for your viewpoint. Remember, forecasting is a quest for truth, and a forecast should not arbitrarily be jacked up in order for a product to pass a corporate milestone that will result in the amplification of a product manager's career, since he/she may have moved on to greater assignments by the time it becomes evident that the product didn't live up to his/her unrealistically high expectations.

SOME FORECASTERS FORGET THE REAL WORLD

So far I have discussed the user's contribution to the corporate politics of business forecasting. There are many preparers who add to this dilemma, especially those who are oblivious to reality. There are forecasters who eat, sleep, and drink with their computer and their models. At times, they forget the real world. Some even begin to worship their models and follow them with a blinder on, believing that they are always correct. Some preparers have taken a narrow view of business forecasting, focusing on statistical techniques instead of organizational complexities.

The technical extremists are one of my favorite. Their goal is to develop the next generation algorithm — one that, in all its mathematical grandeur, will unlock the mysteries of the universe, and will be suitable for forecasting in all situations. They wallow in mathematical complexity, despite the fact that simpler models might work just as well. Their verbosity argues the virtues of time series extrapolation versus regression models, despite the fact that both are good, depending upon the situation. Perhaps more important is that models are developed for the sake of mathematical refinement, despite the fact certain ingredients other than mathematics are required. Furthermore, little attention is given to the nature of the corporate reporting system. The non-quantitative aspects that must be considered are ignored. These same preparers fail to recognize that a business is a system of interacting elements. On the opposite spectrum there are technically incompetent preparers. All disciplines have them, however, they have single handedly created strong doubts in the minds of the users whether or not the field of business forecasting has any positive impact. Their misunderstanding and haphazard application of the methods, specifically designed to assist their efforts, has left the discipline open to questions of integrity. These same preparers believe that one model will fit all circumstances because either they developed it in the first place, briefly learned about it in school, or probably got lucky and were able to forecast a few products accurately at a point in the past.

Finally, some preparers have an attitude that most users are incompetent. They believe that management will never grasp anything more mathematical than simple moving averages or single exponential smoothing. The result, they prejudge what management should be exposed to and what management wants to hear. Users are responsible for this attitude to some degree by asking for ridiculous tasks like trying to correlate pigs slaughtered to pig-iron. Whatever the reason, the effect is that management never recognizes that there are alternative methods available. The end result is the use of extremely simplistic models that don't work very well.

Users need to be more open minded and honest instead of playing the amusing game of waiting to pounce on some inevitable forecast error or seek an opportunity to ridicule because they resent the corporate attention that many business forecasters receive. They must come to grips with the fact that they are not experts in techniques and have only limited exposure to modeling applications. Consequently, they require help from experts in developing proper applications within their organizations. The one area where they can contribute the most is in explaining the relationships among the variables that impact their business.

Preparers need to be open minded, too. In most cases a pet model or method is not all conclusive in solving the forecast problem. Business forecasting is complex, and the ability to adapt techniques to many difficult situations is the key to successful application. In other words, no one model or method is best suited to solve all cases. Preparers need to roll-up their sleeves and get into the trenches with management to learn more about the company for which they work. We, forecasting practitioners, are only one element in the decision process, but have the ability to contribute the most pertinent information.

REFERENCES

1. Brandenburg, George. "Sales Forecasting's Impact on Inventory Management." **Johnson & Johnson International Materials Management Report.** September 10, 1989, pp. 1-5.
2. Forrest, Robert A. "Machiavellian Principles as Applied to Business Forecasting." **The Journal of Business Forecasting.** Fall 1987, pp. 2-5.
3. Gross, Charles W. "Bridging the Communications Gap Between Managers and Forecasters." **The Journal of Business Forecasting**. Winter 1987-88, pp. 6-9.
4. O'Clock, George D, and Priscilla M. O'Clock. "Political Realities of Forecasting." **The Journal of Business Forecasting**. Spring 1989, pp. 2-6.

344

PART XII

FORECAST TRAINING

INTRODUCTION

For a strong and effective forecasting function, a company must have a forecast training program in place. This section describes how to go about to set up such a program. For a program to take off it needs support and commitment from the upper management. If upper management recognizes the importance of forecasts, others will follow. Plus, it is the upper management who can provide resources needed for running such a program. The program should be dynamic — the one that changes with time. Methodology, process, environment and products to be forecasted, they all change with time. The program should call for training not only those who prepare forecasts but also who use them. It is difficult for someone to assess forecasts if he or she does not know at all how they are prepared.

CHAPTER 60

DEVELOPING TRAINING PLANS FOR A FORECASTING ORGANIZATION

Steve Thrift
Springs Industries, Inc.

What is the biggest challenge facing business today? While it is impossible to find a single answer, I find a common thread, which is, finding, keeping, and developing skilled people. In interacting with people in many companies through conferences, teaching classes, and in the normal course of business, it seems the shortage of skilled people may be reaching critical levels, particularly in some areas of expertise and geographic locations. For those of us in forecasting, the explosion in the forecasting function means that the demand for people in this discipline is growing faster than the supply. While the answer for an individual company to fill such a position is to "steal" a skilled person from another company, but it neither solves the global problem nor provides a long-term solution.

KEY CHALLENGES

Businesses face many challenges, some are common and others are unique. Some common ones can be highlighted by the following questions:

- How do we develop accurate forecasts and then ensure they are utilized throughout the organization?
- How do we positively impact corporate performance?
- How do we keep up with increasing expectations of shareholders, customers, and management?

While the answers to these questions may vary from one expert to another, failing to address them will surely prove disastrous. The development of a forecasting organization and forecasting training program can certainly help us to provide answers to these questions.

SKILLS NEEDED FOR A FORECASTING FUNCTION

Before doing anything each forecasting organization must carefully outline and analyze its forecasting philosophy, definition of what constitutes success, and what critical skills are needed at every organizational level. In my view, there are three critical components of a successful business: people, processes, and systems. This chapter is concerned with people and how they can be best "skilled" in the forecasting function. To state it another way, "What are the critical skills necessary to ensure that the forecasting function is adding value and playing a critical role in our organization?" I will propose a model, which can be useful to practitioners.

As with any function, people in forecasting face many challenges, rewards, and frustrations. One of the greatest frustrations is that forecasts aren't used consistently throughout organization. We often hear complaints that "Operations doesn't use our forecast," "Purchasing does its own forecast," or "Finance ignores our numbers." While some of the reasons have to do with human nature (which I won't try to evaluate) or organizational dynamics (which is outside of the scope of this chapter), I would argue that one of the reasons for these complaints is that forecasters may be technically proficient but less than optimally skilled in areas such as process management and persuasiveness. These skills are important but get little or no attention in the forecasting literature. I will suggest that we should take a much broader approach to training and developing our forecasting staff.

BIONIC FORECASTER

The first step to develop a training plan, for an individual or a forecasting organization, is to outline the characteristics of a "Bionic Forecaster," for a particular company or business unit. Of course, no one is likely to have all these characteristics but they will provide a benchmark for a company. They will also provide a basis for doing a "gap analysis," that is, the gap between what people working in this function should have and what they actually have.

Based on my experience, forecast training programs should opt for developing characteristics like the followings:

- A broad understanding of the forecasting function, and ability to apply the concepts and techniques of forecasting, including a wide variety of mathematical models.
- The ability to communicate clearly, logically, assertively, and persuasively with customers, suppliers, and people in a wide variety of levels and functions.
- Knowledge of the company's forecasting software and its supporting infrastructure as well as systems integrating to it, such as order management, manufacturing/MRP, and distribution.
- Understanding of the products being forecast and how end-consumers react to changes in price, advertising, modifications in engineering or construction, and competitive actions.

DEFINING CRITICAL KNOWLEDGE AND SKILLS

The next step is to group the skills into categories. In other words, we should take the characteristics of a Bionic Forecaster and classify them into manageable areas of expertise. This will allow us to come up with a balanced skill set for a forecaster. This will also give order, structure, and simplicity to the model and the analysis. The four areas we have defined for our forecasting experts are:

1. Forecasting and Supply Chain Concepts

2. Technical and Software Skills
3. Process Management and Product Knowledge
4. Personal and Interpersonal Skills

In my view there should be a reasonable balance among these four areas. It's obvious that no amount of persuasiveness can overcome the lack of knowledge of basic forecasting concepts and techniques. However, overlooking the need for interpersonal and organizational skills ignores the realities of power, politics, and the other organizational dynamics of business enterprises which a forecaster has to deal with. What we are looking for is a balanced skill set needed for developing forecasts and other forms of quantitative demand analysis, necessary for the company, its suppliers, and its customers to support its goals and objectives. The skill set for those in the forecasting area will be notably different from those in other areas but it should include some characteristics common to many other areas of expertise.

Here are some of examples of the skills we have identified in our four areas and the resources available.

1. **Forecasting and Supply Chain Concepts.** This includes when, where and how to aggregate and reconcile forecasts, how to manage inventory, and the mechanics of MRP. Resources include creating an in-house course on Forecasting 101 (we have developed a one-day in-house course on the basics of forecasting), Institute of Business Forecasting Tutorials, APICS certification, and spending one-on-one time with the Master Schedulers who plan manufacturing operations.

2. **Technical and Software Skills.** These skills are the hands-on application of the concepts described above. These include ability to: develop simple forecasts from historical data, calculate seasonality and determine trends by various methods, compute and explain different measures of forecast error, use effectively the forecasting software along with its various functions and options, and write basic reports. Resources may include college or continuing education courses, IBF and APICS courses, and training classes offered by forecasting and report-writing software vendors.

3. **Process Management and Product Knowledge.** This includes knowledge of forecasting and supply chain process flows and timing (when the forecast is due, who gets it, and what happens downstream), a thorough understanding of roles and responsibilities (e.g., what is the role of the sales team in forecasting and how do we relate to them), benchmarks of the wholesale and retail pricing structure, basic engineering and construction of the products, and the value of various product options in the marketplace. While some of this knowledge may be acquired from various sources in the industry, much of it must be gained from within the company. It may involve regular training sessions with engineers, designers and product managers. If the company is in retail or sells to retail, regular visits to retail stores may be necessary to see the product and the environment in which it is sold.

4. **Personal and Interpersonal Skills.** This is an area, which is easily overlooked but essential in the ultimate success of a forecasting function. Such skills include time

management, assertiveness/ persuasiveness, and building relationships and communication networks. Fortunately, there is an abundance of classes and workshops available on such topics. Many companies offer internal courses on these subjects. The American Management Association has a host of offerings in the area; well-known programs such as Dale Carnegie may offer value as well.

GAP ANALYSIS AND DEVELOPMENT PLANS

After determining the critical skills needed for success, those leading the forecasting function must determine where gaps exist and how to close them. If the organization is imbalanced, it should be addressed first. Hopefully, staffing and development have been managed in such a manner so that on the whole, individual skill sets are fairly balanced. If not, the training should be focused in the areas of weakness. If the department is, by and large, well balanced, training plans should be developed to balance the skill sets of individuals. These plans may include classes, seminars, workshops, and conferences. But don't ever underestimate the value of mentoring, coaching, and on-the-job training. Sometimes the best training opportunities come as a result of a crisis or emergency situation. For developing plans for training or staff development, we often face many constraints — constraints of time, money and energy. In other words, we can't fill every gap at once. For that reason, priorities must be determined. Training plans must be developed with the realities of the business in mind. An individual shouldn't be scheduled for a 5-day class during the same month he or she is required to complete a major project. Having to cancel a much-anticipated class due to a foreseeable conflict can cause tremendous disappointment and discouragement.

SUPPORTING INFRASTRUCTURE

The infrastructure necessary for the success of a forecasting function includes:

- **Guiding principles.** These are the "self-evident truths" by which we operate and help define priorities. One example is "Know your product: Forecasting is more than just numbers." This directs training efforts to include knowledge of the product.

- **Clearly defined roles and responsibilities.** Define as clearly as possible who is responsible for what, not only the tasks but authority for change and approval.

- **Listening and feedback.** Everyone who participates in the process should give feedback, including what works and what doesn't, and what could be changed to make it better.

- **Defining future expectations.** Expectations from many stakeholders will continue to increase. It should be clear to everyone that what is excellent performance today may be only mediocre tomorrow. Future expectations enable people to set realistic goals and plans for improvement.

SUMMARY

What will the future hold? None of us know for sure. But we can be sure it won't be the same as the past or the present. Expectations of customers, stockholders, management, and associates are increasing constantly and rapidly. Like many plans, the most difficult part of training plans is execution. We all have much more to do every day than what we can physically do. Ensuring that everyone understands expectations (present and future), knows where the skill gaps are and has a personal plan, are tasks which are easy to delay but must be treated as both urgent and important.

We must all make the time and expend the energy to prepare for the future. While training and staff development aren't the only factors for success, they are critical in an increasingly turbulent and competitive environment.

REFERENCES

1. Ellis, Dennis and Jay Nathan. **A Managerial Guide to Business Forecasting**. New York: Graceway Publishing Company, 1990.
2. Jain, Chaman L. "Explosion in the Forecasting Function in Corporate America." **Journal of Business Forecasting**. Volume 18. Number 2. Summer 1999, pp.2, 28.
3. Mentzer, John T. and Carol C. Bienstock. **Sales Forecasting Management.** Thousand Oaks, CA: Sages Publications, Inc, 1998.

CHAPTER 61

FORECASTING TRAINING PROGRAM

Kenneth J. Thompson
American Information Technologies Corp.

(Although this article was written before the telecommunications industry was deregulated, many important lessons can be learned from how AT&T instituted the training program at that time. Ed.)

Undertaking a comprehensive forecaster training program represents a major management commitment to forecasting excellence. As such, conspicuous top management support is a necessary element for waging resource allocation battles. Training exerts a discipline in support of standardized job performance. Training, like forecasting, has its own well-founded theories and techniques. Professional training program development and implementation improve the likelihood of success. Training brings change. If change is not desired, don't train. Proven outstanding forecasters with recognized reputations of excellence should be associated with forecaster training. Overall training program objectives need to be documented and used to guide program development. An individual training course, like any product, has a lifecycle. This should be identified in advance, performance tracked and the course killed with or without replacement at the appropriate moment. These are some of the lessons learned from the Bell System in designing and implementing an in-house forecaster training program.

FORECASTING IN THE BELL SYSTEM

Forecasts of customer demand for telecommunications' services are at least as old as the granting to telephone companies of territorial franchises, which require these companies to meet demands for basic service. Provision of basic telephone service remains a heavily capitalized enterprise. Construction of telephone plant much prior to the time the additional capacity will be used (and generate revenues) puts a financial burden on existing rate payers and a political burden on the regulatory commission (PUC). Construction of a plant after customers need it is a violation of a company's service franchise and results in poor customer relations as well as revenues foregone.

Professional forecasting with small organizations of people dedicated solely to producing forecasts became common within the Bell System companies in the 1950's. Post-World War II service backlogs had largely been cleared and companies no longer could throw telephone plant anywhere on the landscape and find customers waiting for it. It became operationally and financially important to the business to accurately predict where tomorrow's customers were going to locate geographically.

TOWARDS STANDARDIZATION

In 1963, AT&T headquarters staff issued the first system standard forecasting practices entitled The Commercial Forecasting Manual. This manual represented a significant attempt to standardize forecasting methodology and products within the over twenty operating telephone companies. An even greater force leading to standardization was the more widespread use by the mid 60's of digital computers beyond payroll and other accounting functions. Computers began to support operations' functions of business with applications we now call 'decision support systems.' Time sharing of central computer capability through remote terminals made possible the extension of mathematical and statistical methodologies to operating managers from the heretofore protected domain of the specialist.

In 1967, a watershed event occurred. The first joint Bell System conference of forecasters and analytical specialists from statistical research organizations was held in St. Louis, Missouri. Forecasting has never been the same since! For those forecasters present, a 'brave new world' was heralded by discussion of mathematical forecasting models. Later in the year, AT&T's' Operations Vice President sent a letter to all company presidents calling for the establishment of professional forecasting organizations staffed by trained, qualified people dedicated full time to integrated forecast analysis and production. The die was cast!

ESSENTIAL BUILDING BLOCKS

The foregoing narrative highlights three essential building blocks necessary to support the decision that provided a formal training program for Bell's forecasters. First, a stated commitment from senior management to put in place a professional corporate forecasting capability was an essential prerequisite to training. Training is always an expensive solution to a performance problem. Without top management support, training budgets would never have been supported to the degree they were within the Bell System.

Second, standardized methodology was a necessary ingredient for the successful initiation of formal training. Training is cosmetic without a supportive environment to facilitate the transfer to the job of newly acquired skills and knowledge. Without standardization of methods, techniques and reports, there would have been no common 'content' for forecasting to learn.

Third, through an accident of timing, the need for training was recognized by forecasters and their supervisors because of the advent of widespread computer technology and its alliance with mathematical and analytical techniques. Effective forecasting required new skills not widely present within the ranks of existing forecasting organizations. These three forces combined provided a climate necessary to support a formalized forecaster training program. A group of AT&T and company's forecasting managers agreed in 1970 to establish a comprehensive program of forecaster training.

IMPLEMENTING THE PROGRAM

The first decision critical to successful implementation was the decision to actively involve the managers of the community to be trained in program implementation. This arrangement was formalized through the creation of a Forecaster Training Advisory Board (FTAB), chaired by AT&T but staffed by selected heads of company forecasting organizations. The board was responsible for identifying potential training needs; prioritizing training projects; acting on curriculum recommendations from trainers; establishing the training development budget; interacting with training staff on course specifics; approving selections of forecasting training staff and providing overall program support.

The second key decision was to use an existing Bell System management technical training center then called The Bell System Center for Technical Education (BSCTE) in Lisle, Illinois, to provide training administration and support to the program. An alternative to 'go it alone' was highly favored by some, but BSCTE's training administration systems were well tested and their track record was good. Training administration is time consuming. The BSCTE management assumed responsibility to staff the program, to measure and ensure quality of products produced and to worry about details of budgeting, registering conferees into courses, scheduling courses and billing to companies to recover expenses of course development and delivery. If AT&T resources had assumed these and like administrative responsibilities, other necessary headquarters' functions may well have suffered and the quality of training administration provided would not have been as high as it turned out to be.

KEYS TO SUCCESS

A key to any successful business undertaking is appropriate staffing. The initial three forecasters brought to Lisle, Illinois, for two to three year assignments were carefully selected based on successful careers to date in companies with progressive forecasting organizations. A great deal of responsibility and accountability was vested in the initial forecaster trainers. They reacted by designing a highly unorthodox initial training course. To the credit of FTAB, despite strong misgiving about the direction the staff was going, it gave its full support to create the recommended course. In initiating a forecaster training program, the Bell Operating Companies did not cast a vote to maintain the status quo. Clearly, change was called for. This is an important point to recognize for any organization likewise disposed to establish a forecaster training program. Even if not explicitly stated, training is a mandate for change. All subsequent decisions should be consistent with this Mandate.

TRAINING PROGRAM GOALS

The first goal of Bell's training program was to change the perceived emphasis of the forecaster from effect to cause. Historically, forecasters analyzed internal corporate reports and inferred from them what had happened in the immediate past. It was not uncommon to extrapolate the past into the future. The training staff decided to focus forecasters' attention on external, not internal phenomena. After basic familiarization with the dynamics of demographic and economic events, forecasters learned how to analyze components of change, draw conclusions about what these forces were signaling, make assumptions about future changes and predict quantitative results, using the most advanced techniques available.

Second, attention was directed to making forecasts for periods out to twenty years or so. It was believed that improvements would also result in the shorter-term forecasts of one to five years if the forecasters understood the changing structural aspects of markets. Emphasis was placed on the analysis of demographic change and on land use factors. To the degree that forecasters had considered market forces at all, they were preoccupied with business cycle movements. These cyclical movements were naively extrapolated into future periods without due regard for structural factors. By emphasizing longer-term structural forces, when the role of business cycles is subordinated to factors impacting trend, it was believed that the quality of both short and long term forecasts would improve.

Third, the use of proven methodologies was strongly emphasized. One might be surprised to know how many forecasters develop their own homegrown forecasting techniques. Within the Bell system, this activity tended to isolate the practitioner from the rest of the forecasting community. The problem of lack of standardization in forecasting methodology was a serious one inhibiting personnel transfers and effective technical supervision. By introducing a wide variety of accepted analytical procedures to Bell System forecasters, the program greatly increased inter-forecaster communication. In effect, the training program provided a common language.

Fourth, forecast documentation was demanded in order to facilitate both retrospective analysis and staff transfers. Much emphasis was placed in the training courses on how to document forecast rationale and underlying assumptions.

Fifth, to move forecasting from being only intuitive to more of a systematic, analytical science — albeit still informed by judgment, computer based applications of analytical techniques were introduced in the training program. It was believed that the forecasts would be improved by this approach and that forecast users would develop a new respect for forecasters and their outputs.

Sixth, to enlarge the forecaster's territorial perspective, techniques were presented which enabled the forecaster to relate his/her forecast territory to larger and smaller ones. The integration of related forecasts prepared by different forecasters for different pieces of geography were expected to be improved as a result of this initiative. Such were the goals of the forecaster training program. With the benefit of hindsight it can be said that they were all met to a degree not imagined by those involved in initial program formulation. It is very important to establish goals prior to undertaking a program. If one does not know where one is going, there is no way to determine when or if one has arrived at the destination.

THE TRAINING PROCESS

For training to be on target, the instructional content had to match the on-the-job performance requirements. Front-end analysis of the job to be trained resulted in detailed descriptions of all job tasks and their derived skill and knowledge components. A thorough job of data collection and analysis was done. Sources of data were job incumbents, their supervisors, headquarters staff methods' designers and AT&T documentation. Forecasting job tasks were grouped by frequency, difficulty, and criticality. Tasks that were typically performed in a deficient manner became targeted for training attention. This job analysis step was the most important of all steps in the training development.

The next step in the process was the specific design of each training course. Once the design was produced, the training was developed using that design as a specification. For the Bell System, end-of-course objectives were specified (based on the need to correct task performance deficiencies identified during the job analysis) and performance tests were developed. These simulated as closely as possible, actual on-the-job performance requirements and environment. Instructional content was organized into clusters and activities, which were later transformed into lessons and lesson modules. Only then was actual course content written.

The next phase of training consisted of the actual creation of training materials. Lesson objectives were tracked to end-of-course objectives and tests matching the lesson objectives were created. Instructor notes, student workbooks, case materials, media, and course administration documentation were all produced during this phase. Materials were tested prior to live use.

Finally, the first training session of each new course occurred. Its purpose was to evaluate all aspects of the newly developed training under realistic conditions. Students accepted into this 'pilot' course were carefully screened to ensure that they typified characteristics of the entire job population. Careful monitoring of the course pilots evaluated course materials, equipment use, demonstrations, exercise, tests, and live instructions. Test results were carefully reviewed for signs of inadequate performance. Student reactions were systematically collected and evaluated on each module or lesson and its presentation, content and materials.

After the pilots, data were carefully evaluated and decisions were made about what needed to be modified prior to opening each course to the full population to be trained. Modifications were then made and the courses became available for on-going delivery. Evaluations, less detailed than those in the pilot, were made in subsequent course sessions as one indicator of needed modification over time.

It is important to note that the commitment to train is an on-going commitment. If courses had been allowed to get out of date, the initial investment in them would have been compromised. With forecasting technology, electronic database and software development and some economic structures constantly changing, maintenance of current information within training courses became a significant undertaking requiring the continuing attention of responsible trainers. The world of forecaster training was dynamic during the last decade of the Bell System's existence. Almost every year saw the presentation of one or more new courses. Only seven of the twenty-one courses initiated over time are in the active curriculum today. When a training course accomplished its mission, it was terminated. Meanwhile, course content changed to match the level of sophistication of newly appointed forecasters.

CAREFUL MONITORING

The training was targeted at particular populations of existing or anticipated incumbents of specific jobs. Careful monitoring of changes in the job population was important input to decisions to re-write courses. For example, the initial course was for forecasters of small geographic areas. They were 'old pros' in the job, but had not been exposed to formal forecasting training. They tended to be unfamiliar with analytical, market-oriented techniques. When that population had gone through the course, it was rewritten for new forecasters who were more likely to be recent college graduates better versed in economic theory but much less familiar with the telecommunications business and the role of forecasting.

As each forecaster course was developed, a parallel short seminar for their supervisors was also created in the belief that the graduates of full courses would present a potential thread to their bosses who might have been unable to provide effective technical supervision unless also familiar with modern techniques. The seminars were specifically aimed at providing a reinforcing climate on the job for the forecaster behavior change initiated in the classroom. It was felt that training of the forecasters without a concurrent change in the behavior of their supervisors would result in a much less effective program. The supervisor seminars became an essential element of the overall program's success.

358

GLOSSARY OF FORECASTING RELATED TERMS

GLOSSARY

ABF
Account based forecasting.

Adjusted R^2
It is similar to coefficient of determination (R^2). The way R^2 is computed, it increases when more and more independent variables are added to the regression-based model. This may not necessarily mean that the model has improved. To adjust for the number of independent variables, adjusted R^2 is computed to determine whether the improvement is real or not.

AEI
Automatic Equipment Identification technology which is used to collect shipment-tracking information quickly and effectively.

Aggregate Forecast
Sales forecast of a company as a whole.

ATP
Available to promise.

Autocorrelation
Correlation within a series. For example, sales of 2000 are related to the sales of 1999, sales of 1999 are related to the sales of 1998, and so on.

Autocorrelated Time Series
A time series in which the current value of a series depends, at least in part, on the past value.

Auto Regression or Auto-Regressive Process
Where sales of one period are regressed on the previous period.

Auto-Regressive Moving Average (ARMA) Process (Model)
Where the Auto-Regressive and Moving Average Processes are combined. It is often called ARMA (ARIMA) model or the Box-Jenkins Model.

Back Forecasting
Making forecasts of periods for which actuals are known. Also, known as ex-post forecasts.

Base Period
A period in time from which comparisons of other time periods are made.

Best Linear Unbiased Estimator (BLUE)
The criterion used in regression modeling to select the best estimator from a number of Unbiased Estimators.

Bias
It is often referred to an error resulting from a poor data gathering, faulty program design, mistakes on the part of personnel, or invalid data sources.

Bottom-Up Forecasting
Forecasts that originate from the bottom. For example, preparing an aggregate forecast by obtaining forecasts from salespeople of different territories and then adding them together.

Box-Jenkins Model
A time series model named after the developers of this model. It combines the Auto-Regressive Process with a Moving Average.

Bullwhip Effect
In case of stock out, customers tend to order more than they needs which distorts the real sales pattern.

Categorical Variable
A qualitative variable created by classifying observations into categories. For example, a series of household incomes could be classified into categorical variables, low, medium, and high, based on specific ranges of income levels. Many statistical techniques are inappropriate for handling categorical variables. Also, it is referred to as a Qualitative Variable.

Causal Model
It is a type of model where cause and effect relationships are taken into account. For example, sales are a function of price and advertisement. Here sales are the effect, and price and advertisement are the causes. Regression/econometric models are causal models.

Census
A complete enumeration of the universe (population), e.g., the Census of Population and Housing, the Census of Agriculture, and the Census of Manufacturing. In contrast, a sample is a portion of the true but unknown universe.

Census X-11
It is one of the decomposition models. It decomposes time series data into secular (long-term) trend, as well as into seasonal, cyclical, and irregular components.

Classical Decomposition
A time series model which decomposes the data into trend, cycle, seasonality and randomness.

Coefficient Term
It is a slope of the line. It shows how the dependent variable, on the average, changes with a one unit of change in the independent variable.

Coefficient of Determination (R^2)
A common measure of the "Goodness of Fit" used in regression modeling to assess the degree of causation between one or more independent variables and a dependent variable. It is a square of the correlation coefficient and shows the percent of variations in the dependent variable (variable being forecasted) that can be explained by the variations in the independent (explanatory) variable(s). Its value varies between 0 (0%) and 1 (100%). The higher the value is, the better.

Consensus Forecasts
Forecasts which are jointly agreed upon. Or, average of forecasts given by different individuals.

Correlation Coefficient (R)
A standard measure of relationship between a dependent and independent variable. Its value varies between 0 and 1. Zero means that there is no correlation whatsoever, and one means, perfect correlation. The value can be negative or positive. Positive value means that they are positively related, that is, when one goes up, the other also goes up. Negative value means that they are negatively correlated.

Cross-Sectional Analysis
Observation of variables within one time frame.

Customers
Customers of a vendor are distributors, wholesalers and/or retailers.

Customer Service
In production, it is often defined in terms of case fill percentage; that is, the number of cases shipped from the nation-wide network of distribution centers to the customer's warehouses divided by the number of cases ordered by the customers.

Cyclical Fluctuations
Cyclical fluctuations are those, which occur regularly but not periodically. The length of a cycle is always more than one year. For example, economy goes up and down regularly. This is definite. But these fluctuations don't occur at a set time. In one cycle, it may take five years to complete an upswing and in another, three years. The same is true with the downswing. In other words, there is no set time when the upswing or downswing of a cycle will be completed.

Data Warehouse
Where data arc stored. Data may be stored on a mainframe.

Delphi
This is a judgmental technique of forecasting where a panel of experts are asked to give their own forecasts which are then distilled to arrive at the final forecast.

Demand
Booking orders.

Dependent demand
It represents the demand of vendor's factory (e.g., raw material), vendor's distribution center demand which depends on the customer distribution center's demand, and customer retail store's demand which depends on the demand of final consumers.

Dependent Variable
A variable we wish to forecast. In regression analysis, the variable being predicted is the dependent variable.

Dissaggregate Forecasts
When a company level sales forecast is broken down into category and SKU level forecasts.

DRP
Distribution requirements planning — planning regarding shipment, transportation, and warehousing.

DRPS
Distribution requirement planning system.

Dummy Variables
They are used in regression to capture the effect of seasonality, qualitative element such as a strike, and outlier (s). The values used for dummy variables are "0" and "1."

Durbin-Watson Test
Diagnostic tool used to test a regression model. Its value varies between 0 and 4. The model is the best if its value is 2. Normally, the value between 1.5 and 2.5 is acceptable.

Eache
It represents consumer unit of purchase, e.g., a 12 oz bottle of soda and one box of cereal.

Economic Indicator
It provides an indication of how the economy is behaving.

Econometric Forecasting
Here a number of equations are used simultaneously to capture the inter-relationship among different variables — internal and external.

EDI
Electronic Data Interchange is used for transmitting documents such as invoices, orders and status of order, from one computer to another. With this, one computer talks with another.

Efficient Consumer Response (ECR)
Synchronizing consumer demand with production.

End-User
Ultimate user of a forecast.

Estimation
It is referred to the estimation of parameters of an equation. For example, estimating the values of "a" and "b"(s) in a predictive model.

Ex-ante Forecast
Forecast of a period for which actual is not known.

Endogenous Variables
The variables which are under the control of a company. They are also called internal variables. For example, advertising expenditures and price of a product. Either one, the company can change in any way and at any time.

ERP
Enterprise resource planning.

Exogenous Variables
The variables which are external to the system. The company has no control over them. For example, the state of the economy. The company (forecaster) has to accept as it is, because it cannot change it.

Explanatory Variables
The variables that drive the sales. For example, advertising outlay, price and state of the economy. They are used to predict the value of a dependent variable (sales, for example). They are also called independent variables.

Ex-post Forecast
Forecast for a period for which actual is known.

EVA
Economic value added.

Fitted Values
The predicted values of known period, derived from a regression model by applying the regression coefficients to the independent variables.

Forecast Horizon
The number of time periods out to be forecasted, e.g., one month out, one quarter out, and one year out.

Forecasting Process
It is referred to a process which outlines who will provide the information used for preparing forecasts; how it will be gathered; after information is obtained, how it will be processed and used for preparing statistical forecasts; and once statistical forecasts are prepared, who will participate in the process to arrive at consensus forecasts.

Forecast Receivers (Customers)
Ones who receive forecasts (end users).

Forecast System
Mechanizing the forecasting process including the use of software and hardware.

Forward Buy
Occurs when an account buys extra quantity during the deal period to be sold after the deal has ended.

F Statistics
In a regression model, it is used to determine the overall performance of a model. The higher the F value is, the better.

Goodness of Fit
Measure of how well the predicted values match with the actual values.

Historical Fit
The ability of a forecasting model to predict the past values.

Identification
To identify the variables which appear to have a strong relationship with the variable we wish to forecast.

Independent demand
It represents consumption demand. For example, POS based consumption data.

Independent Variables
The variables that drive the sales. For example, advertising outlay, price and state of the economy. They are used to predict values of a dependent variable They are also called explanatory variables or drivers.

Intermittent Demand
These are the products that have no demand for many months and sporadic demand in other months.

IRP
Integrated resource planning model.

Lead Time
Time needed to make any change in production plan or ordering raw materials; the amount of time required to provide (or produce) a product to an inventory location; or time needed to make any change in production plan.

Leading Indicator
Economic indicator whose peaks and troughs during the business cycle tend to occur before the general economy. Stock market prices are generally considered as a leading indicator of the economy.

Linear Model
In a linear model, the relationship between dependent variable (e.g., sales) and independent variable (e.g., advertising expenditures) is considered as linear. If the relationship between sales and advertising expenditures is 1:5, it assumes that it will remain the same for every level of

advertising expenditures. That is, when advertising expenditures increase by one unit, sales will increase by 5 units.

Macro-forecast
Forecast of an economy as a whole. For example, forecasts of GDP and employment.

MAPE
Mean Absolute Percent Error, average percent error with signs ignored.

Micro-forecast
Company level forecast. For example, sales forecast.

Misspecification
Where a forecast model either includes variables, which don't have significant relationship with the variable we wish to forecast, or excludes certain variables, which have a significant effect on the variable to be forecasted.

Matured Products
Products that have passed their growth stage in terms of demand.

MPS
Master Planning Scheduling.

MSE
Mean squared error. Here errors are first squared and then their average is computed.

Multicollinearity
Multicollinearity is referred to a situation where two independent variables are highly associated (correlated) with each other. In forecasting, a model with a problem of multicollinearity may not help in determining the precise contribution of each independent variable to the dependent variable, but it may not have any effect on the model's ability to forecast.

Multiple regression
A regression based model where more than one independent (explanatory) variables are used.

Naive Forecast
Here it is assumed that the next period's forecast is the same as the current period's actual.

Observations
Number of periods used in a forecasting model.

Operational Forecasts
Short term forecasts, usually of less than one year. They are also called tactical forecasts.

Outlier
A value that is outside the norm — unusually too large or too small.

Phasing
Percent of annual sales realized in a given month.

Price Elasticity
How sensitive is the sale to price. It is highly elastic if a small change in price leads to a large change in demand. It is highly inelastic, if a large change in price leads to a small change in demand.

Product Life Cycle
Refers to a life cycle of a product. The product forms a S curve with four stages of development — introduction, growth, maturity, and decline.

Qualitative Forecasting
Refers to judgmental approach to forecasting.

Quantitative Forecasting
Refers to statistical approach to forecasting.

Regression
It is a causal method of forecasting which assumes that the variable to be forecasted exhibits a cause/effect relationship with one or more variables (drivers).

Residual
It is equivalent to a forecast error — the actual minus the fitted (forecast) value.

Round Robin Tournament Approach
Where the same data are subjected to multiple forecasting techniques, e.g., single-, double- and triple exponential smoothing, to reduce the forecast error.

Safety Stocks
Buffer stock used to compensate for uncertainties in demand.

Scenario Forecasting
A judgment technique of forecasting where several set of circumstances are constructed which form the boundaries within which the actual number is expected to lie.

Seasonality
Seasonal fluctuations are those which occur regularly and periodically and the length of a cycle is always less than one year. For example, the sales of a department store reaches peak during November and December because of Christmas. This happens every year and at the same time.

Sell in Forecast
Forecast of shipment from the manufacturer to retailer.

Sell Through Forecast
Forecast of sales to end-use consumers.

Shipping Data
Data of merchandise shipped.

SKU
Stock Keeping Unit (item). For example, shirt, size 15", half sleeves, white color is one SKU. Shirt size 15", half sleeves, blue color is another SKU.

Spatial Autocorrelation
Often arises in a cross sectional data where a change in one region may cause a change in the activity in other region because of close economic linkages.

Standard Deviation
Measure of variations within a series. For example, how errors vary over different periods.

Specification
In a regression based model, it is referred to specifying variables which should be included in a model.

Stock-Out
When inventory isn't available to meet orders.

Strategic Forecasts
Long term forecasts, usually of more than one year.

Structural Change
Where data show an abrupt yet permanent change in the pattern. For example, sales of a company shoots up significantly due to a merger or acquisition.

Tactical Forecasts
Short term forecasts, usually for less than one year. Also called operational forecasts.

Time Series Models
Where it is assumed that past pattern will continue in the future. Here one needs only the data of series to be forecasted. Exponential smoothing, decomposition, and moving averages are some of the time series models.

Top-Down Forecasting
Here the forecast is first prepared of the company as a whole, which is then disaggregated into category and SKU level forecasts.

T Test
It is used to determine in a regression model whether the impact of a certain independent variable is significant or not. In other words, whether we should keep that variable or throw it out. The variable is normally considered significant if its value is 2 or higher.

Trend
It is statistically computed. It shows how, on the average, sale is moving — upward or downward.

Unconstrained Demand

What could have been sold if there were no problem in production or of any other kind which might have affected the sales.

Univariate Models

Here one needs only the data of series to be forecasted. Time series models are univariate models.

Validation

The process of testing whether the model is valid or not.

REFERENCES

1. Business and Economic Research Group, Executive Offices, 6275 Neil Road, Reno, Nevada 89511.
2. Makridakis, Spyros, Steven C. Wheelwright and Victor E. McGee. **Forecasting: Methods and Applications.** New York: John Wiley & Sons. 1983.

NOTES

NOTES

NOTES